MW00997198

Spoken Algerian Arabic

Elizabeth M. Bergman

Spoken Algerian Arabic

Elizabeth M. Bergman

2005
Dunwoody Press

Spoken Algerian Arabic

All inquiries should be directed to:
Dunwoody Press
6564 Loisdale Ct., Suite 900
Springfield. VA 22150. USA

ISBN: 1-931546-10-X
Library of Congress Control Number: 2005921930
Printed and bound in the United States of America

Table of Contents

Acknowledgments

Co-workers and colleagues have been more than generous with advice and aid throughout the writing process. This is my opportunity to thank them. The final product, of course, remains my responsibility.

Karima Roudesli originated this project. She carried out fieldwork in the US and in Algeria, where she conducted many of the interviews that provide text selections for this work. She also did preliminary transcription and translation of the interviews.

Co-workers at LRC/McNeil Technologies have also contributed to the work. Azizeh Babaa was instrumental in the process. Her transcriptions in Arabic and IPA-based Latin script form the basis of later work. The Technical Support staff of Alan Downing, Aung Kyaw Oo, Mark Jeon, and Stephen Poulos did what I cannot. They provided audio recording and editing, support for the use of computer hardware and software, and final production.

For their sharp editing eyes and sharper pens, I owe a debt to Jack Jones and Carol Breakstone. Dr. R. David Zorc has been a constant source of encouragement, as a linguist of exceptional range and a true colleague. Thomas Creamer has offered much support through his lexicographical expertise and his managerial proficiency.

We would like to acknowledge with gratitude the support provided by the African Language Project of the University of Maryland, Eastern Shore, under the directorship of Dr. Chester Hedgepath. We are deeply appreciative as well of Habaka Feghali's many valuable contributions.

Consultants assisted at various stages. They include B.M. Belghachi, R. Goulmamine, and A. Rezig. Dr. Aziza Boucherit's review of the manuscript was all an author could ask for. Her critical judgment and understanding of SAA were invaluable to the final editing process.

Finally, there is my mother, Joyce O. Bergman. I owe her more than I can say.

My thanks to all of you.

i

Preface

About Spoken Algerian Arabic

Arabic as spoken in Algeria is as varied as Algeria's geography and history. The land of Algeria rises from the coastal lowlands and the hills of the Tell to the Atlas Mountains and the High Plateaus. From the mountains, Algeria extends far south into the Sahara Desert. That land has been held by, among others, the Romans, the Arabs, the Turks, and the French. In large part because of its geography and history, Algeria has no dominant variety of Arabic. There is no Algerian equivalent of, for example, Cairene Arabic in Egypt. What we call here Spoken Algerian Arabic (SAA) instead includes a wide range of variation.

This work presents and describes some of the variation that occurs in SAA. The speech that occurs here comes from four of Algeria's five major dialect regions. They are central Algeria (Algiers), eastern Algeria (Annaba and Constantine), western Algeria (Oran, Sidi Bel Abbès, and Tlemcen), and southern Algeria (Biskra, Djelfa, El Bayadh, and El Meghaier). These places cannot, of course, demonstrate the full range of variation that is SAA. The aim of this work is to provide a representative sampling rather than a detailed description or dialect atlas of SAA. Limitations of space mean that some urban areas do not appear here, nor does the region of the Sahara Desert, which forms a separate dialect area. (For overviews of Arabic as spoken in Algeria, see Cantineau's series of articles in _Revue africaine_ and Marçais's contribution on language to "Algeria" in the _Encyclopaedia of Islam_.)

Variation in SAA is regional. It also occurs between urban centers, among speakers from the same place, and in the speech of a single individual. Variation is most obvious when it affects pronunciation (phonology) and vocabulary (lexicon). It can also influence word-formation (morphology) and sentence structure (syntax).

The samples of SAA in this work would not be complete if they did not include French. The inclusion of French in spoken Arabic is characteristic of SAA, as it is of other varieties of Arabic in North Africa. The use of French is a natural result of 130 years of French colonial rule in Algeria. It has persisted post-Independence because of the political, economic, and cultural ties that continue to link Algeria and France. In spite of its persistence, the use of French in SAA varies. A French word may occur as a borrowing that conforms, to a certain extent, to the norms of Arabic. French may also occur, more or less unchanged, as a word, phrase, or sentence within an utterance that is otherwise Arabic (code-switching). Speakers themselves vary in their use of French. A number of factors can affect French usage in SAA. These include a speaker's age, gender, background, education, and political orientation, among others. They also include relative age and status of the speakers, topic, situation, etc.

Readers familiar with Algeria will note that this work does not treat any of the varieties of Berber spoken there. The importance of Berber language and culture in Algeria cannot be denied. This work, however, focuses on Arabic as spoken in Algeria.

The language situation in Algeria, characterized by variation, code-switching, and multilingualism, may seem odd to a reader who has grown up in a monolingual community. It is, however, a natural situation for Algerians. Many Algerians speak SAA as a first language; others speak it as a second language. And most Algerians, even if they do not speak French fluently, use and recognize common French words and phrases. The result is a range of varieties of Arabic that Algerians as well as other speakers of Arabic clearly recognize as "Algerian."

About this work

This work is intended for those who are familiar with Modern Standard Arabic (MSA) and with at least one other variety of spoken Arabic. This is not an elementary-level conversation manual or textbook. Listening comprehension is its focus. This is largely because, in our experience, speakers of one variety of Arabic can usually understand and respond to speakers of other varieties, even though this response can be difficult to understand, both for Arabic speakers of another variety and for non-native speakers of Arabic. Hence, the present emphasis on listening rather than speaking.

This work is made up of three parts. The first part is a grammar that describes the distinguishing features of SAA. This is a sketch or an outline rather than an exhaustive study. It aims to serve as a brief reference for those who need familiarity with SAA and for those whose interest is the comparative study of Arabic dialects.

The second part of this work consists of sample selections transcribed from audio recordings. These recording were made by consultants, all first-language speakers of SAA. SAA speech is transcribed in Latin script, in a modified version of IPA (International Phonetic Alphabet), and in Arabic script. Both transcriptions are largely phonemic, in that they record the primary sounds of SAA rather than the specific variations each sound may have in actual speech. They also preserve the starts, stops, and slips of tongue that occur in spontaneous speech. All French is transcribed using standard French orthography. An English translation accompanies the transcriptions. A glossary follows each selection. Words and phrases that may be new to learners of SAA are listed and defined in the order in which they occur in the selection. Finally, notes provide information about linguistic and cultural features of the selection that may be unclear to those unfamiliar with SAA and Algeria.

The third part of this work is a two-part glossary. The glossary is a list of words and phrases that occur in the audio selections, with the first part consisting of Arabic and the second of French items. The Arabic glossary follows Arabic alphabetical order. The headword or main word of each entry appears in IPA and Arabic script. The French glossary follows Latin script alphabetical order.

How to use this work
Step One: The grammar

It is suggested that the learner begin by reading through the grammar and taking notes of those features of SAA that seem most different from what they know. We recognize that a grammar is not an easy read. It is, however, the fastest and easiest way to get acquainted with the sounds, the word-building system, and the sentence-forming rules of SAA. The grammar is brief. Other than some technical terminology used to orient those with a linguistic background, it describes SAA in terms that should be familiar to most readers.

Step Two: Work through the sample selections in order

We recommend that the learner work through the selections in order. There are two reasons for this recommendation. First, the selections are arranged in order of difficulty (in terms of SAA, in terms of length, complexity, topic, etc., and in terms of the amount of French they contain). Second, features of SAA are described in the notes the first time they occur. Notes are usually not repeated. The learner who goes directly to selections of particular interest will find gaps in her or his knowledge of SAA. These gaps will make learning more difficult than it need be.

Step Three: Find out about the selection

The learner will want to begin by getting as much information about the selection as possible. Each selection is introduced by a short paragraph about the subject matter and any noteworthy features of that selection. The learner will also find it helpful to read through the glossary and the notes before reading the selection. This gives the learner some familiarity with the new material before encountering it in context.

Step Four: Listen to the selection

Having finished the orientation, the learner should close this book. Listening to the selection without following the transcription lets the learner get used to the voices and get a general idea of the topic. What may sound difficult on the first hearing becomes easier on the second, third, or fourth repetition. The learner will soon recognize familiar words and phrases. It then becomes possible to guess the meaning of new words.

Step Five: Work through the selection

The learner can read along in the IPA or the Arabic script transcription while listening to the selection. This is a matter of choice. Some people find it easier to read from left to right in Latin script. This, they say, makes up for the effort involved in learning IPA symbols. Reading the IPA transcription also makes using the glossary and notes easier. Only the main word or headword of each glossary entry appears in Arabic; the notes cite Arabic words and phrases only in IPA. Other people think that reading Arabic in Arabic is a better solution. They can recognize familiar words and phrases more easily. However, some of the sounds specific to SAA cannot be written in Arabic. There is, for example, no commonly used letter to represent the sound /g/.

As the learner progresses through the work, she or he will encounter more and more French. Some find it difficult to rely on Arabic script at this point. It requires the reader to shift from reading left-to-right in Arabic to right-to-left in French and back again. This shifting is an unfortunate but normal effect of reading (and writing) in two languages with different scripts.

As the learner works through the selection, the glossary and notes will be a primary resource. The glossary's translations of new words and phrases are the learner's first source for new words and phrases in each selection. Items in the glossary include words and phrases from SAA and French as well as some from MSA. Some MSA items are glossed because the sound changes of SAA make them difficult for a learner to recognize. Other MSA items are glossed because they cannot easily or readily be found in Wehr's Dictionary of Modern Written Arabic. All French is glossed to allow the learner to focus on learning SAA. The learner should note that SAA words and phrases are glossed the first time they occur; they are not repeated. The alphabetic glossary at the back of this work is a useful way to review items that have occurred in a previous selection.

The notes explain grammatical, linguistic, and cultural features of the selection that may be unclear. They do not provide detailed descriptions of a feature. For further information on a particular grammatical feature treated in a note, the learner will want to consult the grammar. Note that the translation of the selection should be the learner's last resort. Most people learn more when they try to work out answers to their questions than they do when they get the answer without effort.

Step Six: Learn new words and phrases

By this stage, the learner has developed her or his own ways of learning new words and phrases. These may include making flash cards, writing out lists of new items, repeating new items aloud, using new items in sentences, and other strategies. Of course, learners will want to try new methods of learning, if only to vary learning activities.

Key to transcription

Latin	Arabic		Latin	Arabic
ʔ	ء		ḍ	ض
aa	ا		ṭ	ط
ee	ي		ð̣ - ḍ	ظ
oo	و		ʕ	ع
aw	و		ɣ	غ
a - ə			f	ف
b	ب		v	ڤ
p	پ		q - g - k - ʔ	ق
t	ت		k	ك
θ - t	ث		l - ḷ	ل
j	ج		m	م
ḥ	ح		n	ن
x	خ		h	ه
d	د		uu	و
ð - d	ذ		u	
r - ʁ	ر		w	و
z	ز		ii	ي
s	س		i	
ʃ	ش		y	ي
ṣ	ص			

Notes to transcription key

Transcription reduces the linear sound-plus-image of spoken language to text on a page. It necessarily requires choices and compromises. The following may clarify some of the choices made in this work.

Liaison and elision in natural speech

Liaison, the pronouncing of two words in sequence without a clear break between them, and elision, the omission of sounds or entire syllables in the flow of speech, are essential elements of natural speech. In fact, at the time of writing, liaison and elision distinguish natural speech from machine-generated speech. The gaps between words, even though minute, and the pronunciation of words in their full form are clearly audible in even the best machine-generated speech.

Because liaison and elision are characteristic of natural speech, we have elected not to indicate these features in transcripts. Our assumption, and that of the reader as well, should be that words connect unless there is an indication to the contrary. The resulting pages are, we believe, both more readable and more aesthetically pleasing.

Punctuation in IPA and Arabic transcriptions

Spoken language has its own punctuation. It includes, among other things, hesitations, pauses, interruptions, and overlaps. The conventions that represent this punctuation in writing, however, are limited to specialists. For the sake of readability, therefore, we chose to use written punctuation.

Commas separate items in a list. They also separate clauses in a sentence.

Periods precede the beginning of a new topic.

Quotation marks indicate direct quotes.

Question marks denote questions.

Ellipses (...) follow a word that is cut off in the middle of a sentence. They also complete a sentence that is incomplete at the end of a speaker's utterance or turn.

Italics indicate code-switched material. Code-switched material in this work consists of single words as well as longer phrases that occur in an Arabic utterance.

Treatment of word-final long vowels in IPA and Arabic transcriptions

Although, generally speaking, long vowels in SAA and other varieties of Arabic lose their length in word-final position, they are transcribed as long in this work.

Comparing the IPA and Arabic script versions

Note that the two alphabets used in the transcription in this work are radically different. Readers may therefore note that the IPA transcription is not identical to the Arabic script transcription of a given selection. Any differences are due in part to characteristic differences between the two scripts. They are at the same time due to the decision we made to exploit those differences. We decided to build on the flexibility of IPA, which was developed by linguists to represent the sounds of the world's languages. The IPA version of a selection is, thus, a more phonemic representation of speech. The Arabic script, in contrast, evolved over time as the writing system for Classical Arabic (ClA) and Modern Standard Arabic (MSA). It, therefore, provides a visible link between ClA and MSA, on the one hand, and SAA on the other.

Homographs in Arabic transcription

A glance at the transcription key reveals that, in several cases, Arabic has a single symbol where the IPA has two symbols. There is, unfortunately, no easy way to differentiate the two sounds from one another in Arabic. Specialists, of course, can use any number of diacritical marks in Arabic, but we chose to use Arabic script in a more or less conventional form.

Treatment of selected morphological features in Arabic transcription

alif

Transcription in this work retains the <u>alif</u> of the definite article ال, as in المدينه /əlmdiina/ 'the city'.

In addition, it retains the word-final <u>alif</u> (in forms used in MSA), as in الدنيا /ddənyaa/ 'the world'.

taaʔ marbuuṭa

This transcript writes the <u>taaʔ marbuuṭa</u> as ه when not in construct and not sounded as /t/, as in المدينه /əlmdiina/ 'the city'. In contrast, the <u>taaʔ marbuuṭa</u> appears as ة when in construct and pronounced /t/, as in مدينة الجزائر /mdiinət əljazaaʔir/ 'the city of Algiers'.

Symbols and Abbreviations

/text/	text in SAA
text	text in a language other than English
...	incomplete word or sentence
text	code-switched text
1	first-person
2	second-person
3	third-person
adj	adjective
adv	adverbial
ClA	Classical Arabic
conj	conjunction
disc	marker of organization or attitude
f	feminine
fp	feminine plural
Fr	French
fs	feminine singular
imperf	imperfect
interj	interjection
interrog	interrogative
m	masculine
mp	masculine plural
MSA	Modern Standard Arabic
nfp	feminine plural noun
nfs	feminine singular noun
nmp	masculine plural noun
nms	masculine singular noun
np	plural noun
p	plural
particle	particle
prep	preposition
pro	pronoun
prop	proper noun
s	singular
SAA	Spoken Algerian Arabic
s.b.i	supplied by informant
u.d.	unpublished data
v	verb

Glossary of Terms

adverbial – one of a varied group of items that modify the verb

alveolar – a sound made by the front of the tongue and the alveolar ridge, which is just behind the teeth

apical – a sound made by the apex or tip of the tongue

bilabial – a sound made by the coming together of both lips

broken plural – in Arabic, a plural formed by change in syllable structure and/or vowel change rather than by the addition of a suffix, (also called ablaut plural) as opposed to the **sound plural**

cardinal – of a number used for counting, as opposed to the **ordinal**

construct phrase – in Arabic, a structure in which one noun or nominal immediately follows another, so that the second item modifies the first in a relationship generally described as possessive, (also called iḍaafa) as opposed to the **possessive adjective construction**

dental – a sound made by the tip of the tongue against the upper teeth

derived verb form – in Arabic, any verb form other than $C_1vC_2vC_3$

elative – in Arabic, a form that expresses the comparative or superlative, depending on the construction in which it appears

elide – of sounds, to be omitted

epenthetic vowel – an extra vowel that has been added to a word (also called helping vowel)

flap-trill – a sound made by rapid contact between two parts of the mouth, where one instance of contact is a **flap** and multiple contacts make a **trill**

fricative – a sound in which two parts of the mouth come close together and friction results from air passing between them

geminate – doubled

geminate verb/root – a verb or root in which $C_2 = C_3$

glottal – a sound made by the closure or narrowing of the glottis, the opening between the vocal cords

homophone – a word that has the same pronunciation as another word but a different meaning

imperative – a verb form used for commands

imperfect – a verb form that usually expresses duration or continuity of action (also called the present tense), as opposed to the **perfect**

information question – a question that asks for a response more detailed than "yes" or "no", as opposed to the **yes-no question**

intransitive verb – a verb that cannot take a direct object, as opposed to the **transitive verb**

invariable – a word or form that does not undergo change, for example, of number, gender, or person, or a word or form that does not undergo sound change

labiodental – a sound in which one lip is in contact with the teeth

lateral – a sound in which air escapes around a closure in the mouth

moon letter – a letter of the Arabic alphabet to which the l of the definite article al- does not assimilate, a group that includes non-apical consonants and j, as opposed to the **sun letter**

morphology – the word-building process[es] of a language

nasal – a sound produced by the flow of air through the nose

nominal sentence – in Arabic, a sentence that does not contain a verb, generally a copular or possessive sentence (also called equational sentence), as opposed to the **verbal sentence**

ordinal– of a number used for ordering rather than counting, as opposed to the **cardinal**

palatal – a sound made when the tongue touches or comes near to the hard palate

perfect – a verb form that usually expresses completion or a completed action, sometimes called the past tense in descriptions of Arabic, as opposed to the **imperfect**

pharyngeal – a sound made with the pharynx

possessive adjective construction – in Arabic, a structure in which a possessive adjective links two nouns or nominals so that the second item modifies the first in a relationship generally described as possessive, as opposed to the **construct phrase**

post-palatal – a sound made in any part of the mouth behind the palate, including the velum, the uvula, and the pharynx

pre-verb – one of a variety of forms, usually a verb or participle in SAA, that provides additional information about the time frame of the verb (it is aspectual) or about an attitude towards the action of the verb (it is modal)

relative pronoun – in Arabic, a pronoun that introduces a definite relative clause

semivowel – a glide, in SAA /w/ and /y/

sound plural – in Arabic, a noun plural formed by the addition of a suffix (also called suffixed plural), as opposed to the **broken plural**

stem vowel – a vowel in a verb or noun that is not part of a prefix or suffix (also called internal vowel)

stop – a sound made by a complete blocking of the air flow

strong verb form – in Arabic, a verb form in which no root consonant is a semi-vowel, as opposed to the **weak verb form**

sun letter – a letter of the Arabic alphabet to which the <u>l</u> of the definite article <u>al-</u> assimilates, a group that includes apical consonants but not j, as opposed to the **moon letter**

transitive verb – a verb that takes a direct object, as opposed to the **intransitive verb**

unmarked – the more neutral or general form (also called default form)

uvular – a sound made by the back of the tongue against the uvula

velar – a sound made by the back of the tongue against the velum or soft palate

verb form – in Arabic, one of a limited number of patterns for verb derivation, conventionally numbered with Roman numerals

verbal noun – in Arabic, a noun that names the action of the verb and that is usually but not always derived from that verb (also called <u>maṣdar</u>)

verbal sentence – a sentence that contains a verb, as opposed to the **nominal sentence**

voiced – a sound characterized by vibration of the vocal cords, as opposed to the **voiceless**

voiceless – a sound characterized by no vibration of the vocal cords, as opposed to the **voiced**

weak verb form – in Arabic, a verb form in which one or more root consonant is a semi-vowel, as opposed to the **strong verb form**

yes-no question – a question that is best answered by "yes" or "no", as opposed to the **information question**

References

In English

Encyclopaedia Britannica. 1973. Chicago: William Benton.

"Algeria". 1960 - . *Encyclopaedia of Islam.* 2nd edition.

Badawi, El-Said and Martin Hinds. 1986. *Dictionary of Egyptian Arabic: Arabic-English.* Beirut: Librairie du Liban.

Ferguson, Charles A. 1959. "The Arabic *koine.*" *Language* 35 (1959): 616-630. Reprinted in *Readings in Arabic linguistics.* Pp. 49-69. Salman H. al-Ani, ed. Bloomington: Indiana University Linguistics Club, 1978.

Harrell, Richard S. 1962. *A short reference grammar of Moroccan Arabic.* Richard Slade Harrell Arabic Series. Washington: Georgetown UP.

___, ed. 1962. *A dictionary of Moroccan Arabic: Moroccan-English.* Richard Slade Harrell Arabic Series. Washington: Georgetown UP.

Heath, Jeffrey. 1989. *From code-switching to borrowing: foreign and diglossic mixing in Moroccan Arabic.* Library of Arabic Linguistics 9. London; New York: Kegan Paul International.

Metz, Helen Chapin. 1993. *Algeria: A Country Study.* Washington: Library of Congress, 1993. WWW. Federal Research Service. htt://lcweb2.loc.gov/cgi.bin/query/r?frd/cstudy:@field(DOCID+dz). July 1999.

Nydell, Margaret K. [Omar]. 1993. *From Modern Standard Arabic to the Maghrebi dialects (Moroccan and Algerian) Conversion course.* Arabic dialect series. Arlington, VA: DLS.

Wehr, Hans. 1979. *Dictionary of modern written Arabic: Arabic-English.* 4th ed. Ed. J. Milton Cowan. Ithaca, NY: Spoken Language Services.

In French

Beaussier, Marcelin. 1958. *Dictionnaire pratique arabe-français* [Practical Arabic-French dictionary]. 2nd edition. Ed. M. Mohamed Ben Cheneb. Alger [Algiers]: *Maison des livres.*

Bencheneb, Rachid. 1942. *L'argot des Arabes d'Alger* [The slang of the Arabs in Algiers]. *Revue africaine* LXXXVI: 77 - 101.

Boucherit, Aziza. 2002. *L'arabe parlé à Alger: aspects sociolinguistiques et énonciatifs* [Spoken Arabic in Algiers: sociolinguistic & enunciative aspects]. Paris: Peeters.

Cantineau, Jean. 1939. *Les parlers arabes du département d'Alger* [The Arabic dialects of the department of Algiers]. *Revue africaine* LXXXI: 703-711.

___. 1939. *Les parlers arabes du département de Constantine* [The Arabic dialects of the department of Constantine]. In *Quatrième congrès de la Fédération des Sociétés Savantes de l'Afrique du Nord.* 2 vols. v. II, p. 849-863.

___. 1940. *Les parlers arabes du département d'Oran* [The Arabic dialects of the department of Oran]. *Revue africain* LXXXIV: 220-231.

___. 1941. *Les parlers arabes des territoires du Sud* [The Arabic dialects of territories of the south [of Algeria]). *Revue africaine* LXXXV: 72-77.

Caubet, Dominique. 2004. *Les mots du bled: création contemporaine en langues maternelles, les artistes on la parole* [Words from the village: contemporary creation in native languages, the artists speak]. *Espaces discursifs.* Paris: L'Harmattan.

Darmaun, Henri. 1963. *Recueil de textes algériens* [Anthology of Algerian texts]. *Études arabes et islamiques.* Paris: C. Klincksieck.

Dziri, Larbi. 1970. *L'arabe parlé algérien par l'image: vol. III: glossaire* [Spoken Arabic through pictures: vol. III: glossary]. 3 vols. Paris: Maisonneuve.

Grand'Henry, Jacques. 1972. *Le parler arabe de Cherchell (Algérie)* [The Arabic dialect of Cherchell (Algeria)]. *Publications de l'Institut orientaliste de Louvain 5.* Louvain: Institut orientaliste, Université Catholique de Louvain.

___. 1976. *Les parlers arabes de la région du Mzab (Sahara algérien)* [The Arabic dialects of the region of Mzab (Algerian Sahara)]. Studies in Semitic languages and linguistics V. Leiden: E.J. Brill, 1976.

Lentin, Albert. 1959. *Supplément au dictionnaire pratique arabe-français de Marcelin Beaussier* [Supplement to the Practical Arabic-French dictionary of Marcelin Beaussier]. Alger [Algiers]: *Maison des livres.*

Madouni, Jihane. 1994. *De l'auxiliarité dans un parler de Sidi-Bel-Abbès* [On auxiliarity in a dialect of Sidi Bel Abbès]. *Matériaux arabes et sudarabiques-GELLAS* 6: 128-139.

Madouni-La Peyre, Jihane. 2003. *Dictionnaire arabe algérien-français, Algérie de l'ouest* [Algerian Arabic-French dictionary: western Algeria]. Paris: Langues Mondes Asiathèque.

New Cassell's French Dictionary. 1962. New York: Funk and Wagnalls.

Peres, Henri and Paul Mangion. 1961. *Vocabulaire de base de l'arabe dialectal algérien et saharien: Mille et un mots d'usage courant chez les arabophs de l'Algérie et du Sahara* .... [Basic vocabulary in Algerian and Saharan colloquial Arabic: 1,001 words in daily use among the Arabic speakers of Algeria and the Sahara]. Alger [Algiers]: *Maison des livres.*

Quitout, Michel. 1997. *Grammaire berbère: rifain, tamazight, chleuh, kabyle* [Berber grammar: Rifian, Tamazight, Chleuh, Kabyle]. Paris: L'Harmattan.

In German

Singer, Hans-Rudolf. 1984. *Grammatik der arabischen Mundart der Medina von Tunis* [Grammar of the Arabic dialect of the city of Tunis]. Berlin; New York: Walter de Gruyter.

Willms, Alfred. *Einführung in das vulgärarabische on Nordwestafrika* [Introduction to the colloquial Arabic of northwest Africa]. Leiden: E.J. Brill, 1972.

Map of Algeria

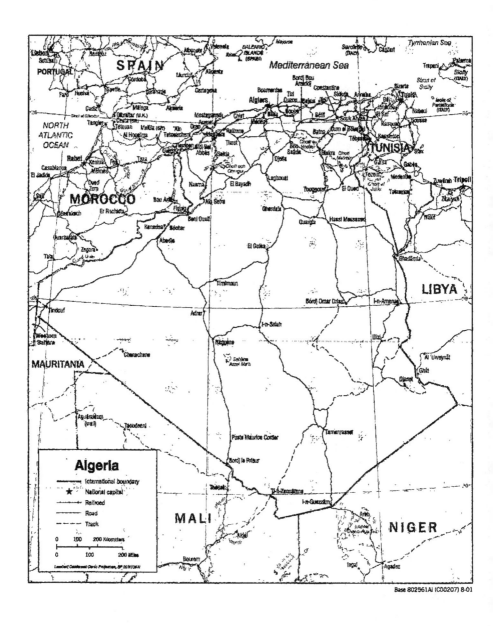

1. The sounds of SAA

1.1. Consonants

1.1.1. The consonants of SAA

Note that symbols between square brackets [ ] indicate consonants limited in their occurrence.

	Bilabial	Labio-dental	Dental	Alveolar	Palatal	Velar	Uvular	Pharyngeal	Glottal
Voiceless Stop	[p]		t - ṭ			k	q		[ʔ]
Voiced Stop	b		d - ḍ			g			
Voiceless Fricative		f	θ	s - ṣ	ʃ	x		ḥ	h
Voiced Fricative		[v]	ð - ọ̌	z - ẓ		ɣ	[ʁ]	ʕ	
Affricate				[tˢ]	j				
Nasal	m			n					
Lateral			l - [ḷ]						
Flap-Trill				r					
Semi-Vowel	w				y				

1.1.2. SAA reflexes of MSA

1.1.2.1. SAA variation in MSA letters ث - ذ - ظ - ض

Variation in the SAA treatment of the MSA letters ث - ذ - ظ - ض are common in SAA. Within the phonology of SAA, two systems operate. In one, the interdentals /θ/ - /ð/ - /ọ̌/ occur, as in /θneen/ 'two', /haaðaa/ 'this (MS near demonstrative)', and /nọ̌ann/ 'I think'. They contrast with the stops /t/ - /d/ - /ḍ/. In the other, the interdentals do not occur; stops replace the interdentals, as in /tneen/ 'two', /haadaa/ 'this (ms near demonstrative')', and /nḍann/ 'I think'. Whichever phonological system dominates, individual speakers may show a good deal of variation, even within a single utterance. An example is /nnaas ʕam-baalhaa haadii hiyya … haaðiik lḥayaat taaʕ *Algérie* yaʕnii/ 'People knew this was it, this is life in Algeria, I mean' (Selection 4).

1.1.2.2. SAA reflexes of MSA ق: /q/ - /g/ - /k/ - /k/

In general, the MSA letter ق is /q/ in SAA. This occurs in words used in formal contexts, such as /iqtiṣaad/ 'economy'. It also occurs in words in daily use, such as /wəqt/ 'time'. There are, however, certain items that have /g/ rather than /q/. These include high-frequency words such as /gaal/ 'to

1

say' (MSA qaala). Other words occur less often, such as /nəggəz/ 'to jump' (MSA naqaza).

Less often, the SAA reflect of ق is /k/. This occurs, for example, in /ktəl/ 'to kill' (MSA qatala). The /ʔ/ occurs in SAA as a reflex of MSA ق in the city of Tlemcen. It is one of the most notable features of Arabic as spoken in that city.

1.1.3. Consonants limited in their occurrence

1.1.3.1. /ʔ/

The /ʔ/ or hamza (voiceless glottal stop) not is not a phoneme or basic sound for most speakers of SAA. It is true that it occurs in SAA. For example, the word transcribed as /aaxər/ 'last' is actually pronounced with an initial /ʔ/ or as [ʔaaxər].

This work, however, omits the initial /ʔ/. It is an automatic sound change; pronouncing a vowel-initial word after a pause without an initial /ʔ/ is impossible. For that reason alone, the /ʔ/ could reasonably be omitted. In addition, there is the question of /ʔ/ as it occurs in MSA words and their SAA analogues. SAA has a number of ways, mostly unpredictable, of replacing this MSA letter.

A word-initial ʔ, as in MSA ʔaaxir 'last', often drops out of the SAA analogue when preceded by the definite article /l/, as in /laaxər/ 'the last'. More often, however, high-frequency words like /aaxər/ add another /l/ to the definite article, as in /llaaxər/ 'the last'. This appears to compensate for the lost ʔ. In other cases, a word-initial ʔ disappears entirely, as does the following vowel. The MSA plural ʔawlaad 'children', for example, is /wlaad/ in SAA.

When ʔ is word-medial, several very different sound changes may take place. The MSA verb saʔala 'to ask, inquire', for example, has two SAA analogues. The SAA verb /saal/ 'to ask, inquire' has no ʔ, while the two short /a/ vowels have merged into the single long /aa/. In contrast, the SAA verb /suwwəl/ 'to ask, inquire' has a doubled /w/ where MSA has a single ʔ. The active participle of /saal/ illustrates another possible sound change, where /y/ stands in the place of the MSA ʔ, as in /saayəl/ 'asking'.

A word-final ʔ is regularly lost in its SAA analogue. In verbs, the resulting final vowel is re-analyzed to make the verb finally-weak. For example, the MSA verb badaʔa 'to begin' is /bdaa/ in SAA, with the 1S perfect form /bdeenaa/ 'we began'.

2

1.1.3.2. /tˢ/

The /tˢ/ (voiceless alveololar affricate) is described in older sources as characteristic of SAA speech. It replaced /t/ in certain environments and in certain sub-varieties of SAA. The /tˢ/ appears to have disappeared from many sub-varieties of SAA. It occurs in this work only in Selection 31. Even there, however, the speaker does not use the sound /tˢ/ in his own speech, that of Annaba. Instead, he uses /tˢ/, together with /č/ (voiceless palatal affricate) to imitate the speakers of nearby Constantine.

1.1.3.3. /ʁ/

The /ʁ/ (voiced uvular fricative) occurs in this work in the speech of Tlemcen (Selection 26). For this speaker, /ʁ/ replaces /r/ (apical flap or trill) in some but not all words. The /ʁ/ occurs in Tlemcen and certain other cities of North Africa, as well as in Baghdad.

1.1.3.4. /ḷ/

The /ḷ/ (emphatic dental lateral, the emphatic version of /l/) occurs in SAA as well as MSA. Its occurrence (as a phoneme) is limited to the word /ḷḷaah/ 'God'.

1.1.3.5. /p/ and /v/

The sounds /p/ and /v/ occur in borrowings from languages other than Arabic. These words have /p/, for example, in /plaaṣa/ 'place, location', and /iṣpaanii/ 'Spanish'. The /v/ occurs in words such as /aanvastaa/ 'to invest' and /vooṭaa/ 'to vote'.

1. 2. The vowels of SAA

1.2.1. The short vowels of SAA

The short vowels of SAA are /a/, /i/, /u/ and /ə/. Two features of short vowels in SAA should be noted. First, one of the most noticeable features of SAA and other varieties of North African Arabic is the loss of short vowels. To the listener new to these varieties, speakers may sound as though they use no vowels at all. Long vowels certainly exist in SAA and other varieties of North African Arabic. Short vowels, however, are problematic. In certain environments, they disappear entirely. Second, distinctions between short vowels are often neutralized.

1.2.1.1. Loss of short vowels

The short vowels of SAA can be considered "lost" only by comparison with MSA. Typically short vowel loss occurs in an open syllable, a syllable that ends in a vowel. Because the loss of short vowels affects and changes

3

syllable structure throughout a paradigm, this subject is discussed under "Syllable structure."

1.2.1.2. Neutralization of short vowels

The distinctions between the three cardinal short vowels of Arabic, /a/, /i/, and /u/, tend to be obscured or neutralized, in SAA, especially in rapid speech. That neutralization is represented in this work by the /ə/ or schwa, as in /təfəssəd/ 'it (fs) ruins' (compare with MSA tufassidu).

1.2.2. The long vowels of SAA

The long vowels of SAA are /aa/, /ii/, /uu/, as in MSA.

1.2.2.1. Lengthening of short vowels

Speakers of SAA may pronounce vowels that are short in MSA as long. The result is the SAA /qaadiim/ 'ancient', as opposed to the MSA qadiim. This lengthening of a short vowel is the SAA strategy for preserving a short vowel in an open syllable. It occurs most often in a formal style or in careful speech.

1.2.3. Diphthongs

In general, SAA has the monophthongs /ee/ and /oo/ where MSA has the diphthongs ay and aw. Thus, we hear SAA /loon/ 'color' and /beet/ 'house' (compare with MSA lawn and bayt).

1.3. Syllable structure and stress

1.3.1. Syllable structure

Following are the permissible syllable structures of SAA:

vv	/aamən/	he believed
vC	/ismii/	my name
vCC	/aşl/	origin
Cv	/baarka/	divine grace (word-final only)
CvC	/bəgra/	cow
CvCC	/dəll/	he indicated
CCvC	/drək/	he understood
CCvCC	/ktəbt/	I wrote
Cvv	/ʕaada/	custom
CvvC	/beet/	house
CvvCC	/maadd/	pulling (ms)
CCvv	/nʕaawəd/	I return
CCvvC	/njiib/	I bring

4

1.3.2. Vowel loss and vowel shift

Vowel loss means the deletion of a short vowel in an open syllable (preceding a single vowel). Vowel shift means that a vowel appears to have changed its position within the word. These two phenomena operate in several ways in SAA.

1.3.2.1. Simple or regular vowel loss

Simple or regular vowel loss refers to the loss of a vowel in the SAA item as compared to its MSA counterpart. It is a distinguishing feature of SAA and other varieties of North African Arabic. Simple vowel loss reshapes basic words. For example, Form I strong verbs have the pattern $C_1C_2vC_3$, as in /ktəb/ 'to write'(compare with MSA kataba).

1.3.2.2. Vowel shift

Some, but not all, simple triliteral nouns show vowel shift when compared with their MSA counterparts. These have the same pattern, $C_1C_2vC_3$, as in /byəl/ 'mule' (compare with MSA baɣl). Vowel shift is not an automatic process, as demonstrated by an item like /gərn/ 'horn' (compare with MSA qarn).

1.3.2.3. Vowel loss plus vowel shift

The loss of short vowels in open syllables makes for some complications when a word containing a short vowel takes a vowel-initial suffix. In certain cases, the resulting vowel shift is predictable. These cases include the following:

1.3.2.3.1. Form I strong verbs of pattern $C_1C_2vC_3$ with vowel-initial suffixes in the perfect

Form I strong verbs of pattern $C_1C_2vC_3$ have vowel shift when they take vowel-initial suffixes in the perfect. Thus, /ktəb/ 'to write' + /ət/ 3FS perfect suffix -> /kətbət/.

1.3.2.3.2. Words of pattern $C_1C_2vC_3$ with vowel-initial suffixes

Words other than Form I strong verbs have the pattern $C_1C_2vC_3$ and have vowel shift when they take vowel-initial suffixes. Thus, /rjəl/ 'foot' + /ii/ 1S suffix -> /rəjlii/.

Words other than Form I strong verbs that have the pattern $C_1C_2vC_3$ show vowel shift when they take the suffix /a/ that marks a feminine noun, adjective, or participle, or a count noun. Thus, /byəl/ 'mule' + /a/ -> /bəɣla/ 'mare mule, female mule' and /hjər/ 'stone (collective) + /a/ -> /həjra/ 'a stone'.

Words of the pattern $C_1C_2vC_3$ show vowel shift when they take the dual suffix /iin/. Thus, /ʃhar/ 'month' + /iin/ dual suffix -> /ʃahriin/.

1.3.2.4. Vowel loss with variation

Both the simple and the predictable results of short vowel loss are in regular use in SAA. In other cases, however, the results of short vowel loss are neither simple nor predictable. They are variable. Variations in the results of short vowel loss are not necessarily linked to specific sub-varieties within SAA. It is not unusual, in fact, to find a single speaker using several of these variations in speech.

Variable results of short vowel loss primarily occur in two situations. The first is the case of a Form I strong verb when it takes vowel-initial suffixes in the imperfect. The second is that of polysyllablic words that take vowel-initial suffixed pronouns.

The following outlines the different results of vowel loss. For the sake of comparison, a single verb /ktəb/ 'to write' and a single noun /rokba/ 'knee' will provide illustrations.

1.3.2.4.1. Complete loss of short vowel

The complete loss of a short vowel in an open syllable results in a sequence of three consonants. Examples include /təktbii/ 'you (fs) write' and /rokbtək/ 'your (S) knee'. (Note that what appears to be an unpronounceable sequence of three consonants becomes pronounceable when a speaker does not fully release stops.)

1.3.2.4.2. Vowel shift

Vowel shift moves the short vowel to the preceding consonant to close an open syllable, as occurs in other cases of short vowel loss. When this occurs, the vowel of the prefix is lost. Examples include /tkətbii/ and /rkobtək/.

1.3.2.4.3. Vowel shift with doubling of C_1

In other cases, the doubling of C_1 preserves the short vowel that would otherwise be lost. The result is, for example, /təkkətbii/ and /rokkəbtək/. This variant is widespread in SAA.

Note, however, that doubling does not necessarily not occur where C_1 is /l - n - r/. Instead, there is simple loss of the short vowel, as in /nəlbsuu/ 'we dress; we wear' and /mənzla/ 'position, status'.

1.3.2.4.4. Vowel shift with vowel lengthening

Vowel shift follows vowel lengthening in another variant that preserves the short vowel. Examples include /taaktəbii/ and /rookbətək/.

1.3.2.5. Case two: Variable results when a word-final syllable of the pattern CvC takes a suffixed pronoun

Another set of variants occurs when a word in which the final syllable has the pattern CvC takes a suffixed pronoun. These variants, in some cases, differ from the variants described above to resolve the problem of short vowel loss. Again, the example will be the same through for the sake of comparison. It is /kətbət/ 'she wrote'.

1.3.2.5.1. Complete loss of short vowel

The complete loss of the short vowel in the syllable that precedes the suffixed pronoun results in a sequence of three consonants. Thus, /kətbtuu/ 'she wrote it (ms)'. As is the case described above, what appears to be an unpronounceable sequence of three consonants becomes pronounceable when a speaker does not fully release stops.

1.3.2.5.2. Vowel shift

Vowel shift results in a 2FS verb that resembles the 1S verb with the same suffixed pronoun, /ktəbtuu/ 'she wrote it (ms)' and 'you (ms) wrote it (ms)'.

1.3.2.5.3. Vowel shift with vowel lengthening

Vowel lengthening is one strategy that preserves the short vowel of the final syllable, as in /kətbaatuu/ 'she wrote it (ms)'.

1.3.2.5.4. Vowel shift with doubling of the stem-final consonant

Another strategy that preserves the short vowel of the final syllable is the doubling of the following consonant, as in /kətbəttuu/ 'she wrote it (ms)'.

1.3.3. Stress rules

The following are the basic rules governing word stress in SAA:

The final syllable takes word stress when it is doubly closed (has the structure CvvC or CvCC).

If the final syllable is not doubly closed (has a structure other than CvvC or CvCC), the penultimate (next to last) syllable takes word stress.

Word stress may shift with the addition of a suffix that makes the final syllable doubly closed. Compare /tənsii/ (stress on the first or penultimate syllable) 'you (ms) forget' with /maa tənsii-ʃ/ (stress on the final syllable) 'don't forget (2S)'.

2. Nouns and adjectives: derivation and inflection

2.1. Noun morphology

Nouns in SAA, in general, resemble the nouns of other varieties of Arabic. They are derived through similar morphological processes and follow similar syntactic rules. Readers seeking details on, for example, nouns of instance, nouns of place, collective and unit nouns, or diminutives will wish to consult the reference grammar of their choice. (In the absence of a standard reference grammar for MSA or a spoken variety of Arabic, many learners rely on the textbook most familiar to them.)

SAA nouns also resemble those of other varieties of spoken Arabic in that they do not inflect for case, as do nouns in MSA. Syntactic relationships are expressed through prepositions, particles, and word order.

In SAA as in other varieties of Arabic, nouns have either a sound (suffixed) plural or a broken (ablaut) plural. For details on the sound (suffixed) plural, see 2.3.4 - 5. The broken plural patterns of SAA are similar to those of other varieties of Arabic and are equally unpredictable. Note, however, that the broken plural of some nouns of SAA differ from the plurals occurring in other varieties of Arabic, such as /xwaataat/ 'sisters' (singular /uxt/). Learners seeking information about the plural of a specific singular noun or the singular of a specific plural noun can consult a dictionary of SAA. It should be noted that the most comprehensive SAA-French dictionary, Beaussier's Dictionnaire pratique arabe-français was last updated in 1959. A more recent (2003) SAA-French dictionary is Madouni-La Peyre's Dictionnaire arabe algérien-français, but it is not comprehensive.

2.2. Adjective morphology

2.2.1. Adjective patterns

The adjectives of SAA, like nouns, resemble those of other varieties of Arabic. The patterns of adjectives, however, are far fewer in number than those of the noun. The following briefly lists the most common adjective patterns and their associated meaning.

2.2.1.1. The adjective pattern $C_1C_2iiC_3$

The pattern $C_1C_2iiC_3$ may be the most commonly-used adjective pattern, as in /sʕiib/ 'hard, difficult'. This pattern is similar for geminate roots, those in which the second and third root consonants are identical. It becomes $C_1C_2iiC_2$, as in /jdiid/ 'new'.

2.2.1.2. The adjective pattern $C_1C_2vC_3$

A specialized adjective has the pattern C_1C2vC_3 to describe a color (/kḥəl/ 'black') or a physical or mental defect (/ṭrəʃ/ 'deaf'). The FS and MP patterns differ from those of other adjectives. The FS has the pattern $C_1vC_2C_3$aa, as in /kəḥlaa/ 'black (fs)' and /ṭərʃaa/ 'deaf (fs)'; the P has the pattern $C_1vC_2C_3$, as in /kəḥl/ 'black (p)' and /ṭərʃ/ 'deaf (p)'.

Some speakers of SAA interpret the final /aa/ vowel of the FS of this adjective pattern (as in /kəḥlaa/ 'black (fs))' as a regular feminine ending. As a result, the final /aa/ vowel becomes /ət/ when the FS of this adjective pattern occurs as the first term of a construct phrase, as in /ḥamrət lwəjh/ 'red-faced (fs)'.

2.2.1.3. The adjective pattern $C_1vC_2C_3$aan

The pattern $C_1vC_2C_3$aan often occurs for adjectives expressing bodily needs or passing states, such as /ʕayyaan/ 'tired, fatigued' and /fənyaan/ 'lazy' (compare Fr. fainéant).

2.2.1.4. The adjective pattern $C_1vC_2C_2$aaC_3

The pattern $C_1vC_2C_2$aaC_3 is the pattern for adjectives describing a habit or character trait (/bəkkaay/ 'crier, weeper'), or a profession (/xəmmaas/ 'sharecropper').

2.2.1.5. The nisba or relational adjective

One pattern for adjectives, the nisba or relational adjective, derives from nouns or other adjectives through the addition of the suffix /-ii/ (/dzaayrii/ 'Algerian'). The suffix /-aanii/ also occurs, as in /taḥtaanii/ 'lower'.

2.2.1.6. The elative pattern $C_1C_2vC_3$

The elative (the pattern shared by the comparative and superlative adjective) has the pattern $C_1C_2vC_3$, as in /ktar/ 'more, most'. This is identical to the pattern for colors and disabilities (see 2.2.1.2). Unlike the pattern for colors and disabilities, however, the elative is invariable for number and gender. On the use of the elative adjective, see 8.1.8.

9

2.3. Gender and number inflection

2.3.1. Gender and number inflections for nouns, adjectives, and participles

The masculine gender is the unmarked gender for most singular nouns and adjectives. Following are the inflectional endings for the feminine, the dual, and the plural.

	Noun	Adjective	Participle
FS	/-a/ /smaana/ 'week'	/-a/ /sˤʕiiba/ 'hard, difficult (fs)'	/-a/ /ḥaabba/ 'liking, wanting (fs)
	/-ət/ /jaarəthaa/ 'her neighbor (fs)'	/-ət/ /ḥamrət lwəjh/ 'red-faced (fs)'	/-aa-/ /ʕaarfaanaa/ 'knowing (fs) us'
Dual	/-iin/ or /-een/ /waaldiin/ 'two parents'		
	/-ee-/ /ʕeeneehaa/ 'her two eyes'		
MP	/-iin/ /xəddaamiin/ 'workers'	/-iin/ /ḥəlwiin/ 'sweet (p)'	
FP	/-aat/ /plaaṣaat/ 'places'	/-aat/ /muuhəmmaat/ 'important (fp)'	/-aat/ /jaayaat/ 'coming (fp)'

2.3.2. The feminine singular inflection

A feminine noun, adjective, or participle, when it derives from a masculine form, marks feminine grammatical gender with the suffix /-a/ or one of its other forms.

2.3.2.1. Forms of the feminine singular inflection

2.3.2.1.1. The form /-a/ occurs with forms that are independent or isolated. These include the noun (/smaana/ 'week'), adjective (/sˤʕiiba/ 'hard, difficult'), and participle (/ḥaabba/ 'thinking; saying'). That is, /-a/ occurs where there is no suffixed pronoun and no noun following in a construct phrase.

10

2.3.2.1.2. The form /-ət/ precedes a suffixed pronoun or a noun in a construct phrase, for nouns (/jaarəthaa/ 'her neighbor (fs)') and adjectives (/ḥamrət lwəjh/ 'red-faced (fs)'). It also occurs with nouns preceding the dual suffix /-een/ (/saaʕteen/ 'two years'). Note that the short /ə/ of /-ət/ elides when it occurs in an open syllable, as it does in /saaʕteen/ 'two years' (from /saaʕəteen/).

2.3.2.1.3. The form /-aa-/ is used with participles that take a suffixed pronoun as direct object (/ʕaarfaanaa/ 'knowing (fs) us').

2.3.3. The dual

Only nouns take the dual suffix /-iin/ or /-een/ to mean "two" of anything; adjectives and pronouns do not take dual suffixes. The dual is not productive in SAA. It occurs with nouns that name persons or objects that typically occur in sets of two. This group of words includes paired body parts (/wədniin/ 'two ears'). It also includes periods of time and may have an approximate meaning (/yoomeen/ 'two days; a couple of days, several days').

See 8.1.6.2 on the agreement of adjectives and participles that modify dual nouns.

2.3.3.1. Forms of the dual inflection

2.3.3.1.1. The form /-iin/ or /-een/ occurs with a noun that is independent or isolated. That is, /-iin/ occurs in the absence of a suffixed pronoun or of a second noun in a construct phrase (/ʕaamiin/ 'two years').

2.3.3.1.2. The form /-ii-/ or /-ee-/ occurs with a noun that takes a suffixed pronoun (/ʕeeniihaa/ 'her two eyes'). It may also occur when a noun with the dual suffix is followed by a second noun in a construct phrase (/saaʕtee lxədma/ 'two hours of work'). This construction is not common. Most speakers use instead a possessive adjective construction (/saaʕteen **taaʕ** lxədma/).

2.3.4. The masculine sound plural

The suffix for the masculine sound plural of nouns, adjectives, and participles is /-iin/. The forms of the broken or ablaut plural in SAA, as in MSA, are not predictable. Note that, the masculine sound plural suffix /-iin/ is homophonous with one variant of the dual suffix /-iin/. The two suffixes are, however, limited in their use: the masculine sound plural occurs most often with nouns naming humans (/xəddaamiin/ 'workers'), while the dual is typically used with nouns that name body parts (/wədniin/ 'two ears') and periods of time (/yoomiin/ 'two days'). In the unlikely event of overlap

11

between the two homophones, context usually makes clear the number intended by the speaker.

2.3.4.1. Forms of the masculine sound plural

2.3.4.1.1. The form /-iin/ occurs with nouns (/xəddaamiin/ 'workers'). It also occurs with adjectives (/ooxriin/ 'other (mp)') and participles (/mwaalfiin/ 'accustomed, used to (mp)') that are independent or isolated.

2.3.4.1.2. In SAA, the /n/ of /-iin/ may be retained preceding a suffixed pronoun, as in /mətfaahmiinuu/ 'mutually understanding it (ms)'. This occurs most frequently with participles that take suffixed pronouns, as in the cited example. Where nouns are concerned, the tendency is to avoid using a masculine sound plural with a suffixed pronoun. The noun and the pronoun are instead linked with the possessive adjective construction, as in /lxəddaamiin taaʕhaa/ 'its [i.e. the company's] workers'.

2.3.5. The feminine sound plural

The suffix for the feminine sound plural of nouns, adjectives, and participles is /-aat/. This form occurs with independent forms. These include nouns (/plaaṣaat/ 'places'), adjectives (/muuhəmmaat/ 'important (fp)'), and participles (/jaayaat/ 'coming (fp)'). Nouns in the feminine sound plural also have the suffix /-aat/ preceding a suffixed pronoun (/xwaataatii/ 'my sisters') and when in a construct phrase (/ḥaajaat lmədrasa/ 'things pertaining to school').

3. Verb morphology

3.1. Affixes of the perfect, imperfect, and imperative

3.1.1. Suffixes of the perfect

/njəm/ 'to be able'				
	Singular	Plural	Singular	Plural
3M		/-uu/	/njəm/ 'he was able'	/nəjmuu/ 'they (p) were able'
3F	/-ət/		/nəjmət/ 'she was able'	
2M	/-t/	/-tuu/	/njəmt/ 'you (ms) were able'	/njəmtuu/ 'you (p) were able'
2F	/-tii/*		/njəmtii/* 'you (fs) were able'	
1	/-t/	/-naa/	/njəmt/ 'I was able'	/njəmnaa/ 'we were able'

*See below on the 2FS suffix of the perfect verb.

12

3.1.1.1. The 2FS suffix of the perfect verb

The 2FS suffix is not general throughout SAA. Some sub-varieties of SAA have only one suffix for 2S, masculine and feminine. That suffix is /-t/ as in /njəmt/ 'you (S) were able.'

3.1.1.2. The 3P and 2P suffixes of the perfect verb

As in certain other varieties of spoken Arabic, SAA has no gender distinction in the 3P and 2P perfect verb. The 3P or 2P form indicates masculine, feminine, and mixed-gender groups, just as the 1P form does.

3.1.2. Affixes of the imperfect

/njəm/ 'to be able'				
	Singular	Plural	Singular	Plural
3M	/yə-/	/yə- -uu/	**/yənjəm/** 'he wrote'	**/yə**njəmuu/* 'they (p) wrote'
3F	/tə-/		/tənjəm/ 'she wrote'	
2M	/tə-/	/tə- -uu/	/tənjəm/ 'you (ms) wrote'	/tənjəmuu/* 'you (p) wrote'
2F	/tə- -ii/		/tənjəmii/* 'you (fs) wrote'	
1	/nə-/	/nə- -uu/	/nənjəm/ 'I wrote'	/nənjəmuu/* 'we wrote'

*Variations in syllable structure are detailed in the treatment of the forms of the verb that follows this section.

3.1.2.1. The 3MS and 3P prefixes of the imperfect /yə-/

Preceding a consonant cluster, the 3MS and 3P prefixes of the imperfect have the form /yə-/, as in **/yə**ktəb/ 'he wrote'. Preceding a single consonant, the 3MS and 3P prefixes often show loss of the short vowel in the open syllable and have the form /ii/, as in /**i**idəll/ 'he points out, indicates'. Some sub-varieties of SAA, however, maintain the short vowel in the prefix, as in /**yə**dəll/ .

3.1.2.2. The 3P and 2P affixes of the imperfect verb

As in certain other varieties of spoken Arabic, SAA has no gender distinction in the 3P and 2P imperfect verb. The plural forms indicate masculine, feminine, and mixed-gender groups.

3.1.2.3. The 1S and 1P affixes of the imperfect verb

In SAA, as in other varieties of North African Arabic, the 1S and 1P affixes of the imperfect verb are as regular as are the 2S and 2P, and the 3S and 3P. That is, the 1S affix is /nə-/, while the 1P affixes are /nə-/ and /-uu/, to result in /nənjəm/ 'I was able' and /nənjəmuu/ 'we were able'.

3.1.3. Affixes of the imperative

/ḥbəs/ 'to stop'				
	Singular	Plural	Singular	Plural
2M	Ø	/-uu/	/ḥbəs/ 'stop (ms)'	/ḥəbsuu/* 'stop (p)'
2F	/-ii/		/ḥəbsii/* 'stop (fs)'	

*Variations in syllable structure are detailed in the treatment of the forms of the verb that follows this section.

The suffixes of the imperative resemble those of the imperfect, so that the imperative /ḥəbsuu/ 'stop (p)' shows a clear link to the imperfect /təbsuu/ 'you (p) stop'.

3.2. Forms of the verb in SAA

The descriptions that follow describe the perfect and imperfect in some detail. The imperative, as it derives from the imperfect through regular processes similar to those of MSA, is described only where regular derivational processes do not apply.

3.2.1. Form I verbs

3.2.1.1. The strong Form I verb

The loss of the short vowel in an open syllable leads to vowel shift in the stem of the strong Form I verb in preceding vowel-initial suffixes. As a result, the strong Form I verb can be said to have two stems, $C_1C_2vC_3$ and $C_1vC_2C_3$.

/xdəm/ - /yəxdəm/ 'to work; to make, do'				
	Perfect		Imperfect	
	Singular	Plural	Singular	Plural
3M	/xdəm/	/xədmuu/	/yəxdəm/	/yexdmuu/
3F	/xədmət/		/təxdəm/	/iixədmuu/
				/yexxədmuu/
				/yaaxədmuu/
2M	/xdəmt/	/xdəmtuu/	/təxdəm/	/texdmuu/
2F	/xdəmtii/		/təxdmii/	/təxədmuu/
			/txədmii/	/texxədmuu/
			/təxxədmii/	/taaxədmuu/
			/taaxədmii/	
1	/xdəmt/	/xdəmnaa/	/nəxdəm/	/nexdmuu/
				/nexədmuu/
				/nexxədmuu/
				/naaxədmuu/

3.2.1.1.1. The prefix of the imperfect has the short vowel /ə/ when it precedes a consonant cluster. Thus, /**yə**xdəm/ 'I work' but /**ii**xədmuu/ 'they work'.

3.2.1.1.2. The variant forms provided for the 2FS and all P forms of the imperfect verb may result from the loss of the stem vowel in an open syllable (see 1.3.2.).

3.2.1.2. Initially-weak or assimilated Form I verbs with /w/

Initially-weak or assimilated verbs Form I verbs with /w/ as C_1 lose the initial /w/ in the imperfect. They have the perfect stems wC_2vC_3 and wvC_2C_3 (or uuC_2vC_3 and uuC_2C_3), and the imperfect stem uuC_2vC_3, as in /wṣəl/ - /yuuṣəl/ 'to find'.

/wṣəl/ - /yuujəd/ 'to find'				
	Perfect		Imperfect	
	Singular	Plural	Singular	Plural
3M	/wṣəl/	/wəṣluu/	/yuuṣəl/	/yuuṣluu/
3F	/wəṣlət/		/tuuṣəl/	/iiwəṣluu/
				/yəwwəṣluu/
2M	/wṣəlt/	/wṣəltuu/	/tuuṣəl/	/tuuṣluu/
2F	/wṣəltii/		/tuuṣlii/	/twəṣluu/
			/twəṣlii/	/təwwəṣluu/
			/təwwəṣlii/	
1	/wṣəlt/	/wṣəlnaa/	/nuuṣəl/	/nuuṣluu/
				/nwəṣluu/
				/nəwwəṣluu/

3.2.1.2.1. The variant forms provided for the 2FS and all P forms of the imperfect verb result from the loss of the stem vowel in an open syllable. (See 1.3.2).

3.2.1.3. Initially-weak Form I verbs with /y/

Initially-weak Form I verbs with /y/ are less common than those with /w/. They have a single pattern for the perfect and the imperfect. That pattern is yiC$_2$vC$_3$ - yiiC$_2$vC$_3$, as in /iibəs/ - /yiibəs/ 'to be dry; to dry up'.

/iibəs/ - /yiibəs/ 'to be dry; to dry up'				
	Perfect		Imperfect	
	Singular	Plural	Singular	Plural
3M	/iibəs/	/iibsuu/	/yiibəs/	/yiibsuu/
3F	/iibəst/		/tiibəs/	/yəyyəbsii/
2M	/iibəst/	/iibəstuu/	/tiibəs/	/tiibsuu/
2F	/iibəstii/		/tiibsii/	/tyəbsuu/
			/tyəbsii/	/təyyəbsuu/
			/təyyəbsii/	
1	/iibəst/	/iibəsnaa/	/niibəs/	/niibsuu/
				/nyəbsu/
				/nəyyəbsuu/

3.2.1.3.1. The variant forms provided for the 2FS and all P forms of the imperfect verb result from the loss of the stem vowel in an open syllable. (See 1.3.2).

16

3.2.1.4. Hamza-initial or glottal stop-initial Form I verbs

Verbs that have an initial <u>hamza</u> or /ʔ/ (glottal stop) as a root consonant or radical in MSA rarely show that /ʔ/ in the perfect in SAA. Instead, the perfect is re-analyzed as finally-weak verb with the perfect stems C_1C_2aa and C_1C_2ii. The imperfect stem, however, has an initial long /aa-/, apparently to compensate for the loss of the /ʔ/, and no final long vowel. The two most common verbs of this type are /klaa/ - /yaakul/ 'to eat' and /xdaa/ - /yaaxud/ 'to take'.

/klaa/ - /yaakul/ 'to eat'				
	Perfect		Imperfect	
	Singular	Plural	Singular	Plural
3M	/klaa/	/klaaw/	/yaakul/	/yaakluu/
3F	/klaat/		/taakul/	
2M	/kliit/	/kliituu/	/taakul/	/taakluu/
2F	/kliitii/		/taaklii/	
1	/kliit/	/kliinaa/	/naakul/	/naakluu/

3.2.1.4.1. The imperative of verbs that have an initial <u>hamza</u> or /ʔ/ (glottal stop) as a root consonant or radical in MSA have been re-analyzed, as have the other tenses of this form. The imperative resembles the medially-weak verb (see 3.2.1.5).

/klaa/ - /yaakul/ 'to eat'		
	Singular	Plural
2M	/kul/ 'eat (ms)'	/kuluu/* 'eat (p)'
2F	/kulii/ 'eat (fs)'	

3.2.1.5. Medially-weak Form I verbs

Medially-weak Form I verbs have two perfect stems in SAA, as in MSA. The perfect stem for 3S and 3P is C_1aaC_3. The perfect stem for 2S and 2P, as well as for 1S and 1P, is C_1vC_3. The imperfect stem is iiC_1vvC_3.

As in MSA, some sub-varieties of SAA have a short vowel in the perfect stem that corresponds to the long vowel of the imperfect stem, as in /ʃaaf/ - /ʃuft/ - /iiʃuuf/ 'to see' and /daar/ - /dirt/ - /iidiir/ 'to do, make'. For certain verbs, of course, the short vowel of the perfect stem does not correspond to the long vowel of the imperfect stem, as in /xaaf/ - /xuft/ - /yaxaaf/ 'to fear'.

Other sub-varieties of SAA have neutralization of the distinctions between short vowels. As a result, the short vowel of the perfect stem is /ə/,

17

whatever the long vowels are, as in /ʃaaf/ - /ʃəft/ - /iiʃuuf/ 'to see'. The presence of pharyngeal consonants or the sounds /ḥ - x - ʕ - ɣ - q - h/, however, may affect the quality of the short vowel even in these sub-varieties. For this reason, one may hear /qaal/ - /qult/ - /iiquul/ as well as /qaal/ - /qəlt/ - /iiquul/ 'to say'.

/ʃaaf/ - /iiʃuuf/ 'to see'				
	Perfect		Imperfect	
	Singular	Plural	Singular	Plural
3M	/ʃaaf/	/ʃaafuu/	/iiʃuuf/	/iiʃuufuu/
3F	/ʃaafət/		/tʃuuf/	
2M	/ʃəft/	/ʃəftuu/	/tʃuuf/	/tʃuufuu/
2F	/ʃəftii/		/tʃuufii/	
1	/ʃəft/	/ʃəfnaa/	/nʃuuf/	/nʃuufuu/

3.2.1.6. Medially-weak Form I verbs as medial-hamza verbs in MSA

Some verbs that have the hamza as C$_2$, in MSA are re-analyzed as medially-weak verbs. This is because the hamza generally does not occur as phoneme or base unit of the SAA sound system. An example is saʔala 'to ask (a question)' in MSA. It becomse /saal/ - /iisaal/ in SAA (also /suwwəl/ - /iisuwwəl/).

3.2.1.7. Finally-weak Form I verbs

Finally-weak verbs in SAA have two stems in the perfect. The 3S and 3P stem is C$_1$C$_2$aa (/ʃraa/ 'to buy'); the stem for other persons and numbers (preceding consonant-initial suffixes) is C$_1$C$_2$ii (/ʃriit/ 'I studied'). Two patterns exist for finally-weak verbs in the imperfect. Some verbs retain the final /-aa/ in the imperfect, as in /bqaa/ - /yəbqaa/ 'to stay, remain'. Other verbs have a final /-ii/ in the imperfect, as in /mʃaa/ - /yəmʃii/ 'to go'.

The final long /aa/ of the perfect stem does not elide preceding a suffix. The 3FS and all P forms of the perfect are, thus /bqaat/ 'she sayed and /bqaaw/ 'they stayed'. Likewise, in some sub-varieties of SAA, the final long /aa/ and /ii/ of the imperfect stem do not elide. The results, in some sub-varieties, are /yəbqaaw/ 'they stayed and /yəmʃiiw/ 'they went'. In other sub-varieties, the long vowels elide, producing /yəbquu/ 'they stayed and /yəmʃuu/ 'they went'.

It should be noted that verbs which in MSA have hamza or /ʔ/ as C$_3$ are reanalyzed as finally-weak in SAA, as in certain other varieties of spoken Arabic. This is because hamza or /ʔ/ does not typically act as a full phoneme in SAA. One example of such a verb is /qraa/ - /yəqraa/ 'to study; to read' (compare MSA qaraʔa 'to read').

18

3.2.1.7.1. Finally-weak Form I verbs with /aa/ in the imperfect

/bqaa/ - /yəbqaa/ 'to read; to study'				
	Perfect		Imperfect	
	Singular	Plural	Singular	Plural
3M	/**bqaa**/	/**bqaa**w/	/yə**bqaa**/	/yə**bqaa**w/
3F	/**bqaa**t/		/tə**bqaa**/	/yə**bqu**u/
2M	/**bqi**it/	/**bqi**ituu/	/tə**bqaa**/	/tə**bqaa**w/
2F	/**bqi**itii/		/tə**bqaa**y/ /tə**bq**ii/	/tə**bqu**u/
1	/**bqi**it/	/**bqi**inaa/	/nə**bqaa**/	/nə**bqaa**w/ /nə**bqu**u/

3.2.1.7.2. Finally-weak Form I verbs with /ii/ in the imperfect

/mʃaa/ - /yəmʃii/ 'to forget'				
	Perfect		Imperfect	
	Singular	Plural	Singular	Plural
3M	/**mʃaa**/	/**mʃaa**w/	/yəm**ʃii**/	/yəm**ʃii**w/
3F	/**mʃaa**t/		/təm**ʃii**/	/yəm**ʃu**u/
2M	/**mʃi**it/	/**mʃi**ituu/	/təm**ʃii**/	/təm**ʃii**w/
2F	/**mʃi**itii/		/təm**ʃii**/	/təm**ʃu**u/
1	/**mʃi**it/	/**mʃi**inaa/	/nəm**ʃii**/	/nəm**ʃii**w/ /nəm**ʃu**u/

3.2.1.7.3. Finally-weak Form I verbs with /uu/ in the imperfect

There are few finally-weak Form I verbs with /uu/ in the imperfect in SAA. One exception is /ḥbaa/ - /yəḥbuu/ 'to crawl'.

3.2.1.8. Doubled or geminate Form I verbs

Geminate Form I verbs are those in which C_2 and C_3 are the same, as in /ʃədd/ - /iiʃədd/ 'to pull'. The perfect stem resembles the imperfect stem with the pattern $C_1vC_2C_3$. The conjugation of doubled or geminate Form I verbs in the perfect resembles that of the finally-weak Form I verb in SAA (see 3.2.1.7). That is, the doubled or geminate consonant is retained throughout the conjugation, and the long vowel /ii/ precedes the suffix of the perfect in 2S and 2P, as well as in 1S and 1P (as in /ʃəddiit/ 'I pulled').

19

/ʃədd/ - /iiʃədd/ 'to pull'				
	Perfect		Imperfect	
	Singular	Plural	Singular	Plural
3M	/ʃədd/	/ʃədduu/	/iiʃədd/	/iiʃədduu/
3F	/ʃəddət/		/tʃədd/	
2M	/ʃəddiit/	/ʃəddiituu/	/tʃədd/	/tʃədduu/
2F	/ʃəddiitii/		/tʃəddii/	
1	/ʃəddiit/	/ʃəddiinaa/	/nʃədd/	/nʃədduu/

3.2.1.8.1. The imperfect prefix of geminate Form I verbs does not have the short /ə/ vowel. The stem begins with a single consonant (as in /-ʃədd/ 'to pull', as opposed to the initial consonant cluster of verbs like /-ftəl/ 'to spin (wool, cotton, etc.)'. For this reason, the 3S and 3P imperfect prefix is /ii-/, rather than /yə-/.

3.2.1.9. Other Form I verbs

3.2.1.9.1. Only one verb in SAA is truly irregular. It is the verb /jaa/ - /iijii/ 'to come'.

/jaa/ - /iijii/ 'to come'				
	Perfect		Imperfect	
	Singular	Plural	Singular	Plural
3M	/jaa/	/jaaw/	/iijii/	/iijiiw/
3F	/jaat/		/tjii/ /tiijii/	/iijuu/
2M	/jiit/	/jiituu/	/tjii/	/tjiiw/
2F	/jiitii/		/tiijii/	/tjuu/ /tiijiiw/ /tiijuu/
1	/jiit/	/jiinaa/	/njii/ /niijii/	/njiiw/ /njuu/ /niijiiw/ niijuu/

3.2.1.9.1.1. Variations in the prefix of the imperfect of /jaa/ 'to come'

Two variations occur in the imperfect prefix of /jaa/ 'to come'. One variation is the addition of the long vowel /ii/ to the imperfect prefix. This appears to compensate for the brevity of the stem. The result, for example, is the 2S form /tiijii/ 'you come'. This variation is listed in the table above. The other variation is the assimilation of the prefix /t/, an unvoiced consonant, to the following /j/, a voiced consonant. The result, for example, is the 2S form /djii/ 'you come'. This variation is not listed, as assimilation is a sound change typical of SAA and other varieties of spoken Arabic.

3.2.1.9.1.2. The imperative of /jaa/ 'to come'

The imperative of /jaa/ 'to come' also shows some variation. It may have no prefix vowel, as in /jii/ 'come (2S)'. Alternatively, it may have the short prefix vowel /i/ or /a/, as in /ijii/ and /ajii/ 'come (2S).

Verb /jaa/ - /iijii/ 'to come'	
Imperative Singular	Imperative Plural
/jii/	/jiiw/
/ijii/	/ijiiw/
/ajii/	/ajiiw/

3.2.2. Derived verb forms

The description that follows assumes that weak and geminate stems of derived verb forms behave like strong stems. Weak and geminate stems of derived verb forms are described only where they behave differently from the corresponding strong forms.

This brief description of SAA does not include discussion of the meanings associated with each of the derived verb forms. For such information, a reference grammar should be consulted.

3.2.2.1. Form II verbs

Form II is one of the most frequently-used of the derived verb forms. With a geminate C_2, it has the pattern $C_1vC_2C_2vC_3$ - $iiC_1vC_2C_2vC_3$, as in /ʕalləm/ - /iiʕalləm/ 'to to learn (s.t.)'.

Form II verbs, like other derived verbs forms, shows vowel loss before vowel-initial suffixes. An example is /tʕalləm/ 'you (ms) learn' but /tʕallmii/ 'you (fs) learn'.

3.2.2.1.1. Medially-weak Form II verbs may show monophthongization (change of a diphthong to a monophthong) where the verbal suffix is vowel-initial. The result is /zowwəq/ 'he decorated' but /zoowqət/ 'she decorated'.

3.2.2.1.2. Finally-weak Form II verbs have the pattern $C_1aC_2C_2aa$ - $yaC_1aC_2C_2ii$. That is, they have a final /-aa/ in the perfect and a final /-ii/ in the imperfect, as in /rabbaa/ - /iirabbii/ 'to bring up, raise (child or animal)'.

21

3.2.2.2. Four-consonant or quadriliteral verbs

Four-consonant or quadriliteral verbs have four, rather than three, root consonants or radicals. They have a pattern similar to that of Form II verbs, except that two different consonants make up the consonant cluster in the middle of the verb. The pattern is $C_1vC_2C_3vC_4$ - ii$C_1vC_2C_3vC_4$, as in /farkət/ - /iifarkət/ 'to search'.

3.2.2.3. Form III verbs

Form III verbs have a long /-aa-/ preceding the second root consonant. The pattern of the Form III verb is $C_1aaC_2vC_3$ - ii$C_1aaC_2vC_3$, as in /waaləf mʕa/ - /iiwaaləf mʕa/ 'to be or become used to, accustomed to'.

Form III verbs, like other derived verbs forms, show vowel loss before vowel-initial prefixes. An example is /twaaləf mʕaah/ 'you (ms) are used to him' but /twaalfii mʕaah/ 'you (fs) are used to him.

3.2.2.3.1. Finally-weak Form III verbs have the pattern C_1aaC_2aa - yaC_1aaC_2ii. That is, they have a final /-aa/ in the perfect and a final /-ii/ in the imperfect, as in /saawaa/ - /iisaawii/ 'to do, make'.

3.2.2.4. Form IV verbs

Form IV verbs, with the pattern ʔa$C_1C_2aC_3$ – yu$C_1C_2iC_3$, such as ʔantaj 'to produce', occur in SAA mainly in words borrowed from MSA. The form is not productive in SAA. Verbs familiar from MSA are usually re-analyzed in SAA as Form I verbs. Compare, for example the SAA verb /ṣbəḥ/ 'to become' to the MSA ʔaṣbaha 'to become'.

3.2.2.5. Form V and Form VI verbs

Form V verbs derive from Form II through the addition of the prefix /t-/. Form V has the pattern t$C_1vC_2C_2vC_3$ - yvt$C_1vC_2C_2vC_3$, as in /tbəddəl/ - /yətbəddəl/ 'to change (o.s. or one's clothing)'. Similarly, Form VI verbs derive from Form III through the addition of the prefix /t-/. Form VI has the pattern t$C_1aaC_2vC_3$ - yvt$C_1aaC_2vC_3$, as in /txaaləṭ/ - /yətxaaləṭ/ 'to associate, go around together'.

Form V verbs and Form VI verbs, like other derived verbs forms, show vowel loss before vowel-initial prefixes. An example of Form V is /tətbəddəl/ 'you (ms) change' but /tətbəddlii/ 'you (fs) change'.

3.2.2.5.1. Finally-weak Form V and Form VI verbs have a final /-aa/ in the perfect and the imperfect. Form V has the pattern t$C_1vC_2C_2aa$ - yvt$C_1vC_2C_2aa$, as in /tḥallaa/ - /yətḥallaa/ 'to be, become sweet, nice'. Form VI has the pattern tC_1aaC_2aa - yvtC_1aaC_2aa, as in /tlaaqaa/ - /yətlaaqaa/ 'to meet, encounter (one another)'.

3.2.2.6. Form VII verbs

Form VII derives from Form I through the addition of the prefix /n-/. It has the pattern $nC_1vC_2vC_3$ - $yvnC_1vC_2vC_3$, as in /nxaṭəb/ - /yənxaṭəb/ 'to get engaged (to be married)'.

Medially-weak Form VII verbs resemble medially-weak Form I verbs because medially-weak Form VII verbs also have two stems for the perfect. The perfect stem for 3S and 3P is nC_1aaC_3. The perfect stem for 2S and 2P, as well as for 1S and 1P, is nC_1vC_3. The imperfect stem is $yvnC_1aaC_3$. The correspondence between the short stem vowel of the perfect and the long stem vowel of the imperfect is frequently neutralized in SAA, so that the vowel of the short stem is /ə/. One example is /nbaaʕ/ (also /mbaaʕ/) - /nbəʕt/ - /yənbaaʕ/ 'to be sold', derived from the Form I verb /baaʕ/ - /iibiiʕ/ 'to sell'.

3.2.2.6.1. Finally-weak Form VII verbs have a final long /-aa/ in the perfect and the imperfect. They have the pattern nC_1vC_2aa - $yvnC_1vC_2aa$, as in /nʕaṭaa/ - /yənʕaṭaa/ 'to be given'. Finally-weak Form VII verbs show the same variation in the plural forms of the imperfect as do finally-weak Form I verbs. An example is /yənʕaṭaa/ 'it (ms) is given' and /yənʕaṭaaw/ or /yənʕaṭuu/ 'they (p) are given'.

3.2.2.7. Form VIII verbs

Form VIII derives from Form I through the addition of an infixed /t/ after C_1. It has the pattern $C_1tvC_2vC_3$ – $yvC_1vC_2vC_3$, as in /ḥtarəm/ - /yəḥtarəm/ 'to respect'. Form VIII verbs occur in SAA, but can be considered borrowings from MSA. The form is not productive in SAA.

Form VIII verbs also show vowel loss before vowel-initial prefixes. An example is /təḥtarəm/ 'you (ms) respect' but /təḥtarmii/ 'you (fs) respect'.

The perfect shows some variation. Some speakers pronounce this form with an initial consonant cluster, as in /ḥtarəm/. Others insert a short /ə/ before that cluster, as in /əḥtarəm/.

3.2.2.7.1. Medially-weak Form VIII verbs have /aa/ as the long vowel of the perfect stem and the imperfect stem. In SAA, these verbs may show variation in the treatment of the long vowel of the perfect before a consonant-initial suffix.

In some cases, the medially-weak Form VIII verb has the pattern C_1taaC_3 – C_1tvC_3 - yvC_1taaC_3, as in /xtaar/ - /xtart/ - /yəxtaar/ 'to choose'. This variant resembles the treatment of the long vowel of the perfect in MSA. Another variant retains the long vowel before the consonant-initial suffixes of the perfect, as in /xtaar/ - /xtaart/ - /yəxtaar/ 'to choose'. Yet another variant preserves the long vowel of the stem and inserts the long vowel /ii/ before a consonant-initial suffix in the perfect. This treatment of the long vowel before a consonant-initial suffix resembles that of the doubled Form I verb. The result, for example is /xtaaruu/ 'they chose' but /xtaariinaa/ 'we chose'.

3.2.2.7.2. Finally-weak Form VIII verbs have a final long /-aa/ in the perfect. They show variation in the final long vowel of the imperfect. It may be /-ii/ or /-aa/. Finally-weak Form VIII verbs thus have the pattern vC_1taC_2aa - yvC_1taC_2aa or yvC_1taC_2ii, as in /əlthaa b-/ - /yəlthaa b-/ or /yəlthii b-/ 'to care for'.

3.2.2.8. Form IX verbs

The Form IX verb of SAA differs from that of MSA in two ways. First, the Form IX verb in SAA has the pattern $C_1C_2aaC_3$. Second, the Form IX verb in SAA describes colors, as in /ḥmaar/ 'to be or become red'. It also describes characteristics derived from common adjectives. Examples include /ṭwaal/ 'to be or become long or tall' and /xlaaṣ/ 'to be finished, completed'.

Form IX verbs, unlike other SAA verbs with a long stem vowel, preserve that long vowel through the paradigm. Sub-varieties of SAA vary in their treatment of the verb stem before the consonant-initial suffixes of the perfect as they do for medially-weak Form VIII verbs. One variant retains the long vowel before the consonant-initial suffixes of the perfect with no change, as in /ḥmaaruu/ 'they turned red' and /ḥmaartuu/ 'you (p) turned red'. Another variant preserves the long vowel of the stem but inserts the long vowel /ii/ before a consonant-initial suffix in the perfect. This treatment of the long vowel before a consonant-initial suffix resembles that of the doubled Form I verb. The result, for example is /ḥmaaruu/ 'they turned red' but /ḥmaartiiw/ 'you (p) turned red'.

3.2.2.9. Form X verbs

Form X verbs have the pattern $əstC_1vC_2vC_3$ - $yvstvC_1C_2vC_3$ such as /stəʕmar/ 'to settle, colonize'. One variant of this form has as /ss/ as the prefix, as in /ssənnaa/ 'to wait', derived from /stənnaa/. Form X is not productive in SAA.

Strong verbs of Form X may show vowel shift before the vowel-initial prefixes of the perfect. An example is /stəʕmar/ 'he colonized' as opposed to /əstʕamruu/ 'they colonized'. The influence of MSA, however, may prevent vowel shift, as in /staʕmaruuhum/ 'they [the Turks] colonized them [the other Arab countries]' (Selection 2).

24

3.2.2.9.1. Initially-weak or assimilated Form X verbs

Initially-weak or assimilated verbs of Form X may or may not show vowel shift preceding the vowel-initial suffixes of the perfect. An example of short vowel preservation is /stowṭənuu/ 'they settled, colonized' (or /stooṭənuu/, with change of the diphthong /aw/ to /oo/). Vowel shift results in /stwəṭnuu/.

3.2.2.9.2. Finally-weak Form X verbs

There appears to be variation in the final vowels of finally-weak Form X verbs, as in other derived forms of the verb. Some Form X verbs have /aa/ as the final long vowel of the imperfect, as in /stənnaa/ - /yəstənnaa/ 'to wait'. Others have /ii/, as in /stədʕaa/ - /yəstədʕii/ 'to invite; to summon, subpoena'.

3.2.2.10. The form $tvC_1C_2vC_3$

3.2.2.10.1. Verbs of the form $tvC_1C_2vC_3$ have the pattern $tvC_1C_2vC_3$ - $yvtC_1C_2vC_3$, as in /təxdəm/ - /yətxdəm/ 'to be done, made'. This form is very productive in SAA as a quasi-passive. That is, it has passive meaning (to be X) without the internal vowels of the MSA passive voice. Note that Form VII (see 3.2.2.6) also occurs with quasi-passive meaning.

There is some variation in this verb form. For example, the single /t/ of the prefix may be doubled, as in /ttəxdəm/.

Verbs of the form $təC_1C_2vC_3$ show vowel loss and vowel shift preceding the vowel-initial suffixes of the perfect. An example is /təxdəm/ 'it (ms) was done' as opposed to /txədmuu/ 'they were done'.

3.2.2.10.2. The finally-weak verb of this form has a final long /-aa/ in the perfect and in the imperfect, as in /təbnaa/ - /yətbnaa/ 'to be built'.

3.3. Other forms derived from verbs

3.3.1. Verbal nouns

Verbal nouns of Form I verbs in SAA, as in MSA, are not predictable. The following list gives patterns and examples of verbal nouns for the derived verb forms. Note that, for many derived verbs, speakers of SAA may use the verbal noun of the corresponding Form I verb, if such a verb exists.

Verb form	Verbal noun pattern	Example
Form II	tvC$_1$C$_2$iiC$_3$	/taḥwiis/ (from /ḥuwwəs/ 'to take a walk, stroll')
	tvC$_1$C$_2$aaC$_3$	/taʕdaal/ (from /ʕaddəl/ 'to prune, trim')
Form III	mC$_1$aaC$_2$C$_3$a	/mwaalfa/ or /wəlf/ (from /waaləf mʕa/ 'to associate with')
Form IV	(not productive in SAA)	
Form V	tvC$_1$C$_2$iiC$_3$	/təbdiil/ (from /bəddəl/ 'to change (s.o., s.t.), rather than from /tbəddəl/ 'to change (o.s. or one's clothing)')
Form VI	mC$_1$aaC$_2$C$_3$a	/mʕaanqa/ (from /ʕaanəq/ 'to embrace, hug (s.o.)' rather than /tʕaanəq/ 'to embrace, hug (one another)')
Form VII	use verbal noun of corresponding Form I	/xəṭba/ (from /xṭəb/ 'to give in marriage, affiance' rather than /nxəṭəb/ 'to be given in marriage, engaged')
Form VIII	(not productive in SAA)	
Form IX	(not productive in SAA)	
Form X	(not productive in SAA)	
SAA form tC$_1$vC$_2$vC$_3$	(not predictable and often derived from correspond-ing Form I verb)	/xədma/ (from Form I /xdəm/ - /yəxdəm/ 'to work; to do, make rather than /txədəm - /yətxdəm/ 'to be done, made')

3.3.2. Active participles

3.3.2.1. The active participle of Form I verbs

3.3.2.1.1. The active participle of strong Form I verbs has the pattern C$_1$aaC$_2$vC$_3$, as in /ḥaabəs/ 'stopped, not moving' (from /ḥbəs/ - /yəḥbəs/ 'to stop').

3.3.2.1.2. The active participle of medially-weak Form I verbs has the pattern C$_1$aayvC$_3$, as in /ʕaayəʃ/ 'living' (from /ʕaaʃ/ - /iiʕiiʃ/ 'to live').

3.3.2.1.3. The active participle of finally-weak Form I verbs has the pattern C$_1$aaC$_2$ii, as in /baaqii/ 'staying, remaining' (from /bqaa/ - /yəbqaa/ 'to stay, remain').

26

3.3.2.1.4. The active participle of geminate verbs has the pattern $C_1aaC_2C_3$, as in /ḥaabb/ 'liking; wanting (ms)' (from /ḥabb/ - /iiḥabb/ 'to like, love; to want'.

3.3.2.2. The active participle of derived verbs

The active participle of derived verbs prefixes /m(v)-/ to the imperfect stem, as in /mwaaləf mʕa/ 'accustomed, used to' (from /waaləf mʕa/ - /iiwaaləf mʕa/ 'to be, become accustomed, used to') and /məddarrəg/ 'having hidden, concealed o.s.' (from /ddərrəg/ - /yəddərrəg/ 'to have hidden, concealed o.s.').

3.3.3. Passive participles

3.3.3.1. The passive participle of Form I verbs

3.3.3.1.1. The passive participle of Form I strong verbs has the pattern $mvC_1C_2uuC_3$, as in /maʕruud/ 'invited' (from /ʕrad̩/ - /yərʕəd̩/ 'to invite').

3.3.3.1.2. Medially-weak Form I verbs form their participle on the pattern mvC_1yuuC_3, as in /məbyuuʕ/ 'sold' (from /baaʕ/ - /iibiiʕ/ 'to sell').

3.3.3.1.3. All finally-weak Form I verbs have a final long /-ii/, with the pattern mvC_1C_2ii, as in /mʃrii/ 'bought' (from /ʃraa/ - /yeʃrii/ 'to buy').

3.3.3.2. The passive participle of derived verbs

The passive participle of derived verbs is homophonous with the active participle. Like the active participle, the passive participle of derived verbs prefixes /m(v)-/ to the stem of the imperfect, as in /mʕammər/ 'full, filled up' (from /ʕammər/ - /iiʕammər/ 'to fill, fill up').

3.4. Uses of the perfect

3.4.1. The perfect expresses the past

The perfect typically indicates action completed before the moment of speaking, that is, in the past, as in /jiit/ 'I came'. In some cases, however, speakers of SAA and other varieties of Arabic use the perfect to refer to events that a speaker of American English thinks of as occurring in the present, such as /fhəmt/ 'I understand, lit. I understood'. Usage like this is often explained as referring to the actual moment of comprehension, an event that preceeded the moment of speaking.

3.4.2. The perfect is the act (the performative)

In some cases, the perfect occurs in an utterance that is equivalent to an action. A familiar example of the performative in English is the statement "I apologize," where the apology takes place only when the words are said.

The performative use of the perfect in SAA often occurs in legal or contractual contexts, such as buying, selling, and divorce. The act of saying /qbəlt/ 'I accept, lit. I have accepted', for example, seals an agreement.

3.5. Uses of the imperfect

3.5.1. The simple imperfect

The simple imperfect is the most usual or default form of the non-past verb of SAA. Note that SAA differs from certain other varieties of spoken Arabic in that it has no prefixed imperfect form of the verb. That is, most sub-varieties of SAA do not use an imperfect marker such as the /bi-/ (as in /bi-yiʃtayil/ 'he works') of spoken Levantine and Egyptian Arabic. The imperfect of SAA has only one form, the simple imperfect with no marker, as in /yəxdəm/ 'he works'.

The time frame of the simple imperfect is not specific. The simple imperfect may make a general statement, as in /lemraa ... təxdəm barra w-təxdəm fə-ddaar/ 'A woman ... works outside the home and works at home' (Selection 32). It may describe repeated or habitual action, as in /diimaa yəḥḥafruu/ 'They are always digging' (Selection 7). It may depict action that takes place at the moment of speech, as in /maaniiʃ ... nguullək bəllii ṭoolga xeer mən biiskra/ 'I'm not telling you that Tolga is better than Biskra' (Selection 21). Finally, it may refer to an event in the near future, as in /taaxud draahəm, naʕṭuukum draahəm/ 'You'll get money, we'll give you money' (Selection 10). Adverbials of time and place, however, can clarify the time frame of the simple imperfect, as in the example from Selection 7 above.

3.5.2. The presentational particle /raa-/ and the imperfect

The presentational particle /raa-/, followed by a suffixed pronoun, may precede an imperfect verb. The exact meaning of this construction is not clear at present. Some sources analyze /raa-/ as an imperfect marker. They describe it as indicating action that is ongoing at the time of speaking, like the imperfect markers of other varieties of spoken Arabic. A more recent source (Boucherit 2003) offers an alternative analysis. It sees /raa-/ as adding expressive value to the utterance in which it occurs. As a result, a question like /ʃkuun llii raah yərbaḥ fiihaa/ may be better translated as 'Who on earth will profit from it', rather than 'Who profits from it?' (Selection 28)

Our data suggest that /raa-/ and the suffixed pronoun, when they precede an imperfect verb or other type of word, adds strength or emphasis to an utterance. This is most noticeable in narratives. See, for example, Selection 12. There the female speaker marks the turning points of her story with /raa-/ and another presentational particle /haa-/.

28

3.5.3. The future

As noted above, the simple imperfect may refer to an event in the near future, as in /**taaxud** draahəm, **naʕṭuukum** draahəm/ 'You'll get money, we'll give you money' (Selection 10). The future time of the simple imperfect, however, must be understood from context.

The future time frame becomes clearer when the active participle /raayəḥ/ 'going' (from /raaḥ/ - /iiruuḥ/ 'to go') precedes the imperfect verb. This participle inflects for gender and number, as most active participles. An example is /ləblaad **raayḥa** təððərr w-wlaad jjazaayər **raayḥiin** yiððərruu/ 'The country will be hurt and the children of Algeria will be hurt' (Selection 28).

3.5.4. Pre-verbs

SAA has a variety of pre-verbs. This is a general term for forms, usually verbs or participles, that precede a verb, the main verb. A pre-verb provides additional information about the time frame of the main verb (it is aspectual) or about an attitude towards the action of the main verb (it is modal). The following lists some of the most commonly-used pre-verbs of SAA.

3.5.4.1. /kaan/ as a pre-verb

For the most part, /kaan/ marks time in a nominal or verbal sentence. The role of /kaan/ is perhaps more clear in non-verbal sentences. For example, when the perfect of /kaan/ precedes a non-verbal construction, it moves the time frame of that construction into the past or future.

Non-verbal
fa-zmaan ddzaayər əlʕaaṣiima **kaan** əsəmhaa *Icosium.*
In the old days, the name of Algiers was *Icosium.* (Selection 1)

The perfect of /kaan/ may also precede the perfect or imperfect to change the time frame of the main verb. It effectively moves the event or action of the main verb into the past or future.

Perfect
yaʕnii fə-llowwəl kaant fiih ḥarb liʔanna **kaanuu jaabuu** diin jdiid.
That is, in the beginning, there was a war because they had brought a
   new religion. (Selection 2)

Imperfect

ssuuma taaʕ əlpətrool kaant mliiḥa, fa-**kaanuu yʃruu** kulləʃ mə-lxaarəj.

The price of oil was good, so they used to buy everything from abroad.
(Selection 3)

3.5.4.2. Verbs of motion as pre-verbs

3.5.4.2.1. Verbs of motion frequently function as pre-verbs. They may precede the imperfect, as in /iijii **yʕalləm**, iiwaasii ʃəɣluu wə-xlaaṣ/ 'He comes to teach, does his job, and that's it' (Selection 33). In verb strings like this, the action of the main verb causes or is the reason for the verb of motion. In other words, the relationship between the two verbs can be translated as 'to, in order to'.

3.5.4.2.2. Where a verb of motion precedes the perfect, the relationship between the two verbs is not one of cause and effect. It is simply a matter of sequence, as in /**jaat** *TF1* **daarət** ... *un reportage*/ 'TF1 [French television channel] came and did a report' (Selection 22). In these cases, the relationship between verbs is best translated as 'and'.

3.5.4.3. Other verbs as pre-verbs

The following lists common pre-verbs of SAA that occur in our data. It is not exhaustive. The translations that appear here are general; further details can be found in the "Glossary" at the end of this work.

♦ /bdaa/ - /yəbdaa/ 'to begin, start'
/**bdaaw** iiduuruu ʕlaa ʃʃaʕb fii əlquura/
'They started turning against the people in the villages.' (Selection 14)

♦ /bɣaa/ - /yəbɣii/ 'to want to; to like, love'
/lḥuukuuma law **bɣaat** tuwəqqəf haaðaa ʃʃii/
'the government, if it wanted to stop this thing' (u.d.)

♦ /xəṣṣ/ - /yxəṣṣ/ 'to be necessary'
/**iixəṣṣ** lmaa yṭiib/
'The water has to boil [lit. be cooked]' (Selection 23)

♦ /ḥabb/ - /iiḥabb/ 'to want to; to like, love'
/wəlla **yḥabb** iiruuḥ plaaṣa xraa *où il se repose*/
'... or he wants to go somewhere else *where he can relax*.' (Selection 35)

30

♦ /zaad/ - /iiziid/ 'to do again (action of main verb); to continue to do (action of main verb)'
/xuuyaa maa ḥabbʃ **iiziid** yahdər mʕaayaa *pendant un bon bout de temps*/
'My brother didn't want to talk to me again for a good long time."   (u.d.)

♦ /ʕaawəd/ - /iiʕaawəd/ 'to do again (action of following imperfect verb); to re-do, replace'
/iiruuḥuu yəḥənnuu w-**iiʕaawduu** yərʃʕuu lə-dyaarhum/
'They go and get henna, and they go back home again.' (Selection 16)

♦ /gaam/ - /iiguum/ 'to begin (to do s.t.); to get, stand up'
/kull ʃʃaʕb əljəzaaʔirii **gaam** ... iiʃaarək/
'All of the Algerians began ... to participate.' (Selection 3)

♦ /qdər/ - /yəqdər/ 'to be able to'
/waaḥəd əlfuqr llii maa **yəqdəruuʃ** iitḥammluu/
'... such poverty that they couldn't bear it' (Selection 4)

♦ /qʕad/ - /yəqʕad/ 'to keep on, continue (to do s.t.); to stay'
/nnaas laazəm yaʕqaluu ʃwiyya, **yəgʕaduu** yahdruu ... mʕa baʕḏhum baʕḏ/
'People need to be a little reasonable and keep talking ... with one another.' (u.d.)

♦ /njəm/ - /yənjəm/ 'to be able to'
/[à] *un certain point* maa **nənjmuuʃ** nərjəʕuu/
'[At] a certain point, we cannot go back.' (Selection 28)

♦ /wəllaa/ - /iiwəllii/ (also /wullaa/ - /iiwullii/) 'to begin, start; to become'
/**wəlliinaa** maa nəntjuu waaluu/
'We began to produce nothing at all.' (Selection 6)

3.5.4.4. Inflecting participles as pre-verbs

♦ /ḥaabb/ 'wanting, intending to' (active participle of /ḥabb/ - /iiḥabb/ 'to want to; to like, love')
/lkull **ḥaabbiin** gaaʕ yəxrujuu w-iiharbuu me-ddzaayər/
'Everyone just wants to leave and get away from Algeria.' (u.d.)

♦ /raayəḥ/ 'going to, will' (active participle of /raaḥ/ - /iiruuḥ/ 'to go'
/wlaad jjazaayər **raayḥiin** yəḏḏərru/
'The children of Algeria will be hurt.' (Selection 27)

31

♦ /gaaʕəd/ 'keeping on, continuing to' (active participle of /gʕad/ -
/yəgʕad/ 'to keep on, continue (to do s.t.); to stay')
/lqraaya **gaaʕdiin** naqraaw fiihaa zaayda/
'Education, we just keep on studying more.' (Selection 35)

3.5.4.5. Invariable forms as pre-verbs

♦ /raa-/ plus suffixed pronoun
/ʃkuun llii **raah yərbaḥ** fiihaa/
'Who on earth will profit from it?' (Selection 28)

♦ /ɣaadii/ 'going to, will'
/en allant vers la plage, **ɣaadii** nwərriilək *le château Santa Cruz/*
'As we go towards the beach, I will show you *the Chateau Santa Cruz.*'
(u.d.)

♦ /laazəm/ 'necessary'
/kaayn ookla xaaṣṣa **laazəm,** laazəm təndaar/
'There is a special food that must, it must be made.' (Selection 17)

♦ /məfruuḍ/ 'ought to, should'
/rabbamaa kaan **məfruuḍ** iixalluu haaðaa lḥizb yəḥkam ʃii ʃhuur
iiʃuufuu kiifaaʃ yədiir/
'Perhaps they should have let this party govern for a few months and see
how it did.' (Selection 11)

♦ /mumkən/ and /yəmkən/ 'possible'
/mumkən twəlliiluu?/
'Can you go back to him?' (u.d.)

/hakdaak martuu **yəmkən** təqdər təxdəm/
'That way, it's possible for his wife to work.' (Selection 33)

3.6. The use of the active participle

The active participle is usually translated as 'doing (the action of the verb)'.
The time frame of the active participle, like that of the prefixed imperfect
(see 3.5.1), is not specific. It may describe action that takes place at the
moment of speech, as in /raahya **qaaʕda** fə-lbiit ʕlaa jaal ddraarii/ 'She's
staying at home because of the kids' (Selection 33). It may refer to action in
the future, as in /ddars taaʕ ... ənnhaar llii **jaay**/ 'the lesson for ... the next
day (lit. the day to come)' (Selection 9). In addition, the active participle
may indicate the result of an action or describe a condition that took place

before the moment of speaking and still holds true. An example is /fiih ktiir mən əljaamaaʕaat llii **daaxliin** f-haaðaa ṣṣiiraaʕ/ 'There are a lot of groups that have gotten involved in this struggle' (Selection 13).

In still other cases, the active participle has taken on the meaning and functions of a noun. Active participles that act as nouns (that have been re-lexicalized) usually take a broken plural. Consider, for example, the active participle /raakəb/ 'riding', with the masculine sound plural /raakbiin/. In contrast, the noun /raakəb/ 'passenger' has the masculine broken plural /rəkkaab/.

4. Pronouns

4.1. Independent personal pronouns

The independent personal pronouns of SAA are listed here in two groups. One group is the default or typical form of the independent personal pronoun. A second group consists of those pronouns that have what we call 'strong forms'.

4.1.1. Independent personal pronouns: the default forms

In SAA, the default or typical forms of the independent personal pronouns show some variation.

	Singular	Plural
3M	/huwa/	/humma/
	/huu/	/humm/
3F	/hiyya/	/huum/
	/hii/	/huuma/
		/hum/
		/ham/
2M	/nta/	/ntuumaa/
2F	/ntii/	
1	/anaa/	/ḥnaa/

4.1.2. Independent personal pronouns: the strong forms

The strong forms of the independent personal pronouns occur only for the 1S form (/anaaya/), the 2MS (/ntaayaa/), the 2FS form (/ntiiyaa/), and the 1P (/ḥnaayaa/). The strong form of the personal pronoun has greater strength or force than the default or typical form. One example of the strong form in use is /kiifaaʃ ndiiruuhaa **ḥnaayaa**?/ 'How do we in particular do it?' (Selection 18).

4.2. Suffixed personal pronouns

There is a certain amount of variation in the forms of suffixed personal pronouns. This variation is conditioned by the sound that precedes the pronoun.

	following C	following v or V
3MS	/-uu/	/-h/ or Ø
3FS	/-haa/	
2MS	/-ək/	/-k/
2FS	/-ək/	/-kii/ or /-k/
1S (after non-verbal forms)	/-ii/	/yaa/
1S (after verbal forms)	/-nii/	
3P	/-hum/	
2P	/-kum/	
1P	/-naa/	

4.3. Demonstratives

4.3.1. Variable demonstratives

Like personal pronouns, some demonstratives change to indicate gender and number. They also show a certain amount of variation in their form. These are the forms that occur most often in our data; other forms may exist in sub-varieties of SAA.

	'this, these' (near demonstratives)	'that; those' (far demonstratives)
MS	/haaðaa/ /haadaa/ /haaðaay/ /haadaay/	/haaðaak/ /haadaak/ /haaðaaka/ /haadaaka/ /ðaak/
FS	/haaðii/ /haadii/ /haaðiyaa/ /haadiyaa/	/haaðiik/ /haadiik/ /haaðiika/ /haadiika/ /ðiik/
MP	/haaðuu/ /haaduu/ /haaðum/ /haadum/	/haaðuuk/ /haaduuk/ /haaðuuka/ /haaduuka/ /duuk/

34

As in MSA, demonstratives in SAA serve as pronouns, as in /haaðaa maa kaaʃ fə-lmaariikaan/ 'This does not exist in the US' (Selection 9). They also serve as adjectives. As such, they precede the noun phrase, as in /haaðaa rrdiim jaa mən kilmət yə ... yərdim/ 'This rdiim comes from the word yərdim "to bury"' (Selection 24). They may also follow the noun phrase, as in /lʕurs haaðaa taaʕnaa kiifaaʃ iitəmm?/ 'This wedding of ours, how does it take place? (Selection 17).

4.3.2. Invariable demonstrative

In addition to the variable demonstratives, SAA has the invariable demonstrative adjective /haad/. It may precede the noun phrase, as in /nʃaa ḷḷah haad ləqtiilaat wə-ddbiiḥaat iiḥabsuu/ 'God willing, these killings and massacres will stop' (u.d.). Less often, it follows the noun phrase, as in /taaʕ ərruumaan haad/ 'belonging to these Romans' (Selection 1).

4.3.3. The demonstrative /haak/

The demonstrative /haak/ occurs as a pronoun, as in /daar iiduu kiimaa haak w-nəggəz/ 'He put his hand like this and jumped' (Selection 25). More often, however, it functions as an adverbial, as in /iidiiruuh haak kbiir/ 'They do it like this, big' (Selection 34).

4.3.4. Adverbial demonstratives

The adverbial demonstratives ('thus, like this, this way' or 'thus, like that, that way') have a number of variants. One variant group includes /haak/, /hakkaa/, and /hakkaak/. A second consists of /haakðaa/ and /haakdaa/, while a third has /haakðaak/ and /haakdaak/. All are used in similar ways, as /haakdaak əljazaayər aṣbaḥt yaʕnii wiilaaya taaʕ, taaʕ ədduula lʕuθmaaniyya/ 'In that way, Algeria became, I mean, a province of, of the Ottoman state' (Selection 2).

4.3.4.1. Another use of the adverbial demonstrative

For some speakers, the adverbial demonstrative appears to function as a placeholder in the utterance. That is, it has no clear connection to the rest of the utterance in which it occurs. It is a filler that gives the speaker time to organize the rest of the utterance. This use of the adverbial demonstrative can be translated as 'like; you know', as in /maa zaal ʕaayʃiin ʃγul a ... haakðaak bərk *à la ... à la nature*/ 'They are still living a kind of, ah ... like that, just in a natural way' (Selection 22).

5. Numbers and number derivatives

5.1 Numbers for counting (cardinal numbers) and ordering (ordinal numbers)

5.1.1. Cardinal numbers 1 – 10

The cardinal numbers, like other elements of SAA, show a good deal of variation. For the most part, variation arises from phonological change. The number 'three' is a good example of variation due to phonological change. Note, however, that SAA has two different words for the number 'two'. Some, but not all of the variations that occur in SAA, are listed here.

1	/waaḥəd/ (ms) /waaḥda/ (fs)
2	/zuuj/ - /zooj/ - /zawj/ - /juuz/, /tneen/ - /θneen/
3	/tlaata/ - /θlaaθa/ - /θəlθ/ - /tlət/
4	/rabʕa/ - /arbaʕa/
5	/xəmsa/
6	/sətta/
7	/sbaʕa/ - /səbʕa/
8	/tmaanya/ - /θmaanya/
9	/təsʕa/
10	/ʕaʃra/

The numbers 3 - 10 may retain the final /a/ when they occur in a counted-noun construction (see 8.1.7). More often, however, the final /a/ drops out, especially in rapid speech. The cardinal numbers of SAA do not change in other ways. In this they differ from the numbers of MSA that have gender inflection.

5.1.2. Cardinal numbers 11 – 20

5.1.2.1. Cardinal numbers 11 – 20: Default form

The forms of the cardinal numbers listed here are the default or typical form used when the number occurs in counting or in isolation. A number occurs in isolation especially as an answer to a question such as "How old are you?" It can be answered with the number alone, as in /tlaṭṭaaʃ/ '13'.

11	/ḥdaaʃ/
12	/ṭnaaʃ/ - /tnaaʃ/ - /θnaaʃ/
13	/tlaaṭṭaaʃ/ - /θlaaṭṭaaʃ/
14	/rabˁaṭaaʃ/ - /arbaˁṭaaʃ/
15	/xəmsaṭaaʃ/
16	/səṭṭaaʃ/
17	/sbaˁṭaaʃ/ - /səbˁaṭṭaaʃ/
18	/tmaanṭaaʃ/ - /θmaanṭaaʃ/
19	/tsaˁṭaaʃ/ - /təsˁaṭaaʃ/
20	/ˁəʃriin/

5.1.2.2. Cardinal numbers 11 - 19 in combination

The cardinal numbers 11 - 19 in SAA take a different form when they occur in combination. The form adds the suffix /-ən/ to the defaut form of the number. The combination form is usually found in a counted noun construction. It would, for example, answer the question "How old are you?" with /tlaṭṭaaʃən səna/ '13 years old'.

11	/ḥdaaʃən/
12	/ṭnaaʃən/ - /tnaaʃən/ - /θnaaʃən/
13	/tlaaṭṭaaʃən/ - /θlaaṭṭaaʃən/
14	/rabˁaṭaaʃən/ - /arbaˁṭaaʃən/
15	/xəmsaṭaaʃən/
16	/səṭṭaaʃən/
17	/sbaˁṭaaʃən/ - /səbˁaṭṭaaʃən/
18	/tmaanṭaaʃən/ - /θmaanṭaaʃən/
19	/tsaˁṭaaʃən/ - /təsˁaṭaaʃən/

5.1.3. Cardinal numbers 10 – 100

Numbers in SAA compound as in MSA: /waaḥəd w-səttiin/ 'sixty-one'.

10	/ˁaʃra/
20	/ˁaʃriin/
30	/tlaatiin/ - /θlaaθiin/
40	/rəbˁiin/ - /arbaˁiin/
50	/xəmsiin/
60	/səttiin/
70	/sbaˁiin/ - /səbˁiin/
80	/tmaaniin/ - /θmaaniin/
90	/təsˁriin/
100	/mya/

37

5.1.4. Cardinal numbers 100 – 1000

100	/mya/
200	/miitiin/
300	/tlaatmya/ - /θlaaθmya/
400	/rabʕamya/ - /arbaʕmya/
500	/xəmsmya/
600	/səttmya/
700	/sbaʕmya/ - /səbʕamya/
800	/tmaanmya/ - /θmaanmya/
900	/tsaʕmya/ - /təsʕamya/
1000	/alf/

5.2. Ordinal numbers

5.2.1. Ordinal numbers 1 – 10

The ordinal numbers 1 - 10 are those used to order items from first to last. The form of the ordinal number in SAA resembles that of MSA and also inflects for gender and number.

first	/uwwəl/ - /owwəl/ (ms), /uulaa/ (fs), /uwwəliin/ (p)
second	/taanii/ - /θaanii/
third	/taaləl/ - /θaaləθ/
fourth	/raabəʕ/
fifth	/xaaməs/
sixth	/saadəs/
seventh	/saabəʕ/
eighth	/taamən/ - /θaamən/
nineth	/taasəʕ/
tenth	/ʕaaʃər/

38

5.3. Days of the week and months of the year

5.3.1. Days of the week

The names of most of the days of the week derive from numbers.

Sunday	/yoom əl-ḥədd/
Monday	/yoom əttneen/ - /yoom θθneen/
Tuesday	/yoom əttlaata/ - /yoom əθθlaaθa/
Wednesday	/yoom l-arbʕa/
Thursday	/yoom əlxmiis/
Friday	/yoom əl-jəmʕa/
Saturday	/yoom əssəbt/

5.3.2. Months of the year

The months of the secular or solar calendar in SAA derive from French or a related language. As with other word groups, the month names show some variation. The months of the Islamic or lunar calendar are as in MSA.

January	janvier	/jaanvyee/
February	février	/feevryee/
March	mars	/maarəs/ - /maars/
April	avril	/abriil/ - /avriil/
May	mai	/mee/
June	juin	/jwaan/
July	juillet	/jwiiyee/
August	août	/uut/
September	septembre	/səbtəmbər/
October	octobre	/ktoobər/
November	novembre	/noovaambər/
December	decembre	/diisaambər/

6. Prepositions

Prepositions occur with definite and indefinite nouns, or take suffixed pronouns as objects. A number of prepositions may occur in isolation when they have an adverbial function, as in /gəddaam/ 'in front'.

The following lists the most common prepositions of SAA. The translations given here are general; more precise translations can be found in the general glossary to this work or in the glossaries to individual selections.

Preposition	English translation
/bḥaal/	like, as
/baʕd/	after
/barraa/	outside of, outside
/bə-/ - /bii-/ - /b-/ (/bii-/ or /bə-/ with suffixed pronoun)	with (by means of)
/biin/ - /biinaat/	between, among
/blaa/	without
/təḥt/	underneath, downstairs
/ḥattaa/	until
/ḥdaa/	next to, beside
/xaarəj/	outside; overseas
/daaxəl/	within, inside
/siwaa/	other than, except
/ʃɣul/	like, as
/ɖ̣ədd/	against
/ʕand/ - /ʕan/ - /ʕad/	at (place or s.o.'s home)
/ʕlaa/ - /ʕal-/ - /ʕa-/ (/ʕlee-/ with suffixed pronoun)	on; about
/fii-/	at; on
/fooq/	above, on top of
/gṣaad/	opposite; across from
/qbəl/	before
/qədd/	as much as
/qəddaam/	in front, in front of
/kiif/ - /kii-/	like, as
/kiimaa/	like, as
/laawṭaa/	underneath; downstairs
/lə-/ - /l-/	to; for
/mʕa/ (/mʕaa-/ with suffixed pronoun)	with (accompanying)
/mən/ - /məm/ - /mə-/	from
/muur/	behind, in back of
/wraa/	behind, in back of

Many of these prepositions may occur in compounds, as in /mən baʕad/ 'after'.

7. Interrogatives

Following is a list of the interrogatives of SAA. As in other word classes, SAA interrogatives show a good deal of variation. Not all variants appear here. See 8.2.7 on the use of interrogatives in information questions.

Interrogative	English translation
/aamaa/	which?
/aaʃ mən/	which?
/ʃtaa/	what?
/ʃḥaal/	how many?; how much?
/ʃkuun/	who?
/ʃlaa qəddaaʃ/	when?
/ʃlaah/ - /ʃlaaʃ/	why?
/qəddaaʃ/	how much, how many?
/kiif/ - /kiifaaʃ/ - /kiifaah/ - /kii/	how?
/mniin/	when?
/mniin/	from where, whence?
/waaʃ/ - /wəʃ/ - /waaʃnuu/ - /wəʃnuu/	what?
/wiin/ - /ween/	where?

8. Phrases and sentences

8.1. Nouns and noun phrases

In general, the noun phrases of SAA resemble those of other varieties of Arabic. In addition to the definite article /l-/, however, SAA has two indefinite articles, /waaḥəd/ and /ʃii/. SAA also has an alternative to the construct phrase or ʔIḍafa, the possessive adjective construction.

8.1.1. The definite noun

8.1.1.1. The definite noun and the definite article

8.1.1.1.1. The definite noun may be marked by the definite article /l-/, as in /əlmsiid/ 'the mosque' or /ədduwaa/ 'the medication'. (The /l/ of the definite article assimilates to /j/ and to "sun letters" or apical consonant.)

8.1.1.1.2. The status of the definite article with code-switched words and phrases (usually from French) in SAA is not always clear. In certain contexts, the SAA definite article /l-/ can sound very much like the French MS definite article *le*. For the most part, it seems that speakers include the definite article in the switch, as in /qbəl *le quatrième*/ 'before the fourth one' (Selection 23). In some cases, however, the definite article assimilates as in Arabic to the following code-switched noun, as in /kaayən s-*sport*/ 'there are sports' (Selection 35).

41

8.1.1.2. The definite noun and a suffixxed pronoun

A noun with a suffixed pronoun is also definite, as in /əsəmhaa/ 'its (fs) name' or /daarnaa/ 'our house'.

8.1.1.3. The definite noun in the construct phrase

The first noun of a construct phrase (see 8.1.1.3) is definite when the second noun is definite, as in /mdiinət **ljazaayər**/ 'the city of Algiers'. When the second noun is indefinite, the first is also indefinite, as in /wəld **ʕaam**/ 'cousin; a cousin (lit. father's brother's child)'.

8.1.1.4. The definite noun as proper noun

Proper nouns, such as /tləmsaan/ 'Tlemcen' and /faaṭma/ 'Fatima (woman's name)', are definite.

8.1.2. The indefinite noun

8.1.2.1. The unmarked indefinite noun

The unmarked indefinite noun in SAA lacks an indefinite article. It also lacks a definite article /l-/ or suffixed pronoun, and is not part of a construct phrase, as in /maaḥabba/ 'love; a (kind of) love' or /ʕaayla/ 'family; a family'. The unmarked indefinite noun is the usual or default form of the indefinite noun in SAA.

8.1.2.2. The indefinite article /waaḥəd/

8.1.2.2.1. The indefinite article /waaḥəd/ with a singular noun

The indefinite article /waaḥəd/ precedes a noun that is both definite and singular, as in /waaḥəd əlmakla/ 'a dish; a certain dish, a particular dish'. As the translation "a certain' and 'a particular' suggest, the noun phrase that consists of the indefinite article /waaḥəd/ with a singular noun indicates not just any members of that group of items. It refers instead to a particular member of the group.

For this reason, the construction often occurs when a speaker wants to introduce a new character or element to a story or description. An example is /waaḥəd əlmakla/ 'a dish; a certain dish, a particular dish'. It occurs in the utterance that ends /kiimaa ḥnaa nsəmmuuhaa fə-ddzaayər ʔa … **waaḥəd əlmakla** ysəmmuuhaa garanṭeeṭa/ 'as we call it in Algeria, a certain dish they call <u>garanteta</u>' (Selection 9). The speaker goes on to describe the dish.

8.1.2.2.1.1. The indefinite article /waaḥəd/ with a borrowed singular noun

There are two strategies for the treatment of a singular noun from a language other than Arabic when it follows /waaḥəd/. In some cases, the definite article is omitted before the borrowed noun, as in /waaḥəd *protocole/* 'a particular *protocol*'. In other cases, however, the definite article is maintained, as in /waaḥad *l'affection/* 'a certain *affection*'. The reasons for this variation are not yet clear.

8.1.2.2.2. The indefinite article /waaḥəd/ with a number or counted noun construction

The indefinite article /waaḥəd/ may also precede the dual or a counted noun construction.

8.1.2.2.2.1. The indefinite article /waaḥəd/ with a dual

When the indefinite article /waaḥəd/ precedes a dual noun, that noun is usually definite, as in /waaḥd əlʕaameen/ 'about two years'. As the translation indicates, the use of /waaḥəd/ turns the dual from an exact number to an approximation.

8.1.2.2.2.2. The indefinite article /waaḥəd/ with a counted-noun construction

In SAA, the indefinite article /waaḥəd/ may also follow a number or counted noun construction (see 8.1.7), as in /baabaa ʕanduu **waaḥəd sətta w-səbʕiin səna**/ 'my father is about 76 years old' (u.d.). This structure resembles the use of /waaḥəd/ with a dual noun. Note, however, that the counted noun construction is indefinite.

8.1.2.2.3. The adjectival use of /waaḥəd/

8.1.2.2.4. As an adjective, /waaḥəd/ 'one' may precede an indefinite noun and agree with that noun in gender. Note, however, that /waaḥəd/ as an adjective does not indicate indefiniteness. The adjective /waaḥəd/ 'one' instead points out the "oneness" or "singleness" of the item, as in /lmaariikaan fiihaa waaḥəd … **ḥaaja waaḥda** taʕjəbnii fiihaa/ 'America, there is one … one thing that I like here'(Selection 32).

8.1.2.3. The indefinite article /ʃii/

The indefinite article /ʃii/ precedes a noun that is indefinite. The noun is sometimes singular, as in /ʃii marra/ 'some time'. The noun is often plural, as in /ʃii ʃhuur/ 'some months; a few months'. Whether the noun is singular or plural, the indefinite article /ʃii/ indicates potential existence rather than the existence of a specific thing, as does /waaḥəd/.

The indefinite article /ʃii/ occurs less frequently in our data than the other indefinite constructions of SAA.

8.1.3. Demonstrative phrases

A demonstrative phrase consists of a definite noun and a demonstrative that agrees in number and gender with that noun (see 4.3). In SAA, the demonstrative may precede the noun, as in /**haaðii** nnaas/ 'these people'

(Selection 10). The demonstrative may also follow the noun, as in /nnaas **haadii**/ 'these people' (Selection 28). The difference between the structure in which the demonstrative precedes the noun and that in which the demonstrative follows the noun appears to be largely stylistic.

8.1.4. Expressing possession

SAA has two ways to express possession and other kinds of close relationships between nouns. One of these is the construct phrase or ʔidaafa familiar from MSA and other varieties of Arabic. The other is the possessive adjective construction, in which an adjective, usually invariable, expresses the link between the two nouns.

8.1.4.1. The construct phrase

The construct phrase or ʔidaafa consists of two nouns standing next to one another. The first of these two nouns may not have the definite article /l-/ or a suffixed pronoun; that is, it must be indefinite. The second noun may be either definite or indefinite. The status of the second noun of the construct phrase determines that of the first noun. That is, when the second noun of the construct is definite, the first noun of the construct is considered to be definite, as in /**mdiinət** ljazaayər/ 'the city of Algiers'. When the second noun is indefinite, the first is also indefinite, as in /**wəld** ʕaam/ 'cousin; a cousin (lit. father's brother's child)'.

8.1.4.2. The possessive adjective construction

The possessive adjective construction has three elements. The first is the possessed noun, which is modified by the second element, the possessive adjective. The possessive adjective used most commonly in urban SAA is /taaʕ/, as in /aaxər qətra **taaʕ** əddamm/ 'the last drop of blood' (Selection 13). In non-urban areas, the possessive adjective is often /ntaaʕ/, as in /ʃʃeex **ntaaʕ** əljaaməʕ/ 'the sheikh of the mosque'. Other possessive adjectives occur in SAA, but /taaʕ/ and /ntaaʕ/ are the most widespread.

These possessive adjectives in urban areas do not usually inflect for gender, number, or definiteness. The possessive adjective stands in a construct phrase with the third element of the construction, the possessor noun or pronoun suffix. As is the case with the construct phrase, the possessed noun may be indefinite, as in /wiilaaya taaʕ, **taaʕ** ədduula lʕuθmaaniyya/ 'a province of, of the Ottoman state'. The possessed noun may also be definite, as in /ddraahəm **taaʕ** əlpətrool/ 'the oil money'.

Note, however, that in non-urban areas, the possessive adjective may inflect for gender and number to agree with the first or possessed noun of the phrase. The inflecting forms are /taaʕ/ (ms), /taaʕət/ (fs), and /taawaʕ/ (p), or are /ntaaʕ/ (ms), /ntaaʕət/ (fs), and /ntaawaʕ/ (p). The result, for example, is /les produits **taawaʕ**hum/ 'their products; the products belonging to them' (u.d.).

44

8.1.4.3. The use of the construct phrase and the possessive adjective construction

Although the construct phrase and the possessive adjective construction both express a relationship of possession, the two constructions are not used interchangeably by speakers of SAA. Usually the construct phrase expresses relationships of inherent possession. Inherently possessed items are, for example, family members, body parts, one's name and nationality, material from which something comes or is made, and other elements that are permanent or essential. The construct phrase can express other kinds of relationships, but speakers of SAA typically restrict it to relations of inherent possession. They use the possessive adjective phrase for other relationships, those that are not inherently possessed.

8.1.5. The noun-adjective phrase

The noun-adjective phrase is made up of a noun that is followed by an adjective that modifies or qualifies the noun. The adjective agrees with the noun in definiteness as it agrees in gender and number. See 8.1.6 for details of number and gender agreement.

A definite adjective has the definite article /l-/. It can modify a noun that also has the definite article, as in /ttaariix əlqədiim/ 'ancient history'. It can also modify a noun in an ʔiḍaafa or construct phrase, as in /maʕnaahaa lʔaṣliyya/ 'its (fs) original meaning'. A definite adjective may, finally, modify a noun in a possessive adjective construction. In such a construction, the placement of the adjective varies. The phrase /ttaariix taaʕ ələ ... taaʕ əljazaayər əlqaadiim/ 'the history of the ... of Algeria, the ancient kind' shows placement of the adjective /əlqaadiim/ 'the ancient' that resembles that of the idaafa or construct phrase. That is, the adjective modifying the first noun of the construction, /ttaariix/ 'history', appears at the end of the entire construction. In contrast, an adjective modifying the first noun of the construction may immediately follow that noun, as in /əlmuuṣiiqaa lʔandaaluusiyya taaʕnaa/ 'our Andalusian music'.

8.1.6. Gender and number agreement

See 2.3 for gender and number inflections for nouns, adjectives, and participles. The following description is a general outline of agreement. It does not cover all of the variations that can occur in spontaneous speech. Note that, in the discussion of agreement that follows, "modifiers" include all elements that usually show agreement in Arabic. These are adjectives, participles, pronouns, and verbal predicates.

8.1.6.1. Agreement of singular nouns

Modifiers of a singular noun are also singular. They agree with the noun in gender, as in /diin jdiid/ 'a new religion' and /xədma mliiḥa/ 'a good job'.

They also agree with the noun in definiteness, as in /əlklaam əṭṭwiil/ 'the long speech' and /lxədma lmliiḥa/ 'the good job'.

8.1.6.2. Agreement of dual nouns

Only nouns may take the dual ending /-iin/ or /-een/. Nouns that take a dual ending in SAA are limited to nouns of measure and those that name body parts (see 2.3.3). Nouns of other types, those that do not typically take the dual, are counted using the counted-noun construction (see 8.1.7). In such a construction, the noun counted as "two" is plural. Its modifier is also plural, as in /zuuj ḥaalaat ṣʕaab/ 'two difficult situations'.

8.1.6.3. Agreement of plural nouns

8.1.6.3.1. Plural nouns generally take plural modifiers. This is the case whether the plural noun refers to male human beings (/ərrjaal lxəddaamiin ʕand əlḥkuuma/ 'the men who work for the government'), female human beings (/nnsaawiin haahum yəʃtḥuu/ 'The women, they dance.'), or to human beings in general (/nnaas wullaaw msəlmiin/ 'The people became Muslims.'). It is also the case for nouns that refer to inanimate objects, as in /əlḥwaayj llaazmiin/ 'the things that are necessary'.

8.1.6.3.2. There is some variation in agreement patterns for plural nouns referring to inanimate objects. This variation occurs most often when the plural noun takes the feminine plural inflection /-aat/. Especially in high-frequency expressions and frozen forms, the use of FS modifiers familiar from MSA occurs, as in /jjaamaaʕaat lʔislaamiyya/ 'the Islamic groups'. In other phrases, the adjective that modifies a plural noun with the feminine inflection /-aat/ takes the same feminine inflection, as in /ḥaajaat muuhəmmaat/ 'important things'. This echo form of agreement may be stylistic.

8.1.6.4. Agreement of /kaan/ in clauses with /fiih/ and /ʕand-/

Like certain other varieties of spoken Arabic, SAA usually does not show agreement of /kaan/ with /fiih/ 'there is; there are' and /ʕand-/ 'to have'. In other words, /kaan/ is generally invariable, as in /kaan fiih lubnaaniyyiin/ 'there were Lebanese' (u.d.), and /kaan ʕanduu llarḍ/ 'he had land' (Selection 6). Agreement of /kaan/ is possible, however. This occurs most often in formal speech or a formal situation, as in /kaant fiih ḥarb/ 'there was war' (Selection 2), and /kaa[n]t ʕan[d]naa waaḥd ənnəxla/ 'we had a date-palm tree' (Selection 25).

8.1.7. Counted-noun constructions

SAA has several structures that combine a number and a counted noun. SAA numbers are invariable. They do not undergo changes of gender or sound change. The exception is /waaḥəd/ 'one', which functions as an adjective in counted-noun constructions and takes gender inflections as do other adjectives.

8.1.7.1. The number "one"

The number "one" is most often expressed by an indefinite singular noun, as in /kaar/ 'a bus; one bus' or /smaana/ 'a week; one week'.

Where a speaker wants to express the number "one" or "a single" with greater clarity or emphasis, the word /waaḥəd/ 'one' follows the noun. The word /waaḥəd/ agrees with the noun in gender and definiteness, as in /ʕaam **waaḥəd**/ 'one year' or /ḥaaja **waaḥda**/ 'one single thing'.

8.1.7.2. The number "two"

SAA has two ways to express the number "two". They are the morphological dual and the counted noun construction.

8.1.7.2.1. The morphological dual takes the form of the suffix /-een/ or /-iin/, as in /yoomeen/ 'two days'.

8.1.7.2.2. The use of the morphological dual is limited in SAA to nouns of measure and to paired body parts, as in /ʃahreen/ 'two months' and /iideen/ 'two hands'. For nouns of other class, the counted-noun construction expresses the number "two," /zuuj draarii/ 'two children'.

8.1.7.3. Numbers larger than "one"

8.1.7.3.1. The counted-noun construction for the numbers 2 - 10 consists of the number followed by a plural noun, as in /ʕaʃra sniin/ 'ten years'. This structure becomes definite when the definite article precedes the number only, as in /lʕaʃra sniin/ 'the ten years'.

8.1.7.3.2. Some counted-noun construction for the numbers 2-10 have the counted noun as a singular. This occurs most often when the counted noun is borrowed. One example is /ʕaʃra **duuroo**/ 'ten <u>douros</u>' (Selection 9).

8.1.7.3.3. The counted-noun construction for numbers over 10 consists of the number followed by a singular noun, as in /ʕaʃriin səna/ '20 years'. This structure becomes definite when the definite article precedes the number only, as in /lʕaʃriin səna/ 'the 20 years'.

8.1.7.4. Ordinal numbers in phrases

8.1.7.4.1. The ordinal numbers of SAA usually function as adjectives. They follow the noun they modify and agree in number and gender, as in /nnhaar llowwəl/ 'the first day' or /ssana ttaanya/ 'the second year'.

8.1.7.4.2. The ordinal numbers, plus the word /aaxər/ 'last', also occur as the first noun of a construct phrase where the second noun is indefinite or where the ordinal takes a suffixed pronoun. The resulting phrase is another way of expressing order, as in /awwəl yoom/ 'the first day' or /aaxər qətra/ 'the last drop'.

8.1.8. Expressions of comparison and superlative

The form that expresses the comparative and the superlative in SAA is the elative. It has the pattern $C_1C_2vC_3$. The elative is invariable for number and gender.

8.1.8.1. The comparative

8.1.8.1.1. Comparison in a phrase consists of an indefinite singular noun followed by an elative, as in /daʕwa ḥsən/ 'a better situation'.

8.1.8.1.2. Comparison in a clause consists of three elements. The first element is an indefinite elative, the second is the preposition /mən/, and the third is the noun or suffixed pronoun that is the object or person to which the comparison is made. An example is /haad lijtiimaaʕ kaan **qṣar mən lloww**əl/ 'This meeting was shorter than the first one'.

8.1.8.1.3. Adjectives derived from other forms, including participles as well as adjectives of the form $C_1C_2vC_3$, do not form an elative. These adjectives form comparatives using the elative /ktar/ as an intensifier. The result is an explicit comparative structure, as in /ṭoolga maʕruufa ktar mən biiskra/ 'Tolga is better known than Biskra. (Selection 21).'

8.1.8.2. The superlative

8.1.8.2.1. The elative followed by an indefinite singular noun expresses an absolute superlative, as in /akbar sadd/ 'the largest dam'.

8.1.8.2.2. The elative followed by a definite plural noun or a suffixed pronoun expresses a relative superlative, as in /ḥsən lmuuduun/ 'the best of the cities'.

8.2. Sentences and clauses

8.2.1. The verbal sentence

The verbal sentence, in its simplest form, consists of two elements. The subject is a noun or pronoun, and the predicate is a verb. The subject typically precedes the verb, as in /huwwa yʕarrəf ruuḥuu dərk/ 'He's going to introduce himself now' (Selection 36).

The pronoun subject of a verbal sentence is usually expressed in the inflected form of the verb rather than as an independent pronoun. When the pronoun subject appears as an independent pronoun it typically conveys emphasis or contrast, as in /lḥaqt ʕleeh anaa/ 'I (personally) am aware of it (ms)' (Selection 3).

48

8.2.2. The equational sentence

The nominal or equational sentence has two basic elements. The subject is a noun or pronoun. The predicate may be a noun, a pronoun, an adjective, an adverb, or a prepositional phrase. No verb or other copular element links subject and predicate, and the subject usually but not always precedes the predicate. Equational sentences express a range of relationships, including identification, description, location in time or space, existence, and possession. Equational sentences of existence and possession, sentences that SAA expresses somewhat differently, are described below.

8.2.2.1. The equational sentence of existence

The equational sentence of existence is introduced by an existential. SAA has two existentials, /kaayən/ and /fiih/. Of the two, /kaayən/ occurs more frequently, as in **/kaayən** ɣeer lḥuut/ 'There are only fish' (u.d.). The form /fiih/ also occurs, as in **/fiih** durk ljeeʃ/ 'Now there's the army' (Selection 13). When /kaan/ occurs to change the time frame of an existential sentence, settiing it in the past or the future, the form /fiih/ is preferred, as in **/kaan fiih** lḥuut/ 'There was fish' (Selection 5).

Note that /fiih/ is invariable, as in other varieties of spoken Arabic. The form /kaayən/, however, may agree in gender and number with the grammatical subject of the sentence. The FS is /kaayna/, as in /lmaaʃaakəl lli **kaayna** fə-lblaad/ 'the problems that there are in the country' (Selection 8). The P form is /kaayniin/. Our data suggest that this form may be in some kind of transition, as the inflected forms seldom occur. Instead, the invariable /kaayən/ is more usual, as in **/kaayən** ookla xaaṣṣa/ 'There is a special dish' (Selection 17).

8.2.2.2. The equational sentence of possession

The equational sentence of possession relies on a specialized use of the preposition /ʕand-/ 'of, belonging to, lit. at, at the home of'. The possessive use of this preposition differs from its use in expressing spatial relations in two ways. First, the preposition takes a suffixed pronoun whose referent is the possessor. This pronoun occurs even when a noun phrase in the same sentence names the possessor, as in **/nnaas** ʕand**hum** draarii/ 'People have children' (Selection 7). Second, the possessive prepositional phrase precedes the grammatical subject of the sentence, the item possessed, as in /duuka ləmraa ʕandhaa ... *double travail*/ 'Now a woman has ... *two jobs*' (Selection 32).

8.2.3. Expansion of the simple sentence

The following describes some of the ways in which a simple sentence in SA can be expanded.

8.2.3.1. The topic-comment sentence

The topic-comment sentence consists of a topic that is a noun or a pronoun, and a comment that is itself a complete sentence. Note also that the topic contains a pronoun, suffixed pronoun, or verb inflection whose referent is the topic. The sentence that is the comment may be verbal, as in /ḥnaa maa naʕtarfuu b-haað lḥizb haaðaa/ 'We do not acknowledge this party' (Selection 13). The comment may also be a nominal sentence, as in /huu maa ʕlaa baaluuʃ bə-lmustaqbəl/ 'He doesn't know about the future' (Selection 35).

8.2.3.2. The relative clause

A relative clause in SA is another kind of sentence embedded in a second sentence. The embedded sentence modifies a noun or pronoun in the main sentence. A relative clause is called definite when the noun it modifies, the head noun, is definite. It is indefinite when the head noun is indefinite.

8.2.3.2.1. The definite relative clause modifies a definite noun. It is indicated by the relative pronoun /llii/. The relative clause contains a resumptive pronoun. This is a pronoun, suffixed pronoun, or verb inflection whose referent is the head noun, as in /ttaariix taaʕ əljazaayər llii lḥaqt ʕleeh/ 'The history of Algeria that I am aware of, lit. The history of Algeria that I am aware of it' (Selection 19).

8.2.3.2.2. The indefinite relative clause modifies an indefinite noun. There is no indefinite relative pronoun in SA. The indefinite relative clause, like the definite relative clause, contains a resumptive pronoun. This is a pronoun, suffixed pronoun, or verb inflection whose reference is the head noun, as in /waalii waaḥəd aaxər iiguuluu[h] siidii mḥamməd ləkbiir/ 'another saint whom they call Sidi Muhammad al-Kabir, lit. another saint whom they call him Sidi Muhammad al-Kabir' (Selection 19).

8.2.4. Conditional sentences

The presence of a conditional particle marks a conditional sentence or clause in SAA. The conditional particles of SAA are /iðaa/ (also /idaa/), /ilaa/, /luu/ (also /loo/) and, rarely, /kuun/ and /kaan/. The differences between these conditional particles and the clauses in which they occur, however, are not as clear-cut in SAA as they are in MSA or in other varieties of Arabic. It is possible that variation is a result of differences between sub-varieties of SAA. The discussion that follows is based on the conditional sentences and clauses that occur in our data.

The uses of the particles /iðaa/ (also /idaa/) and /ilaa/ overlap. Both may mark real or predictive conditions to describe events that do occur or will occur. Both may also mark unreal or contrary-to-fact conditions, those that have not occurred or will not occur. The particles /luu/ (also /loo/) and /kuun/ tend to mark unreal conditionals.

8.2.4.1. Real or predictive conditionals

Real or predictive conditionals describe events as they usually occur or will occur. The conditional particle in such sentences can often be translated with 'when' as well as 'if'.

The if-clause generally contains a perfect verb. The verb or non-verbal structure of the result clause is usually non-perfect. It may be imperfect, as in /ilaa maa xaantəkʃ ṣaḥḥtək kull ʃii **yjuuz**/ 'If your health does not let you down, anything is possible' (u.d.). The result clause may also contain a non-verbal structure, as in /**maa fiiʃ** maasaakəl [maaʃaakəl] ilaa kaan ʔa ... ykuunuu ʔa ... lfluus moojuudiin/ 'there are no problems if there is money' (Selection 23). Finally, the verb of the result clause may be imperative, as in /iðaa jaʕt **kulluuh**/ 'If you get hungry [in the desert], eat him [your riding camel]' (u.d.).

Less frequently, the verb of the if-clause is imperfect. The verb of the result clause is also non-perfect. An example comes from the speaker who produced the previous example. This, too, describes the usefulness of the camel: /iðaa **yxlaaṣlək** lmaa ḥaʃʃluu rəjleeh/ 'If your water runs out, cut into his [your riding camel's] legs.' (u.d.).

8.2.4.2. Unreal or contrary-to-fact conditionals

Unreal or contrary-to-fact conditionals describe events that have not taken place or will not take place. Note that any of the conditional particles (/iðaa/ (also /idaa/), /ilaa/, /luu/ (also /loo/) and, rarely, /kuun/) may introduce the if-clause of an unreal conditional.

The feature that appears to mark a conditional as unreal is a compound past (past perfect or past imperfect) verb in the if-clause. The verb of the result clause varies. It, too, may be past perfect, as in /loo **kaan məʃii huumaa** loo **kaan** raanii *déjà* raanii rfətt ruuḥii w-ruḥt lə-ʕand Michelle/ 'If it weren't for them, I would *already* have gone ahead and gone to Michelle's.' (u.d.). (Note that /kaan/ may be invariable following /loo/ or /luu/.) The verb of the result clause may also be past imperfect, as in /ilaa **kunt ruḥnaa, ruḥnaa** l-fransaa, **kaant tkuun** lḥaala ʔaṣʕab/ 'If we had gone to France, gone to France, things would have been harder' (Selection 33). (Note that /kunt/ 'I was' is 1S, while /ruḥnaa/ 'we went' is 1P, the result of a change of reference or slip of the tongue.). The verb of the result clause may also be imperfect, as in /luu **kaan məʃii**, mahsuub **məʃii** ddraarii **nərfəd ruuḥii** wə-nʕayyətlaa ʕaad/ 'If it weren't for, I mean, it weren't for the kids, I'd just go right ahead and call her.' (u.d.),

51

8.2.4.3. Hypothetical conditionals

Hypothetical conditionals describe events that might or might not happen. Certain other varieties of Arabic mark hypothetical conditionals, but SAA often does not. Only context differentiates between events that might take place and those that do or do not.

8.2.5. Conjunctions

8.2.5.1. Commonly-used conjunctions of SAA

Other expansions of the simple sentence rely on the use of conjunctions. The following lists some of the more common conjunctions of SAA.

Conjunction	English translation
/baaʃ/ - /bəʃ/	for; so that, in order to
/b-ḥeet/	since, as
/b-ṣaḥḥ/ - /bə-ṣṣaḥḥ/	but
/bəllii/	that (after verbs of speaking and considering)
/ḥattaa w-loo/	even if
/ḥattaa w-maa/	even if not
/xaaṭ/ - /xaaṭʃ/ - /laa xaaṭʃ/	because, due to the fact that
/xaaṭər/ - /laa xaaṭər/ - /ʕlaa xaaṭər/	because, due to the fact that
/xaaṭʃii/ - /laa xaaṭʃii/	because, due to the fact that
/ʃkuun llii/	who; what
/ʕlaa jaal/	because of, due to
/fii ʕood/	instead of, rather than
/kii/	like, as
/kii/	when, whenever
/kii/	when, at the time that
/kiifaaʃ/	how
/kii llii/	as if
/kii ... kii/	the same for ... as for
/laakən/	but
/liʔannuu/ - /liʔann/ - /liyyan/	because
/məllii/	when, at the time
/məllii/	since, from the time that
/wəllaa/	if, when, whenever
/iiðaa/	if, when, whenever
/iimmaalaa/ - /mmaalaa/	so, therefore

8.2.5.2. Other conjunctions that may occur

Some speakers of SAA use conjunctions from French. These may occur in isolation, that is, where no other French is used in the utterance, as in /haadii *parce que* ssiiyaasa hiyya llii həlkət a ... lfəllaaḥiin/ 'This is *because* politics are what destroyed ah ... the peasants' (Selection 7). Conjunctions from French that occur in this work include the following.

Conjunction	English translation
donc	thus, so
à part (que)	apart from
mais	but, however
parce que	because
puisque	since, due to the fact that
sinon	otherwise
soit ... soit	either ... or

8.2.6. The negative sentence

8.2.6.1. The negative /maa ... ʃ/

The negative /maa ... ʃ/ is the all-purpose negative particle of SAA. It occurs in verbal sentences (/**maa** nəqdərʃ nəkdəb ʕleeh/ 'I can't lie to him.'(Selection 8)) and nominal sentences (/xlaaṣ, **maa** fiiʃ mədxuul yaʕnii / 'That's it, there is no income' (Selection 4)). The imperative in SAA is also negated with /maa ... ʃ/, as in /**maa** tziidʃ dduur biihaa./ 'Don't take care of it again' (Selection 25).

8.2.6.2. The negative particle /maaʃii/

The negative particle /maaʃii/ usually negates equational sentences, as in /**maaʃii** laataay llii nʃruuhaa ḥnaa/ 'It's not the tea that we buy' (Selection 23).

8.2.7. The question

8.2.7.1. The yes-no question

The yes-no question in SAA is indicated only by intonation. The speaker's voice rises as it approaches the end of the utterance, as in /tʃarbuu laataay?/ 'Will you drink tea?' (Selection 23).

8.2.7.2. The information question

Questions that ask for information rely on interrogatives to do so (see 7 for a list of the most commonly-used interrogatives of SA). In SAA, as in certain other varieties of spoken Arabic, the interrogative typically occurs at the front of the utterance, as in /waaʃ daar ʃʃiibaanii? hjaṛ/ 'What did my old man do? He ran away' (Selection 25).

9. Markers of organization and attitude

In addition to the types of words discussed, SAA has a category we call "markers". Markers are words or phrases that differ from other classes. They are not well integrated into an utterance through agreement (as are adjectives) or dependence (as are suffixed pronouns). In addition, they do not really affect the content or meaning of the utterance. These markers, however, play two very important roles in utterances. One group of markers consists of devices that organize. Another group is made up of devices that indicate the speaker's attitude. In both groups, translation is not the best indicator of function. The flow of speech, sometimes stretching over a page of transcript, demonstrates marker function. Following are some of the more common markers of SAA that occur in our data.

9.1. Markers of organization

Markers of organization are of three types, clarifiers, correctives, and resumptives.

9.1.1. Clarifiers

Clarifiers have a variety of literal meanings, among them /yaʕnii/ 'lit. it (ms) means', /maḥsuub/ 'lit. considered to be', /zaʕmaa/ 'really', /iiguullək/ 'he will tell you', and /tsəmmaa/ (and its variants) 'it is called'. Whatever their literal meaning, clarifiers function in the same way. Like "you know" or "I mean" in English, they indicate that explanation or amplification of a statement. They also, like their English counterparts, hold the speaker's place and fill in what would otherwise be silence.

♦ /ttaariix taaʕ ələ ... taaʕ əljazaayər əlqaadiim **yaʕnii** taaʕ wəqt ələ ... əlfiiniiqiyyiin w-taaʕ ələ ... -yuunaan w-taaʕ ərroomaan haad/

  'the history of the ... of Algeria, the ancient kind, you know, of the time of ... the Phoenicians and of the Greeks and of the Romans, this one' (Selection 1)

♦ /yxəddmuuhum, **maḥsuub** yaʕṭiiw ṣadaqa/

  'They employ them, that's to say, they give them charity.' (Selection 25)

♦ /raak *limité*, raak baayən **zaʕmaa** ʕandək s-*sport* taaʕək wəllaa qraaytək. *à part ça* maa ʕandəkʃ ḥaaja xraa/

  'You are limited. You are, it's obvious. That is, you have your *sports* or your studies. *Aside from them* you've got nothing else.' (Selection 35)

54

♦ /iixawwfuuk. **iiguulləҟ** maa taʕrafʃ ... maa təʕrafʃ illaa, illaa *barrage* haakδaa wəllaa *barrage* haakδaak/

'[They] scare you, that is, you don't know, you don't know if it's this kind of *roadblock* or that kind of *roadblock*.' (Selection 29)

♦ /lfiilaahaa maa kaayna waaluu, **tsəmmaa** fii *les environs* ntaaʕ a ... bəʃʃaar kaaynət ʃwiyya/

'There is no agriculture at all. That is, *surrounding*, ah ... Béchar there is a little.' (Selection 20)

9.1.2. Correctives

The corrective /haaqiiqa/ 'in fact' lets the speaker indicate an upcoming correction or attempt at greater precision.

♦ /hnaa ʕadnaa waahd əlʕaadaat a ... hiyya **haaqiiqa** fə-ddiin maahiiʃ məqbuula/

'We have some customs. ah ... they are, in fact, unacceptable in Islam.' (Selection 16)

9.1.3. Resumptives

The resumptive /lmuuhəmm/ 'the point is, lit. the important thing is' lets the speakers indicate a return to the main topic or thread of the narrative after a digression. The utterance that appears below follows a list of those female relatives who could apply henna for the bride and groom before the wedding and precedes the speaker's return to his topic, wedding customs.

♦ /**lmuuhəmm** llii maa zaalt kbiira hiyya llii tə ... thənniilhum/

'The point is that someone who is old, she is the one who ... she applies henna for them.' (Selection 16)

9.2. Markers of attitude

9.2.1. Mitigators

The mitigators /waaqiil/ and /waaqiilatan/ appear to derive from the verb /qaal/ 'to say'. In spite of this, they function as mitigators, softening what the speaker has to say. They are best translated as 'perhaps, maybe; apparently'.

◆ /la *température* taaḥḥaa təlḥag aḷḷaah aʕlam **waaqiil** waaḥəd
cinquante wəllaa *cinquante-cinq degrés*/

'*Its temperature* reaches, God knows, maybe *50* or *55 degrees*.'
(Selection 24)

◆ /kaayn əlgirbaaʕii, ənnaas iiʕayyṭuuluu maaʃii digla. kaayən naas
iiʕayyṭuuluu a … **waaqiilatan** tmuuʃənt/

'There is the girba'i, people call it "not degla", there are people who call
it, ah … maybe Temouchent.' (Selection 21)

56

Selections

ttaariix taaʕ əljazaayər əlqadiim

This selection provides a general introduction to the history of Algeria in the
classical period. It also illustrates some of the characteristic linguistic features
of SAA.

A: anaa naqṣud yaʕnii ttaariix taaʕ ələ ... taaʕ əljazaayər[1] əlqaadiim[2,3]
     yaʕnii taaʕ wəqt ələ ... əlfiiniiqiyyiin w-taaʕ ələ ... -yuunaan w-taaʕ
     ərroomaan haad.[4] awwəl llii jaaw[5] ələ ... manṭiiqa haadiik huum
     əlfiiniiqiyyiin ləmmaa bdaaw[6] iitaajruu mʕa lʕaaləm. məm-baʕdhum
     jaaw a ... lyuunaan. b-ṣaḥḥ lyuunaan maa, maa qaʕduuʃ[7] yaʕnii maanuuʃ[8]
     taariix kbiir fə-ljazaayər. huum ərroomaan huum əllii ʕandhum taariix
     kbiir fə-ljazaayər.

B: ḥattaa lʔaataar taaḥḥum bqaat fə-ljazaayər.

A: yaʕnii lə ... bə-maa huum əllii bnaaw əlʔawwəl, llii bnaaw ələ ...
     mdiinat ljazaayər [xxx] ʕleenaa, ddzaayər[9] lʕaaṣiima, w-bnaaw ʕannaaba
     w-bnaaw a ... a ... qṣamṭiina. fa-zmaan ddzaayər əlʕaaṣiima kaan əsəmhaa
     Icosium. w-kaant a ... yaʕnii a... miinaaʔ kbiir yaʕnii taaʕ əttiijaara
     w-kaanuu a ... ii ... kull yaʕnii lmaaḥaaṣiil taaʕ əzziraaʕa[10] llii kaanət
     tkuun fə-ljazaayər kaanuu yədduuhaa lə ... lə-roomaa. w-baʕd roomaa a
     ... jaa waaḥəd lə ... -naas[11] iisəmmuuhum mə ... *les Vandales,*[12] huum
     əllii ḥaṭṭamuu roomaa. qaʕduu ʃwiyy yaʕnii fə, fə-ljazaayər ...

التاريخ تاع الجزاير القديم

أ: أنا نقصد يعني التّاريخ تاع الـ ... تاع الجزاير[1] القاديم[2, 3] يعني تاع وقت الـ ... إلفينيقيّين وتاع اليونان وتاع الرومان هاد.[4] اوّل اللّي جاوا[5] الـ ... منطقه هذيك هم الفينيقيّين لمّا بداوا[6] يتاجروا مع العالم. مم بعدهم جاوا ا ... اليونان. بصحّ اليونان ما، ما قعدوش[7] يعني مانوش[8] تاريخ كبير فالجزاير، هم الرّومان همّ اللّي عندهم تاريخ كبير فالجزاير.

ب: حتّى الاتار تاعهم بقات فالجزاير.

أ: يعني الـ ... بما هم اللّي بناوا الأوّل، اللّي بناوا الـ ... مدينه الجزاير [xxx] علينا، الدّزاير[9] العاصيمه، وبناوا عنّابه وبناوا ا ... ا ... قسنطينه، فزمان الدّزاير العاصيمه كان اسمها *Icosium*. وكانت ا ... يعني ا ... ميناء كبير يعني تاع التّيجاره وكانوا ا ... إيـ ... كلّ يعني الماحاصيل تاع الزّراعه[10] اللّي كانت تكون فالجزاير كانوا يدّوها الـ ... لروما. وبعد روما ا ... جا واحد الـ ... ناس[11] يسمّوهم مـ .... *Les Vandales*،[12] هم اللّي حطّموا روما. قعدوا شويّ يعني فـ فالجزاير ......

Vocabulary:

anaa انا [*also* anaayaa] *pro* I (1S)

qṣəd قصد *v* to mean, intend {*imperf:* yəqṣəd}

yaʕnii يعني *disc* I mean; that is to say (lit. it (ms) means)

taaʕ تاع [*also* ntaaʕ] *possessive adj; invariable* of, belonging to

ljazaayər الجزاير [*also* ddzaayər] *prop* Algeria; Algiers

fiiniiqii فينيقي *adj* Phoenician {*fs:* fiiniiqiyya, *pl:* fiiniiqiyiin}

lyuunaan اليونان *prop* Greece

59

roomaanii روماني *adj* Roman {*fs:* roomaaniyya, *pl:* roomaan}

haad هاد [*also* haað] *pro* this (invariable near demonstrative)

əllii اللي [*also* llii] *pro* who, what (definite relative pronoun)

jaa جا *v* to come, come to, arrive at; to be located (past tense or active participle) {*imperf:* iijii}

haadiik هديك [*also* haadiika; haaðiik; haaðiika] *pro* that (FS far demonstrative) {*fs:* haadaak, *pl:* haaduuk}

ləmmaa لَا *conj* when

məm-baʕd ممبعد [*also* mən baʕd; m-baʕda; m-baʕd] *conj* after

b-ṣaḥḥ بصحّ *conj* but; actually (lit. with truth)

maa : ش – ما not

qʕad قعد *v; pre-verb* to remain; to sit; to continue (to do s.t.) {*imperf:* yəqʕad}

maanuuʃ مانوش [*also* maahuuʃ] he is not; it (ms) is not

huum هوم [*also* humm(a); ham; huuma] *pro* they (3P)

ʕand + suffixed pronoun عند [*also* ʕad; ʕan] *prep* to have

ḥattaa حتّى *adv* even

taaḥ- + suffixed pronoun with initial /h/ تاح [*also* taaʕ] *possessive adj; invariable* of, belonging to

ddzaayər الدّزاير [*also* ljazaayər] *prop* Algiers ; Algeria

ddzaayər lʕaaṣiima الدّزاير العاصيمه *prop* the capital Algiers

ʕannaaba عنّابه *prop* Annaba (city in eastern Algeria)

qṣamṭiina قسنطينه [*also* qṣanṭiina] *prop* Constantine (city in eastern Algeria)

zmaan زمان *adv* a long time ago; in the old days

ddaa ادّى *v* to take; to bring; to send {*imperf:* yəddii}

roomaa روما *prop* Rome

waaḥəd + plural noun واحد some, approximately, about; a, an (indefinite article)
les Vandales *nmp* the Vandals

Notes:

1. The phrase /ttaariix **taaʕ** ələ ... taaʕ əljazaayər/ 'the history of the ... of Algeria' illustrates the possessive adjective construction of SAA. The possessive adjective /taaʕ/ 'of, belonging to' links two nouns in a relationship broadly described as possessive. The first noun may be definite, as /ttaariix/ 'history, lit. 'the history' is here. That noun is followed by the possessive adjective /taaʕ/. The second noun of the construction follows /taaʕ/ to produce a phrase like /ttaariix taaʕ əljazaayər/ 'the history of Algeria'.

   Two features of the possessive adjective construction should be noted. First the possessive adjective is invariable; it generally does not agree in number, gender, or definiteness with the first noun of the construction. Second, the possessive adjective construction is synonymous in meaning with the idaafa or construct phrase, as in /**ḥaajaat lmadrasa**/ 'things pertaining to school'. Note that the two structures are synonymous but not interchangeable.

2. The phrase /ttaariix taaʕ ələ ... taaʕ əljazaayər **əlqaadiim**/ 'the history of the ... of Algeria, the ancient kind,' shows placement of the adjective /əlqaadiim/ 'the ancient' that resembles that of the idaafa or construct phrase. That is, the adjective modifying the first noun of the the the construction, /ttaariix/ 'history', appears at the end of the entire construction. Adjective placement in the possessive adjective construction is not fixed as it is in the idaafa. An adjective modifying the first noun of the construction may immediately follow that noun, as in /əlmuuṣiiqaa **lʔandaaluusiyya** taaʕnaa/ (u.d.) 'our Andalusian music'.

3. Speakers of SAA sometimes pronounce vowels that are short in MSA as long. The result is the SAA /əlq**aa**diim/ 'the ancient', as opposed to the MSA alq**a**diim. This lengthening of a short vowel is the SAA strategy for preserving a short vowel in an open syllable. Compare, for example, the first long vowel of /q**aa**diim/ 'ancient' with the initial consonant cluster of /**kb**iir/ 'large'.

4. As the phrase /ərroomaan **haad**/ 'these Romans' shows, the demonstrative in SAA may follow the noun it modifies. The demonstrative may also precede the noun, as in /**haadaa** ʃʃii/ 'this thing' (Selection 2). The phrase in which the demonstrative precedes the noun is synonymous in meaning with the phrase in which the demonstrative follows the noun. Differences in usage appear to be stylistic.

61

5. The final /w/ of /jaaw/ 'they came' is a regular suffix for plural forms of the perfect and imperfect of finally-weak verbs. The same suffix appears in this selection with the verbs /bdaaw/ 'they began' and /bnaaw/ 'they built'.

6. At first glance, the form /bdaaw/ 'they began' looks very different from its MSA counterpart bada?uu. The differences between these forms, however, are regular. First, SAA omits a short vowel in an open syllable, resulting in the initial consonant cluster /bd/ (/bdaaw/) rather than bad (bada?uu). Second, SAA lacks hamza (glottal stop) as a phoneme or full member of the consonant set. Thus, the SAA form has the long vowel /aa/ (/bdaaw/) where the MSA has the sequence a? (bada?uu). Finally, the suffix /w/ is the SAA suffix for the plural forms of the perfect and imperfect of the finally-weak verb (/bada?uu/) in place of the MSA uu (bada?uu).

7. The combination of /maa/ and /ʃ/ in /maa qaʕduuʃ/ 'they did not stay' signals negation in SAA and certain other varieties of spoken Arabic. In verbal negation, /maa/ precedes the verb; the particle /ʃ/ follows the verb and any direct object suffix. These two particles also negate certain non-verb structures, such as /nnaas maahuumʃ fəllaaḥiin/ 'the people are not peasants' (Selection 20). To negate other non-verbal structures, the two particles fuse to become /maaʃii/, as in /fə-diin maaʃii məqbuula/ 'in Islam, it is not acceptable' (Selection 17).

8. The form /maanuuʃ/, in the statment /yaʕnii maanuuʃ taariix kbiir fəljazaayər/ 'you know, they [the Greeks] don't have a long history in Algeria' is a variant of /maaluuʃ/ 'he doesn't have, it doesn't have'.

9. The form /ddzaayər/ 'Algiers; Algeria' derives from /əljazaayər/ by means of two sound changes. One change is dissimilation, in which two similar sounds become less alike. Dissimilation is common in SA, especially when the two similar sounds are fricatives, as /j/ and /z/ are in /əljazaayər/. The voiced fricative /z/ is unchanged, but the voiced affricate /j/ becomes the voiced stop /d/. The other change is the loss of the short vowel /a/ in the open syllable of /əljazaayər/. The resulting /ddzaayər/ is the usual, informal SAA pronunciation of the name of the country and its capital.

10. The speaker does not exaggerate in the phrase /kull yaʕnii lmaahaaṣiil taaʕ əzziraaʕa/ 'all of the agricultural products'. North Africa was an important resource for the Roman Empire, as it was later for France. It was called "the granary of the Empire." In addition to grain, North Africa exported fruits, especially grapes and figs, as well as beans.

11. In the phrase /waaḥəd lə ... naas/ 'a certain (group of) people', /waaḥəd/ functions as an indefinite article. The noun it precedes is definite and singular, as is /lə ... naas/ 'the people' (or /ənnaas/, with no hesitation between the definite article and the noun).

The indefinite noun phrase with /waaḥəd/ differs from the indefinite noun phrase of MSA (as in kitaabun 'a book') in meaning as well as structure. The indefinite noun phrase of MSA is usually translated as 'a, an'. The indefinite noun phrase with /waaḥəd/, in constrast, is translated as 'a certain, a particular'.

Note also that the word /naas/ 'people' in the context of this particular phrase may be considered grammatically singular (as a collective). The following clause, however, treats /naas/ as grammatically plural: /yəsəmmuuhum/ 'they call them'.

12. The Germanic tribe known as /les Vandales/ 'the Vandals' sacked the city of Rome in 428 CE.

The Ancient History of Algeria

A: I mean, you know, the history of the ... of Algeria, the ancient kind, you know, of the time of ... the Phoenicians and of the Greeks and of the Romans, this one. The first who came to this region, they were the Phoenicians when they began to trade with the world. After them came ah ... the Greeks. Really, the Greeks did not, did not stay, you know, they don't have a long history in Algeria. It is the Romans, they are the ones who have a long history in Algeria.

B: Also, their ruins are still found in Algeria.

A: I mean, the ... inasmuch as they are the ones who built the first, who built the ... the city of Algiers [xxx] to us, Algiers the capital, and built Annaba, and built ah ... Constantine. In the olden days the capital Algiers was called Icosium. There was ah ... you know, ah ... a large harbor, you know, for trade, and they used to, ah, all of the agricultural products that Algeria used to have, they used to take them to Rome. After Rome ah ... there came a ... people called *the Vandals*, who were the ones who destroyed Rome. They stayed a short time, you know, in, in Algeria.

lʕarab jaabuu mʕaahum əlʔislaam

This broad outline of Algerian history in the Islamic period notes historical elements that Algeria shares with the Arab and Islamic world, as well as the ways in which it differs.

A: baʕdəhum jaaw əl ... lʕarab w-jaabuu mʕaahum əlʔislaam. a ... lʕarab yaʕnii fə-llowwəl[1] kaant fiih ḥarb[2] liʔanna kaanuu jaabuu diin jdiid.

wə... illaa anna baʕdmaa nnaas wəllaaw musləmiin fa-xlaaṣ yaʕnii maa, maa bqaat[3] ayy ʃii,[4] maa bqaatʃ ḥarb beenhum, maa bqaatʃ nə ... ṣiraaʕ mʕa lə ... mʕa lʕarab. ḥattaa fə-lʔaaxər yaʕnii f-ḥaawaalii alf wə-rbaʕ miya w-tneen wə-təsʕiin, xamsa wə-tsʕiin baʕdmaa saqṭat a ... ɣarnaaṭa fə-lʔaandaaluus, jaaw əl ... əl ... lʔiṣpaan. jaaw əlʔiṣpaan[5] a ... ḥtəlluu lə ... təqriibən kull əʃʃaamaal taaʕ, taaʕ əljazaayər, a ... baʕdmaa kaan listi ... lə ... listiʕmaar taaʕ əlʔiṣpaan, a ... ddzaayriyyiin yaʕnii ndərruu ktiir mən listiʕmaar taaʕ əṣṣpaanyool. fa ... baʕtuu jmaaʕa mən a ... mən əl ... yaʕnii nnaas taaʕ əl ... lkbaar yaʕnii taaʕ əl ... taaʕ əlmadiina, taaʕ əlʕaaṣiima wə... w-baʕḍ əlmudun looxriin.[6] raaḥuu w-ʃaafuu[7] lə ... a ... ssulṭaan taaʕ əl ... taaʕ əlʕutmaaniyyiin, suuliimaan lqaanuunii,[8] w-ṭalbuu mənnuu baaʃ iisaaʕadhum. wə-baʕat mʕaahum yaʕnii jeeʃ, wə-b-haadaa ʃʃii llii huuma qadruu yaʕnii yḥarruu[9] ljazaayər. w-haakdaak əljazaayər aṣbaḥt[10] yaʕnii wiilaaya taaʕ, taaʕ ədduula lʕuθmaaniyya. haaðaa ʃii yaʕnii yəxaalf lə ... kiifaaʃ yaʕnii dduwwəl lʕarabiyya looxraa wəllaat yaʕni ... dduwwəl lʕarabiyya looxraa kullhaa lə ... lʔatraak staʕmarhum yaʕnii, staʕmaruuhum[11] illaa ljazaayər llii[12] ...

B: kaant ḥiimaaya[13].

A: kaant yaʕnii ḥiimaaya w-ʔaṣbaḥt yaʕnii ... kaan ʕandhaa yaʔnii waḍaʕ xaaṣṣ biihaa. w-baʕdhuum baʕd əl ... əl ... lʔatraak jaaw lfiiraansiyyiin.

العرب جابوا معهم الإسلام

أ: بعدهم جاوا الـ ... العرب وجابوا معهم الإسلام. ا ... العرب يعني فالاوّل[1] كانت فيه حرب،[2] لأنّ كانوا جابوا دين جديد. و ... إلّا انّ بعدما النّاس ولّوا مسلمين فخلاص يعني ما، ما بقات[3] ايّ شي،[4] ما بقاتش حرب بينهم مابقاتش نـ ... صراع مع الـ ... مع العرب. حتّى فالآخر يعني فحاوالي الف واربع ميه واتنين وتسعين خمسه وتسعين بعد ما سقطت ا ... غرناطه فالآندالس، جاوا الـ ... الـ ... الإصبان. جاوا الإصبان[5] ا ... احتلّوا الـ ... تقريبًا كلّ الشّامال تاع، تاع الجزاير، ا ... بعدما كان الاست ... الـ ... الاستعمار تاع الإصبان، ا ... الدّزيريّين يعني انضرّوا كثير من الاستعمار تاع الإصپانيول. فا ... بعثوا جماعه من ا ... من الـ ... يعني النّاس تاع الـ ... الكبار يعني تاع الـ ... تاع المدينه، تاع العاصيمه وبعض المدن الاوخرين.[6] راحوا وشافوا[7] الـ ...ا ... السّلطان تاع الـ ... تاع العتمانيّين، سوليمان القانوني،[8] وطلبوا منّه باش يساعدهم. وبعث معهم يعني جيش وبهذا الشّي اللّي هم قدروا يعني يحرّروا[9] الجزاير. وهكذاك الجزاير اصبحت[10] يعني ويلايه تاع، تاع الدّوله العثمانيّه. هذا الشّي يعني يخالف الـ ... كيفاش يعني الدّوّل العربيّه الاخرى ولّأت يعني ا ... الدّوّل العربيّه الاخرى كلّها الـ ... الأتراك استعمرهم يعني، استعمروهم[11] إلّا الجزاير اللّي... .[12]

ب: كانت حيمايه.[13]

أ: كانت يعني حيمايه وأصبحت يعني ا ... كان عندها يعني وضع خاصّ بيها. وبعدهم بعد الـ... الـ ... الأتراك جاوا الفيرانسيّين.

Selection 2

Vocabulary:

jaab جاب *v* to bring {*imperf:* iijiib}

owwəl اول [*also* uwwəl; awwəl] *adj* first {*fs:* uulaa, *pl:* uuwliin}

aaxər اخر [*also* ooxər] *adj* other {*fs:* axraa, *pl:* axriin}

fə-l?aaxər فالاخر [*also* fə-llaxxər] at the end, in the end

wullaa ولّى [*also* wəllaa] *v* to become; to end up; to return; to start (as pre-verb) {*imperf:* iiwullii}

xlaaṣ خلاص *interj* that's it; that's the way it is

ḥaawaalii حاوالي *adv* about, approximately

ɣarnaaṭa غرناطه *prop* Granada (city in Andalusia in Spain)

l?aandaaluus الاندالوس *prop* Andalusia (region of southern Spain)

iṣpaanii اصپاني *adj* Spanish, Spaniard {*fs:* iṣpaaniyya, *pl:* iṣpaan}

dzaayrii دزايري [*also* jazaayii] *adj* Algerian {*fs:* ddzaayriyya, *pl:* dzaayriyyiin}

ṣpaanyoolii صپانيولي *adj* Spanish, Spaniard {*fs:* ṣpaanyooliyya, *pl:* ṣpaanyool}

ʃaaf شاف *v* to see, look at; to consider, think {*imperf:* iiʃuuf}

raaḥ راح *v* to go {*imperf:* iiruuḥ}

ʕutmaanii عتماني [*also* ʕuθmaanii] *adj* Ottoman Turkish {*fs:* ʕutmaaniyya, *pl:* ʕutmaan}

suuliimaan lqaanuunii سوليمان القانوني *prop* Suleiman the Magnificent (lit. Suleiman the Lawgiver; 16th century ruler of the Ottoman Empire)

baaʃ باش [*also* bəʃ] *conj* for; so that, in order to

haadaa هدا [*also* haad; haað; haaðaa] *pro* this (MS near demonstrative) {*fs:* haadii, *pl:* haaduu}

ʃii شي *nms* matter, situation; thing, object {*pl:* aʃyaa}

huuma هوم [*also* humm(a); ham; huum] *pro* they (3P)

haakdaak هكداك [*also* haakðaak] *adv* like that, in that way

haaðaa هذا [*also* haadaa; haaðaayaa; haaðaay] *pro* this (MS near demonstrative) {*fs:* haaðii, *pl:* haaðuu}

kiifaaʃ كيفاش [*also* kiifaah] *interrog; conj* how; how much (also exclamatory)

turkii تركي *adj* Turk, Turkish {*fs:* turkiyya, *pl:* turk, *pl:* traak}

Notes:

1. The noun in the phrase /fə-llowwəl/ 'at first' is not /lowwəl/ but /owwəl/, with no initial /l/. The /l/ of the defininite article /əl/ is doubled here. This doubling may offset the absence of the hamza (/ʔ/ glottal stop) that is present in the MSA counterpart of this word, ʔawwal. The hamza is not a regular phoneme of SAA. This doubled /l/ occurs in SAA and other varieties of spoken Arabic where the MSA counterpart of the noun has an initial hamza. It is especially common in high-frequency words like /owwəl/.

2. Note the agreement of /kaant/ 'it (fs) was' with its grammatical subject, the grammatically feminine noun /ḥarb/ 'war' in the phrase /kaant fiih harb/ 'there was war'. This would be unusual in certain other varieties of spoken Arabic, in which /kaan fiih/ 'there was' is invariable. In SAA, however, /kaan/ may show agreement with its grammatical subject, as it does here. It may also occur invariably, as in /kaan fiih lubnaaniyyiin/ 'there were Lebanese' (u.d.).

3. The long vowel /aa/ preceding the perfect suffix of /bqaat/ 'it (fs) remained' is the long vowel of the finally-weak root /bqaa/. Certain varieties of spoken Arabic, including certain varieties of SAA, retain the long vowel of the finally-weak root throughout the verb conjugation. The two stems of the perfect of the verb /bqaa/ 'to stay, remain' are /bqaa/ and /bqii/, as in /**bqaat**/ 'it (fs) remained' and /**bqiinaa**/ ' we remained'. The two stems of the imperfect are /bqaa/ and /bq/, as in /yə**bqaa**/ 'he remains' and /nə**bquu**/ 'we remain'. There is, however, variation in the treatment of the long vowel in plural forms.

   The feminine inflection of the verb /bqaat/ 'it (fs) remains', which does not agree in gender with its grammatical subject /ayy ʃii/ 'anything', appears to be a slip of the tongue. It may look ahead to the grammatical subject of the following clause, the grammatically feminine noun /ḥarb/, as in /maa bqaatʃ **ḥarb** beenhum/ 'there was no longer war between them'.

4. The clause /**maa** bqaat ʔayy ʃii/ 'there was nothing left' lacks the negative morpheme /ʃ/. This morpheme usually accompanies /maa/ in a negative construction (as in /**maa** qaʕduuʃ/ 'they did not stay'). The negative morpheme /ʃ/, however, may be replaced by another negative form. Among the negative forms that can replace /ʃ/ include /ayy ʃii/ 'nothing, lit. anything' /waaluu/ 'nothing', /ḥattaa ḥaaja/ 'nothing at all', /ḥattaa waaḥəd/ 'no one'.

5. As the speaker says, /baʕdmaa saqṭat ʔa ... ɣarnaaṭa fə-lʔandaaluus jaaw əl ... əl ... lʔispaan/ 'after Grenada in Andalusia fell, the ... the ... the Spanish came'. The fall of Grenada to the Spanish in 1492 marked the end of the Spanish Christian reconquest of Spain. Following that victory in Spain, the Spanish began to expand into North Africa. Fortified outposts or presidios were built on the coast and tribute was collected.

6. Agreement of adjectives, verbs, and pronouns with plural nouns in SAA is typically plural, as in /əlmudun **looxriin**/ 'the other cities'. There is, however, some variation. This will be noted as it occurs.

7. The clause /raaḥuu w-ʃaafuu/ 'they came and saw' contains two medially-weak verbs, /raaḥ/ 'to go' and /ʃaaf/ 'to see'. These two verbs occur in many varieties of spoken Arabic. Either one is a reliable indicator that the Arabic in use is a variety of spoken Arabic (here, SAA) rather than MSA.

8. The ruler that the speaker calls /suuliimaan lqaanuunii/ 'Suleiman the Lawgiver' is known in English as Suleiman the Magnificent or Suleiman I. As stated, he sent a contingent of some 2,000 janissaries to Algeria under to the beylerbey (provincial governor) Khayr al-Din or Barbarossa.

9. The form /yḥarruu/ 'they liberate' is a Form II verb with the 3MS perfect /ḥarrar/ and imperfect /yḥarrar/. The second syllable of the verb stem /ḥarrar/ is lost through regular phonological change. When that stem takes the long /uu/ suffix of the 3P imperfect, the short vowel in the open syllable. The result should be /iiḥarruu/, with a cluster of three consonants. This is similar to, for example, /iiʕallmuu/ 'they learn'. The difference is that a cluster of three unlike consonants such as /llm/ is permissable in SAA, but a cluster of three identical consonants is not. For that reason, the sequence of three identical consonants /rrr/ is reduced to two. The result is /iiḥarruu/ or, as here, /yḥarruu/.

10. The form /aṣbaḥt/ 'it (fs) became' derives from the 3FS perfect /aṣbaḥət/. The short vowel /ə/ of the 3FS perfect suffix /ət/ often drops out in the stream of speech. It does again in the utterance of the female speaker, /kaant ḥiimaaaaya/ 'it was a protectorate'. Note that in its current form /aṣbaḥt/ is homophonous with the 2MS and 1S forms. Context, however, typically makes confusion unlikely.

70

11. The speaker stops to correct himself during the utterance /lʔatraak staʕmarhum yaʕnii, staʕmaruuhum/ 'the Turks, he occupied them, I mean, they occupied them'. That correction is signalled by the repetition of the verb /staʕmar/ 'to occupy', as well as by the use of the word /yaʕnii/ "I mean; that is'. The word /yaʕnii/ often acts as linguistic filler like this. It gives the speaker time to collect her or his thoughts without leaving a gap in the stream of speech.

12. The relative pronoun /llii/ is invariable; it does not change to reflect the gender or number of the noun or noun phrase it modifies. It follows a definite noun and precedes a relative clause modifying that noun. An example occurs here: /B: ljazaayər llii ... A: kaant ḥiimaaya./ 'B: Algeria, which .... A: it (fs) was a protectorate.'

13. As the female speaker points out, Algeria for the most part was not under direct rule by the Ottoman Empire. Instead, /kaant ḥiimaaya/ 'it (fs) was a protectorate.' This system began in 1720, when the Ottoman sultan recognized the dey of Algiers as regent. Algeria remained part of the Ottoman Empire, but the sultan's government had little or no direct authority in the country.

The Arabs Brought Islam with Them

A: After them came the, the Arabs and they brought Islam with them. Ah ...
the Arabs, I mean, at first there was a war because they had brought a new
religion. However, after people became Muslims, that was it. I mean, there
was nothing left, there was no more war between them, there was no more
... struggle with, with the Arabs until the end, I mean, in about 1492 after,
ah, Granada fell in Andalusia. The, Spain came, Spain, ah ... occupied the
... nearly all of the north of, of Algeria. Ah ... after the col ... the
colonialism of Spain, ah ... the Algerians suffered a lot from the colonialism
of the Spanish, so they sent a group of, of ... influential people, I mean,
from, from the capital city and some other cities. They went to see the, ah
... the sultan of those Ottomans, Sulayman the Magnificent, and asked that
he help them. They sent, I mean, ah ... an army with them. In this way
they were able to, I mean, liberate Algeria, and in this way Algeria became,
I mean, a province of, of the Ottoman state. This, I mean, differs ... how, I
mean, the other Arab states became, I mean, all of, I mean, the other Arab
states were colonized by the Turks, I mean, it occupied them, except for
Algeria which ...

B: It was a protectorate.

A: It was, I mean, a protectorate and it became, I mean, it had, I mean, its own
special situation, I mean. After them, after the Turks came the French.

huwwa taaʕ fraansaa

In their brief discussion of the Algerian war of independence, speakers emphasize the political unity that made the war of independence possible. Their speech, in contrast, introduces some of the variations occurring in SAA.

A: ttaariix taaʕ əljazaaʔir llii lḥaqt ʕleeh anaa, huwwa taaʕ fraansaa. kaanuu məstaʕmariinnaa[1] miya w-tlaatiin sana. a… məm-baʕd bdaaw iiḥaḍḍruu lə-θoora[2] w-ləmmaa qaamuu l-ttoora[3] kull ʃʃaʕb əljazaaʔirii qaam yə… yaʕnii …

B: iiʃaarək yaʕnii.

A: iiʃaarək a… lwasaṭ a … lɣarb a… maa kaanʃ fiih yaʕnii waaḥəd iiquul haadaa qbaaylii wəllaa haadaa qṣamṭiinii wəllaa mə … kullhum kaanuu f-iid wəḥda[3] w-ḥaarbuu fraansaa. ḥattaa xarjət, aṣbaaḥuu[4] yəthaarbuu biinaathum.[5]

هوّ تاع فرانسا

أ: التّـاريخ تـاع الجـزائر اللّـي لحـقت عليـه انـا، هوّ تاع فـرانسـا. كـانوا
مـستعمرينّا¹ ميـه وثلاثين سنـه ا ... ممبعد بداوا يحضّروا للثّوره² ولمّا
قامـوا للثّوره² كلّ الشّعب الجزائري قام يـا ... يعني ....

ب: يشارك يعني.

أ: يشارك ا ... الوسط ا ... الغرب ا ... مـا كانش فيـه يعني واحد يقول هذا
قبـايلي ولاّ هاد قسنطينـي ولاّ مـ ... كلّهم كانـوا فيـد واحـده³ وحاربـوا
فرنسا. حتّى خرجت، اصبـاحوا⁴ يتحاربـوا بيناتهم.⁵

Vocabulary:

lḥaq ʕlaa لحق على *v* to keep up with, be on top of {*imperf:* yəlḥaq ʕlaa}

huwwa هوّ [*also* huu; huwa] *pro* he (3MS)

qaam قام *v; pre-verb* to begin (to do s.t.); to get, stand up; to revolt, rebel {*imperf:* iiquum}

qṣamṭiinii قسنطيني [*also* qṣantiinii] *adj* Constantinois (from Constantine, city in eastern Algeria) {*fs:* qṣamṭiiniyya, *pl:* qṣamṭiiniyyiin}

wəllaa ولاّ *conj* or

qbaaylii قبايلي *adj* Kabyle, of or from Kabylia (region of west central Algeria) {*fs:* qbaayliyya, *pl:* qbaayliyyiin}

biinaat بينات [*also* biin] *prep* among, between *with P noun or suffixed pronoun*

Notes:

1. Note the doubled /n/ of /məstaʕmariinnaa/. The first /n/ is that of the sound masculine plural suffix /iin/. The second /n/ is that of the 1P suffix /naa/. In SAA as in certain other varieties of spoken Arabic, the /n/ of the sound

75

masculine plural suffix does not always drop before a suffixed pronoun or when the noun is the first term of a construct phrase, as it does in MSA (musta\'miriinaa 'occupying (p) us').

2. Two variants of the MSA letter ث occur here, in /θθoora ... ttoora/ 'the revolution ... the revolution'. The first variant, in /θθoora/, is the interdental fricative /θ/. The second variant, /ttoora/ is the dental stop /t/. Some speakers of SAA use the interdental fricative /θ/, as well as /ð/ and /ð̣/. Other speakers replace the interdental fricatives with the relevant stops /t/, /d/, and /ḍ/. Whichever system a speaker may use, a good deal of variation usuall occurs.

3. The form /wəḥda/ 'one (fs)' that occurs here derives from /waaḥda/. The short vowel /ə/ that occurs in the first syllable is a variant. Although SAA tends to drop short vowels in open syllables (as in /kbiir/ 'large', as compared with MSA kabiir), it usually maintains long vowels, even when followed by a sequence of two consonants (as in /waaḥda/).

4. The form /aṣbaaḥuu/ 'they became', with a long /aa/ as the stem vowel, is related to the MSA form ʔaṣbaḥuu. The long /aa/ vowel of the SAA form /aṣbaaḥuu/ is one SAA strategy (see Selection 1, note 3) for preserving the short stem vowel of the MSA form ʔaṣbaḥuu. That short vowel would otherwise drop out because it is in an open syllable. The result would be something like /ṣabḥuu/ 'they became' (Selection 13), with loss of the initial syllable and vowel shift in the stem. The form here, however, is an MSA-like variant, which lengthenf the short vowel.

5. The form /biinaat/ 'amongst, between', as in /biinaathum/ 'among themselves' occurs in SAA and certain other varieties of spoken Arabic. It is the form taken by the preposition /biin/ 'amongst, between' when it precedes a plural suffixed pronoun or plural noun. This occurs, however, only when the preposition indicates location within a particular group of persons or things. When the preposition /biin/ links two groups, as in /biinnaa w-biin wahraan/ 'between us and Oran' (Selection 29), the plural form of the preposition is not used. It should also be noted that the variant /been/ is invariable (see Selection 2).

76

It's about France

A: The history of Algeria that I am aware of is about France. They colonized us for 130 years, ah .... Later, they began preparing for the revolution and when they began the revolution all of the Algerian people began to, I mean ....

B: To participate, that is.

A: To participate, ah .... The central region, the west, ah .... There was, I mean, no one who said, "This person is from the Kabyle" or "This person is from Constantine" if .... They were hand in hand and they fought against France until it left. They began to fight among themselves.

ləmmaa ṭaaḥt suumət lpətrool, xlaaṣ

As the speaker describes it here, Algeria at the height of the oil boom was totally dependent on foreign imports. The language used, with the use of French and borrowed items, reflects expressed opinion.

yaʕnii l-ḥadd əlʔaan, lḥaala liqtiṣaadiyya fə-ddzaayər ṣʕiiba bəzzaaf.[1] a ... fə-lluwwəl yaʕnii qabəl ttaamaaniinaat yaʕnii kaant ... kaan fiih[2] pətrool,[3] ssuuma taaʕ əlpətrool kaant mliiḥa, fa-kaanuu yəʃruu kulləʃ mə-lxaarəj,[4] yaʕnii maa kənnaa nəntjuu ḥattaa ḥaaja, ɣeer əlpeetrool. fa-kaan kulləʃ iijiibuu mə-lxaarəj, nnaas ʕam-baalhaa haadii hiyya ... haaðiik lḥəyaat taaʕ *Algérie* yaʕnii. kulləʃ iijjaab[5] mən əlxaarəj, lmaakla, lmaaʃiinaat, a ... lmaawaad lʔowwəliyya yaʕnii llii yəstaʕməluuhum fəl ... fə-lmaaṣaaniʕ, fa-ləmmaa ṭaaḥt suumət lpətrool, xlaaṣ, maa fiiʃ mədxuul yaʕnii, fa-kull ʃii llii kaan yəttʃəraa mə-lxaarəj wəllaaw maa yjiibuuhʃ.[6] wə-nnaas ... wə-nnaas wəllaaw yaʕnii maa iiṣiibuu ḥattaa ḥaaja[7] fə-lmaarʃii, iiruuḥuu lmaarʃii yəʃryuu lḥaajaat llii kaanuu mwaalfiin iiṣiibuuhaa, xlaaṣ. yaʕnii ṭaaḥt ʕliihum waaḥəd lə ... waaḥd lmiiziiriyya, waaḥəd əlfuqr llii maa yəqdəruuʃ iitḥammluu.

لمّا طاحت سومة البترول، خلاص

يعني لحدّ الآن، الحاله الاقتصاديّه فالدّزاير صعيبه بزّاف[1] .. ... فالأوّل يعني قبل التّامانينات يعني كانت ا ... كان فيه[2] بترول،[3] السّومه تاع البترول كانت مليحه، فكانوا يشروا كلّش مالخارج،[4] يعني ما كنّا ننتجوا حتّى حاجه، غير البيترول. فكان كلّش يجيبوه مالخارج، النّاس عم بالها هذي هيّ ... هذيك الحياه تاع *Algérie* يعني. كلّش يتجاب[5] من الخارج، الماكله، الماشينات، ا ... الماواد الاوّليّه يعني اللّي يستعملوهم فـ ... فالمصانع، فلمّا طاحت سومه البترول، خلاص ما فيش مدخول يعني، فكلّ شي اللّي كان يتشرى مالخارج ولّوا ما يجيبوهش.[6] والنّاس ا ... والنّاس ولّوا يعني ما يصيبوا حتّى حاجه[7] فالمارشي، يروحوا المارشي يشريوا الحاجات اللّي كانوا موالفين يصيبوها، خلاص. يعني طاحت عليهم واحد الـ ... واحد الميزيريه، واحد الفقر اللّي ما يقدروش يتحمّلوه.

Vocabulary:

ṣʕiib صعيب *adj* hard, difficult {*fs:* ṣʕiiba, *pl:* ṣʕaab}

bəzzaaf بزّاف *adv* a lot, very much

uwwəl اوّل [*also* awwəl; owwəl] *adj* first {*fs:* uulaa, *pl:* uuwliin}

pətrool بترول [*also* peetrool; piitrool] *nms* oil, petroleum

suuma سومه *nfs* price

mliiħ مليح *adj* good, nice {*fs:* mliiḥa, *pl:* mlaaḥ}

kulləʃ كلّش *nms* all, everything

mə- م [*also* mən; məm-] *prep* from, of

xaarəj خارج *prep* overseas, outside the country; outside

peetrool پتـرول [*also* pətrool; piitrool]   *nms* oil, petroleum

ʕam-ḥaal- + suffixed pronoun عـم بـال [*also* ʕlaa baal]   in s.o.'s opinion, s.o. thinks

haadii هـدي [*also* haaðii; haadiyyaa; haaðiyyaa]   *pro* this (FS near demonstrative) {*ms:* haadaa, *pl:* haaduu}

hiyya هِـي [*also* hii; hiya]   *pro* she (3FS)

haaðiik هـذيـك [*also* haadiika; haadiik; haaðiika]   *pro* that (FS far demonstrative) {*ms:* haaðaak, *pl:* haaðuuk}

jjaab اتجـاب *v* to be brought {*imperf:* yəjjaab}

maaʃiina مـاشـيـنـه *nfs* machine, engine, machinery {*pl:* maaʃiinaat}

ṭaaḥ طـاح *v* to fall, drop {*imperf:* iiṭiiḥ}

ṣaab صـاب *v* to find, discover {*imperf:* iiṣiib}

maarʃii مـارشـي *nms* market (large or European-style marketplace) {*pl:* maarʃiyyaat}

mwaaləf mʕa مـوالـف مـع   used to, accustomed to {*fs:* mwaalfa mʕa, *pl:* mwaalfiin mʕa}

miiziiriya مـيـزيـريـه *nfs* destitution, extreme poverty; misery, despair

Notes:

1. The adverbial intensifier /bəzzaaf/ 'a lot, very much' is one of the words that distinguishes SAA (and certain varieties of spoken Moroccan Arabic) from other varieties of spoken Arabic.

2. The time frame of an existential clause changes when /kaan/ is present, as occurs here in /**kaan** fiih pətrool/ 'there was oil'. The simple or present existential version of this clause would be /**fiih** pətrool/. Note that speakers of SAA use the existential /kaayən/ as well as /fiih/. The tendency, however, is to use /fiih/ rather than /kaayən/ when a change of time or time frame is required.

3. Note that the speaker in this selection uses several words of non-Arabic origin, such as /pətrool/. Arabic speakers from all parts of the Arabic-speaking world regularly use words of non-Arabic origin, such as /kumbyuutar/ 'computer' and /tiliifuun/ 'telephone'. According to stereotypes, however, speakers from Algeria, Morocco, and Tunisia, all former French colonies, use large amounts of French when they speak Arabic. The use of French in

North African Arabic is perhaps a natural result of over 100 years of French colonialism and of continuing close ties with the Francophone world.

4. The preposition /mən/ is reduced to /mə-/ in the phrase /mə-lxaarəj/. The loss of the /n/ in /mən/ regularly occurs in SAA when /mən/ precedes the definite article.

5. The form /iijjaab/ 'it (ms) could be brought' derives from /tjaab/ 'to be brought'. The /t/ of the /tjaab/ is the affix of the quasi-passive form $tC_1C_2vC_3$. That /t/ becomes the first /j/ of /jjaab/ through total assimilation, in which one consonant, /t/, becomes identical with another, /j/.

The quasi-passive in SAA and other varieties of spoken Arabic, replaces the ablaut or vocalic passive of ClA and MSA (as in <u>kutiba</u> 'to be written', derived from <u>kataba</u> 'to write'). The quasi-passive takes the form $tC_1C_2vC_3$, as seen in /jjaab/ or Form VII, as in /nqaal/ 'to be said'.

6. The 3MS suffixed pronoun is represented by /h/ when it follows a vowel, as in /maa yiijiibuuhʃ/ 'they do not get'. The sound is not noticeable when it occurs in word-final position. Here, however, preceding /ʃ/, it is clearly pronounced.

7. The verb /wullaa/ (also /wəllaa/) acts as a pre-verb meaning 'to begin, start', as here in /**wullaaw** yaʕnii maa yṣiibuu ḥattaa ḥaaja/ 'they started, I mean, to find nothing at all'. This verb may also serve as the main verb of a clause, when it means 'to become', as in /nnaas **wullaaw** musləmiin/ 'people became Muslims' (Selection 2).

When the Price of Oil Dropped, That Was It

I mean, so far, the economic situation in Algeria is very difficult. At ... at first, I mean, before the 80s, I mean, there was oil. The price of oil was good, so they used to buy everything from abroad. I mean, we produced nothing at all except for oil, so they brought everything in from abroad. People knew this was it, this is life in Algeria, I mean. Everything was brought in from abroad, food, machinery, ah ... raw materials, I mean, what they use in factories. When the price of oil dropped, that was it, I mean, there was no revenue, I mean. Everything that had been purchased abroad, they began not getting it. People started, I mean, to find nothing at all in the market. They would go to the market to buy the things they were used to finding there. That was it. I mean, such a, such a state of poverty befell them, such poverty that they couldn't bear it.

yyaamaat əlbaanaan

This selection contrasts the prosperity of the speaker's childhood memories with Algeria's current economic conditions.

A: anaa nəʃfaa lbaanaan[1] fii haaðaa lə ... məllii kənt ṣɣiir yaʕnii kənt nruuḥ nəqḍii mʕa yəmmaa[2] f-haaðaak əl *marché* llii qəddaam wiin[3] nəsknuu, kən- nʕayyəṭuuluu[4] *Marché Clauzel*[5] yaʕnii wə...

B: mmm.

A: *Clauzel* ʕalaa asəm taaʕ waaḥəd a ... *général* taaʕ ... fiiraansii llii dxəl fə-ddzaayər fə-ʔalf wə-tmənmya wə-tlaatiin. əlmuuhəmm,[6] kaan haaðaa lə *marché* haaðaa fiih lxeer yaʕnii, kiimaa yguuluu a ... kənnaa ... llii-kaant fiih əlxuṭra,[7] kaan fiih əlḥuut kaan fiih a ... kaan waaḥəd əlxəḍḍaar[8] ʕanduu mə ... yaʕnii mwaalf mʕaanaa yə ... an ... yəʕrafnaa ḥnaa kənnaa nruuḥuu ʕanduu kull yoom yaʕnii, təqriibən kull yoom. fa-kull-maa nruuḥuu ʕanduu yaʕṭiinii, yaʕṭiinii ḥabba baanaan[9] yaʕnii, zyaada yaʕnii qaal a ... yaʕnii kaan iiḥabbənii haaðaak lə ... ssiyyid haaðaak yaʕnii wə-maa, maa ... lə ... bə-ṣṣaḥḥ[10] maa nððəkkarʃ lə ... lwəjh taaʕuu yaʕnii maʕ lʔasəf yaʕnii. əlmuuhəmm, ləmmaa kssaruu haaðaak əl *marché*, bnaaw a *marché* waaḥəd aaxor[11] jdiid bnaawa bəl ... bə-lbeeṭoon wə-ssiimaan w-raaḥ kulləʃ. maa ... aḷḷaah yəṣṭar[12] yaʕnii kuulləʃ raaḥ, laa ... laa xuḍra, laa faakiya, laa ḥuut,[13] kaayn ɣeer lḥəyuuṭ, nnaas truuḥ dduur fə-l *marché* haaðaak, dduur ʕal ... *à gauche, à droite* wə-twəllii, maa kaayn waaluu. yaʕnii, yaʕnii haaðaak əl *marché*, traaḥət ʕleeh lbaaraaka kiimaa yguuluu nnaas yaʕnii. laa raah ... kii raaḥt fraansaa, raaḥ mʕaahaa lḥuuṭ, raaḥ mʕaahaa lə ... lə ... lxeer, raaḥ mʕaahaa kuulləʃ, aḷḷaah yəṣḍar[12] yaʕnii.

ايامات البانان

أ: انا نشفى البـانان[1] في هذا الـ ... مـاللّي كنت صغير يعني كنت نروح
نقضي مع يمّا[2] فهذاك الـ marché اللّي قدّام وين[3] نسكنوا، كنا نعيّطوله[4]
Marché Clauzel يعني و ...

ب: ام.

أ: Clauzel على اسم تاع واحد ا ... général تاع ا ... فـرنسي اللّي دخل
فالدّزاير فألف وثمنميه وثلاثين. الموهمّ،[6] كان هذا الـ marché هذا فيه
الخير يعني، كيما يقولوا. ا ... كنّا ... اللّي كانت فيه الخطره،[7] كان فيه
الحوت كان فيه ا ... كان واحد الخضّار[8] عنده مـ .... يعني موالف معنا يـ
... أن ... يعرفنا، احنا كنّا نروحوا عنده كلّ يوم يعني، تقريبًا كلّ يوم.
فكلّ ما نروحوا عنده يعطيني، يعطيني حبّه بانان[9] يعني، زياده يعني.
قال ا ... يعني كان يحبّني هذاك الـ ... السّيّد هذاك يعني وما ... لا
... بالصّحّ[10] ما نذّكرش الـ ... الوجه تاعه يعني مع الأسف يعني. الموهمّ،
لمّا كسّروه هذاك الـ marché، بناوا ... marché واحد اخر[11] جديد بناوه
بالـ ... بالبيطون والسّيمان، وراح كلّش. مـا ... اللّه يصطر[12] يعني
كلّش راح، الـ ... لا خضره، لا فاكيه، لا حوت،[13] كاين غير الحيوط. النّاس
تروح تدور فالـ marché هذاك، دّور عـالـ à droite, à gauche..، وتولّي مـا
كاين والو. يعني، يعني هذاك الـ marché، تراحت عليه البـاراكـه كيما
يقولوا النّاس يعني. لا راه ا ... كي راحت فرنسا، راح معها الحوت، راح
معها الـ ... الـ ... الخير، راح معها كلّش، اللّه يصطر[12] يعني.

Vocabulary:

ʃfaa شـفـى *v* to remember, recall {*imperf:* yəʃfaa}

baanaan بـانـان [*also* baanaanaa] *nms* banana

məllii مـلـلـي *conj* when, at the time that; since, from the time that

qḍaa قـضـى *v* to shop; to buy, get {*imperf:* yəqḍii}

yəmmaa يـمّا *nfs* mother; s.o.'s mother (reference clear from context) {*pl:* yəmmaat}

haaðaak هـذاك [*also* haadaaka; haadaak; haaðaaka] *pro* that (MS far demonstrative) {*fs:* haaðiik, *pl:* haaðuuk}

qəddaam قـدّام *prep* in front of

wiin ويـن *interrog; conj* where, the place that

ʕayyəṭ عـيّـط *v* to call (by the name of); to call out, shout {*imperf:* iiʕayyəṭ}

marché nms market

Clauzel prop Clauzel, Bertrand (1772 - 1842; governor-general of Algeria from 1835 - 36)

asəm اسـم *nms* name {*pl:* aasmaaʔ, *pl:* aasaamii, *pl:* smaawaat}

général nms general

xuṭra خـطـره [*also* xuḍra] *nfs; collective* vegetables {*pl:* xḍaarii}

kaayən كـايـن *adj; existential; also invariable* there is, there are {*fs:* kaayna, *pl:* kaayniin}

ḥuut حـوت *nms; collective* fish {*fs:* ḥuuta, *pl:* ḥuutaat}

ɣeer غـيـر *prep* only, just

ḥnaa احـنـا [*also* ḥnaayaa; ḥanaa] *pro* we, us (1P)

waaləf mʕa والـف مـع *v* to be or become used to, accustomed to {*imperf:* iiwaaləf mʕa}

ḥabba حـبّـه *nfs* piece (of fruit); grain (of wheat, etc.) {*pl:* ḥabbaat}

bə-ṣṣaḥḥ بالصّـحّ [*also* b-ṣaḥḥ] *conj* but (lit. with the truth)

ððəkkar اذّكـر *v* to remember, recall {*imperf:* yəððəkkar}

lmuuhəmm الـمـهـمّ *disc* the point is, the essential thing is

haaðiika هـذيـك [*also* haadiika; haadiik; haaðiik] *pro* that (FS far demonstrative) {*fs:* haaðiika, *pl:* haaðuuka}

beetoon بيتون *nms* concrete, cement

siimaan سيمان *nms* cement, concrete

ṣṭar صطر [*also* ṣḍar] *v* to protect (of the deity); to cover, conceal {*imperf:* yaṣṭar}

aḷḷah yaṣṭar الله يصطر [*also* aḷḷaah yaṣḍar] *v* may God protect

faakiya فاكيه *nfs* fruit {*pl:* fwaakiih}

ḥiiṭ حيط *nms* wall {*pl:* hyuuṭ}

à gauche, à droite to the left, to the right

wallaa ولّى [*also* wullaa] *v* to end up; to become; to return; to start (as pre-verb) {*imperf:* iiwallii}

traaḥ ʕlaa تراح *v* to slip away {*imperf:* yatraaḥ}

baaraaka باراكه *nfs* divine blessing, divine grace

kiimaa كيما *prep* like, as ; *conj.*

gaal قال [*also* qaal; ʔaal] *v* to speak, talk {*imperf:* iiguul}

kii كي *conj* when, whenever; like, as

xeer خير *nms* goodness, bounty

ṣḍar صضر [*also* ṣṭar] *v* to protect (of the deity); to cover, conceal {*imperf:* yaṣḍar}

aḷḷah yaṣḍar الله يصضر [*also* aḷḷaah yaṣṭar] *v* may God protect

Notes:

1. The status of a form such as /lbaanaan/ 'banana' is uncertain. That is, the word may be a borrowing of the French word la banane 'banana' that can be considered Arabicized. On the other hand, it may result from code-switching, in which a speaker moves from Arabic into French. With no sounds in the form /lbaanaan/ that are definitively Arabic (such as /q/) or French (such as the r grassayé), the observer can only rely on judgments by speakers of SAA. There is some agreement that /lbaanaan/ is borrowed into SAA and exists side by side with the ClA and MSA word /mooz/ 'banana'.

2. The word /yəmmaa/ has the general meaning 'mother'. More specifically, it refers to someone's mother. Usually, as here, that someone is the speaker. The same is true in English. Written English uses a capital letter to distinguish (my) Mother from (anyone's) mother, but a similar distinction in Arabic is dependent on context.

3. The word /wiin/ 'where' may function as a preposition, as it does here in /qəddaam wiin nəsknuu/ 'across from where we live'. It also serves as in interrogative or question word, as in /wiin iiruuḥuu?/ 'where do they go?'

4. The phrase /kən- nʕayyəṭuuluu/ 'we used to call it' would otherwise be pronounced /kənnaa nʕayyəṭuuluu/. The loss of the syllable /naa/ from /kənnaa/ can be explained as the result of two regular processes. First, the sequence of three identical consonants /n/ forces the long /aa/ of /kənnaa nʕayyəṭuuluu/ to drop out. The resulting intermediate form would be /kənn-nʕayyəṭuuluu/. The sequence of three identical consonants, however, is unusual in SAA, even though a sequence of three non-identical consonants may occur. For that reason, one /n/ drops out. The end result is the phrase that occurs here.

5. The namesake of the Marché Clauzel, located in central Algiers, is Bertran Clauzel. He was governor-general of Algeria from 1835 to 1836. Since Algerian independence, the Algerian government has changed a number of place names from French to Arabic, as when it changed the of the name of the city from Phillipeville to Skikda. Some people, however, continue to use the old Francophone names.

6. The form /əlmuuhəmm/ 'the point is; the important thing' is not adjectival here. It is a marker of organization. Its function is resumptive, as it indicates that the speaker is resuming or returning to the main topic. Here, for example, the speaker uses /əlmuuhəmm/ to mark his return from identifying the namesake of the Marché Clauzel to his description of the market itself.

7. The form /lxuṭra/ 'vegetables' is a varient within SAA for /lxuḍra./

8. The phrase /waaḥəd əlxəḍḍaar/ 'a certain produce vendor' is a more typical example of the indefinite noun phrase with /waaḥəd/ than /waaḥəd nnaas/ 'a certain (group of) people' (see Selection 1, note 11). Here, the noun /əlxəḍḍaar/ 'produce vendor' is singular in grammatical function and in meaning.

9. The noun /ḥabba/ 'banana' in the phrase /**ḥabba** baanaan/ 'a banana' lacks the /t/ of the feminine ending. This /t/ typically occurs at the end of a feminine noun, when that noun is the first noun of a construct phrase, as in /ḥabbat baanaan/. In SAA and certain other varieties of spoken Arabic, however, the occurrence of the /t/ is optional under certain conditions. The condition that applies here is that the first noun of the construct must name a container or measure, as does /ḥabba/ 'piece (of fruit); grain (of wheat, etc.)'. Thus, both /**ḥabba** baanaan/ and /**ḥabbat** baanaan/ occur.

10. The phrase /bə-ṣṣaḥḥ/ (also /b-ṣaḥḥ/) 'but, lit. truly' is a marker of organization like /əlmuuhəmm/ 'the point is'(see this selection, note 6). The phrase /bə-ṣṣaḥḥ/, however, marks an explanatory comment or even a digression, as it does here. The speaker notes about the produce vendor whose kindness he remembers that /**bə-ṣṣaḥḥ** maa nððəkkarʃ l ... lwəjh taaʕuu/ 'but I don't remember the ... his face'. He then return to his main point and marks that return with /əlmuuhəmm/.

11. The phrase /waaḥd aaxor/ is an adjectival compound that means 'other, another'. Note that the element /waaḥd/ (also /waaḥəd/) does not change to reflect gender or number. The element /aaxor/ does change, as in /waaḥd ooxraa/ (fs) and /waaḥd ooxriin/ (p).

12. The phrases /aḷḷaah yəṣṭar/ and /aḷḷaah yəṣḍar/ are variants of one another. The variant /aḷḷaah yəṣḍar/ shows dissimilation, in which two sounds become less alike. The two sounds are /ṣ/ and /ṭ/ in /yəṣṭar/. The voiceless /ṭ/ of /yəṣṭar/ becomes the voiced /ḍ/ of /yəṣḍar/. Note that the ClA and MSA counterpart of these phrases is ʔaḷḷaah yasṭur, with no pharyngealized or emphatic sounds.

13. The phrase /laa xuḍra, laa faakiya, laa ḥuut/ 'no vegetables, no fruit, no fish' appears to be incomplete. The negative /laa/ often accompanies /wə-laa/, as in /laa pətrool wə-laa ṭaraab/ 'neither oil nor dust'. In this case, however, the speaker uses /laa/ three times without using /wə-laa/ to mark the last item in the series.

The Time of Bananas

A: I remember bananas at that ... when I was young, I mean. I used to go shopping with my mother at that *market* that was across from where we lived. We used to call it the *Marché Clauzel*, I mean.

B: Yes.

A: Clauzel, after some ah ... *general* from ... a Frenchman who came to Algeria in 1830. The point is that this *market* had everything. I mean, as they say, ah ... we were ... What it had was vegetables, it had fish, it had ... There was a produce vendor who had ... I mean, who saw us all the time, he ... that .... He knew us, we used to go to him every day, I mean, nearly every day. Every time we went to him, he used to give me, he would give me a banana, I mean, an extra one, I mean, he said. I mean, that ... man liked me, I mean, and I don't .... But I don't remember his ... his face, I mean, unfortunately. The point is that when they tore down that *market*, they built another *market*, a new one. They built it out of ... out of concrete and cement. Everything was gone, there was no .... God protect us, I mean, everything was gone -- no, no vegetables, no fruit, no fish. Just the bare walls. People go there, they walk around that *market*. They turn *right and left*, they go home. There is nothing, I mean. The blessing has gone out of that market, as people say. I mean, if they .... When the French left, the fish left with them, the ... the ... the goodness left with them, everything left with them, I mean, God protect us.

llii ysəmmuuhaa ttoora zziraaʕiyya

Algeria's agricultural revolution, described here as a complete disaster, was discontinued in 1978 after large financial losses and the low productivity that the speaker notes.

immaalaa fiin yaʕnii, maaniiʃ[1] ʕaarf[2] anaa, lpiitrool haaðaa yguulləK[3] a... bə-lʕaam lə-lʕaam raahum[4] iiṣiibuu yaʕnii *des* ... kiimaa yquuluuhum iḥtiiyaaṭaat yaʕnii taaʕ əlpətrool kbiiraa fiihaa lə ... fiihaa lə ... lɣaaz, fiihaa ddahab, fiihaa liiraanyoom yaʕnii yguulk əljazaayər blaad ɣaaniyya. w-maa fhamnaaʃ yaʕnii mə-ljiiha yguul blaad ɣaaniyya w-mən jiiha xraa nnaas ʕaayʃiin fii, fii, fii fuqər, kii llii tquulii ʕaayʃiin fii blaad maa fiihaa waaluu[5] yaʕnii. laa, laa. laa pətrool wə-laa ṭaraab wə-laa .... zmaan kaant lə ... ddzaayər yaʕnii tṣəddər lqamḥ, tṣəddər lə ... lfaakiya, haaðii ttʃiinaa, ttəmar kaan fə-fraansaa, f-*l'Europe* yaʕnii, kaan kull ʃii. wə-mʕa nnhaar daaruu haaðiik llii ysəmmuuhaa ttoora zziraaʕiyya[6] haaðiik taaʕ alf wə-tsaʕmiya w-waaḥd w-səbʕiin. fii ʕaamiin təlt sniin yəhhəlkuu[7] gaaʕ əlziraaʕa[8] taaʕ əddzaayər. llii kaan ʕanduu llarḍ yəxdəmhaa naḥḥaawhaaluu,[9] aʕṭaawhaa lwaaḥd oxriin a... wəllaaw aʃɣul xəddaamiin[10] ʕand lḥuukuuma. yaʕṭuuhum ʃahriyya, yaʕnii yəxdəm wəllaa maa yəxdəmʃ, ʕanduu ʃʃahriyya taaʕuu. fa-lʔiintaaj yaʕnii wəllaa *zéro*, xlaaṣ. lə ... lə ... lə ... ṭṭmar kənnaa nə ... kənnaa yaʕnii mə ... mən biin lʔarbaʕa lbəldaan lluwwəliin[11] fə-lʕaaləm, wəlliinaa maa nəntjuu waaluu. kulləʃ raaḥ yaʕnii, lə ... ʃʃjar haaðuuk marḍuu, wəllaaw maa yəthalloʃ[12] fiihum, kulləʃ fsəd.

اللّي يسمّوها الثّوره الزّراعيّه

امّالا فين يعني، مانيش[1] عارف[2] انا. البيترول هذا يقولّك[3] ا ... بالعام للعام
راهم[4] يصيبوا يعني *des* ... كيما يقولوهم إحتياطات يعني تاع البترول
كبيره فيها الـ ... فيها الـ ... الغاز، فيها الذّهب، فيها الـ ... إيرانيوم يعني
يقولك الجزاير بلاد غانيّه. وما فهمناش يعني من جيهه يقول بلاد غانيّه
ومن جيهه اخرى النّاس عايشين في، في، في فقر، كي اللّي تقولي عايشين
في بلاد ما فيها والو[5] يعني، لا، لا، لا بترول ولا طراب ولا ا .... زمان كانت
الـ ... الدّزاير يعني تصدّر القمح، تصدّر الـ ... الفاكيه، هذي التّشينه،
التّمر كان فـفرانسا فـ *l'Europe* يعني كان كلّ شي. ومع النّهار داروا هذيك
اللّي يسمّوها الثّوره الزّراعيّه[6] هذيك تاع ألف وتسعميه وواحد وسبعين.
في عامين ثلث سنين يهلّكوا[7] قاع الزّراعه[8] تاع الدّزاير. اللّي كان عنده
اللأرض يخدمها نحّاوهاله،[9] عطاوها لواحد اخرين ا .... ولّوا شغل خدّامين[10]
عند الحوكومه. يعطوهم شهريّه، يعني يخدم ولّا ما يخدمش، عنده الشّهريّه
تاعه. فالاينتاج يعني ولّى *zéro*، خلاص. الـ ... الـ ... التّمر كنّا نـ ... كنّا
يعني مـ ... من بين الاربعه البلدان اللأوّلين[11] فالعالم، ولّينا ما ننتجوا
والو. كلّش راح يعني، الـ ... الشّجر هذوك مرضوا، ولّوا ما يتهلّوش[12] فيهم،
كلّش فسد.

93

Vocabulary:

immaalaa امّالا [*also* mmaalaa] *conj* so, therefore

maaniiʃ مانيش I am not

maa + suffixed pro + ʃ ما – ش [*also* muu + suffixed pro + ʃ] is not, are not

piitrool پيترول [*also* pətrool; peetrool] *nms* oil, petroleum

iiguullək يقولّك *disc* that is to say, I mean (lit. they tell you)

raa + suffixed pro را *disc* there is, there are

d e s of the (indefinite article)

iḥtiiyaaṭ احتياط *nms* reserve, supply {*pl:* iḥtiiyaaṭaat}

ɣaaz غاز *nms* gas, gasoline; gas, gaseous element {*pl:* ɣaazaat}

iiraanyoom ايرانيوم *nms* uranium

blaad بلاد *nfs* country; region; city {*pl:* bəldaan, *pl:* blaadaat}

ɣaanii غاني *adj* rich, wealthy {*fs:* ɣaaniyya, *pl:* aɣniyaa}

jiiha جيهه *nfs* side; direction {*pl:* jiihaat, *pl:* jwaayəh}

mən jiiha من جيهة on the one hand; as for, as to (lit. from a side)

mən jiiha xraa من جيهه اخرى on the other hand (lit. from another side)

kii llii كي اللي *conj* as if, like

waaluu والو *part.* nothing, not a thing

taraab تراب *nms* earth, dust, dirt

ṣəddər صدّر *v* to export {*imperf:* iiṣəddər}

haaðii هذي [*also* haadii; haaðiyyaa; haadiyyaa] *pro* this (FS near demonstrative) {*ms:* haaðaa, *pl:* haaðuu}

tʃiina تشينه *nfs: collective* orange (fruit) {*pl:* tʃiinaat}

tmar تمر *nms; collective* dates (fruit) {*fs:* təmra, *pl:* təmraat}

Europe *prop* Europe

daar دار *v* to do, commit; to make {*imperf:* iidiir}

gaaʕ قاع *adv* all; every, each; not at all, never (with negative constructions)

səna سنه *nfs* year {*pl:* sniin}

arḍ ارض *nfs* land, plot of land, piece of real estate {*pl:* aaraaḍii}

xdəm خــدَم *v* to work; to do, make; to weave; to plant, cultivate, grow {*imperf:* yəxdəm}

nəḥḥaa نـحّــى [*also* naḥḥaa] *v* to take away, remove; to eliminate, remove (i.e., from a post) {*imperf:* iinəḥḥii}

wəllaa ولّـى [*also* wullaa] *v* to become; to end up; to return; to start (as pre-verb) {*imperf:* iiwəllii}

ʃɣul شَــغل *prep* like, as, in the form of; a kind of, type of

xəddaam خدّام *nms* worker, employee {*fs:* xəddaama, *pl:* xəddaamiin}

ʃahriyya شـهريّــه *nfs* salary {*pl:* ʃahriyyaat}

biin بـين [*also* biinaat] *prep* among, between

zéro *nms* zero

arbaʕa اربــعه [*also* rabʕa] *nfs* four

ʃajara شـجره *nfs* tree {*pl:* ʃjar}

haaðuuk هـذوك [*also* haaduuka; haaduuk; haaðuuka] *pro* that (P far demonstrative) {*ms:* haaðaak, *fs:* haaðiik}

thallaa fii تـهلّى فـي *v* to take care of, care for {*imperf:* yəthallaa}

Notes:

1. The form /maaniiʃ/ 'I am not' combines the negative morphemes /maa/ and /ʃ/ with the 1S suffixed pronoun. Except for the 1S pronoun, the negated pronoun is the independent form. All of the personal pronouns of SAA may be negated in the same way, as in /maahuuʃ/ 'he is not' and /maahiiʃ/ 'she is not'. A nominal sentence negated with a negative pronoun (as in /**maaniiʃ** ʕaarf/ 'I don't know') is synonymous with one negated by /maaʃii/ or /muʃ/'is not, are not' (as in /muʃ ʕaarf/ 'I don't know', Selection 7). Differences in usage appear to be stylistic.

2. The participle /ʕaarf/ in the phrase /maaniiʃ **ʕaarf**/ 'I don't know' is synonymous with the imperfect verb in the phrase /maa **naʕraʃʃ**/ 'I don't know'. In SAA as in other varieties of spoken Arabic, participles may have verbal force. Note, however, that not all participles are equivalent to verbs. The use of a participle is a matter of style as well as meaning.

3. The form /yguullək/ 'they say, lit. he says to you' sometimes functions as linguistic filler. It functions much like /yaʕnii/ 'I mean, lit. it means'. In

95

rapid speech, it has the variant /iiguulk/.

4. In the phrase /raahum iiṣiibuu/ 'they find', the imperfect verb /iiṣiibuu/ follows the presentational particle /raa/ 'here is, here are' with the 3P suffixed pronoun /hum/. This phrase is essentially synonymous with the simple imperfect /iiṣiibuu/ 'they find'.

   The meaning and function of the presentational particle /raa/ in this context is not at the moment clear. Some sources call it an imperfect prefix, similar to the imperfect prefix that occurs in other varieties of spoken Arabic (as in Moroccan /**ka**-yṣiibuu/ 'they find'). Others simply refer to it as a presentational particle, whether it occurs in a nominal or verbal sentence. It seems likely that the particle /raa/ plays a role in discourse, that is, in the organization of a stretch of talk. As a discourse particle, /raa/ appears to mark or to add prominence to a new topic of conversation.

5. The phrase /maa fiihaa **waaluu**/ 'there is nothing in it (fs)' lacks the negative /ʃ/ that usually accompanies /maa/ (as in /**maa** fhamnaaʃ/ 'we don't understand'. The /ʃ/ is omitted when another morpheme, usually with a negative meaning, is paired with /maa/ in the phrase, as /waaluu/ is here. Note also that the use of /waaluu/ identifies a North African variety of Arabic.

6. The Algerian /ttoora zziraaʕiyya/ 'agricultural revolution' began under President Houari Boumedine in 1971. The program broke up large farms and redistributed the land to those who agreed to join government agricultural cooperatives. By 1974, the program has given 10 hectares of land to each of 60,000 people. The program ended after Boumediene's death in 1978 after large financial losses and poor agricultural productivity.

7. The imperfect verb /yəhhəlkuu/ 'they ruin', with a double /h/, is acceptable in SAA. This imperfect derives from the Form I verb /hlək/ 'to destroy, ruin', with the 3MS imperfect /yəhlək/. The doubling of C_1 (here of /h/) in the P forms of the imperfect is one of several strategies used in SAA. These strategies all avoid leaving a short vowel stranded in an open syllable. Some speakers of SAA leave the short vowel in an open syllable, saying /yəhləkuu/. One strategy simply drops the short vowel, resulting in /yəhlkuu/, with a sequence of three consonants. Another relies on a vowel shift to re-distribute consonants into two two-consonant clusters, as in /thəlkuu/ 'you (p) ruin'. The other common strategy is vowel shift with the doubling of C_1, as seen here.

8. The phrase /gaaʕ əlziraaʕa/ 'all of the agriculture' shows no assimilation of the /l/ of the definite article /əl/. The /l/ of the definite article usually assimilates or becomes identical to a following consonant when that consonant is apical or pronounced wit the tip of the tongue. The lack of assimilation here may be the result of hesitation.

9. The form /naḥḥaawhaaluu/ 'they eliminated him from it' is made up of the perfect 3P verb /naḥḥaaw/ 'they eliminated', followed by the 3FS suffixed pronoun /haa/, which is followed by the indirect object marker /l/ with the 3MS suffixed pronoun /uu/. This order is usual in SAA and certain other varieties of spoken Arabic for a verb that has two objects. It can be written as a formula: verb + suffixed pronoun + indirect object marker + suffixed pronoun.

10. The phrase /ʃɣul xəddaamiin/ 'like employees' contains the preposition /ʃɣul/. This preposition is a homonym of the noun /ʃɣul/ 'work, job, task'. The preposition, however, precedes a noun to mean 'like, as; a kind of'.

11. The phrase /lʔarabʕa lbəldaan lluwwəlliin/ 'the four greatest countries' is a counted-noun construction that has been made definite. It differs from an indefinite counted-noun construction, such as /arbaʕa bəldaan/ 'four countries' only because of the presence of the definite article /əl/. Note that each element of the phrase takes the definite article: /lʔarabʕa lbəldaan lluwwəlliin/.

12. The verb of the phrase /maa ythallooʃ fiihum/ 'they don't take care of them' derives from the 3P imperfect verb /yəthallaaw/ 'they take care'. In rapid speech and when a diphthong such as /aaw/ precedes a consonant, that diphthong may become a monophthong, as it becomes /oo/ here. Note, however, that the same speaker does not monophthongize the diphthong in other forms, such as /nḥḥaawhaaluu/ 'they took it from him'.

What They Call the Agricultural Revolution

So, where, I mean, I certainly don't know. This oil, they say, ah ... from year to year, they keep finding, I mean, *some* ... As they say, they, reserves, I mean, of oil are large. There is natural gas, there is gold, there is uranium. I mean, they say, Algeria is a rich country. We don't understand, I mean, on the one hand they say it's a rich country. but on the other hand, people live in, in, in poverty, as if you were to say that they live in a country that has nothing, I mean, no, no, no oil or even dust or ... In the old days, the ... Algeria, I mean, used to export wheat, export the ... fruit, those lemons, dates were in France, in *Europe*, I mean, there was everything. Then one day they set up what they call the agricultural revolution, that was in 1971. Within two or three years, they had ruined all of Algeria's agriculture. Anyone who had land that he worked, they took it from him and gave it to other people. They became, ah, like employees of the government, they gave them a salary. I mean, whether or not he worked, he got his salary. So production, I mean, became *zero*. That was it. The ... the ... dates which we were ...,we were ..., I mean, among the ... four greatest producers in the world, we began producing nothing at all. It all disappeared, I mean, the ... those trees fell ill, they stopped taking care of them and everything rotted.

iixəddəmuu nnaas, yaʕʈuuhum ʃahriyya wə-lʔintaaj qliil

This selection describes the economic and employment policies of the agricultural revolution in more detail.

A: iih, haadii *parce que* ssiiyaasa hiyya llii həlkət a ... lfəllaaḥiin. arjjəʕathum,[1] yəxxədmuu wəllaa maa yəxxədmuuʃ, ʃʃahriyya taaḥḥum[2] ʈaalʕa, fii aaxər ʃʃahar djiihum[3] a ... ʃʃahriyya dyaalhum.[4] a ...

B: [xxx].

A: wəllaaw maa ʕandhumʃ ḥattaa ʃajaʕa baaʃ yəxxədmuu, wəllaa lkasal a ...

B: yaʕnii nəʃfaa[5] anaa kətt[6] fə-ddzaayər ləmmaa nʃuufuu,[5] njuuzuu ʕlaa kaaʃ ʈriiq w-kaayən[7] naas yəxxədmuu fə-ʈʈriiq haaðiika. diimaa yəḥḥafruu wəllaa məʃ ʕaarf, wəllaa təʃfaay[8] fə-ddzaayər nnaas fə-lkull ... kull ʈriiq wə-llaa kaayən ḥafra,[9] iiʕaawduu haaðuuk əl ... əlquwaadəs haaðuuk taaʕ, taaʕ əlmaa w-taaʕ əl *gaz*, tʃuufii rabʕa waaqfiin w-waaḥəd yəḥfar [laugh], yaʕnii də ... də ... fii ʕooḍ iixallaʂuu waaḥəd wəllaa zooj bəʃ iidiiruu lxədma haadiik, iixallaʂuu xamsa wəllaa sətta. fa-yaʕnii fə-lluwwəl, lyalʈa bdaat mə-lluwwəl yaʕnii, fii ʕooḍ iixəddəmuu nnaas ʕlaa ḥsaab lkaafaaʔa taaḥḥum wəllaa ḥsaab lʔintaaj taaḥḥum, humma kaanuu yə... yaʕnii yəxəddəmuu nnaas, yaʕʈuuhum ʃahriyya wə-lʔintaaj qliil yaʕnii siiz ... haadiyaa lmuuʃkiila lkbiira. ddraaham kaanuu yətʂarfuu[10] bəzzaaf ʕa-nnaas fə-l ... xaaʂʂatan fə-l ... fə ... fə lxalaaʂ taaḥḥum wə-lʔiintaaj kaan qliil, nnaas tʕawwduu ʕlaa haaðiik lḥaala wa ... wə ... ḥasbuu anna haaðiik lḥaala, lə ... lə ... haaðiik hiya lə ... lə ... lwəðʕiyya yaʕnii lə ... kiimaa yquuluu bə-lfransiyya *normal* yaʕnii.

يخدّموا النّاس، يعطوهم شهريّه، والانتاج قليل

أ: ايه، هذي *parce que* السّياسه هيّ اللّي هلكت ا ... الفلاّحين. ارجّعتهم[1] يخدّموا ولاّ ما يخدّموش، الشّهريّه تاعهم[2] طالعه، في آخر الشّهر تجيهم[3] ... الشّهريّه ديالهم[4]....

ب: [xxx]

أ: ولاّوا ما عندهمش حتّى شجعه باش يخدّموا، ولّى الكسل ....

ب: يعني نشفى[5] انا كنت[6] فالدزاير لمّا نشوفوا،[5] نجوزوا على كاش طريق وكاين[7] ناس يخدّموا فالطّريق هذيك. ديما يحَفروا ولاّ ماش عارف ولاّ تشفاي[8] فالدّزاير النّاس فالكلّ ا ... كلّ طريق ولاّ كاين حفره،[9] يعاودوا هذوك الـ ... القوادس هذوك، تاع، تاع الما وتاع الـ *gaz*، تشوفي اربعه واقفين وواحد يحفر [laugh] يعني د .... د ... في عوض يخلّصوا واحد ولاّ زوج باش يديروا الخدمه هذيك، يخلّصوا خمسه ولا ستّه. فيعني فاللاّوّل، الغلطه بدات مالـلاوّل يعني، في عوض يخدّموا النّاس على حساب الكفاءه تاعهم ولاّ حساب الانتاج تاعهم. همّا كانوا يـ ... يعني يخدّموا النّاس، يعطوهم شهريّه، والانتاج قليل يعني سيـز ... هذيا الموشكيله الكبيره. الدّراهم كانوا يتصرفوا[10] بزّاف عالنّاس، فلـ ... خاصّةً ...فلـ ... فـ ... فالخلاص تاعهم والانتاج كان قليل، النّاس تعوّدوا على هذيك الحاله و ... و ... حسبوا انّ هذيك الحاله الـ .... الـ ... هذيك هي الـ ... الـ ... الوضعيّه يعني الـ ... كيما يقولوا بالفرنسيّه *normal* يعني.

wə-laakən məm-baʕd xlaaṣ ləmmaa xlaaṣuu ddraaham taaʕ əlpətrool,
xlaaṣ kull ʃii. qaallhum yaa wuddii xlaaṣ, kull waaḥəd iiruuḥ l-daaruu,
xlaaṣuu[11] ddraaham. *mais* lmuuʃkiila anna nnaas ʕandhum draarii, ʕandhum
ʕaayiilaat laazəm yəṣṣarfuu ʕleehum. wə-ʕlaa haaðii yaʕnii lə ... ḥattaa
lə ... lḥaala lə ... llii ḥnaa ʕaayʃiin fiihaa taaʕ əl ... lə ... lḥa ... lḥarb
lʔahliyya haaðiyaa, maa ḥabbətʃ təxlaaṣ, laa xaaṭʃ lə ... lfuqər maa
yḥabbʃ yəxlaaṣ.

ولكن من بـعد خلاص لمّا خـلاصوا¹¹ الدّراهم تـاع البـترول خـلاص كلّ شـي.
قـالّهم يا ودّي خـلاص، كلّ واحـد يروح لداره، خـلاصـوا الدّراهم. *Mais*
الموشكله انّ النّـاس عندهم دراري، عندهم عـايلات لازم يصـرّفـوا عليـهم.
وعلى هذي يعني الـ ... حتّى الـ ... الحاله الـ ... اللي احنا عـايشين فيـها
تاع الـ ... الـ ... الحـ ... الحرب الأهليّه هذيّا، مـا حبّتش تخلاص لا خاطشي
الـ ... الفقر مـا يحبّش يخلاص.

Vocabulary:

iih ايه *interj* yes

parce que *conj* because

llii اللي [*also* əllii] *pro* who, what (definite relative pronoun)

rajjaʕ رجّع *v* to give, pay (money); to return, make return {*imperf*: iirajjaʕ}

ṭaaləʕ طـالـع *adj* coming, arriving {*fs*: ṭaalʕa, *pl*: ṭaalʕiin}

dyaal ديـال *possessive adj*; *invariable* of; belonging to

kaaʃ كاش [*also* kəʃ] *part*. some, any

diimaa ديـما *adv* always

məʃ مـاش [*also* maaʃ] *part*.; *negates nominal structures* not

ʕaawəd عـاود *v; pre-verb* to re-do, replace; to do again (action of following imperfect verb); to begin, start (to do the action of the following imperfect verb) {*imperf*: iiʕaawəd}

wə-laa ولا *there has to be*

qaaduus قـادوس [*also* qaaḍuus] *nms* pipe, drainpipe {*pl*: quwaadəs}

maa مـاه *nms* water {*pl*: myaa}

gaz *nms* gas, natural gas

rabʕa اربـعه [*also* arbaʕa] *nfs* four

fii ʕood في عود *conj* instead of, rather than

xallaṣ خـلّص *v* to pay, have paid; to finish, complete (s.t.) {*imperf*: iixallaṣ}

zooj زوج [*also* zuuj; juuz; zawj] *nfs* two

baʃ باش [also baaʃ] *conj* for; so that, in order to

xədma خدمه *nfs* work, job, employment; task {*pl:* xədmaat}

bdaa بدا *v* to start, begin {*imperf:* yəbdaa}

humm هُمّ [also huum; ham; huuma] *pro* they (3P)

haadiyaa هديا [also haadii; haaðii] *pro* this (FS near‧demonstrative) {*ms:* haadaay, *pl:* haaduu}

muuʃkiila موشكيله [also muuʃkila] *nfs* problem, difficulty {*pl:* mʃaakəl}

dərham درهم *nms* derham (basic Algerian unit of currency) {*pl:* draaham}

draaham دراهم *np* money (from /dərham/ derham, Algerian unit of currency)

ətṣraf اتصرف [also əṣṣrəf] *v* to be spent (of money) {*imperf:* yətṣraf}

ʕa- ـع [also ʕlaa; ʕa-] *prep* on, at; concerning; at, about (of time); incumbent on, necessary

xalaaṣ خلاص *nms* pay, salary

ḥsəb حسب *v* to think, consider, suppose {*imperf:* yəḥsəb}

wədʕiyya وضعيّه *nfs* situation, position {*pl:* wədʕiyyaat}

normal adj normal

xlaaṣ خلاص *v* to be ended, finished {*imperf:* yəxlaaṣ}

yaa wuddii يا ودّي o my friend (term of address)

mais conj but, however

dərrii درّي *nms* child {*pl:* draarii}

laazəm لازم *adj* it is necessary that ; *invariable preverb*

ʕaayiila عاييله [also ʕaayla; ʕaaʔiila] *nfs* family {*pl:* ʕaayiilaat}

ḥabb حبّ *v; pre-verb* to want to; to like, love {*imperf:* iiḥabb}

laa xaatʃ لا خاطش [also laa xaatər; ʕlaa xaatər; laa xaatʃii] *conj* because, due to the fact that

Notes:

1. The form /arjjaʕəthum/ 'they (3FS) paid them (3P)' derives from the Form II verb /rajjəʕ/ 'to pay, give', which is followed by the 3P suffixed pronoun /hum/. The reason for the unusual shape of this verb is not clear. It may be that hesitation has caused a vowel shift. from the more typical /rajjaʕəthum/

104

to /arjjaʕəthum/.

2. The form /taaḥ/ 'of, belonging to', as in /taaḥḥum/ 'belonging to them', is a regular variant of /taaʕ/. It occurs before the /h/ of a 3S or 3P suffixed pronoun. Note that assimilation in this case affects both the /ʕ/ of /taaʕ/ and the /h/ of the suffixed pronoun /hum/. Both consonants become /ḥ/ in /taaḥḥum/.

3. The form /djiihum/ 'it (3FS) comes to them (3P)' is the imperfect 3FS of the verb /jaa/ 'to come', which is followed by the 3P suffixed pronoun /hum/. The /d/ of /djii/ began as the /t/ of the imperfect prefix, as in /tjii/. The /t/ becomes /d/ through assimilation. Note that the form /tjii/ also occurs in SAA.

4. The possessive adjective /dyaal/ 'of, belonging to' is synonymous with the possessive adjective /taaʕ/. The form heard here, /dyaal/, may occur in SAA, especially in western Algeria.

5. The stretch of talk that includes /nəʃfaa anaa kətt fə-ddzaayər ləmmaa nʃuufuu,/ 'I remember I was in Algeria, when we'd see' shows two characteristic features of SAA and other varieties of North African Arabic. They are the 1S imperfect prefix /n/, as in /nəʃfaa/ 'I remember' and the 1P imperfect affixes /n/ and /uu/, as in /nʃuufuu/ 'we see'. These are not, of course, the affixes of other varieties of spoken Arabic, such as the Egyptian /azkur/ 'I recall' and /niʃuuf/ 'we see'.

6. The form /kətt/ 'I was' derives from the 1S perfect /kənt/ 'I was'. The assimilation of /n/ to the /t/ of the perfect suffix occurs in fast or informal speech.

7. Speakers of SAA use the existential /kaayən/ 'there is, there are'. It is usually invariable. That is, it does not change to reflect gender or number of its grammatical subject, as in /kaayən waaḥəd/ 'there is someone', /kaayən ḥafra/ 'there is a hole', and /kaayən ʃii kəlmaat/ 'there are certain words'. The existential /fiih/ also occurs in SAA. As noted in Selection 4, note 3, /fii/h tends to occur where /kaan/ indicates a change in time frame.

8. The 3F imperfect verb /təʃfaay/ 'you (fs) remember' demonstrates the regular conjugation of finally-weak verbs in some sub-varieties of SAA. The verb stem does not change even when the verb suffix is vowel-initial. Thus, the 3F and 3P imperfect verb has a regular /y/ ending, as in /təʃfaay/ 'you (fs) remember' and /təʃfaaw/ 'you (p) remember'. The 3F and 3P perfect verbs are also regular in this way.

9. The form /llaa/ in the utterance /kull ṭriiq wə-**llaa** kaayən ḥafra/ 'every road, there's got to be a hole' appears to be related to the MSA ʔillaa 'unless, if not; except'. In a context like this one, however, the function of /llaa/ in SAA and certain other varieties of spoken Arabic is very different. Inserted between two clauses (or following an oath or vocative phrase), /llaa/ indicates that the second clause must or should occur, as it does here.

10. The form /yətṣarfuu/ 'they are spent' illustrates how SAA and certain other varieties of spoken Arabic express passive meaning. Few varieties of spoken Arabic have an ablaut or vocalic passive voice (the "true" passive) of ClA and MSA. The vocalic passive contrasts, for example, the active kataba 'he wrote' with the passive kutiba 'it (ms) was written'. Instead of the vocalic passive, SAA has Form $tC_1C_2vC_3$, as in /yətṣarfuu/, which functions as a quasi-passive, being passive in meaning without having its own conjugation. Form VII, as in /ndaar/ 'to be done, made' also has a quasi-passive meaning and function.

11. The form /xlaaṣuu/ 'they were gone' derives from the SAA Form IX verb /xlaaṣ/ 'to be finished, done'. The Form IX verb in SAA and certain other varieties of spoken Arabic differs from the Form IX of ClA and MSA in two ways. First, the shape of the SAA Form IX verb is $C_1C_2aaC_3$, with a long stem vowel and single final consonant rather than the short stem vowel and doubled final consonant of the Form IX of ClA and MSA, $C_1C_2aC_3C_3$. Second, the Form IX of SAA of course includes verbs of color (as in /byaaḍ/ to be, become white') and physical afflictions (as in /ʕwaaj/ 'to be bent, twisted'). It also derives from common adjectives, such as /xlaaṣ/ 'done, finished' (with the resulting verb /xlaaṣ/ 'to be done, finished') and /smiin/ 'plump, fat' (with the resulting verb /smaan/ 'to be, become plump, fat').

They Put People to Work, Give Them a Salary, and Production Is Low

A: Yes .... This is *because* politics are what destroyed ah ... the peasants. They paid them whether they worked or not. Their salary was coming, at the end of the month, ah ... their salary came to them, ah ....

B: [xxx].

A: They got no encouragement to work and laziness became, ah ....

B: I mean, I remember I was in Algeria, when we'd see, we'd be going along some road and there were people working on that road. They are always digging, or I don't know, or you remember in Algeria, people in every ... every road, there's got to be a hole. They were repairing ah ... those ... those pipes for, for water or for *gas*. You see four standing around and one digging [laugh]. I mean, ah ... ah ... instead of paying one or two to do that work, they pay five or six. So, I mean, in the beginning, the mistake started at the beginning. I mean, instead of putting people to work according to their ability or according to their production, they were, I mean, they put people to work, give them a salary, and production is low. This is the big problem. They would spend a lot of money on people, on the ... especially on the ... on their pay, and production was low. People got used to that situation and ... and ... they thought that the situation, this ... this is the ... the ... the state of affairs, I mean, the... it is as they say in French, *normal*, I mean. But later, it was over. When the oil money was gone, it was all gone. They told them, well, it's over, everyone go home, the money is gone. But the problem is that people have children, they have families they have to support, and for that reason, I mean, the ... even the ... the situation that we are living through, of this ... this civil war, it is not going to end because ... poverty is not going to end.

kull smaana laazəm nruuḥ lə-ssiineemaa

The speaker's memories of a childhood spent both at and in the movies produces
some optimism about Algeria's future as well as nostalgia for the past.

A: anaa kii kənt ṣɣiir nəʃfaa kənt a ... nəqraa mliiḥ, kaan baabaa yaʕṭiilii
diimaa draaham baaʃ nruuḥ ... kaan daaymən iiʃəjjəʕnii baaʃ nruuḥ nʃuuf
les ... *les films* fə-ssiineemaa. daaymən, kull smaana laazəm nruuḥ
l-ssiineemaa. ḥattaa w-maa, maa nḥabbʃ arruuḥ,[1] iiquullii[2] laazəm truuḥ
tʃuuf[3] haaðaak əlfiilm wə-kii twəllii ləzəm təḥkiilii wəʃ ʃəft. bəʃ[4] maa
nəqdərʃ nəkdəb ʕleeh nquulluu maa ... annii raḥt[5] wə-maa ... yaʕnii
lḥamdu llaah ḥattaa haaðaak a ... ʃʃii yaʕnii ʃəjjaʕnii yaʕnii ykuun
ʕandii ʃwiyya yaʕnii θaaqaafa yaʕnii lʔinsaan iiḥabb ssiineemaa. xaatʃ
huwwa kaan yə... yəxdəm fə-ttiiliifiizyoon taaʕ, taaʕ, taaʕ ddzaayər
wə-yaʕnii wəlliit nḥabb *les films* wə-kaan dii ... iiʕallimnii kiifaaʃ a ...
yiidiiruu *film*, a ... yaʕnii ḥattaa mən naaḥiyət ṭṭiqniya yaʕnii.

B: w-kaan yəddiikum tməttəluu?

A: eeh, lʕabt anaa, lʕabt fə-ddzaayər f-baʕḍ əlʔaflaam yaʕnii a ... ʕandii
door ṣɣiir yaʕnii, muuhuuʃ[6] ḥaaja kbiira kaant taaʕ ... kaan ʕandii
tlaṭṭaaʃən səna, ṭnaaʃən səna[7] wəllaa. yaʕnii lə ... kii nətfəkkar yaʕnii
kaant yyaam yaʕnii mliiḥa wə ... yaʕnii haaðuuk huwa ʃii qaaʕədəlnaa
lḥadd əlʔaan yaʕnii, mʕa lmaaʃaakəl llii kaayna fə-lblaad a ... haanaa[8]
ʕaayʃiin mʕa haaðuuk lə ... lə ...

108

كلّ سمانه لازم نروح للسينيما

أ: انا كي كنت صغير نشفى كنت ا ... نقرا مليح، كان بابا يعطيلي ديما دراهم باش نروح ... كان دايما يشجّعني باش نروح نشوف les ... les films فالسّينيما. دايما، كلّ سمانه لازم نروح للسينيما. حتّى وما، ما نحبّش ارّوح،[1] يقولّي[2] لازم تروح تشوف[3] هذاك الفيلم وكي تولّي لازم تحكيلي واش شفت. باش[4] ما نقدرش نكذب عليه نقولّه ما ا ... أنّي رحت[5] وما.... يعني الحمد للّه حتّى هذاك ا ... الشّي يعني شجّعني يعني يكون عندي شويّه يعني ثقافه يعني الأنسان يحبّ السّينيما. خاطش هوّ كان يـ ... يخدم فالتّيليفيزيون تاع، تاع، تاع الدّزاير ويعني ولّيت نحبّ les films وكان ديـ ... يعلّمني كيفاش ا ... يديروا film، يعني حتّى من ناحية الطّقنيّه يعني.

ب: وكان يدّيكم تمثّلوا؟

أ: ايه، لعبت انا، لعبت فالدّزاير فبعض الأفلام يعني ا .... عندي دور صغير يعني، موهوش[6] حاجه كبيره كانت تاع ا ... كان عندي تلتّاشن سنه طناشن سنه[7] ولا. يعني الـ ... كي نتفكّر يعني كانت ايّام يعني مليحه و ... يعني هذوك هو شي قاعدلنا لحدّ الآن يعني، مع المشاكل اللّي كاينه فالبلاد ا ... هانا[8] عايشين مع هذوك الـ ... الـ ....

109

B: ððikraayaat.

A: ððikraayaat lmliiḥa haaðiik uu ... wə-nʃaa llaah yaʕnii mənnaa[9] lə-ʃii
sniin wəllaa ləmma ddaʕwaa tḥassan, nʕaawduu nruuḥuu lə-ddzaayər
wə-n ... nʃuufuu haaðuuk lmanaa ... lplaayəṣ wiin kənt ʕaayəʃ, wəloo ...
lmədrasa llii qreet fiihaa w-daarnaa w-kull ʃii.

ب: الذّكرايات.

أ: الذّكرايات المليحـه هذيك و... وانشـا اللّه يعني منّا⁹ لشي سنين ولاّ لمّا الدّعوى تحسّن ا ... نعاودوا نروحـوا للدّزاير ون ... نشوفـوا هذوك المنا ... الـ... البلايص وين كنت عايش، ولو .... المدراسه اللّي قريت فيها ودارنا وكلّ شي.

Vocabulary:

qraa قرا *v* to study, get an education; to read {*imperf:* yəqraa}

baabaa بابا *nms* father {*pl:* baabaawaat}

daaymən دايماً *adv* all the time, always

les ... les films the... the movies

siineemaa سينيما *nfs* cinema, movie theater {*pl:* siineemaat}

smaana سمانه *nfs* week {*pl:* smaanaat}

ḥattaa w-maa حتّى وما *conj* even if not

fiilm فيلم *nms* movie, film {*pl:* aflaam}

wullaa ولّى [*also* wəllaa] *v* to return; to start (as pre-verb); to end up; to become {*imperf:* iiwullii}

ḥkaa حكى *v* to say, tell {*imperf:* yəḥkii}

wəʃ واش [*also* waaʃ] *interrog* what

qdər قدر *v* to be able to {*imperf:* yəqdər}

kdəb ʕlaa كذب على *v* to lie, speak untruthfully to s.o. {*imperf:* yəkdəb}

lḥamdu ḷḷaah الحـمـد لله thank God, thanks be to God (indicates or responds to fortunate event)

xaaṭʃ خاطش [*also* xaaṭ; xaaṭʃii; xaaṭər] *conj* because, due to the fact that

les films *nmp* the movies

daar دار *nfs* house {*pl:* dyaar}

film *nms* movie

ṭiqniyya طقنيّه [*also* təqniyya] *nfs* technique {*pl:* ṭiqniyyaat}

eeh ايه [*also* iih] *interj* yes

111

muuhuuʃ موهوش [*also* maahuuʃ] he is not; it (ms) is not

muu + suffixed pro + ʃ مو : ش ـ ـ ش [*also* maa + suffixed pro + ʃ] is not, are not

ḥaaja حاجه *nfs* thing, object {*pl:* ḥaajaat, *pl:* ḥwaayəj}

tlaaṭṭaaʃən تـلاطّـاشـن [*also* tlaṭṭaaʃ] *nms; form used in construct phrase* thirteen

tlaṭṭaaʃ تـلاطّـاش [*also* tlaaṭṭaaʃən] *nms* thirteen

ṭnaaʃən طـنـاشـن [*also* ṭnaaʃ] *nms; form used in construct phrase* twelve

ṭnaaʃ طـنـاش [*also* ṭnaaʃən] *nms* twelve

wəllaa ولّى [*also* wullaa] *v* to start (as pre-verb); to end up; to become; to return {*imperf:* iiwəllii}

wəllaa ولّا [*also* wə-ʔillaa] *part.* or something like that, or whatever (at end of sequence)

yoom يـوم *nms* day {*pl:* yyaam}

qaaʕəd قـاعـد *adj* staying, remaining {*fs:* qaaʕda, *pl:* qaaʕdiin}

muuʃkila موشكله [*also* muuʃkiila] *nfs* problem, difficulty {*pl:* maaʃaakəl}

haa + suffixed pronoun ها look here; here is, here are

haanaa هانا here I am

daʕwaa دعـوى *nfs* affair, matter, business {*pl:* dʕaawii}

mənnaa منّا *adv* beginning now, from now; from here; over here

nʃaa ḷḷaah ان شـاء الله God willing, if God wills (of hoped-for event)

ʕaawəd عـاود *v; pre-verb* to do again (action of following imperfect verb); to re-do, replace; to begin, start (to do the action of the following imperfect verb) {*imperf:* iiʕaawəd}

plaaṣa پلاصه *nfs* place, location {*pl:* plaaṣaat, *pl:* plaayəṣ}

ʕaayəʃ عـايـش *adj* living, residing {*fs:* ʕaayʃa, *pl:* ʕaayʃiin}

Notes:

1. The form /aṛṛuuḥ/ 'I go' derives from the 1S imperfect /ṇruuḥ/ 'I go'. The doubled /r/ of /aṛṛuuḥ/ is the result of assimilation, of one consonant become like or, as here, identical to another.

2. The form /iiquullii/ 'he says to me' consists of three elements. The first is

the 3MS imperfect verb /iiquul/. The second is the indefinite object marker /l/ and the third is the 1S suffixed pronoun /ii/. In SAA, as in certain other varieties of spoken Arabic, the indefinite object marker and suffixed pronoun are pronounced with the verb as a single word (the indefinite object is cliticized). That is, there is no audible break between the verb and the indirect object, and stress placement rules apply to the entire complex.

3. The phrase /laazəm truuḥ tʃuuf/ 'you (ms) have to go to see' is a verb string. It consists of the invariable pre-verb /laazəm/ 'necessary' and the conjugated pre-verb /truuḥ/ 'you (ms) go'. These are followed by the main verb /tʃuuf/ 'you (ms) see'/. Verb strings most often consists of two verbal forms, as in /laazëm truu§/ 'you (ms) have to go'. Strings of three or, less often, four verbs may also occur.

4. The utterance that includes /ləzəm təḥkiilii wəʃ ʃəft. bəʃ ... / 'you (ms) have to tell me what you (ms) saw. So that ...' contains a sequence of the short vowel /ə/ where the long vowel /aa/ usually occurs. This can be seen in /ləzəm/ for /laazəm/ 'necessary', /wəʃ/ for /waaʃ/ 'what', and /bəʃ/ for /baaʃ/ 'so that'. Some of these replacements occur in other contexts as well.

5. The forms /raḥt/ 'I went' and /ʃəft/ 'I saw' in the previous sentence have the short stem vowels /a/ and /ə/. This is usual in SAA. Certain other varieties of spoken Arabic, in contrast, have the short stem vowel /u/ in these and similar forms, as in /ruḥt/ and /ʃuft/. In SAA, distinctions between the short vowels /a/, /i/, and /u/ tend to be neutralized, although they are not completely eliminated. The neutral short vowel /ə/, however, occurs as often or more often than the other short vowels in SAA.

6. The form /muuhuuʃ/ 'it (ms) is not' is a variant of /maahuuʃ/ 'it (ms) is not'. The negative pronoun of SAA typically consists of the negative particle /maa/ followed by a pronoun, which is in turn followed by the negative particle /ʃ/. The result is, for example, /maahuuʃ/ or /maahuwaaʃ/ 'he is not; it (ms) is not'. Stress in the negative pronoun falls on the vowel immediately before /ʃ/. The form /muuhuuʃ/, however has /muu/ in the place of /maa/.

7. The forms /tlaṭṭaaʃən/ '13, thirteen' and /ṭnaaʃən/ '12, twelve' are variants of /tlaṭṭaaʃ/ and /ṭnaaʃ/. In some sub-varieties of SAA, the numbers 11 - 19 regularly take this /ən/ suffix when used in a counted-noun construction. Thus, the answer to a question like "How old are you?" can be /tlaṭṭaaʃən sənა/ '13 years old' or simply /tlaṭṭaaʃ/ '13'.

8. The form /haanaa/ 'we are' consists of the presentational particle /haa/ and

the 1P suffix /naa/. When followed by a verb or active particle, the combination of /haa/ and pronoun add force or emphasis to an utterance, as it does here in /haanaa ʕaayʃiin mʕa haaðuuk lə ... ððikraayaat lmliiḥa/ 'We are living with those good memories'.

9. The form /mənnaa/ 'from now, as of now' derives from the phrase /mən hnaa/ 'lit, from here'. Note that the counterpart of /mənnaa/ is /mənhee/ 'from there; over there'.

Every Week I Had to Go to the Movies

A: I, when I was little, I remember I would, ah ... study hard and my father always used to give me money so I could go .... He always used to encourage me to go see *movies* at the theater. Always, every week I had to go to the movie theater, even if I didn't want to go. He would tell me, "You have to go and see that film, and when you get home you have to tell me what you saw." So I couldn't lie to him and tell him what, that I had gone and not .... I mean, thank God, even ah ... that thing, I mean, it encouraged me, I mean, to acquire a little bit of culture. I mean, a person likes films because he used to .... He worked in Algerian television. I mean, I started to like *movies* and he used to ... teach me how, ah ... they make a *movie*, ah ... I mean, even from the technical point of view, I mean ....

B: And he use to take you to act?

A: Yes, I acted, I acted in Algeria in some movies. I mean, ah ... I had a small role, I mean, not a big thing, it was .... I was 13 or 12 or something. I mean, the .... When I think, I mean, they were times, good ones and, I mean. That's what stays with us now, I mean, in spite of the problems there are at home, ah ... we live with these ....

B: Memories.

A: These good memories and .... God willing, I mean, in a few years or when the situation improves, I mean, we'll go back and go to Algeria and .... We'll see those places where I used to live and ... the school I went to and our house and everything.

115

kunnaa nəqraaw, nruuḥuu l-lmsiid

This description of childhood in Algeria features elements familiar to America children, such as school, snacks, and after-school cartoons.

A: anaa nəʃfaa kii kənt ṣɣiir, haaðii kaant yaʕnii daʕwaahaa mliiḥa[1] yaʕnii. kənnaa nəqraaw, kunnaa nəqraaw, nruuḥuu l-lmsiid,[2] a ... yaʕnii liinsaan dii ... yaʕməlluu[3] llii ʕleeh yaʕməl a .... daaymən lwaaldiin yaʕnii yəṭṭalbuu mənnaa bəʃ nəqraaw mliiḥ, iiquullək 'bəʃ tə ... kii tkbər maa, maa ttʕabʃ bəʃ iikuu[4] ʕandək xədma mliiḥa.' kənnaa mʕa ṣṣbuḥ nnooḍuu, a ... yəmmaa hiya twə ... tnowwəḍənaa. a ... tnowwəḍənaa[5] tuujjədəlnaa kulləʃ, a ... tləbbəsənnaa,[6] ddiirnaa lqahwa taaʕnaa, yṭiiybnaa lə ... ləxfaaf a ... bə-zzbiib.

B: m ...

A: kiimaa ysəmmuuh.

B: ah.

A: wə-kunnaa nəʃrabuu lqahwa taaʕnaa. haaðii fə-lluwwəl yaʕnii kii kənt sana lə ... sana uulaa, sana taanya kaant a ... tələbbəsənnaa, nəʃrabuu lqahwa taaʕnaa wə-baʕd təddiinaa hiya l-lmsiid, xaaṭʃ kə ... ləmsiid taaʕii kaan ʃwiyya, ʃwiyya baʕiid. a ... yaʕnii nəqraaw, taʕṭiilii kaaskrooṭ.[7]

B: uhum [laugh].

A: baaʃ naakluu ʕal-ṭṭanaaʃ, xaaṭʃ kənnaa nəqraaw mə-ṣṣbuḥ ḥattaa lə ... ḥattaa lʕaaʃiyya. a ... kaaskrooṭ wə-taʕṭiilii ʕaʃra duuroo, baaʃ a ... wə-llaa jaʕt wəllaa məḥsuub maa kaanʃ *des casse-croûtes*, nəqdər mʕa ṭṭanaaʃ nəxruj wə-nəʃrii ... kiimaa ḥnaa nsəmmuuhaa fə-ddzaayər a ... waaḥəd əlmakla ysəmmuuhaa garanṭeeṭa.

B: m ...

كنّا نقراوا، نروحوا اللّمسيد

أ: انا نشفى كي كنت صغير، هذي يعني دعواها مليحه[1] يعني. كنّا
نقراوا، كنّا نقراوا، نروحوا اللّمسيد،[2] ا ... يعني الانسان ديـ ... يعمله[3]
اللّي عليه يعمل ا ... دايماً الوالدين يعني يطَلبوا منّا باش نقراوا مليح،
يقولّك، «باش تـ ... كي تكبر مـا ... مـا تتعبش باش يكو[4] عندك خدمـه
مليحه.» كنّا مع الصّبح نّوضوا، ا ... يمّا هي تو ... تنوّظنا.[5] ا ... تنوّظنا
توجدلنا كلَّش، ا ... تلبّسنّا،[6] تديرنا القهوه تاعنا، كانت تطيّبنا الـ ...
الخفاف ا ... بالزّبيب.

ب: مــ...

أ: كيما يسمّوه.

ب: اه.

أ: وكنّا نشربوا القهوه تاعنا. هذي فالأوّل يعني كي كنت سنه الـ ... سنه
اولى، سنه ثانيه كانت ... تلبّسنّا، نشربوا القهوه تاعنا وبعد تدّينا هي
للّمسيد، خاطشي كـ ... المسيد تاعي كان شويّه، شويّه بعيد. ا ... يعني
نقراوا، تعطيلي كاسكروط.[7]

ب: اهم [laugh].

أ: باش ناكلوا عالطّناش، خاطش كنّا نقراوا مالصّبح حتّى الـ ... حتّى
الّعاشيّه ا ... كاسكروط وتعطيلي عشره دورو، باش ا ... ولا جعت ولا
محسوب مـا كانش des casse-croûtes, نقدر مع الطّناش نخرج ونشري ا
... كيما احنا نسمّوها فالدّزاير واحد ا ... المكله يسمّوها قرنطيطه.

ب: مــ...

117

A: gaaʕətiik[8] ʕal-ṭṭənaaʃ nruuḥuu nʃruuhaa, hiya yxədmuuhaa bəl ... bə ... bə ... bə-lfaariina taaʕ, taaʕ əlḥmeeṣa. haaðaa maa kaaʃ fə-lmaariikaan, maa, maa jam ... maa ʃəfthaaʃ gaaʕ. əlmuuhəmm, lʕaaʃiyya njuu nə ... nṣiibuu taanii twujjtənnaa lə ... lqahwa taaʕnaa, nkuunuu njuu jiiʕaaniin, da ... nəʃfaa njii nəjrii baaʃ a ... baaʃ nwəllii lə-ddaar. əlmuuhəmm, nəlḥəquu lə-ddaar, nʃarbuu lqahwa taaʕnaa wə-m-baʕd a ... nriyyḥuu ʃwiyya, nruuḥuu nʃuufuu ... kiimaa ysəmmuuhum fə-ttiiliifiizyoon, nʃuufuu *des animés.*

B: ah.

A: kaanuu ʕandaa[9] *les animés* yaʕnii, yḍaḥḥkuu bəzzaaf. wə-lʕaaʃiyya nə ... ndiiruu lə ... le... kiimaa yquuluu *devoirs* taaʕnaa lxədma llii laazəm ndiiruuhaa. wə-nwəjjduu da ... ddars taaʕ, taaʕ ənnhaar llii jaay wə-hiyya raayḥa haakðaak.[10] njuuzuu mtiiḥaanaat taaʕnaa, -naa nʃfaa kənt yaʕnii nəqraa mliiḥ, kənt a ... kənt daaymən njii lluwwəl. muuʃ daaymən wə ... yaʕnii, llaɣlaabiyya taaʕ əl ... taaʕ əlfaṣəl njii lə ... njii lʔowwəl.

B: mliiḥ.

A: w-yaʕnii nəʃfaa yaʕnii, yaʕnii wə-ḷḷaah kaant hiyya yyaam yaʕnii mliiḥa kii liinsaan iiðəkkarhaa.

أ: قاعتيك[8] عالطّناش نروحوا نشروها، هي يخدموها بالـ ... بـ ... بـ ...
بالفارينه تاع، تاع الحميصه. هذا ما، ما كاش فالماريكان، ما جمـ ... ما
شفتهاش قاع. الموهمّ، العاشيّه نجوا نـ ... نصيبوا تاني توجّتنّا الـ ...
القهوه تاعنا، نكونوا نجوا جعانين، د ... نشفى نجي نجري باش ا ... باش
نولّي للدّار، الموهمّ نلحـقـوا للدّار نشربوا القهوه تاعنا ومبعد ا ...
نريّحوا شويّه، نروحوا نشوفوا ا ... كيما يسمّوهم فالتّيليفيزيون،
نشوفوا des animées.

ب: اه.

أ: كانوا عنده les animés [9] يعني، يضحكوا بزّاف والعاشيّه نـ ... نديروا الـ
... الـ ... كيـما يقـولوا devoirs تاعنا، الخـدمـه اللّي لازم نديروها.
ونوجّدوا د ... الدّرس تاع، تاع النّهار اللّي جاي وهيّ رايحه هكذاك.[10]
نجوزوا امتحانات تاعنا، انا نشفى كنت يعني نقرا مليح، كنت ا ... كنت
دايماً نجي الأوّل. مـوش دايماً و ... يعني، الاغلبيّه تاع الـ ... تاع الفصل
نجي الـ ... نجي الأوّل.

ب: مليح.

أ: ويعني يشفى اعني، يعني واللّه كانت هيّ ايّام مليحه كي الانسان
يذكّرها.

119

Selection 9

Vocabulary:

msiid مسيد *nms* mosque {*pl:* msaayəd}

iinsaan اينسان [*also* insaan] *nms* person, human being {*pl:* naas}

ʕlaa على [*also* ʕal; ʕa] *prep* incumbent on, necessary; on, on top of; at, about, around (of time)

waaləd والد *nms* parent, father {*fs:* waalda, *pl:* waaldiin}

mʕa مع *prep* at, about, around (of time); with

ṣbuḥ صبح *nms* morning; dawn {*pl:* ṣubḥaat}

naaḍ ناض *v* to get up, be up; to jump {*imperf:* iinuuḍ}

nowwəḍ نوّض *v* to awaken, wake o.s. up {*imperf:* iinowwəḍ}

wəjjəd وجّد *v* to prepare, make preparation {*imperf:* iiwəjjəd}

daar دار *v* to make; to do, commit {*imperf:* iidiir}

ṭiyyəb طيّب [*also* ṭayyəb] *v* to cook, prepare (food) {*imperf:* iiṭiyyəb}

xfaafa خفافه *nfs khfaf* (kind of fried pastry) {*pl:* xfaaf}

ʃwiyya شويّه *nms* a little (of anything); a short time

kaaskrooṭ كاسكروط *nms* sandwich, snack {*pl:* kaaskrooṭaat}

klaa كلى *v* to eat {*imperf:* yaakəl}

ʕal عل [*also* ʕlaa; ʕa] *prep* at, about (of time); incumbent on, necessary; on, at; concerning

ʕaaʃiyya عشيّ *nfs* late afternoon, early evening {*pl:* ʕaaʃiyyaat}

ʕaʃra عشره *nfs* ten

duuroo دورو *nms* douro (unit of currency equal to 5 centimres) {*pl:* dwaara}
des casse-croûtes snacks

ʃraa شرى *v* to buy, purchase {*imperf:* yəʃrii}

makla ماكله *nfs* food, edible item; meal {*pl:* maklaat, *pl:* mwaakəl}

garanṭeeṭa گرنطيطه *nfs garantita, carantita* (kind of pastry made from chickpea flour)

gaaʕətiik قاعتيك [*also* gaaʕiitiik] *adj* all; every, each; not at all, never (with negative)

faariina فارينه *nfs* flour

ḥmeeṣa حميصـة‎ *nfs; collective* chickpeas

maa kaaʃ مـا كانش‎ [*also* maa kaanʃ] there was not, there were not; she or he is not, it is not

lmaariikaan المـاريكان‎ *prop* America

gaaʕ قـاع‎ *adv* not at all, never (with negative); all; every, each

jraa جرى‎ *v* to run {*imperf:* yəjrii}

wəllaa ولّى‎ [*also* wullaa] *v* to return; to start (as pre-verb); to end up; to become {*imperf:* iiwəllii}

lḥaq لحق‎ *v* to reach, arrive at; to catch up with, overtake {*imperf:* yəlḥaq}

m-baʕd مبـعد‎ [*also* məm-baʕd; mən baʕd; m-baʕda] after ; *conj.*

m-baʕda مبـعد‎ [*also* məm-baʕd; m-baʕd; mən baʕd] *conj* after

riyyəḥ ريّح‎ *v* to rest, relax; to be left to rest, left fallow {*imperf:* iiriyyiḥ}

tiiliifiizyoon تيليفيزيـون‎ *nms* television {*pl:* tiiliifiizyoonaat}

des animés cartoons

les animés *nmp* cartoons

devoirs *nmp* homework

nhaar نهار‎ *nms* day {*pl:* nhaaraat}

jaay جـاي‎ *adj* coming, arriving {*fs:* jaaya, *pl:* jaayiin}

raayəḥ رايـح‎ *adj* going to, will; going, on one's way {*fs:* raayḥa, *pl:* raayḥiin}

muuʃ مهوش‎ *part.* not *negates non-verbal structures*

faṣəl فصـل‎ *nms* term, semester; section, part {*pl:* fṣuul}

Notes:

1. The word /daʕwaa/ 'situation' is grammatically feminine. This is demonstrated by the clause /daʕwaahaa mliiḥa/ 'its (fs) situation is good", where the modifying adjective /mliiḥa/ is FS. A few other words in certain varieties of spoken Arabic resemble /daʕwaa/. That is, they end in /aa/ (alif maqṣuura) and may be treated as feminine. The best-known of these is /maʕnaa/ 'meaning'.

   Note that the referent of the 3FS suffixed pronoun of /daʕwaahaa/ is not clear. It is likely to be /ddzaayər/ 'Algeria; Algiers' or /lblaad/ 'our country'. Both of these nouns are grammatically feminine and fit the context.

2. The speaker's education began at /lmsiid/ 'the mosque' or 'the school'. The SAA word has both meanings, because primary schooling used to (and still does in some places) take place at the local mosque.

3. The form /yaʕməlluu/ 'he does it for himself' consists of the 3MS imperfect verb /yaʕməl/ 'he does', followed by the 3MS indirect object pronoun suffix /luu/ 'for himself'. the object pronoun suffix in this case does not add to the mean of the form. It is a stylistic element, much like the element "myself" in an utterance like "I'll get **myself** some lunch". Like its English analogue, the SAA /yaʕməlluu/ has a greater force and colloquial feel than the simple /yaʕməl/. This construction is sometimes called the "ethical dative".

4. The form /iikuu/ 'he is; it (ms) is' in the phrase /bəʃ **iikuu** ʕandək/ 'so you will have' derives from the 3MS imperfect /iikuun/. The loss of the final /n/ in /iikuu/ is not a regular feature of SAA. It may be a slip of the tongue.

5. The speaker corrects himself here. He begins by saying /tnowwəðənaa/ 'she wakes us up', with stress on the next-to-last syllable. This is not typical for SAA, as stress falls on a short vowel in an open syllable. His next try is more successful, resulting in /tnowwəðənnaa/ 'she wakes us up'. For discussion of the 1P indirect object suffix /ənnaa/ 'for us' in this and several other forms in this selection, see Note 6 below.

6. The two forms /tnowwəðənnaa/ 'she wakes us up' and /tləbbəsənnaa/ 'she dresses us' are similar. Each consists of a 3FS imperfect verb of Form II, /tnowwəð/ and /tləbbəs/. Each is followed by the 1P indirect object suffix /ənnaa/ 'for us'. That suffix derives from /əlnaa/, wish assimilation of the /l/ to /n/. Another feature shared by these two forms is that both verbs normally take a direct object, as in /tnowwəðnaa/ 'she wakes us up' and /tləbbəsnaa/ 'she dresses us'. The use of the indirect rather than the direct object here is a stylistic variation. It adds greater force and colloquial feel (see Note 3) to these forms. It also makes these two forms parallel to that of /tuujədənnaa/ 'she prepares for us'.

7. The word /kaaskroot/ 'snack' derives from the French word casse-croûte. The borrowed SAA form of this word contrasts with the French usage des casse-croûtes 'snacks' later in the same sentence.

8. The form /gaaʕətiik/ 'all [of us]' is an adverbial. It consists of /gaaʕ/ 'all, each' and the adverbial suffix /ətiik/ (or /iitiik/). This adverbial suffix appears to be productive in SAA.

9. The form /ʕandaa/ 'he has; it (ms) has' is a regional variant of /ʕanduu/.

10. The pronoun /hiyya/ in the phrase /uu-**hiyya** raayḥa haakðaak/ 'and so it (fs) goes' has no clear referent. This pronoun instead refers generally to "it" or "things". The 3FS pronoun commonly occurs in Arabic in such a situation.

We Used to Study and We Went to School

A: I remember when I was young, this, I mean, the situation was good, I mean. We used to study, we used to study and we went to school, ah .... I mean, a person ... he does what he must, he works. My parents, I mean, they always used to ask us to study hard, that is, "So when you grow up you will not have to work too hard, so that you will have a good job." In the morning we used to get up, ah ... My mother would ... she would wake us up, ah .... She would wake us up and prepare everything for us. She got us dressed, made coffee for us, and made us ... xfaf with raisins.

B: Mm ....

A: As they call them.

B: Ooh.

A: And we would drink our coffee. This was in the, I mean, in first grade and second grade. She would get us dressed, and we drank our coffee, and then she took us to the school because the school I went to was a little, a little far away. Ah ... I mean, we studied .... She used to give me, ah ... a snack.

B: Mmm .... [laugh].

A: So we could eat at noon because we were in class from morning to ... to late afternoon, ah .... A snack and she would me 10 douros in case I got hungry or there weren't snacks ... I could go out at noon and buy ... what we call in Algeria garantita.

B: Yes.

A: All of us, we went to buy it at noon. It, they make it with ... with chickpea flour. This doesn't exist in America, I haven't ... haven't ever seen it. The point is, in the afternoon, we came and .... We'd find again that she had made us coffee again. We were, we would come in hungry, ah ... I remember I used to run to, ah ... to get home. Anyway, we'd get home and drink our coffee and later ah .... We would relax a little and go to watch what they call cartoons on television.

B: Yes.

A: There were cartoons, I mean, they were really funny. In the evening, we did the ..., what they call *homework*, the work we had to do and we prepared our lessons for the next day and so it went. We took our exams. I remember I was, I mean, I studied hard. I was, ah .... I always came in first, not always and .... I mean, most of the time I came in, I came in first.

B: Good.

A: And, I mean, I remember, I mean, God, I mean, they were days, I mean, good ones when a person remembers them.

yruuḥuu ʕlaa jaal ddraaham

As the speaker here describes it, economic concerns as well as ideology have fueled the continuing conflict in Algeria.

A: eeh, liʔannuu a … lii a … kull ʕaaʔiila yəlqaaw waaḥəd iiquullhum, a … 'ruuḥuu qətluu wəllaa ruuḥuu a … əssərquu wə-taaxduu draaham, naʕṭuukum draaham.'[1] iiruuḥuu ʕlaa jaal a … ddraaham.

B: iih, haaδaa ʃʃii yaʕnii ṭa … ṭabiiʕii yaʕnii. lənsaan iidaa kaan ʕanduu a … ʕaayla kbiira w-laazəm iiṣṣarf[2] ʕleehaa w-maa kaaʃ ḥattaa waaḥəd llii yʕaawnuu,[3] ḥattaa waaḥd ʃkuun llii[4] ysaaʕduuh. fa-lʔawwəl llii yjii liih[5] w-iiquulluu, 'anaa naʕṭiik ʃwiyya draaham.' fa-yruuḥ mʕaah yaʕnii. rubbamaa fə-lluwwəl maa yruuḥʃ, liyanna tkuun a … ʃwiyya yaʕnii djiih ṣʕiiba, yquullək, 'anaa maa ndiirʃ haad ʃʃii w-anaa xaaṭiinii.' rubbamaa yəṣbər ʃhaar, ʃahreen,[6] w-laakən kii maa ykuunʃ yaʕnii, maa fiiʃ ḥall, fa-yaʕnii yruuḥ məḍṭarr yaʕnii. fa-lii-haaδaa qəltlək yaʕnii haaδii nnaas, llii həm iidiiruu haad ʃʃii, naas ʕandhum lə … humma ʕaarfiin bəllii wiin iiḥəbbuu yruuḥuu yaʕnii kii yjiibuu naas baaʃ yəqqətluu wəllaa yruuḥuu ii … yəjjəssuu wəllaa ydiiruu ayy ʃii, yaʕnii maa ʕliihum illaa yruuḥuu lə-zzənqa w-iijiibuu kiimaa yḥəbbuu yaʕnii.

يروحوا على جال الدّراهم

أ: اي، لأنّه ا ... لي ا ... كلّ عائيله يلقاوا واحد يقولّهم، ا ... «روحوا قتلوا ولاّ روحوا ا ... سّرقوا وتاخدوا دراهم، نعطوكم دراهم.»[1] يروحوا على جال ا ... الدّراهم.

ب: ايه، هذا الشّي يعني ط... طبيعي يعني، الانسان إذا كان عنده ا ... عايله كبيره ولازم يصرّف[2] عليها وما كاش حتّى واحد اللّي يعاونوه[3] حتّى واحد شكون اللّي[4] يساعده، فالأوّل اللّي يجي ليه[5] ويقولّوه، «انا نعطيك شويّه دراهم.» فيروح معه يعني. ربّما فالأوّل ما يروحش، لأنّ ا ... شويّه يعني تجيه صعيبه، يقولّك، «انا ما نديرش هاد الشّي وانا خاطيني.» ربّما يصبر شهار، شهرين،[6] ولكن كي ما يكونش يعني، ما فيش حلّ، فيعني يروح مضطّر يعني. فلهذا قلتلك يعني هذي النّاس، اللّي هم يديروا هاد الشّي، ناس عندهم ال... هم عارفين باللّي وين يحبّوا يروحوا يعني كي يجيبوا ناس باش يقّتلوا ولاّ يروحوا يـ... يجسّوا ولاّ يديروا ايّ شيّ، يعني ما عليهم الاّ يروحوا للزّنقه ويجيبوا كيما يحبّوا يعني.

127

Vocabulary:

jəssəs جسّس *v* to spy, keep secret watch { *imperf:* iijəssəs }

liʔannuu لأنّه *conj* because ; *invariable*

ʕaaʔiila عائـلـه [*also* ʕaayla; ʕaayiila] *nfs* family { *pl:* ʕaaʔiilaat }

ʕlaa jaal على جال *conj* because of, due to

ʕaayla عايـلـه [*also* ʕaaʔiila; ʕaayiila] *nfs* family { *pl:* ʕaaylaat }

əṣṣrəf اصرّف [*also* ətṣraf] *v* to be spent (of money) { *imperf:* yəṣṣraf }

ʃkuun شكون *interrog* who

ʃkuun llii شكون اللي *conj* anyone who, someone who; who is it that

liyanna لـيـنّ [*also* liʔanna] *conj* because

xaaṭii + suffixed pro خـاطـي it doesn't concern s.o., leave s.t. alone ; *invariable*

ʃhaar شهار *nms* month { *pl:* ʃhuur, *pl:* ʃhur, *pl:* ʃhahraat }

məḍṭarr مضـطـرّ *adj* forced to, compelled to { *fs:* məḍṭarra, *pl:* məḍrarriin }

zənqa زنقه *nfs* street, road; alley { *pl:* znəq }

Notes:

1. The phrase /taaxduu draaham, naʕṭuukum draaham/ 'you'll get money, we'll give you money' refers to the future. There is, however, no explicit reference to future time here. In SAA as in other varieties of spoken Arabic, the imperfect verb may refer to an event taking place in the near future. Context is the best guide to meaning.

    Unlike certain other varieties of spoken Arabic, however, SAA does not mark future action. Except for the near future, as here, SAA uses explicit time reference in combination with the imperfect verb to indicate the future. An example appears in Selection 8: /mənnaa lə-ʃii sniin wəllaa ləmma ddaʕwaa thassan, **nʕaawduu nruuḥuu** lə-ddzaayər/ 'in a few years or when the situation improves, I mean, we'll go back and go to Algeria'. The verb /raaḥ/ 'to go' may also indicate future action, as in /ləblaad raayḥa ḍḍarr w-wlaad jjazaayər raayḥiin yəḍḍərruu/ 'the country will be hurt, and the children of Algeria will be hurt' (Selection 28).

2. The form /yəṣṣərf/ 'he spends', with its doubled /ṣ/ and stress on the first syllable, is unusual in SAA. The more typical form for the 2MS imperfect of /ṣrəf/ 'to spend' is /yəṣraf/.

3. The form /yʕaawnuuh/ 'he aids him' has a suffixed pronoun that expresses the direct object. That suffixed pronoun, however, is not noticeable when it occurs in word-final position. This is typical of SAA verbs.

4. The phrase /ʃkuun llii/ 'someone who, anyone who' consists of the interrogative /ʃkuun/ 'who' and the relative pronoun /llii/. This phrase literally means 'who is it that'. Over time, however, it has come to function not as an interrogative but as a relative, as it does here.

5. The phrase /yjii liih/ 'he comes to him' has the indirect object /liih/ as a separate word with its own words stress. This occurs in SAA, but is not as common as its alternative. That alternative links the verb (here, /yjii/ 'he comes') with the indirect object (here, /liih/ 'to him'). The result, /yjiiliih/ sounds like a single word and has stress on the second syllable.

6. The phrase /ʃhaar, ʃahreen/ 'a month or two' illustrates the changes that can occur in a noun in SAA. The singular /**ʃhaar**/ 'month', when compared with its MSA counterpart **ʃahr**, shows both vowel shift and lengthening of the short stem vowel /a/ to /aa/. The dual form, however, has a more recognizable form.

They Go Because of the Money

A: Yes, because, ah ... for ah ... every family finds someone who tells them, ah ... "Go kill people or go, ah ... steal, and you'll get money, we'll give you money." They go because of the, ah ... the money.

B: Yes, I mean, it's natural. I mean, a person, if he has, ah ... a big family, he has to spend money on it and there is no one to aid him, no one to help him. So the first person who comes to him and tells him "I'll give you a little bit of money," he goes along with him. I mean, maybe at the start he doesn't go because it is ah ... a little, I mean, it comes hard for him. He'll tell you, "I won't do this thing, it doesn't concern me." Maybe he will be patient for a month or two, but when there isn't, I mean, there is no solution, I mean, he will be forced to go, I mean. For this reason, I'll tell you, I mean, these people, who do this thing, are people who have the .... They know where they want to go, I mean, when they get people to kill or to go to ... to spy, or do anything. I mean, they don't have to do anything but go out on the street and get whatever they want, I mean.

rabbamaa kaan məfruuḍ iixalluu haaðaa lḥizb yəḥkam ʃii ʃhuur

Algeria's experiments with democratic elections have not been entirely successful. The elections of 1991 in which Islamist parties won a majority ended in the dissolution of parliament and the resignation of the president. In the elections of 1999, six of seven candidates withdrew the day before the election. The speaker here suggests another possible alternative.

A: baʕḍ əlʔislamiyyiin lʔaḥzaab kiimaa haaðaak ḥizb taaʕ ənnahḍa[1] w-lii ... llii duuk[2] ʕanduu ... ḥattaa yaʕnii nnaas taaʕuu fə-lparlaamaan taaʕ əddzaayər a ... nnuwwaab yaʕnii fə-lparlaamaan. iiquullək, ʰhaanaa[3] nə ... ʕan ntəbbʕuu[4] lʔislaam lmətfəttaḥ llii lmaraa təqdar truuḥ təqraa fiih wə-lmraa təqdər taʕməl tiijaara, lmaraa təqdər ... yaʕnii ʕandaa ḥuquuq kiimaa rraajəl yaʕnii fii ḥuuduud yaʕnii ...

B: lmaʕquul.

A: ḥuduud lmaʕquul. kiimaa qultii ntii yaʕnii liinsaan ... anaa nḍunn bə-ʔanna nnaas vuuṭaaw[5] ʕlaa haaðaa lḥizb haaðaa fa-kaan mən məfruuḍ yaʕni, ḥattaa w-loo yaʕnii ... əntii tquulii bəllii[6] maa yxəlluuhumʃ, iixəlluuʃ nnsaa w-raayḥiin iidiiruu ... yəḥaggəruu nnsaa w-iinḥuu[7] lḥquuhum[8] yaʕnii, ka-ʔannamaa nnaas ḥakmuu ʕliihum qbəl maa ydiiruu ḥattaa ḥaaja. fa-kaan mə-lməfruuḍ rubbamaa, rubbamaa yaʕnii maa ḥnaa nquuluu a ... maa yqədruuʃ [xxx] lə-lwraa, *à part* ..., rabbamaa kaan məfruuḍ iixalluu haaðaa lḥizb yəḥkam ʃii ʃhuur, iiʃuufuu kiifaaʃ iidiir. b-ḥeet ljeeʃ muujuud muujuud. yaʕnii ljeeʃ huu qbəl wəllaa məm-baʕd huwa muujuud muujuud[9] yaʕnii. iiðaa kiimaa daaruu fə-tturk[10] kaan haadaak ḥizb əlʔiislamiyyiin ʃaafuu tḥarrak ʃwiyya ʕa-lyaamiin, ʕa-lyaasaar naḥḥaawaa, yaʕnii maa fiihaaʃ ...

ربّما كان مفروض يخلّوا هذا الحزب يحكم شي شهور

أ: بعض الإسلميّين، الأحزاب كيما هذاك حزب تاع النّهضه[1] وليـ ... اللّي دوك[2] عنده ... حتّى يعني النّاس تاعه فالبرلامان تاع الدّزاير، ا ... النّوّاب يعني فالبرلامان. يقولَك هانا[3] نـ ... عن نتبّعوا[4] الإسلام المتفتّح، اللّي المراه تقدر تروح تقرا فيه والمراه تقدر تعمل تيجاره، المراه تقدر ... يعني عندها حقوق كيما الرّاجل يعني في حدود يعني ....

ب: المعقول.

أ: حدود المعقول. كيما قلتي انتي يعني الانسان ... أنا نظنّ بأنّ النّاس قوطاوا[5] على هذا الحزب هذا فكان من مفروض يعني، حتّى ولو يعني ... انتي تقولي باللّي[6] ما يخلّوهمش، يخلّوش النّسا ورايحين يديروا ... يحقّروا النّسا وينحوا[7] لحقوقهم[8] يعني، كأنّما النّاس حكموا عليهم قبل ما يديروا حتّى حاجه. فكان مالفروض ربّما، ربّما يعني ما احنا نقولوا ا ... ما يقدروش [xxx] للورا à part, ا .... ربّما كان مفروض يخلّوا هذا الحزب يحكم شي شهور، يشوفوا كيفاش يدير بحيت الجيش موجود موجود[9] يعني الجيش هو قبل ولاّ ممبعد هو موجود موجود يعني. إذا كيما داروا فالتّرك[10] كان هذاك حزب الإسلميّين شافوه تحرّك شويّه عاليامين، عالياسار، نحّاوها. يعني ما فيهاش ....

133

Vocabulary:

duuk دوك [*also* durk; duuka; durka] *adv* now

parlaamaan پرلامان *nms* parliament, legislature {*pl:* parlaamaanaat}

naayəb نايب *nms* deputy, representative {*pl:* nuwwaab}

ḥanaa احنا [*also* ḥnaa; ḥnaayaa] *pro* we, us (1P)

təbbaʕ تبّع *v* to follow, pursue; to imitate {*imperf:* iitəbbaʕ}

raajəl راجل *nms* man, person {*pl:* rjaal}

ḍənn ظنّ [*also* ðənn] *v* to think, consider, deem {*imperf:* iiḍənn}

vuuṭaa ڤوطى [*also* vooṭaa] *v* to vote {*imperf:* iivuuṭii}

məfruuḍ مفروض *nms; pre-verb* supposed, assumed; it is supposed, it is assumed

mən məfruuḍ من مفروض it is supposed, it is assumed

loo لو *part.* if

ḥattaa wə-loo حتّى ولو *conj* even if

bəllii بللي *conj; after verbs of speaking, thinking, etc.* that

xəllaa خلّى *v* to allow, let {*imperf:* iixəllii}

ḥaggər حقّر *v* to despise, scorn, treat with contempt {*imperf:* iiḥaggər}

nḥaa انحى *v* to attack, assail {*imperf:* yənḥii}

rubbamaa ربّما [*also* rabbamaa] *adv* maybe, perhaps

wraa ورا *prep* behind, in back of

à part *prep* separately, apart from

rabbamaa ربّما [*also* rubbamaa] *adv* maybe, perhaps

b-ḥeet بحيث *conj* since, as, due to the fact that

iiðaa اذا *conj* if; when, whenever

haadaak هداك [*also* haadaaka; haaðaak; haaðaaka] *pro* that (MS far demonstrative) {*fs:* haadiik, *pl:* haaduuk}

Notes:

1. The phrase /ḥizb taaʕ ənnahḍa/ 'a Nahda Party', with no definite article on the first noun of the construction, is an apparent slip of the tongue. The speakers seem to refer here to the Algerian Nahda Party or /lḥizb taaʕ ənnahḍa/. This Islamist party featured prominently in the 1999 election when it backed Abdelaziz Bouteflika, the choice of the military and security establishment. The other six candidates in the election withdrew the day before voting.

   Note also the interdental fricative /ḍ̵/ of /ənnahḍa/, as compared to the stop of its MSA counterpart al-nah<u>ḍ</u>a. Many speakers of SAA have a single pronunciation for the Arabic letters ض and ظ. For some, that pronunciation is the stop /ḍ/. For others, like this speaker, it is /ḍ̵/.

2. The form /duuk/ is only one of several variants of the word that means 'now'. Others that appear in this work include /duuka/, /durk/, /durka/, /daaruuk/, and /daarwək/. Those unfamiliar with SAA are fortunate that context provides an aid to comprehension.

3. The form /haanaa/ 'we are' consists of the presentational particle /haa/ and the 1P suffix /naa/. When followed by a verb, the combination of /haa/ and pronoun add force or emphasis to an utterance, as in /haanaa nə ... ʕan ntəbbʕuu lʔislaam lmətfəttaḥ/ 'We follow an open-minded Islam'.

4. The phrase /ʕan ntəbbʕuu/ 'we follow' is not typical in SAA. The imperfect verb in SAA has no prefix. The phrase that occurs here is reminiscent of another variety of spoken Arabic. It is the Levantine spoken Arabic construction /ʕam/ + imperfect verb that regularly indicates ongoing action. Alternatively, it may be a slip of the tongue.

5. The 3P perfect verb /vooṭaaw/ 'they voted' has the 3MS perfect /vooṭaa/ and imperfect /iivooṭii/. This verb derives from the French <u>voter</u> 'to vote'. SAA often borrows French verbs as complete units. That is, the stem of the borrowed verb may be unaltered (and may not resemble an Arabic stem at all). These borrowings are usually treated, as is the verb /vooṭaa/ - /iivooṭii/, as finally-weak verbs.

6. The form /bəllii/ can be translated as 'that'. Its usage, however, is more limited than the translation indicates. It occurs only with expressions of saying (as here, /tquulii **bəllii** maa yxəlluuhumʃ/ 'you say that they will not let them') and knowing (as in Selection 12, /nʕarfuu **bəllii** la télévision taaʕ əddzaayər taaʕ əlḥuukuuma/ 'we know that Algerian television belongs to the government').

7. The form /iinḥuu/ 'they attack' is not Form I but Form IV. Form IV is not productive in SAA, as it closely resembles Form I. This is because the hamza or glottal stop of MSA is not a regular consonant in SAA and because differences between short vowels are often neutralized. When Form IV verbs occur, like this example, they can be considered borrowings from MSA.

8. The form /ḥquuhum/ 'their rights', with a single /q/ is a slip of the tongue for /ḥquuqhum/. Such slips are more apparent in transcripts than in speech, as the reader can check every element of the transcript. Speech, which moves in linear time, has repetition and redundancy to help the listener past slips and other problems.

9. The speaker sums up the role of the military in Algeria with the statement that /ljeeʃ huu qbəl wəllaa məm-baʕd huwa muujuud muujuud/ 'the army is very much present, before the fact and after'. The Algerian ANP (Armée Nationale Populaire or People's National Army) has been a constant in political life since the war of independence. In addition, the military is well-represented in regional as well as international affairs.

10. The speaker alludes to events of 1996 - 1997 when he suggests that the Algerian military do /kiimaa daaruu fə-tturk/ 'as they did in Turkey'. Islamic leader Necmettin Erbakan became Turkish prime minister in June, 1996. Approximately a year later, he resigned under pressure from the Turkish military. Military leaders stated that Islamic fundamentalist threatened Turkey's secular and democratic institutions.

Perhaps They Should Have Let This Party Govern for a Few Months

A: Some of the Islamists, the parties like that, a party of the Nahda and that ... that now has ... even, I mean, people belonging to it in the Algerian Parliament, ah ... deputies in Parliament. They'll tell you, we ... a, "We follow an open-minded Islam in which a woman can go get an education, and a woman can work in business, a woman can ...." I mean, she has rights like a man, I mean, within the limits, I mean ...

B: What's reasonable.

A: Reasonable limits. Like you yourself said, I mean, a person .... I think that inasmuch as people voted for this particular party, then it should, I mean, even if, I mean ..., you say that they will not let them, they will not let women and they are going to do ..., to humiliate women and attack their rights. I mean, it is as if people passed judgment on them before they did anything at all. So it should perhaps, I mean, we could say they can't, [xxx] back. Aside from ... Perhaps they should have let this party govern for a few months and see how it did. Given that the army is very much present, I mean, the army is very much present, both before and after the fact. I mean, if, as they did in Turkey, there was that Islamist party. They saw it move a little to the left and a little to the right, and they removed it. I mean, there isn't any ....

ddzaayǝr raahya raaḥat twǝllii fii miiziiriyya kbiira

Speakers here discuss how Algerians learned about the worsening economic situation. The language used here mixes SAA usage with features associated with MSA and other varieties of spoken Arabic.

A: haanii[1] ntǝðǝkkǝr anaayaa nhaar, marra a ... lǝ ... a ... zaahiyya bǝlʕaaruus llii tahi ... tquul axbaar fǝ-ttiiliiviizyoon qaalǝt innuu a ... 'ddzaayǝr raahiya raaḥǝt twǝllii fii miiziiriyya kbiira liʔann ǝlpiitrool ṭaaḥǝt lʔasʕaar taaʕuu[2] wǝ-xlaaṣ.' a ... nnaas gaaʕ thǝwwluu w-xaafuu, a ... w-baʕdeen a ... baʕd zuuj dqaayǝq, a ... mǝllii aanoñṣaaw haaðaak lxabar, a ... jaat a ... muuðiiʕa taanya fǝ-ttiiliiviizyoon qaalǝt innuu a ... 'xlaaṣ a ... haaðiyaa ɣalṭa, maaʃii ṣaḥḥ.' aḍǝnn annuu kaanuu ḥaabbeen iiquuluu lǝ-ʃʃaʕb innuu a ... lmuʃkiila raahya jaayitkum w-maa ʕaarfuuʃ kiifaah iiquuluuhaa wǝ-rmaawhaa hakkaa fǝ-ttiiliiviiizyoon fajʔatan a ...

B: yaʕnii yǝtmǝsxǝruu bǝ-nnaas yaʕnii [cough], yaʕnii yǝtmǝsxǝruu bǝ-nnaas yaʕnii, nʕarfuu bǝllii *la télévision* taaʕ ǝddzaayǝr taaʕ ǝlḥuukuuma.[3] maa tǝnqaal[4] ḥaaja ḥattaa iillaa w-ʃaafhaa kǝʃ waaḥǝd mǝl ... mǝl ... mǝ-lḥuukuuma wǝllaa mǝ-lḥizb bǝʃ iiwuqqaʕ ʕliihaa w-iiquul bǝllii tǝqdar djuuz. fa-iiða qaalǝthaa laazǝm iikuun nʕaṭaat lmwaafqa taaḥḥaa mǝ-lluwwǝl.

A: aah.

B: fa-rubbamaa yaʕnii kaan fiih, maa tfaahmuuʃ biinaathum, fǝ ... fǝ ... fǝ-lḥuukuuma, fǝ-lwiizaara wǝllaa. waaḥǝd qaal, 'laazǝm nʕallmuu ʃʃaʕb.' wǝ-llaaxǝr qaalluu, 'laa.' faa ... fǝ-llaxxar yaʕnii wǝqʕat fiihaa ʃɣul ... txǝllṭǝt yaʕnii lǝ ... lwǝdʕiyya *mais* lmuuhǝmm yaʕnii huwwa anna lǝ ... nnaas ʕarfuu bǝllii lǝ ... wǝʃ huwwa jaayhum yaʕnii. ṣaḥḥ wǝllaa ... wǝllaa fǝʃtii? ǝlmuuhǝmm ʕaarfiin bǝllii ddaʕwaa ḥa-ttɣǝyyǝr wǝ-maaʃii lǝ-lʔǝḥsǝn yaʕnii diima lǝ-lʔaswa yaʕnii.

الدّزاير راهي راحت تولّي في ميزيريه كبيره

ب: هاني¹ نتذكّر انايا نهار، مرّه ا ... الـ ... أ ... زاهيّ بالعاروس اللّي تـه
... تقول اخبار فالتّلفزيون. قالت إنّه ا ... «الدّزاير راهي راحت تولّي
في ميزيريه كبيره لأنّ البيترول طاحت الأسعار تاعه² وخلاص.» أ ...
النّاس قاع تهوّلوا وخافوا، ا ... وبعدين، ا ... بعد زوج دقايق، ا ... مللّي
آنونصاوا هذاك الخبر، ا ... جات ا ... موذيعه تانيه فالتّلفزيون قالت
إنّه ا ... «خلاص آ ... هذيّا غلطه، ماشي صحّ.» اظنّ انّه كانوا حابّين
يقولوا للشّعب إنّه ا ... المشكيله راهي جايتكم وما عرفوش كيفاه
يقولوها ورماوها هكّا فالتّلفيزيون فجأةً ....

أ: يعني يتمسخروا بالنّاس يعني [cough]، يعني يتمسخروا بالنّاس
يعني، نعرفوا باللّي *la télévision* تاع الدّزاير تاع الحوكومه.³ ما تنقال⁴
حاجه حتّى ألّا وشافها كاش واحد ملـ.. ملـ ... مالحوكومه ولا مالحزب
باش يوقّع عليها ويقول باللّي تقدر تجوز. فإذا قالتها لازم يكون انعطات
الموافقه تاعها ماللّوّل.

ب: اه.

أ: فربّما يعني كان فيه، ما تفاهموش بيناتهم، فـ ... فـ ... فالحوكومه،
فالويزاره ولاّ. واحد قال، «لازم نعلّموا الشّعب.» واللّاخر قالّه، «لا.» فـا
... فالاّخر يعني وقعت فيها شغل ... تخلّطت يعني الـ ... الوضعيّه *mais*
الموهمّ يعني هوّ انّ الـ ... النّاس عرفوا باللّي الـ ... واش هوّ جايهم
يعني. صحّ ولاّ ... ولاّ فشتي؟ الموهمّ عارفين باللّي الدّعوى حتّتغيّر
وماشي للّاحسن يعني ديما للّاسوا يعني.

139

Vocabulary:

anaayaa انايا [*also* anaa] *pro* I (1S)

zaahiya bəlʕaaruus زاهيه بالعاروس *prop* Zahiyya Belarouse (Algerian television personality)

thəwwəl تهوّل [*also* thawwəl] *v* to be alarmed, be frightened {*imperf:* yəthəwwəl}

baʕdeen بعدين *adv* afterwards, then

zuuj زوج [*also* zooj; juuz; zawj] *nms* two

məllii مللي *conj* since, from the time that; when, at the time that

aanoñsaa انونصى *v* to announce, make public {*imperf:* yaanoñsii}

taanii ثاني [*also* θaanii] *adj* another; again ; *adv* {*fs:* taanya, *pl:* taanyiin}

haaðiyaa هذيا [*also* haadii; haadiyyaa; haaðii] *pro* this (FS near demonstrative) {*ms:* haaðaaya, *pl:* haaðuu}

maaʃii ماشي *part.; negates nominal structures* not

ḥaabb حاب *adj; pre-verb* wanting, intending to; liking, loving {*fs:* ḥaabba, *pl:* ḥaabiin}

kiifaah كيفاه [*also* kiifaaʃ] *interrog* how; how much (interrogative or exclamatory)

hakkaa هكّا [*also* hakkaak; haak] *adv* thus, in this way

tməsxər تمسخر *v* to trick, fool; to laugh at, ridicule {*imperf:* yətməsxər}

la télévision *nfs* television

nqaal انقال *v* to be said; to be able to be said, be sayable {*imperf:* yənqaal}

kəʃ كاش [*also* kaaʃ] *part.* some, any

waaḥəd واحد *nms* someone, a certain person; oneself

jaaz جاز *v* to be permitted, be allowed; to pass by, travel {*imperf:* iijuuz}

nʕaṭaa انعطى *v* to be given {*imperf:* yənʕaṭaa}

fə-llaxxər فالأخّر [*also* fə-lʔaaxər] in the end, finally

txəlləṭ تخلّط *v* to be confused, mixed up; to be mixed, mingled {*imperf:* yətxəlləṭ}

mais *conj* but, however

fəʃtii فشتي [*also* fəstii] *nms* lie, untruth; untrue, lying

Notes:

1. Note the female speaker's use of /haa/ and /raa/ structures in this utterance. She begins with /**haa**nii ntəðəkkər anaayaa nhaar, marra/ 'I remember one day, one time'. A second occurrence announces the bad news: /ddzaayər raahya **raa**ḥat twullii fii miiziiriya kbiira/ 'Algeria was going to go through great poverty'. A third occurrence is her interpretation of events: /lmuʃkiila **raa**hya jaayitkum w-maa ʕarfuuʃ kiifaah yəquuluuhaa ʔuu-rmaawhaa haakkaa fə-ttiiliiviiizyoon fajʔatan/ '"There is trouble coming for you," and they didn't know how to say it. So they put it on television with no warning'.

   These three uses of /haa/ and /raa/ mark the three main points of her story. They illustrate the use of /haa/ or /raa/ as a discourse marker that adds strength or emphasis to an utterance, as noted in selection 6, note 4.

2. The clause /əlpiitrool ṭaaḥət lʔasʕaar taaʕuu/ 'the price of oil had fallen' is a topic-comment sentence. The topic is /əlpiitrool/ 'oil'. The comment is /ṭaaḥət lʔasʕaar taaʕ**uu**/ 'its price (lit. their prices) had fallen'. The link between topic and comment is the suffixed pronoun of /taaʕuu/, which refers back to /əlpiitrool/. This topic-comment sentence, which adds no new information and is not a main point of the story, stands in contrast to the /haa/ and /raa/ structures discussed in note 1.

3. The speaker reminds us here that /la télévision taaʕ əddzaayər taaʕ əlḥuukuuma/ 'Algerian *television* belongs to the government'. As a government-owned enterprise, Algerian television is controlled by the state. Alternative sources of information and opinion can be found in the press and satellite television.

4. The quasi-passive /tənqaal/ 'it (fs) can be said' is a Form VII imperfect with the perfect /nqaal/ 'to be said; to be able to be said, be sayable'. Form VII is one verb form available in SAA to express passive meaning. The other verb form is the SAA form $tC_1C_2vC_3$, as in /tṣraf/ 'to be spent; to be spendable'. Although the two forms are synonymous, Form VII has a more formal or classical feel.

Algeria Was Going to Go Through Great Poverty

A: I remember one day, one time I, ah ... the ... ah ... Zahiyya Belarouse, who used to do the news on television, said that, ah ... Algeria was going, going to go through great poverty because the price of oil had fallen and that was that. Ah ... everyone was worried and got scared, ah ... and later, ah .... Two minutes later, ah ... after they made that announcement, ah ... another announcer came ah ... on television. She said, forget it. This was a mistake, it isn't true. I think it was because they wanted to tell people, "There is trouble coming for you," and they didn't know how to say it. So they put it on television with no warning, ah ....

B: They're just fooling people, I mean, [cough] they're just fooling people, I mean. I mean, we know that Algerian *television* belongs to the government. Nothing can be said unless someone from the ... from the ... from the government, from the party has seen it to sign off on it or says it can be allowed. So, if she said that, it must have been agreed upon from the start.

A: Yes.

B: So, perhaps, I mean, there was, they had not come to an understanding among themselves in, in the government, in the ministry or whatever. Someone said, "We have to inform the people," and someone else said to him, "No," so .... In the end, I mean, some ... happened, the situation ... got mixed up, I mean .... *But* the point is, I mean, that the ... the people knew the ... what would happen to them, I mean, is that the truth or no? The point is that they knew that the situation was going to change and not for the better, I mean. It's always for the worse, I mean.

fiih ktiir mən ljaamaaʕaat llii daaxliin f-haaðaa ṣṣiraaʕ

The male speaker here begins by explaining the complexities of the ongoing struggle in Algeria. By the end of this selection, however, he and the female speaker are clear about the basic principles that underlie that struggle.

A: yaʕnii baaʃ əlʔiinsaan yə... yaʕṭii raay yaʕnii ṣaariiḥ w-iikuun waaqiiʕii, ʃʃii ṣʕiib. liyanna fiih ktiir mən a ... mə-lʔaḥzaab, fiih ktiir mən əljaamaaʕaat llii daaxliin f-haaðaa ṣṣiraaʕ.[1] fiih əljeeʃ, fii daaxəl ljeeʃ fiih a ... ʕəddət aḥzaab, ʕəddət tiyyaaraat. fə ... ḥattaa fə-lʔaḥzaab yaʕnii kiimaa ysəmmuu haaðaak *le ... le FIS,* əlḥizb taaʕ jəbhat lʔinqaaḍ.[2] a ... fiih əl ... nnaas llii ḥa ... llii yḥabbuu yəmʃuu mʕa lḥuukuuma baaʃ iidiiruu yaʕnii muuṣaalaaḥa.[3] kaayən fiih nnaas llii maahumʃ ḥaabbiin, iiquullək,[4] 'ḥnaa ndiiruu lkiifaaḥ ḥattaa lə ... ḥattaa aaxər qəṭra taaʕ əddamm.' a ... fiih baʕḍ lʔiislaamiyyiin waaḥd ooxriin llii jəbduu ruuḥhum,[5] lkull yaʕnii ʕan əl *FIS,* iiquullək, 'ḥnaa maa naʕtarfuu b-haað lḥizb haaðaa.' w-huuma ḥizb əja ... taaʕ, taaʕ əlxaarəj, jaabuuh mən iiraan w-maaniiʃ ʕaarf mən ayy blaad w-iiquullək, 'əḥnaa msəlmiin w-laakən məʃii kiimaa haaðuu, ḥnaa maa nəqtluuʃ, ḥnaa maa ndəbḥuuʃ.' yaʕnii lə ... nḍunn lmooḍuuʕ yaʕnii ṣʕiib wə... w-ʕamiiq bəzzaaf bəzzaaf yaʕnii. w-laakən, lxuulaaṣa yaʕnii hiya anna fiih durk ljeeʃ wə-fiih yaʕnii haað ənnaas llii hum iidiiruu haad əlqatl wə-haad lə ... lboombaat. a ... yaʕnii nquuluu kaayən fiih zooj yaʕnii a ... aḥzaab llii ʕandhum ʃwiyya wəzən yaʕnii fə ... fə ... fə-ddzaayər. huwwa *le FIS* llii naḥḥaawaah[6] *mais* yaʕnii ʕand əʃʃaʕb ... maa zaaluu yaʕnii waajəd haaðaa lḥizb haaðaa.

فيه كثير من الجَماعات اللّي داخلين فهذا الصّيراع

أ: يعني باش الأَينسان يـ ... يعطي راي يعني صاريح ويكون واقيعي، شّي
صعيب. لين فيه كثير من ... مالأحزاب، فيه كثير من الجَماعات اللّي
داخلين فهذا الصّراع.[1] فيه الجيش، في داخل الجيش فيه ا ... عدّة أحزاب،
عدة تيّارات. فـ ... حتّى فالأحزاب يعني كيما يسمّوا هذاك *le ...le FIS,*
الحزب تاع جبهة الإنقاض.[2] ... فيه الـ ... النّاس اللّي حـ ... اللّي يحبّوا
يمشوا مع الحوكومه باش يديروا يعني موصالحه.[3] كاين فيه النّاس اللّي
ماهمش حابّين، يقولّك،[4] «احنا نديروا الكيفاح حتّى الـ ... حتّى آخر
قطره تاع الدّم.» ا ... فيه بعض الإيساميّين واحد اوخرين اللّي جبدوا
روحهم،[5] الكلّ يعني عن الـ *FIS،* يقولّك، «احنا ما نعترفوا بهاذ الحزب
هذا.» وهوم حزب اجا ... تاع، تاع الخارج، جابوه من إيران ومانيش
عارف من ايّ بلاد ويقلّك، «احنا مسلمين ولكن ماشي كيما هذو، احنا ما
نقتلوش.احنا ما نذبحوش.» يعني الـ ... نظنّ الموضوع يعني صعيب و
... وعميق بزّاف بزّاف يعني. ولكن، الخولاصه يعني هي انّ فيه درك
الجيش وفيـه يعنـي هذا النّاس اللّي هم يديروا هاد القتله وهاد الـ ...
البومبات. ا ... يعني نقولوا كاين فيه زوج يعنـي ا ... احزاب اللّي
عندهم شويّه وزن يعني فـ ...فـ ... فالدّزاير. هوّ *le FIS* اللّي نحّاواه[6]
mais يعني عند الشّعب ... ما زالوا يعني واجد هذا الحزب هذا. يعني
النّاس ما زالهم يقالّك،

145

yaʕnii nnaas maa zaalhum iiquullək, 'haanaa lə ... llii vooṭeenaa ʕleeh
fə ... f-waaḥd wə-tsʕiin, ʕlaah naḥḥaawaah?' iiquullək maa ʕandhumʃ
əlḥaqq iinaḥḥyuu ḥizb llii ʃʃaʕb qaal laazəm haaðaa lḥizb haaðaa yaḥkəm
fa-ləmmaa anna ʃʃaʕb ntaxbuuh fa-laazəm yəḥkəm.

B: laakən anaa mən raaʔyii lḥamdu llaah llii naḥḥaawaah liʔannuu ləmmaa
tʃuuf lʔiislamiyyiin wəʃ daayriin fə-lbuldaan lʕarbiyya a ... ttaanya wə-
kiifaah yəḥḥakmuu a ... yəḥkəmuu b-ṭaariiqa wəḥʃiyya.

«هانا الـ ... اللّي ڤوطينا عليه فـ ... فواحد وتسعين، علاه نحّاواه؟» يڤلّك
ما عندهمش الحقّ ينحّيوا حزب اللّي الشّعب قال لازم هذا الحزب هذا
يحكم فلمّا انّ الشّعب انتخبوه فلازم يحكم.

ب: لكن انا من رايي، الحمد لله اللّي نحّاواه لأنّه لمّا تشوف الإيسلاميّين واش
دايرين فالبلدان العربيّه ا ... الثّانيه وكيفاه يحكموا ا ... يحكموا
بطاريقه وحشيّه.

Vocabulary:

wjəd وجد *v* to find, come across {*imperf:* yuujəd}

raay راي *nms* opinion {*pl:* ruyyaan}

daaxəl داخل *adj* belonging to, part of; entering {*fs:* daaxla, *pl:* daaxliin}

daaxəl داخل *prep* within, inside

le FIS *prop* FIS (*Front Islamique du Salut*, Islamic Salvation Front)

jəbhat lʔinqaaḍ جبهه الانقاض *prop* (Islamic) Salvation Front (*FIS, Front Islamique du Salut*)

mʃaa مشى *v* to go; to go away, leave {*imperf:* yəmʃii}

waaḥd aaxər واحد اخر other; another *pro; adj* {*fs:* waaḥd ooxraa, *pl:* waaḥd ooxriin}

jbəd جبد *v* to pull; to pull back {*imperf:* yəjbəd}

ruuḥ + suffixed pronoun روح self

jbəd ruuḥ + suffixed pronoun جبد روح *v* to withdraw oneself {*imperf:* yəjbəd ruuḥ-}

məʃii ماشي [*also* maaʃii] *part.; negates nominal structures* not

haað هاذ [*also* haað] *pro* this (invariable near demonstrative)

haaðuu هذو [*also* haadum; haaduu] *pro* this (P near demonstrative) {*ms:* haaðaa, *fs:* haaðii}

dbəḥ ذبح *v* to murder; to kill, slaughter {*imperf:* yədbəḥ}

hum هم [*also* huum(a); ham; humm] *pro* they (3P)

boomba بومبه *nfs* bomb {*pl:* boombaat}

147

wəzən وزن *nms* influence; weight, poundage

mais *conj* but, however

naḥḥaa نحّٰ [*also* nəḥḥaa] *v* to eliminate, remove (i.e., from a post); to take away, remove {*imperf:* iinaḥḥii}

maa zaal ما زال *v: invariable, conjugated, or with pronoun suffix* still; not yet

waajəd واجد *adj* ready, available, prepared {*fs:* waajda, *pl:* waajdiin}

vooṭaa ڤوطى [*also* vuuṭaa] *v* to vote {*imperf:* iivooṭii}

təsʕiin تسعين *nms* ninety

durk درك [*also* duuk; duuka; durka] *adv* now

Notes:

1. If anything, the speaker underestimates when he states that /fiih ktiir mən a ... mə-lʔaḥzaab, fiih ktiir mən ljaamaaʕaat llii daaxliin f-haaðaa ṣṣiraaʕ/ 'there a lot of, of parties and there are a lot of groups that are taking part in this struggle'. He specifically mentions internal divisions in the army and in the FIS. The political diversity of Algeria is demonstrated by the 30 political parties that came into being within a year of their legalization in 1989 and the nearly 60 that existed by the time of the first multiparty national elections in 1991.

2. The Algerian political party known as /le FIS, əlḥizb taaʕ jəbhat lʔinqaaḍ/ 'the FIS [*Front islamique du salut*], the party of the [Islamic] Salvation Front' is one of several Islamist parties in Algeria. Soon after the legalization of political parties, however, the FIS emerged as the only serious challenger at the national level to the government party, the FLN (*Front de la libération nationale*). The FIS took 180 of 430 electoral districts in the elections of 1991, while the FLN took only 15. The parliament that resulted was dissolved shortly after the election and the FIS was banned.

3. The male speaker here makes noticeable use of factitive constructions. These consist of the verb /daar/ 'to do; to make' with a following direct object. Constructions occurring here include /baaʃ **iidiiruu** yaʕnii **muuṣaalaaḥa**/ 'for the sake of, I mean, reconciliation; lit. in order that they do, I mean, a reconciliation'; /ḥnaa **ndiiruu lkiifaaḥ** ḥattaa l ... ḥattaa ʔaaxər qəṭra taaʕ əddamm/ 'we will fight, to ... ah ... to the last drop of blood, lit. we will

148

do the fight ...'; and /haaðaa nnaas llii hum **iidiiruu haad** əlqatl **uu-haad** 1 ... **lboombaat**/ 'these people who are killing and setting off these bombs; lit. these people who do this killing and these ... bombs'. Reliance on factitive constructions occurs in other varieties of Arabic. They are also common in French.

4. The form /iiquullək/ 'they say, lit. he says to you' is not linguistic filler. Here and in other selections, especially Selection 13, it is a discourse marker. It marks quoted speech. The form /iiquullək/ thus functions as does "like" in informal English, as in, "So I said, like, I think you're crazy." Note that /yguullək/ is invariable for the 3P, 3MS, and 3FS forms.

5. In SAA, as in certain other varieties of spoken Arabic, the word /ruuḥ/ is commonly used to mean 'self'. The synonym nafs, also used in MSA, occurs as well in SAA.

6. The 3MS suffixed pronoun /aah/, as in /naḥḥaawaah/ 'they got rid of it (ms)' is one of two SAA variants for this form. The other is /uu/, as in /ʃaafuu/ 'he saw it (ms)'. Both /aah/ and /uu/ occur as suffixes to consonant-final words. The form /h/ replaces both of these after a vowel, as in /jaabuuh/ 'they brought it (ms)'.

There Are a Lot of Groups That Are Taking Part in This Struggle

A: I mean, for a person to ... to give a frank, I mean, opinion and be realistic is difficult. Because there a lot of ... of parties, there are a lot of groups that have gotten involved in this struggle. There is the army. Within the army there are a number of parties and a number of movements. So .... Even within the parties, I mean, what they call this *FIS*, the party of the [Islamic] Salvation Front, ah ... there are ... people who ... who want to go along with the government for the sake of, I mean, reconciliation. There are people who don't want that. They say, "We will fight, to ... ah ... to the last drop of blood." Ah ... there are some Islamists, some others who have withdrawn, all of them, I mean, from the *FIS*. They say, "We do not acknowledge this party. They are a party ... from, from elsewhere." They brought it from Iran or I don't know what country. They say ... "We are Muslims but not like those people. We don't kill, we don't slaughter." I mean, the ... I think the question is, I mean, hard and very complex, I mean. But the long and the short of it is, I mean, that now there is the army and there are, I mean, these people who are killing and setting off these ... bombs. Ah .... I mean, we say there are two, I mean, ah ... parties that have some influence in ... in ... Algeria. They are the *FIS*, which they got rid of *but*, I mean, the people have ... they still find this party. I mean, people still will tell you, "We are the ones who voted for it in ... in '91. Why did they get rid of it?" They say they don't have the right to get rid of a party that the people said has to govern. And when the people elect it, it has to govern.

B: But I think, thank God they got rid of it, because when you see the Islamists and what they are doing in other ... Arab countries, and how they govern, ah .... They govern brutally.

150

hiyya aktar mən misʔalat islaam

The two speakers do not agree on many of the issues surrounding the conflict in Algeria. They do, however, agree that both sides have committed serious offences.

A: yaʕnii anaa aðənn lmooḍuuʕ muuʃ ɣeer mooḍuuʕ iislamiyyiin. mooḍuuʕ aðənn mooḍuuʕ taaʕ *mafia*, taaʕ əljeeʃ llii kaanuu ḥaabbiin lblaad tədxul fii ḥarb ahliyya ttxəlləṭ əlkull ḥattaa huuma yəqədruu yaʕnii yəssərquu w-iiḥḥakmuu kiimaa yḥabbuu yɣanyuu.[1] llii yətḥarrak taanii[2] yquul, 'haaðaa ɣaalaṭ w-raakum sərqtuu w-raakum dərtuu haad ʃʃii.' yəqtluuh yaʕnii, yləṣṣquuluu kaaʃ a … tuhma yaʕnii yquuluu, 'nta islamii w-ənta dərt əlboombaat w-ənta qtəlt.' w-iiqətluuh. yaʕnii kaayn ktiir mə-nnaas llii maa ʕandhum ḥattaa ʕaalaaqa maʕa lʔislaamiyyiin wə-qətluuhum.

B: ʕalaa kulli ḥaal, anaa mwaafqa mʕaak ənnuu a … lmisʔalaa misʔala xaaṭiira w-hiyya aktar mən misʔalat islaam wəllaa. a … laakən ləmmaa nʃuuf lḥuukuuma məm bəkrii w-hiyya taḥkəm a … laakən ʕaamaarhaa maa qatlət ənnaas. ʕaamaarhaa maa a … maa …

A: raakii mətyəqqna ʕaamaarhaa maa qətlət nnaas, anaa maa aðənn.

B: laa, qatlət nnaas laakən maa tʕaarḍətʃ ʕlaa a … ḥuuruumaat taaʕ əlbuuyuut,[3] maa kaanətʃ tədbaḥ a … maadaarəs fə … lmuuʕalliimat fə-lmaadaaris. ṣaḥḥ ləmmaa tkuun qətlaa mən ṭaaraf a … fə … fəʃʃə … fələ … fə-lḥuukuuma nafshaa nʕarfuu ənnuu waaḥəd maa yəqdər yə … yaṣəl lə … a … lḥukkaam illaa biinaathum. yaʕnii məm barra ṣaʕb w-haadaa yaʕnii lxaaṭaaʔ llii nnaas kulluuhum fə-lʔawwəl leeh … wə-ʕlaah ʃʃaʕb kaanuu yə … yʃəjjəʕuu lʔiislaamiyyiin wə-vooṭaaw ʕleehum baaʃ yəṭləʕuu l-lḥukum? liiʕənnuu kaan ʕandhum aaməl innuuhuum … ṣṣiiraaʕ llii ykuun a … mən əlʔiislaamiyyiin iikuun ḍədd lḥuukuuma məʃii ḍədd əʃʃaʕb.

152

هيّ اكتر من مسألة إسلام

أ: يعني انا اظنّ الموضوع موهوش غير موضوع إيسلميّين. موضوع اظنّ
موضوع تاع mafia، تاع الجيش اللّي كانوا حابّين البلاد تدخل في حرب
اهليّه تتخلّط الكلّ حتّى هوم يقدروا يعني يسرّقوا ويحكّموا كيما
يحبّوا يغنّيوا،[1] اللّي يتحرّك تاني[2] يقول، «هذا غالط وراكم سرقتوا
وراكم درتوا هاذ الشّي.» يقتلوه يعني، يلصّقوله كاش ا ... تهمه يعني
يقولوا، «انت إسلامي وانت درت البومبات وانت قتلت ... » ويقتلوه.
يعني كاين كتير مالنّاس اللّي ما عندهم حتّى عالاقه مع الإسلاميّين
وقتلوهم.

ب: على كلّ حال، انا موافقه معك انّه ا ... المسأله مسأله خاطيره وهيّ اكثر
من مسألة إسلام ولاّ. ا ... لكن لمّا نشوف الحوكومه مم بكري وهيّ تحكم ا
... لكن عامارها ما قتلت النّاس، عامارها ما... ما....

أ: راكي متيقّنه عامارها ما قتلت النّاس، انا ما ظنّ.

ب: لا، قتلت النّاس لكن ما تعارضتش على ا ... حورومات تاع البيوت،[3] ما
كانتش تدبح ا ... مادارس فـ ... الموعلّيمت فالمادارس. صحّ لمّا تكون قتلى
من طارف ا ... فـ ... فالشّـ ... فلـ ... فالحوكومه نفسها نعرفوا انّه واحد
ما يقدر يـ ... يصل الـ ... أ ... الحكّام إلاّ بيناتهم ... يعني مم برّه صعب
وهذا يعني الخاطاء اللّي النّاس كلّوهم الأوّل فالـ ... وعلاه الشّعب كانوا
يـ ... يشجّعوا الإيسلاميّين وڤوطاوا عليهم باش يطلعوا للحكم؟ لينّه كان
عندهم امل انّهم ... الصّيراع اللّي يكون ا ... من الإيسلاميّين يكون ضدّ
الحوكومه ماشي ضدّ الشّعب.

153

hə ... haad ssaabab a ... lə ... ʃʃaʕb fə-lʔawwəl ayyəd lə ... lʔislamiyyiin
wə-vooṭaaw ʕleehum[4] wə-ṭləʕuu a ... nəjḥuu. laakən a ... mʕa llaxxar[5]
kii bdaaw iiduuruu ʕlaa ʃʃaʕb fii əlquura. w-haadaa məʃii klaam qriinaah
fə-ljaraaʔəd wəllaa, smaʕnaah mən naas ṣraatləhum haað əlʔaʃyaa.

A: m ...

B: maθalan anaayaa mətyəqqna haadaa klaam sməʕtuu mən a ... maθalan
bnaat kaanuu yəqraaw mʕaayaa fə-lmadrasa, ṣraaw l-ʕammaathum[6] wə-
l-xaalaathum llii yəsknuu fə-lquuraa daaxəl a ... wasaṭ ljazaaʔər.

A: m ...

B: fə-lʔawwəl qaallək kaanuu yəʔayyduu lə ... ljamaaʕaat lʔiislaamiyya
ləmmaa bdaat kaanuu yə... kaanuu ləmmaa yətəxabbaaw fə-lmaazaarəʕ
wəllaa, nnaas llii yəsknuu f-haaduuk əlquuraa yaʕṭuuhum lʔakəl,
yaʕṭuuhum a ...

A: ədduwaa, ləḥwaayəj.

B: ədduwaa, lə ... ləḥwaayəj, mə ... lə ... bə-ṣṣaḥḥ mʕa llaxxər lə ...
ləmmaa ṭawwələt əlmudda ṣabḥuu haaduuk ənnaas llii yjuu yəṭṭalbuu
lʔakəl, yəṭṭəlbuu aktar mə-lʔakəl yië... yəntahkuu ḥuuruumaat bnaathum,
yəd ... yə ...yəntahkuu ḥuuruumaat taaʕ a ... nsaahum. *alors,* nnaas
daaruu ʕleehum, ṣabḥuu maa, maa yqabluuʃ haad ʃʃee, w-kii daaruu
ʕleehum nnaas wəllaaw a ... yəqtluu fii haaduuk nnaas bə-ddaat llii
kaanuu ysaaʕduu fəhum[7] w-iiaʕṭuuhum lʔakəl wə-lmafruuḍ annuhum maa
yqətluuʃ nnaas. a ... biimaa anna ʃʃaʕb kaan iiḥiss innuu lḥuukuuma
kaant ṭḍalmuuh lmafruuḍ a ... kaanuu yəʔəyydu lʔislamiyyiin baaʃ yə...
yə ... yjaahduu ðədd ... kiimaa yquuluu huuma yjaahduu yaʕnii yḥaarbuu
ðədd lḥuukuuma. laakən llii ʃaafuuh ənnaas innuu wə-laa waaḥəd fə-
lḥuukuuma maa ṣraaluu ḥattaa ḥaaja. yaʕnii llii maat ɣeer llii kaayn
yə... llii maat mən aṣḥaab lḥuukuuma ɣeer llii huum ḥabbuu yəqtluuh
fə-lḥuukuuma nafshaa.

هـ ... هاد السّـابب ا ... الـ ... الشّعب فـالأوّل ايّد الـ ... الإسلميّين وڤوطاوا عليهم⁴ وطلعوا ا ... نجحوا. لكن ا ... مع ا الأخّر⁵ كي بداوا يدوروا على الشّعب فـالقورى ... وهذا مـاشي كلام قريناه فـالجرائد ولاّ سمعناه من ناس صراتلهم هاذ الأشيا.

أ: مـ ....

ب: مثلاً انايا متيقّنه هذا كلام سمعته من ا ... مثلاً بنات كانوا يقراوا معايا فـالمدرسه، صراوا لعامّاتهم⁶ ولخالاتهم اللّي يسكنوا فـالقورى داخل ا ... وسط الجزائر.

أ: مـ ....

ب: فـالأوّل قالّك كانوا يأيّدوا الـ ... الجماعات الإيسلاميّه لمّا بدات كانوا يـ ... كانوا لمّا يتخبّاوا فـالمازارع ولاّ، النّاس اللّي يسكنوا فـهذوك القورى يعطوهم الأكل، يعطوهم ا ....

أ: الدّوا، الحوايج.

ب: الدّوا، الـ ... الحوايج، مـ ... الـ ... بالصّحّ مع الأخّر لـ ... لمّا طوّلت المدّه صبحوا هذوك النّاس اللّي يجوا يطلّبوا الأكل، يطلّبوا اكثر مالأكل، يـ ... ينتهكوا حورومات بناتهم، يد ... ينتهكوا حورومات تاع ا ... نساهم. alors، النّاس داروا عليهم، صبحوا مـا، مـا يقبلوش هاد الشّيّ. وكي داروا عليهم النّاس ولاّوا ا ... يقتلوا في هذوك النّاس بالذّات اللّي كـانوا يساعدوا فـهم⁷ ويعطوهم الأكل والمفروض انّهم مـا يقتلوش النّاس. ا ... بيما انّ الشّعب كان يحسّ انّه الحوكومه كانت تضلموه المفروض ا ... كانوا يأيّدوا الأسلاميّين بـاش يـ ... يـ ... يجاهدوا ضدّ ... كيما يقولوا هوم يجاهدوا يعني يحاربوا ضدّ الحوكومه. لكن اللّي شافوا النّاس انّه ولا واحد فـالحوكومه مـا صراله حتّى حاجه. يعني اللّي مـات غير اللّي كاين يـ ... اللّى مـات من اصحاب الحوكومه غير اللّي هم حبّوا يقتلوه فـالحوكومه نفسها.

155

Vocabulary:

mafia ‏نفس‏ *nfs* mafia

ɣnaa ‏غنى‏ *v* to be or become rich {*imperf:* yəɣnii}

taanii ‏ثاني‏ [*also* θaani] *adv* again; another ; *adj.*

ləṣṣəq ‏لصّق‏ *v* to stick on, attach to, glue on to {*imperf:* iiləṣṣəq}

nta ‏انت‏ *pro* you (2MS)

məm ‏مم‏ [*also* mən; mə] *prep* from, of

bəkrii ‏بكري‏ *adv* earlier; in the old days; at first

ʕaamaar + suffixed pronoun + maa ‏عامار ما‏ never (lit. in s.o.'s life)

tʕarrəḍ ʕlaa ‏تعرّض على‏ *v* to attack, assault {*imperf:* yətʕarrəḍ}

ḥurma ‏حرمه‏ *nfs* woman; honor; that which is sacred or is taboo {*pl:* ḥuuruumaat}

ṭləʕ ‏طلع‏ *v* to rise, go up, ascend {*imperf:* yəṭləʕ}

mʕa llaxxər ‏مع الآخر‏ finally, in the end

daar ʕlaa ‏دار على‏ *v* to turn away from, turn one's back on {*imperf:* iiduur ʕlaa}

qraa ‏قرا‏ *v* to read; to study, get an education {*imperf:* yəqraa}

ṣraa ‏صرى‏ *v* to happen, occur {*imperf:* yəṣraa}

txabbaa ‏تخبّى‏ *v* to hide, conceal oneself {*imperf:* yətxabbaa}

məzraʕ ‏مزرع‏ *nms* planted field; farm {*pl:* maazaariiʕ}

haaduuk ‏هدوك‏ [*also* haaduuka; haaðuuk] *pro* that (P far demonstrative) {*ms:* haadaak, *fs:* haadiik}

duwaa ‏دوا‏ *nms* medication, medicine {*pl:* dwaayaat, *pl:* dwiyya, *pl:* dwaawii}

ḥwaayəj ‏حوايج‏ *np* clothes, clothing

ṣbəḥ ‏صبح‏ *v* to become {*imperf:* yəṣbəḥ}

ntahək ‏انتهك‏ *v* to infringe, violate {*imperf:* yəntahək}

bə-ddaat ‏بالذّات‏ none other than, of all people, of all things

ḍlam ‏ضلم‏ *v* to oppress {*imperf:* yəḍlam}

ḍədd ‏ضد‏ *prep* against

ṣaaḥəb ‏صاحب‏ *nms* follower, adherent; entrusted with; friend {*pl:* ṣḥaab}

mən ṭaraf ‏من طرف‏ on the side of, on the part of

Notes:

1. The verb /yɣanyuu/ 'they sing' is used metaphorically in the phrase /kiimaa yḥabbuu **yɣanyuu**/ 'however they like'. In proverbs and idiomatic expressions, singing describes any kind of carefree behavior unconcerned with the consequences of its actions.

2. The SAA relative pronoun /llii/ does not always have a referent. It does not here, in /**llii** ytḥarrak taanii/ 'whoever else makes a move'. Without a referent, /llii/ is best translated as 'whoever, anyone who, the one who'. The relative pronoun more often occurs with a referent, as in /**nnaas llii** ysknuu fii haaduuk əlquuraa/ 'the people who live in those villages', in this selection.

3. The phrase /ḥuuruumaat taaʕ əlbuyuut/ 'the honor of the house' is a euphemism for the women of the house. The use of /ḥuuruumaat/ to refer to women is clearer later in this selection, as in /yəntahkuu ḥuuruumaat bnaathum/ 'they attacked the honor of their daughters'. The use of physical assault and rape is a common terror tactic in Algeria and elsewhere

4. The female speaker uses the phrase /mʕa lla**xx**ər/ 'in the end' twice in this selection. The doubled /x/ of /a**xx**ər/ appears to take the place of the long vowel /aa/ of the more typical /**aa**xər/. The phrase /mʕa lla**xx**ər/ appears to have been re-analyzed, perhaps by analogy with /fə-llu**ww**əl/ 'in the beginning', also with a double consonant.

5. The two phrases /vooṭaaw ʕleehum/ 'they voted for them' and /bdaaw iiduuruu **ʕlaa** ʃʃaʕb/ 'they turned against them' illustrate two of the possible translations of the preposition /ʕlaa/. It can mean 'for' as well as 'against', among others. Context is the best guide to correct translation.

6. The subject of the verb /ṣraaw/ 'they happened' in the phrase /sraaw l-ʕaamaathum/ 'they happened to their paternal aunts' does not occur in this utterance. It is /haað əlʔaʃyaa/ 'these things' in the preceding utterance. The female speaker underlines the reliability of what she says, stating that /smaʕnaah mən naas **ṣraat**ləhum haað əlʔaʃyaa/ 'we heard it from people these things happened to'. When the verb /ṣraa/ occurs here, in /sraaw l-ʕaamaathum/ 'they happened to their paternal aunts', it is in the 3P form. The second occurrence of the verb, however, suggests that it has the same subject as the first occurrence.

157

7. Two uses of a partive structure occur in /yəqtluu **fii** haaduuk nnaas bə-ddaat llii kaanuu ysaaʕduu **fə**hum/ 'they [began] killing those people, specifically the ones who had been helping them'. The partitive occurs when the preposition /fii/ separates a verb , like /yətluu/ or /iisaaʕduu/, from the direct object. The use of /fii/ implies that the action of the verb took place over a period of time. This structure is found in SAA and certain other varieties of spoken Arabic.

It Is More Than a Question of Islam

A: I mean, I think the matter is not just a matter of Islamists. It is a matter, I think, a matter of the *Mafia* in the army that wanted the country to get into a civil war and muddle everything so they can, I mean, steal and govern however they want. Anyone else who makes a move to say, "This is wrong. You are stealing and doing this thing," they kill him. I mean, they accuse him ... of anything. I mean, they say, "You are an Islamist and you have set off bombs and killed people and you have said ...." And they kill him .... I mean there are a lot of people who don't have any connection at all to the Islamists and they have killed them.

B: In any case, I agree with you that ... the question is a serious one and it is more than a question of Islam or whatever, ah ... But when I look at the government, it's been in power for a long time, ah .... But it never killed people, it never, ah ... not ....

A: You're convinced that it never killed people. I don't think so.

B: No, it killed people, but it didn't attack the honor of the house, it never slaughtered ah ... schools in ... teachers in schools. True, when there is killing by one side ah ... in ... in the ... in the ... in the government itself, we know that no one can ... get at ... those in power unless he is one of them. I mean, from outside it's hard. This, I mean, is the mistake that everyone at the start, why ... And why were people ... they encouraged the Islamists and voted for them so that they came to power? Because they hoped that they ... the struggle that would be, ah ... on the part of the Islamists, it would be against the government, not against the people.... This is the reason, ah ... the ... the people at first supported the Islamists and voted for them. They rose, ah ...the ... they won. But in the end, ah ...

159

when they started turning against the villages .... This is not something we read in the papers or whatever, we heard it from people these things happened to.

A: Mmm ....

B: For example, I am sure. This is a story I heard from ... for example, girls who studied with me in school. It happened to their aunts who live in villages in ... the center of Algeria.

A: Mmm ....

B: At the beginning, they say, they supported ... the Islamic groups when they started would ... they would, when they would hide in the fields or whatever, the people who live in those villages would give them food and give them ....

A: Medicine, clothes.

B: Medicine ... clothes ... The truth is that in the end, ... when things had gone on for a while, the people who came to ask for food started asking for more than food. They attacked the honor of their daughters ... they attacked the honor of ... their wives. *So* people turned against them, they refused to accept this kind of thing. When the people turned against them, they started, ah ... they killed those people, specifically the ones who had been helping them and giving them food. They shouldn't kill people. Given that the people felt the government oppressed them, they should, ah .... They supported the Islamists so ... they would fight against, as they say, they would fight against, I mean, they would make war on the government. But what these people saw is that nothing at all happened to anyone in the government. I mean, anyone who died, there .... The only ones on the government side who died were the ones that those the government itself wanted to kill.

baʕd maa yətxaaṭbuu, waaʃ iidiiruu?

This selection describes wedding preparations in a traditional, non-urban Algerian community. Note that the male speaker's usage differs from that heard previously. Markers of his speech include the regular use of the interdentals / θ/ and /ð/, as well as the possessive adjective /ntaaʕ/.

A: kiimaa ləʕraas ntaaʕnaa[1] durk, ḥattaa lə ... baalaak[2] a ... ḥattaa biidaayt a ... ttəsʕiinaat,[3] ləʕraas ntaaʕnaa a ... tfuut fii a ... ʕabra maraaḥəl. əlbiidaaya ḥnaa ʕadnaa[4] lʕaayla, maθalən umm lʕaariis w-umm lʕaaruus fii muddət əlʕaam baʕd maa yətxaaṭbuu, waaʃ iidiiruu? yəbduu yəḥaḍḍruu lə ... lə-lʕərs ntaaḥḥùm, d-uuliidum. maθalan kiimaa laʕjuuz yəmmaat əṭṭfəl tuujjədluu nguuluu ḥnaa a ... ḥuulii, təsjəhuuluu[5] hiyya iiðaa kaant taʕraf, iiðaa maa kaaʃ[6] taʕṭiih l-əxthaa[7] wə-ʔillaa l-jaarəthaa wə-ʔillaa kaðaa, iidiiruuh fii daar mə-ddyaar. iidiiruu lḥuulii haaðaak mnəssəja, maa yəttʃərəʃ lḥuulii haaðaak, iidiiruuh ɣiir mə-ddaar. wə-kaayn θaanii ḥaaja xraa llii hiya fii lqiiṭaaʕ llii huwa lbərnuuṣ. ḥnaa fə-lʕərs ntaaʕnaa laʕriis laazəm iikuun nhaar lʕərs ntaaʕuu yəlbəs lbərnuuṣ,[8] w-haaðaak lbərnuuṣ maa yəttəʃrəʃ, laazəm taanii kiif kiif iitəxdəm fə-ddaar.

B: ʃuuf.

A: laazəm təxdəm a ... ḷḷaah iixalliik.[9] təxdəmuuluu yəmmaa wəllaa xtuu wə-lmuuhəmm ʕlaa ḥsaab əlʕaayla. hiya lkuθra lʔumm hiya llii təxdəm iiðaa kaant taʕraf, iiðaa maa naʕrafʃ,[10] djiib uxthaa wəllaa jaarəthaa wə-ʔillaa, ʕlaa ḥsaab maa ... ð̣ð̣uruuf ntaaʕum.[11] haaðaak əlbərnuuṣ yəxxədmuuh haaðaa qbəl lʕərs, baʕd maa tə ... tətʕiyyən lxuuṭuuba w-kull ʃii iiwəjjduuluu haað əlʔaʃyaa haaðiyaa. əlbənt mən jiihəthaa baʕd nguuluu ḥnaa maa tnəxṭab,[12] waaʃ iidiiruu? əl ... lʔumm ntaaḥḥaa təbdaa tuujjədəlhaa llowaazəm ntaaḥḥaa, maθalən ḥattaa yəddiilhaa[13] ḥuulii, yəddiilhaa nguuluu ḥnaa zuuj a ... a ... kiimaa ḥnaa nsəmmuuhum mṭaaraaḥ.

162

بعد ما يتخاطبو،ا واش يديروا؟

أ: كيما الأعراس نتاعنا درك[1]، حتّى الـ ... بالاك[2] ا ... حتّى بيداية ا ... التّسعينات،[3] الأعراس نتاعنا ... تفوت في ا ... عبر مراحل. البيدايه احنا عندنا[4] العايله، مثلاً امّ العاريس وامّ العاروس في مدة العام بعد ما يتخاطبوا، واش يديروا؟ يبدوا يحضّروا الـ ... للعرس نتاعهم، دوليدهم، مثلاً كيما العاجوز يمّاة الطّفل توجّدوله نقولوا احنا ا ... حولي تنسّجوله[5] هيّ إيذا كانت تعرف، إيذا ما كاش[6] تعطيه لأختها[7] وإيلّا لجارتها وإيلّا كذا، يديروه في دار مالدّيار. يديروا الحولي هذاك منسّجه، ما يتّشريش الحولي هذاك، يديروه غير مالدّار. وكاين تاني حاجه اخرى اللّي هي في القيطاع اللّي هو البرنوص. احنا فالعرس نتاعنا العاريس لازم يكون نهار العرس نتاعه يلبس البرنوص،[8] وهذاك البرنوص ما يتّشريش، لازم تاني كيف كيف يتخدم فالدّار.

ب: شوف.

أ: لازم تخدم ا ... اللّه يخلّيك.[9] تخدمولوه يمّاه ولاّ اختـه والموهمّ على حساب العايله هي الكثره الأمّ هي اللّي تخدم إيذا كانت تعرف، إيذا ما نعرفش،[10] تجيب اختها ولاّ جارتها وإلا، على حساب ما ... الظّروف نتاعهم.[11] هذاك البرنوص يخّدموه هذا قبل العرس، بعد ما تـ ... تتعيّن الخوطوبه وكلّ شي يوجّدوله هاذ الأشيا هذيا. البنت من جيهتها بعد نقولوا احنا ما تنخطب،[12] واش يديروا؟ الـ ... الأمّ نتاعها تبدا توجّدلها اللّوازم نتاعها، مثلاً حتّى يدّيلها[13] حولي، يدّيلها نقولوا احنا زوج ا ... ا ... كيما احنا نسمّوهم مطاراح.

163

B: ṣaḥḥ.

A: waaqiilaatən durk ndiiruu mṭaaraaḥ.

B: ḥnaa taanii nguuluu mṭaaraaḥ.

A: mṭaaraaḥ a ... zuuj, arbaʕa, ʕlaa ḥsaab mməqdaar taaʕ əlʕaayla wə-ʕlaa
ḥsaab əl ... lə ... lʔimkaaniyyaat ntaaḥḥaa, a ... tuujjədhaa nguuluu
ḥnaa luusaayəd haaðiik əlʔuumuur taaʕ əṣṣanduu ... wəllaa taʕrfuu baalaak
a ... kull manṭiiqa muujuuda fiihaa wsaayəd wə-mṭaaraaḥ a ... a ...
zzarbiyya haaðii taanii fə-lqiiṭaaʕ liiʔanna zzarbiyya ḥaaja aasaasiyya a
... wə-zzarbiyya fə-lɣaalb tkuun maxduuma maa ttəʃərəʃ taanii kiimaa
taaʕ əlraajul, maa yəʃruuhaaʃ, haaðiik laazəm iixadmuuhaa. təxdəmhaa
nguuluu ḥnaa yəmmaahaa fii muddat alxuṭuuba haaðiik, laazəm
təxxədəmhaalhaa, *soit* hiyya w-uxuu ... *soit* lbənt təxdəmhaa mʕa
ṣḥaabaathaa.

B: iih.

A: maθalən taʕrəḍ ṣḥaabaathaa kull yoom iijuu yxədmuu[14] saaʕteen wəllaa
θlaaθa fə-zzarbiyya.

B: iih.

A: wə-ʔillaa əlʔumm mʕa ḥbaabaathaa wə-xwaataathaa, yətʕaa ...
yətʕaawnuu fə-zzarbiyya haaðiik bəʃ iixədmuuhaa, xaaṭ zzarbiyya ṭṭowwəl
baʕd maa yəʃruu ṣṣuuf wə-kull ʃii, fiihaa xədma ṭṭowwəl ʃwiyya wə-ʕlaa
haaðaa yətʕaawnuu ʕleehaa baaʃ iiwəjjduuhaa. w-fii nəfs əlwəqt taanii
twujjəd aʃyaaʔ uuxraa xaaṣṣa biihaa, a ... mə ... təʃrii nguuluu ḥnaa
zzuwaar llaazmiin. haaðuuk əlḥwaayj llaazmiin taaʕ əl ... lə ... llii
təddiihum kull ʕaaruusa mʕaahaa.

ب: صحّ.

أ: واقيلةً درك نديروا مطاراح.

ب: احنا تاني نقولوا مطاراح.

أ: مطاراح ا ... زوج، اربعه، على حساب المّقدار تاع العايله وعلى حساب الـ
... الـ ... الامكانيّات نتاعها، ا ... توجّدها نقولوا احنا الوسايد هذيك
الأومور تاع الصّندو ... ولاّ تعرفوا بالاك ا ... كلّ منطيقه موجوده فيها
وساید ومطاراح ا ...ا ... الزّربيّه هذي تاني فالقيطاع لـين الزّربيّه
حاجه آساسيّه ا ... والزّربيّه فالغالب تكون مخدومه ما تّشريش تاني
كيما تاع الراجل، ما يشروهاش، هذيك لازم يخدموها. تخدمها نقولوا
احنا يمّاها في مدّة الخطوبه هذيك، soit لازم تخّدمهالها، هيّ واخو ...
soit البنت تخدمها مع صحاباتها.

ب: ايه.

أ: مثلاً تعرض صحاباتها كلّ يوم يجوا يخدموا[14] ساعتين ولاّ ثلاثه
فالزّربيّه.

ب: ايه.

أ: وإلاّ الأمّ مع حباباتها وأخواتاتها، يتاعا ... يتعاونوا فالزّربيّه هذيك
باش يخدموها، خاط الزّربيّه تطوّل بعد ما يشروا الصّوف وكلّ شي،
فيها خدمه تطوّل شويّه وعلى هذا يتعاونوا عليها باش يوجّدوها. وفي
نفس الوقت تاني توجّد اشياء اخرى خاصّه بيها، ا ... مـ ... تشري
نقولوا احنا الزّوّار اللاّزمين. هذوك الحوايج اللاّزمين تاع الـ ... الـ ...
اللّي تدّيهم كلّ عاروسه معها.

165

Vocabulary:

ʕarṣ عرس *nms* wedding party, wedding fesitivities {*pl:* aʕraas}

ntaaʕ نتاع [*also* taaʕ] *possessive adj; invariable* of, belonging to

baalaak بالاك *adv* maybe, perhaps; about, approximately

təsʕiinaat تسعينات *np* nineties

faat فات *v* to pass, elapse (of events, time) {*imperf:* iifuut}

ʕad + suffixed pronoun عند [*also* ʕand; ʕan] *prep* to have

txaaṭəb تخاطب *v* to become engaged (to be married to one another) {*imperf:* yətxaaṭəb}

ntaah- + suffixed pronoun with initial /h/ نتاح [*also* ntaaʕ] *possessive adj; invariable* of, belonging to

d- د *part.* of, belonging to

uuliid وليد [*also* wliid] *nms* child {*pl:* uuliidaat}

ʕaajuuz عاجوز *nfs* mother of the bridegroom; old woman {*pl:* ʕjaayəz}

ṭfəl طفل *nms* child {*fs:* ṭəfla, *pl:* ṭfaal}

ḥuulii حولي *nms* blanket, coverlet {*pl:* ḥwaalii}

maa kaanʃ ما كانش [*also* maa kaanʃ] he is not, she is not, it is not; there was not, there were not

əxt اخت *nfs* sister {*fpl:* xwaataat}

wə-ʔillaa والاّ [*also* wəllaa] *part.* or something like that, or whatever (at end of sequence)

mnəssəj منسّج *adj* woven

ətʃraa اتشرى *v* to be bought {*imperf:* yətʃraa}

qiiṭaaʕ قيطاع *nms* segment, section {*pl:* qiiṭaaʕaat}

bərnuuṣ برنوص *nms* burnous {*pl:* braanəṣ}

kiif kiif كيف كيف just alike, the same

txədəm اتخدم *v* to be made, done, worked {*imperf:* yətxədəm}

ʃuuf شوف *interj* really, my goodness

ḷḷaah iixallii- الله يخلّي thank you (lit. may God keep s.o.)

166

xdəm خدم *v* to weave; to do, make; to plant, cultivate, grow {*imperf:* yəxdəm}

ſlaa ḥsaab على حساب according to

lkuθra الكثره *nfs* mostly (lit. the majority)

mən jiiha من جيهه on the one hand; as for, as to (lit. from a side)

nxəṭab انخطب *v* to get engaged (to be married) {*pl:* yənxaṭab}

waaʃ واش [*also* wəʃ] *interrog* what

laazma لازمه *nfs* necessary thing, requisite {*pl:* lwaazəm}

maṭraḥ مطرح *nms* mattress {*pl:* mṭaaraḥ}

waaqiilaatən واقيلاة [*also* waaqiil] *disc* maybe, perhaps; apparently

uusaada وساده [*also* wsaada] *nfs* pillow {*pl:* uusaayəd}

zarbiya زربيه *nfs* carpet, rug {*pl:* zraabii}

fə-lɣaaləb فالغالب in general, mostly

məxduum مخدوم *adj* woven; made, done {*fs:* məxduuma, *pl:* məxduumiin}
soit ... soit ... *conj* either ... or

ṣaaḥba صاحبه *nfs* female friend {*fpl:* ṣhaabaat, *fpl:* ṣaaḥbaat}

ſrəḍ عرض *v* to invite {*imperf:* yaſraḍ}

θlaaθa ثلاثه [*also* tlaata; tlət; θəlθ] *nfs* three

ḥbiiba حبيبه *nfs* female friend; female relative {*pl:* ḥbaabaat, *fpl:* ḥbiibaat}

xaaṭ خاط [*also* xaaṭʃ; xaaṭʃii; xaaṭər] *conj* because, due to the fact that

ṭowwəl طوّل *v* to take, require a long time {*imperf:* iiṭowwəl}

zaawra زاوره *nfs* bedcover, bedspread, blanket {*pl:* zaawraat, *pl:* zwaar}

Notes:

1. The form /ntaaſ/ in the phrase /ləſraas ntaaſnaa/ 'our weddings' is another possible form for the possessive adjective in SAA. Other forms have occurred earlier in this work, including /taaſ/ (Selection 1) and /dyaal/ (Selection 7). Another variant of /ntaaſ/ occurs in SAA. It is /mtaaſ/, which does not occur in this work.

2. The male speaker here uses the form /baalak/ 'you (ms) know' in the same way that other speakers use /yaſnii/ 'I mean, lit. it (ms) means'. It is a kind

of linguistic filler that holds the speaker's turn as he hesitates in his speech or puts some linguistic distance between himself and what he is saying.

3. The male speaker describe wedding practices as changes after /biidaayt a ... ttəʕiinaat/ 'the beginning, ah ... of the nineties'. The events he alludes to began shortly before the 1991 elections, after which the military dissolved the parliament dominated by the FIS and civil war began. The economic situation in Algeria, in decline since the fall of oil prices in 1986, played a part in discouraging wedding festivities. Escalating violence, however, made large-scale gatherings and travelling to these gatherings dangerous.

4. The form /ʕadnaa/ 'we have' is a variant of /ʕandnaa/. In this variant, the /n/ of /ʕand/ drops out, perhaps under pressure from the /n/ of the 1P suffixed pronoun /naa/. It tends to occur in rapid or casual speech.

5. The form /təsjəhuuluu/ 'she weaves it for him' is a slip of the tongue for /tnəsjəhuuluu/ Slips like these are more noticeable on the written page than they are in the stream of speech.

6. The phrase /maa kaaʃ/ means 'she was not' as well as 'he was not', 'it was not' and 'they (fp) were not'. That is, /maa kaaʃ/ negates /kaan/ 'he was' and /kaanət/ 'she was'. This form tends to occur in rapid or casual speech. Slower or more formal speech has /maa kaanʃ/ 'he was not' or /maa kaanətʃ/ 'she was not'.

As seen in Selection 9, /maa kaaʃ/ can also negate /kaayən/ 'there is; there are'. It is, thus, a variant of /maa kaayənʃ/. This kind of fusion, in which one item stands in for others that are not obviously related in sound or meaning, is unusual in SAA.

7. The statement /təsjəhuuluu hiyya ʔiiðaa kaant taʕraf, ʔiiðaa maa kaaʃ taʕṭiih l-əxthaa/ 'She weaves it for him herself if she knows how, if not she gives it to her sister' contains two examples of factual conditional sentences. These are conditional sentences that describe (or predict) actual events. The two examples are /təsjəhuuluu hiyya ʔiiðaa kaant taʕraf/ 'she weaves it for him herself if she knows how', where the result clause comes before the condition clause, and /ʔiiðaa maa kaaʃ taʕṭiih l-əxthaa/ 'if she doesn't, she gives it to her sister', with more typical clause order.

Note that the verb of the condition clause (the "if" clause) is usually perfect, as in these examples. There are no restrictions on the verb of the result clause (the "then" clause). It takes the form that fits the time frame of the result.

8. The phrase /iikuun nhaar lʕɘrs ntaaʕuu ylbɘs lbɘrnuuṣ/ 'he should wear a burnous on the day of his wedding' illustrates one of the uses of the imperfect of /kaan/. The imperfect of /kaan/ precedes another imperfect (here /ylbɘs/ 'he wears'). It adds the sense of 'should, ought to' to the main verb.

In this context, the male speaker uses two structures with the same meaning, in /laʕriis **laazɘm iikuun** nhaar lʕɘrs ntaaʕuu yɘlbɘs lbɘrnuuṣ/ 'the groom has to wear a burnous on the day of his wedding'. The combination of /laazɘm/ and the imperfect of /kaan/ in the same verb phrase is not typical. This speaker, however, makes frequent use of synonymous pairs in his speech.

9. It is not clear why the male speaker interrupts himself to say /ḷḷaah iixalliik/ 'thank you, lit. may God keep you safe.' This phrase is usually used to express the speaker's thanks for a favor. Note that speakers of SAA and other varieties of spoken Arabic use a number of different expressions to mean "thank you".

10. The phrase /maa naʕrafʃ/ 'I don't know' is clearly a slip of the tongue. The speaker would not mean to refer to himself when he says /iiðaa kaant taʕraf, ʔiiðaa **maa naʕrafʃ**,[10] djiib ʔuxthaa/ 'if she knows, if I don't, she brings her sister'. In context, the slip is easy to understand and to ignore.

11. The form /um/ for the 3P suffixed pronoun, as here in /ntaaʕum/ 'belong to them', is not typical in SAA. This suffixed pronoun usually has an initial /h/, as in /ntaaʕhum/ or an initial /h/ that through assimilation becomes /ḥ/, as in /ntaaḥḥum/.

12. The phrase /nguuluu ḥnaa/ 'as we say' breaks up the conjunctive /baʕd maa/ in the phrase /**baʕd** nguuluu ḥnaa **maa** tnɘxṭab/ 'after, as we say, she gets engaged'. This would be unlikely in written Arabic. Spoken Arabic can be more flexible.

13. The verb /ddaa/ - /yɘddii/, as in /ḥattaa **yɘddiilhaa** ḥuulii/ 'to give her a houli' can be translated 'to give' and 'to take'. The sense of 'to give' often occurs, as here, with the indirect object marker /l/. The sense of 'to take' is illustrated at the end of this selection, in /llii **tɘddii**hum kull ʕaruus mʕaahaa/ 'what every bride takes with her'.

14. In the phrase /iijuu yɘxɘdmuu/ 'they come to work', the verb /oojuu/ 'they come' is a pre-verb. In verb strings like this, the action of the main verb is the reason for that of the verb of motion. In other words, the relationship between the two verbs can be translated as 'to, in order to'.

After They Get Engaged, What Do They Do?

A: As our weddings now, until ... I mean ... until the beginning, ah ... of the nineties our weddings, ah ... they go in, ah ... through stages. At the beginning, we have the family. For example, the mother of the bride and the mother of the groom during the year after they get engaged, what do they do? They begin preparing for .... for their wedding, of their children. For example, like the mother-in-law, the boy's mother, prepares him what we call, ah ... a <u>houli</u>. She weaves it for him herself if she knows how, if not she gives it to her sister or her neighbor or whatever. They do it in one of the houses. They make the <u>houli</u> by weaving. This <u>houli</u> is never bought, they only make it at home. There is something else that is found in the region which is the burnous. At our weddings, the groom has to wear a <u>burnous</u> on the day of his wedding. This <u>burnous</u> cannot be bought, it also in the same way has to be made at home.

B: Really.

A: She has to do, ah .... Thank you. His mother or his sister makes it for him. The point is, it depends on the family. Most of the time, the mother is the one who does it, if she knows, if I don't know [sic], she gets her sister or her neighbor or whatever, depending on what ... their situation. They make this <u>burnous</u> before the wedding, after ... the engagement is set. They prepare all of these things. On the girl's part, after as we say she gets engaged, what do they do? Her mother starts preparing the things she needs. For example, she also gives her a <u>houli</u>, she gives her what we call two, ah ... ah ... as we say, <u>mtarah</u>.

B: Right.

A: Perhaps now we make <u>mtarah</u>.

B: We call them <u>mtarah</u>, too

A: <u>Mtarah</u>, ah ... two, four, depending on the scope of the family and on the ... their possibilities. Ah .... She prepares her what we call pillows. These things belong in .... Or you know, ah ... every region has pillows, <u>mtarah</u>, ah ... ah ... the rug. This is also found in the region because this rug is essential, ah .... The rug mostly should be made, it can't be bought, just like the ... the man's. They don't buy it, they have to make it for her. As we say, her mother makes it during the engagement. She has to make it for her. *Either* her and ... *or* the girl makes it with her friends.

B: Yes.

A: For example, she invites her friends. Every day they come to work for two or three hours on the rug.

B: Yes.

A: Or her mother, with her friends and her sisters they ... they work together on this rug to make it, because a rug takes time. After they buy the wool and everything, the work on it takes kind of a long time. So they work together on it to get it ready. At the same time other things are specially prepared for her. Ah ... she buys what we call the <u>zwar</u> that are necessary. These things are necessary for ... the ... the ... which every bride brings with her ....

fə-lliilla haaðiik laazəm iiḥənnuu

The custom of henna decoration described in this selection, is widespread. Less typical, however, is for the wedding party to pay a visit to the saint or saints of the region.

A: ḥnaa ʕadnaa waaḥd əlʕaadaat a ... hiyya ḥaaqiiqa fə-ddiin maahiiʃ məqbuula.[1] naqdər nquullək fə-ddiin maaʃii məqbuula w-baalaak ḥattaa fə-lmanṭəqa məʃ məqbuula. waaʃ ndiiruu? kii lʕiriis, kii lʕaaruus ... fii ðaak ... əlliila haaðiik, əlʕaaʃiyya, baʕd maa yətʕəʃʃaaw,[2] iijuu ahl lʕaariis w-maa ... mən mʕaahum, kii yjuu waaḥədhum muuʃ ləkbaar nguuluu ḥnaa yaʕnii mṣaaɣar wə-kulləʃ wə-nnsaawiin kiif kiif. yədduuhum bə-ṭṭəbəl bə ... bə-lməzwəd haaðaak, ḥnaa ...

B: [xxx] eeh.

A: nsəmmuuh, ḥnaa nsəmmuuhaa ʃʃəkwa wə-hnaayaa ysəmmuuhaa lməzwəd[3] wə-ʔillaa bə ... bə-zzurna, ḥnaa nsəmmuuhaa lɣayṭa, lɣayṭa, ʕlaa ḥsaab əmta ... w-laakən duuka fə-lɣaalb ʕaad duuka b-kəθra ʕaad kaayn a ... lməzwəd *parce que* lməzwəd xfiif w-maa ytəʕʕabʃ w-kulləʃ. yədduuhum bə-lməzwəd wə-ṭṭbəl wə-kaðaa, wə-nnsaawiin hum yəʃṭḥuu mənhee wə-rrjaal yəʃṭḥuu mənnaa, faariiq mənnaa w-faariiq mənnaa w-raayḥiin. wiin iiruuḥuu? ʕadnaa wulyaa, haaðaa kiimaa ysəmmuuhum lwulyaa ṣṣaalḥiin,[4] haaðuuk iiruuḥuu, laazəm fə-lliila haaðiik laazəm iiruuḥuu yəḥənnuu, laazəm iiruuḥuu yḥənnuu fə-lliila haaðiik. fə-lliila muuʃ fə-nnhaar, fə-lliila haaðiik laazəm iiḥənnuu, iiruuḥuu ... kaayn wulyaa mə ... maʕruufiin iiruuḥuu θəmmaa[5] yəḥənnuu fiih wə-ḥnaa, maθalən lə ... lʕaarʃ ntaaʕnaa ʕadnaa a ... əlwaalii llii yruuḥuuluu siidii mə ... siidii ʕliyyaa, haaðaa laazəm ənnaas lkull iiruuḥuuluu wə-laazəm iiḥənnuu fiih, iiguuluu waalii siidii ʕliyyaa wə-kaayən waalii waaḥəd aaxər iiguuluu siidii mḥamməd ləkbiir. haaðaa fə-lyoom əlʔawwəl,[6] wə-laazəm iiruuḥuu θəmmaa w-laazəm iiḥənnuu. wə-ʃkuun llii yḥənnii lʕaariis wə-lʕaaruusa?

فاللّيله هذيك لازم يحنّوا

أ: احنا عندنا واحده العادات ا ... هيّ حاقيقه فالدّين ماهيش مقبوله.[1]
نقدر نقالّك فالدّين ماشي مقبوله وبالاك حتّى فالمنطقه ماش مقبوله.
واش نديروا؟ كي العاريس، كي العاروس ... في ذاك ... اللّيله هذيك،
العاشيّه، بعد ما يتعشّاوا،[2] يجيوا اهل العاريس وما ... من معهم، كي
يجوا واحدهم مهوش الكبار نقولوا احنا يعني مصاغر وكلّش
والنّساوين كيف كيف. يدّوهم بالطّبل بـ ... بالمزود هذاك، احنا ...

ب: [xxx] ايه.

أ: نسمّوه، احنا نسمّوها الشّكوه وهنايا يسمّوها المزود[3] وإلاّ بـ ... بالزّرنه،
احنا نسمّوها الغيطه، الغيطه، على حساب امتــ ... ولكن دوك فالغالب
عاد دوك بكثره عاد كان ا ... المزود parce que المزود خفيف وما يتعّبش
وكلّش. يدّوهم بالمزود والطّبل وكذا، والنّساوين هم يشطحوا منهي
والرّجال يشطحوا منّا، فاريق منّا وفاريق منّا ورايحين. وين يروحوا؟
عندنا وليا، هذا كيما يسمّوهم الوليا الصّالحين،[4] هذوك يروحوا، لازم
فاللّيله هذيك لازم يروحوا يحنّوا، لازم يروحوا يحنّوا فاللّيله هذيك.
في اللّيله موش فالنّهار، فاللّيله هذيك لازم يحنّوا، يروحوا ... كاين وليا
مــ ... معروفين يروحوا ثمّا[5] يحنّوا فيه واحنا، مثلاً الـ ... العارش
نتاعنا عدنا .... الوالي اللّي يروحوله سيدي مــ ... سيدي عليّا، هذا لازم
النّاس الكلّ يروحوله ولازم يحنّوا فيه، يقولوه والي سيدي عليّا وكاين
والي واحد اخر يقولوه سيدي محمّد الكبير. هذا فاليوم الأوّل،[6] ولازم
يروحوا ثمّا ولازم يحنّوا. وشكون اللّي يحنّي العاريس والعاروسه؟

173

akbar waaḥda fə-lʕaaʔiila, yaa lʕəmma, yaa ljədda yaa ... lmuuhəmm llii maa zaalt kbiira hiyya llii tə ... tḥənniilhum baaʃ yətbərrkuu biihaa wə-ḥnaa .... lbaaraaka ntaaḥḥaa təbqaa fii yoomuu w-təbqaa maa, maaʃ iiṭuul.[7] wə-haaðaa baʕd maa tə ... yəlbəs lʕaaruus wə-kulləʃ. iiðən, iiruuḥuu yəḥənnuu w-iiʕaawduu yərjʕuu lə-dyaarhum.

اكبر واحده فالعائليه، يا العمّه يا الجدّه يا ... الموهمّ اللّي ما زالت كبيره
هيّ اللّي تـ ... تحنّيلهم باش يتبرّكوا بيها واحنا ... الباراكه نتاعها
تبقى في يومه وتبقى ما، ماشي يطول،[7] وهذا بعد ما تـ ... يلبس
العاروس وكلّش. إيذًا، يروحوا يحنّوا ويعاودوا، يرجعوا لديارهم.

Vocabulary:

ḥaaqiiqa حاقيقه *disc* actually, in fact (lit. reality)

ḥənnaa حنّى *v* to apply henna {*imperf:* iiḥənnii}

diin دين *nms* religion (specifically Islam) {*pl:* dyaan, *pl:* dyaanaat}

kii كي *conj* like, as; when, whenever

kii ... kii كي ... كي *conj* the same for ... as for ...

məṣyar مصـغر *nms* young person; bull calf {*pl:* mṣaayar}

mraa مراه *nfs* woman {*fpl:* nsaawiin, *fpl:* nsaa}

ṭəbəl طبـل *nms* drum {*pl:* ṭbuul}

məzwəd مزود *nms* mezoued (kind of bagpipe) {*pl:* mzaawəd}

ʃəkwa شكوه *nfs* chekoua (kind of bagpipe) {*pl:* ʃəkwaat}

hnaayaa هنايا [*also* hnaa] *adv* here

zurna زرنه *nfs* zurna (kind of reed instrument) {*pl:* zurnaat}

ɣaayṭa غايطـه *nfs* ghayta (kind of reed instrument) {*pl:* ɣwaayəṭ}

duuka دوك [*also* durk; duuk; durka] *adv* now

ʕaad عاد *adv* just now, only now

parce que conj because

təʕʕab تعّب *v* to tire out, make tired, fatigue {*imperf:* iitəʕʕab}

ʃṭəḥ شطح *v* to dance {*imperf:* yəʃṭəḥ}

mənhee منهي *adv* there, over there

waalii والي *nms* holy person; saint (in Islamic context) {*pl:* wulyaa}

mənnaa منّا *adv* from here; over here; beginning now, from now

θəmmaa ثمّا [*also* təmma; tsəmma; səmmaa] *adv* there, over there

Selection 16

ʕarʃ عرش [also ʕaarʃ] *nms* tribe; throne {*pl:* ʕraaʃ}

siidii سيدي *nms* Sidi (title before name of Muslim male saints); Mr., sir (respectful term of adddress to adult males)

tbərrək تبرّك *v* to be blessed, receive a blessing from {*imperf:* yətbərrək}

Notes:

1. It is unclear what the male speaker means when he notes that certain customs are /fə-ddiin maahiiʃ məqbuula/ 'unacceptable in Islam'. It may be that he is referring to mixed-sex dancing. Note that he is careful to point out that women and men dancę separately. There are those, who feel that dancing in mixed company is not appropriate. The speaker may also be referring to the custom of visiting the saints. This is a significant popular practice but is frowned on in stricter circles.

2. The meal referred to here is the traditional wedding feast. It is described in the previous selection, Selection 16.

3. Note that the speaker supplies two names for this reed instrument. He calls it <u>mezoued</u> and <u>chekoua</u>. He does the same for the bagpipes, calling them <u>γayta</u> and <u>zurna</u>. In each case, he is careful to point out the differences between the two names. One is the term used in his region. The other is used in other areas of Algeria.

4. The persons called /lwulyaa ṣṣaalḥiin/ or simply /lwulyaa/ are usually referred to in English as 'saints'. The veneration of saints is a popular practice and institutional Islam may disapprove of it. In spite of this disapproval, people make visits to the shrine or tomb of a local holy person as described here. They do so to share in the <u>baraka</u> 'divine blessing, divine grace' granted to the saint by God.

5. The form /θəmmaa/ 'there' is an alternative to /hnaak/.

6. The events described here, as well as the wedding feast, take place on /lyoom əlʔawwəl/ 'the first day'. As noted in the previous selection, Selection 16, wedding festivities in the male speaker's home region used to last a week or more.

7. The phrase /maaʃ iiṭuul/ 'it doesn't last' is apparently a slip of the tongue. The negative /maaʃ/ negates non-verbal structures. The more usual form for this phrase is /maa yṭuulʃ/.

176

On That Night They Have to Go for Henna

A: We have some customs, ah ... they are in fact, unacceptable in Islam. I can tell you that according to Islam they are unacceptable, and maybe they are unacceptable even in our region. What do we do? When the bride, when the groom ... on that night, in the evening, after they eat, the groom's family comes and ... whoever is with them. When they come by themselves, not the older people, we call them, I mean, "youngsters" and all that, and the women, too. They take them with drums, with ... with the mezoued. We ....

B: Yes.

A: We call it, we call it the chekoua and here they call it the mezoued or with ... with the zurna. We call it a ghayta a ghayta, according to the ... But now mostly, now only now mostly, there is only, ah ... the mezoued because the mezoued is light, it is not tiring and all that. They take them with the mezoued and the drum and such. The women dance on one side and the men dance on the other, one group here and one group here, as they go off. Where do they go? We have saints, they are as we call them "the pious saints." These people, they go, on that night they have to, they have to go for henna, they have to go for henna on this night. At night and not during the day, that night, they have to go .... There are saints ... who are well-known, they go there for henna. We, for example, ... our tribe has, ah ... the saint to whom we go, Sidi ... Sidi 'Aliyya. Everyone has to go to, to this guy and they have to get henna there. They call him Sidi 'Aliyya. There is another saint whom they call Sidi Muhammad al-Kabir. This is on the first day, and they have to go there and they have to get henna. Who puts henna on the bride and groom? The oldest woman in the family, either the paternal aunt or the grandmother or .... The point is that someone who

177

is old, she is the one who ... she applies henna for them so they get a blessing from it. We ... The blessing lasts for that day, it lasts, it doesn't last long. This is after the ... the groom gets dressed and all. So they go and get henna, and they go back home again.

qbəl maa nəbdaaw lʕərs fiih ʕaadaat mahalliyya

The description of the wedding continues with this selection. The male speaker is careful to list the foods considered necessary to the celebration and to give the names by which they are known in his community.

A: fii nafs əlwoqt, kii yqarrəb ... təbqaa mudda qliila lə-lʕərs, ṭabʕan əl ... nguuluu ḥnaa lʕaariis, nguuluu ḥnaa lə ... baabaat lʕaariis wə-kəðaa, iiwəjjduu lʔuumuur taaʕ lə ... taaʕ əlʕars llii hiya, nguuluu ḥnaa yəfətluu bərbuuʃa,[1] ḥnaa nsəmmuuhaa lbərbuuʃa.

B: eeh.

A: yəftluu lbərbuuʃa illii huuma nə ... lmənṭiiqa ....

B: lbərbuuʃa [xxx].

A: ḥnaa ....

B: nnaʕma taaʕnaa.

A: ən ... ənnaʕma llii ysəmmuuhaa ḥnaa fə-lmənṭiiqa ṭṭʕaam.

B: ṭṭʕaam.

قبـل مـا نبـداوا العرس فيـه عادات محلّيّه

أ: في نـفـس الوقت، كي يقـرّب ... تبـقى مـدّه قليله للعـرس، طبـعًـا ال ...
نقولوا احنا العاريس، نقولوا احنا الـ ... بابات العاريس وكذا، يوجّدوا
الأومـور تاع الـ ...تاع العـرس اللّي هي ... نقـولوا احنا يفـتلوا
البربوشه،1 احنا نسمّوها البربوشه.

ب: ايه.

أ: يفتلوا البربوشه اللّي هم نـ ... المنطيقه ....

ب: البربوشه [xxx].

أ: احنا ....

ب: النّعمه تاعنا.

أ: نـ ... لنّعمه اللّي يسمّوها احنا فالمنطيقه الطّعام.

ب: الطّعام.

A: haaðii lbərbuuʃa ywəjjduuhaa ʕlaa ḥsaab əlʕaayla ywəjjduu qunṭaar
   wə-ʔillaa θneen wə-ʔillaa ʃʃee llii yqadruu ʕleeh ʕlaa ḥsaab əl ... lə ...
   lkaaθaafa taaʕ əlʕaayla. wə-ḥnaa fə-lɣaalb yə ... maa kaaʃ aqall mən
   juuz qnaaṭər,[2] liiʔanna lʕaayla sə ... kibiira wə-fə-lʕərs iijuu lə ... lə ...
   lə ... lə ... əl ... wəḥnaa lɣaaʃii kiimaa nsəmmuuh bə-lmənṭiiqa, ḥnaa
   nsammuuh lɣaaʃii. lɣaaʃii bəzzaaf wə-ʕlaa haaðaa ywəjjduu lə ... nnaʕma
   bəzzaaf, [burp] zaaʔəd uumuur uuxraa,[3] ḥaalaawiyyaat wə-ɣeerhaa. haaðiik
   llii ywəjjduuhaa, ywəjjduu lʔuumuur llaazma. iiðan ənnhaar llii yəlḥaq
   lʕərs yəðḥarlii a ... tkuun a ... lʔuumuur haaðii kull waajda. [tongue
   click] nəbdaaw məθələn b-kiifiit lʕərs,[4] awwələn a ... qbəl maa nəbdaaw
   lʕərs a ... fiih ʕaadaat maḥalliyya, haaðiik əlʕaadaat wəʃnuu hiyya? əl
   ...awwalan nʕarḍuu lʔaahaalii bə-ṣiifa rasmiyya. maθalən lbənt, lʕaaruusa
   ta...taʕrəḍ ... nguuluu ḥnaa ḥannhaa w-kulləʃ. wə-lʕaariis yaʕnii yəmmaat
   əlʕaariis taʕrəḍ iigaal fiih. 'bnuu fuulaan raahii ndiiruu lʕurs.'

B: ṣaḥḥ.

A: iiðan əl ... baaʃ əʃʃaʕb iikuun lkull ʕalaa baaluu, yaʕnii ... .

B: heeh.

A: nnaas kull lɣaaʃii lkull iikuun ʕalaa baaluu. yaḥḍruu nhaar lʕərs wə-kull
   ʃii θəmmaa a ... taṣbaḥ lʔuumuur rəsmiyya. lʕurs haaðaa taaʕnaa kiifaaʃ
   iitəmm? awwalan a ... fə-lɣaaləb ḥnaa bəkrii ... duuka yənqəṣṣ fə ...
   bəkrii lʕərs ntaaʕnaa maa yqəlləʃ ʕalaa uusbuuʕ, sə ... ʕlaa smaana.

B: ʕlaa smaana.

182

أ: هذي البربوشه يوجّدوها على حساب العايله، يوجّدوا قنطار وإلّا اثنين وإلّا الشّي اللّي يقدروا عليه على حساب الـ ... الـ ... الكاثافه تاع العايله. واحنا فالغالب يـ ... ما كاش اقالّ من جوز قناطر،[2] لينّ العايله سـ ... كبيره وفالعرس يجوا الـ ... الـ ... الـ ... الـ ... الـ ... واحنا الغاشي كيما نسمّوه بالمنطيقه، احنا نسمّوه الغاشي. الغاشي بزّاف وعلى هذا يوجّدوا الـ ... النّعمه بزّاف، [burp] زائد اومور اوخرى،[3] حالاويّات وغيرها. هذيك اللّي يوجّدوها، يوجّدوا الاومور اللّازمه. إيذًا النّهار اللّي يلحق العرس يظهرلي ا ... تكون ا ... الأومور هذي كلّ واجده. [tongue click] نبداوا مثلاً بكيفية[4] العرس، اوّلاً ا ... قبل ما نبداوا العرس ا ... فيه عادات محلّيّه، هذيك العادات واشنه هيّ؟ الـ ... أوّلاً نعرضوا الآهالي بصيفه رسميّه. مثلاً البنت، العاروسه تـ ... تعرض ... نقولوا احنا حنّها وكلّش. والعاريس يعني يمّات العاريس تعرض يقال فيه «بنو فولان راهي نديروا العرس.»

ب: صحّ.

أ: إيذًا الـ ... باش الشّعب يكون الكلّ على باله، يعني....

ب: هيه.

أ: النّاس كلّ الغاشي الكلّ يكون على باله. يحظروا نهار العرس وكلّ شي ثمّا ا ... تصبح الومور رسميّه. العرس هذا تاعنا كيفاش يتمّ؟ اوّلاً ا ... فالغالب احنا بكري ... دوك ينقصّ فـ ... بكري العرس نتاعنا ما يقلّش على اوسبوع، سـ ... على السّمانه.

ب: على السّمانه.

A: laazəm smaana ʕa-lʔaaqall yaʕnii, duuk nfəṣṣəllək kiifaaʃ, əlklaam ṭwiil laakənnii maaʕləʃ nfəṣṣəllək. əssmaana haaðiik a … ḥnaa fə-lmənṭiiqa fə-lʕaadaat *soit* bə-nnəsba lə-lʕaariis wəllaa lʕaaruus,[5] fə-ssmaana haaðiik wəʃ ndiiruu? a … əl … fii awwəl yoom, awwəl yoom ḥnaa, kaayn ookla xaaṣṣa laazəm, laazəm təndaar, lmaakla yaʕnii laazəm ndiiruuhaa fii ðaak nnhaar, a … kaayn ḥaaja a … ḥnaa nsəmmuuhaa bə-rrfiis.

B: ḥnaa taanii.

A: rrfiis.

B: ʕannaa rrfiis.

A: arrfiis taaʕ əlkəsra, mooʃ taaʕ əl … looxər, mooʃ ʃoom taaʕ əl … mooʃ taaʕ əlḥəlwa, llii yəttəkəl ….

B: [xxx] *non, non,* ḥnaa taanii ….

A: taaʕ nnəʕma, ṣaḥḥ.

B: taaʕ əlkəsra.

A: xlaaṣ baaʃ nkuunuu mətfaahmiinuu …

B: lbaarəḥ kunnaa …

A: eeh.

B: naʕməl fiih [xxx].

A: eeh, ərrfiis, haaðii fii awwəl yoom əlʕərs, ṣaḥḥ, *soit, soit* mən jiiht əlʕaaruusa wəllaa mən jiihət lʕaariis, kii … ttneen iidiiruuwaa.[6]

B: hiih.

أ: لازم سـمـانه عـالأقلّ يعـني، دوك نفصّلّك كيـفـاش، الكلام طويل لكنّي مـاعليش نفصّلّك. السّمـانه هذيك ا ... احنـا فالمنطيـقه فـالعـادات soit بـالنّسبه للعـاريس ولاّ العـاروس،⁵ فـالسّمـانه هذيك واش نديروا؟ ا ... ألـ ... في اوّل يـوم، اوّل يوم احنـا، كاين أوكله خاصّه لازم، لازم تنـدار، الماكله يعني لازم نديروها في ذاك النّهـار، ا ... كاين حاجه ا ... احنا نسمّوها بـالرّفيـس.

ب: احنـا تاني.

أ: الرّفيس.

ب: عندنا الرّفيس.

أ: الرّفيس تاع الكسره، مهوش تاع الـ ... الاوخر، مهوش تاع الـ ... مهوش تاع الحلوه، اللّي يتّكل.

ب: [xxx] *non, non*، احنا تاني ....

أ: تاع النّعمه، صحّ.

ب: تاع الكسره.

أ: خلاص باش نكونوا متفاهمينوا ....

ب: البارح كنّا....

أ: ايـه.

ب: نعمل فيه [xxx].

أ: ايه، الرّفيس، هذي في اوّل يـوم العـرس، صحّ، *soit, soit* من جيهـة العاروسه ولاّ من جيهة العاريس، كي ... التّنين يديروها.⁷

ب: هيه.

A: ərrfiis w-iidiiruu wə ... ʃurba ʕaadiyya, nguuluu ḥnaa ʃərba, ḥnaa fə-lɣaalb
ndiiruuhaa bə-lfriik, ḥnaa nsəmmuuhaa ttʃiiʃa fə-lmanṭiiqa taaḥnaa, ḥnaa
nsəmmuuhaa ttʃiiʃa w-laakən hiya tʃiiʃa, ləfriik kiimaa ysəmmuuhaa
ʕlaa ḥsaab əttəsmiyyaat. w-fii nəfs əlwaqt iidiiruu ṭṭʕaam, maʕnaah θəlθ
ooklaat haaðii laazəm tkuun fii nhaar llowwəl. iiðən a ... haaðaak lə ...
rrfiis, yəthəllaaw biih yaʕnii baaʃ, nguuluu ḥnaa lʕərs haaðaa yjii ḥluuw
wə-lʕaaruusa djii ḥluuwa yaʕnii ʕlaa ḥsaab əlʕaadaat wə-kull ʃii ...

186

أ: الرّفيس ويديروا ا ا ... شـربـه عـاديّـه، نقـولـوا احنـا شـربـه، احنـا فـالـغـالـب
نـديـروهـا بـالفـريك، احنـا نسـمّـوهـا التّـشيـشـه فـالمنطيـقـه تـاحـنـا، احـنـا
نسـمّـوهـا التّـشيـشـه ولكن هـي تشيشـه الفـريك كيمـا يسـمّـوهـا عـلـى حسـاب
التّـسـمـيّـات. وفي نفس الـوقـت يديـروا الطّعـام، مـعـنـاه ثلث اوكـلات هـذي
لازم تكـون في نـهـار الأوّل. إيـذًا مــ ... هـذاك الــ ... الـرّفـيـس، يتـحـلّـوا بـيـه
يـعـني بـاش، نقـولـوا احنـا، الـعـرس هـذا يجـي حلـو والـعـاروسـه تجـي حلـووه
يـعـني علـى حسـاب الـعـادات وكلّ شـي ....

Vocabulary:

ftəl فتل *v* to roll (into beads of couscous); to spin (into thread) {*imperf:* yəftəl}

bərbuuʃa بربوشه *nfs* couscous

naʕma نعمه *nfs* grain, cereal (especially couscous); prosperity

ʈʕaam طعام *nms* couscous (cooked and ready to eat); food

qunʈaar قنطار *nms* hundredweight (traditional measure of approximately 100 pounds) {*pl:* qnaaṭiir}

θneen اثنين [*also* tneen] *nms* two

kaaθaafa كاثافه *nfs* capacity; thickness, density

juuz جوز [*also* zooj; zuuj; zawj] *nms* two

ɣaaʃii غاشي *nms* people, group of people, crowd

ḥaalaawiyyaat حالاويات *np* s.t. sweet; candy; pastry

wəʃnuu واشنه [*also* waaʃnuu] *interrog* what

hal اهل *nms* family, relatives, relations {*pl:* aahaalii}

hənnaa هنّا *nfs* grandmother {*pl:* hənnaawaat}

bən fuulaan بن فولان so-and-so, what's his name {*fs:* bənt fuulaan, *pl:* bnuu fuulaan}

ʕlaa baal على بال aware of, alerted to

ḥḍar حضر *v* to attend, be present at {*imperf:* yəḥḍar}

bəkrii بكري *adv* in the old days; at first; earlier

maaʕliiʃ ما عليش [*also* maʕliiʃ] it's nothing, don't worry, it's OK

nqəṣṣ انقصّ *v* to be cut, cut short {*imperf:* yənqəṣṣ}

soit conj either

ookla اوكله *nfs* dish (speciality of the house or region) {*pl:* ooklaat}

ndaar اندار *v* to be made, done, prepared {*imperf:* yəndaar}

maakla ماكله *nfs* food, nourishment {*pl:* maaklaat, *pl:* mwaakəl}

ðaak ذاك *pro* that (MS far demonstrative) {*fs:* ðiik, *pl:* ðuuk}

rfiis رفــيـس *nms* rfiss (kind of savory pastry made with flat bread); rfiis (kind of sweet pastry)

ʕan + suffixed pronoun عند [*also* ʕad; ʕand] *prep* to have

kəsra كسره *nfs* flat bread {*pl:* kəsraat, *pl:* ksuur}

mooʃ مهوش [*also* muuʃ] *part.; negates non-verbal structures* not

ooxər اخر [*also* aaxər] *adj* other {*fs:* ooxraa, *pl:* ooxriin}

ḥəlwa حلوى *nms* sweet pastry; candy {*pl:* ḥəlwaat, *pl:* ḥaalaawiyyaat}

ttəkəl اتّكل *v* to be eaten, be able to be eaten {*imperf:* yəttkəl}

non, non no, no

lbaarəḥ البارح *adv* yesterday; the previous evening

soit, soit conj either, either

tneen اتنـين [*also* θneen] *nms* two

friik فريك *nms* frik (kind of coarse-ground wheat or barley)

tʃiiʃa تشيشه [*also* dʃiiʃa] *nfs* dchica (kind of coarse-ground barley or wheat)

təsmiyya تسميه *nfs* name, naming practice {*pl:* təsmiyyaat}

θəlθ ثلث [*also* tlət; θlaaθa; tlaata] *nms* three

tḥallaa تحلّى *v* to become sweet, make o.s. sweet {*imperf:* yətḥallaa}

ḥluu حلو *adj* sweet; pleasant, nice {*fs:* ḥluuwa, *pl:* ḥəlwiin}

Notes:

1. The male speaker describes the making of grains of <u>berboucha</u> as /yfətluu bərbuuʃa/ 'they roll <u>berboucha</u>'. This process involves rolling flour and coarse grains of semolina between the palms of the hands to coat the

semolina with flour. The resulting grains are then steamed and served as the base for a stewlike dish. This dish, generally known as couscous, takes a variety of forms (large grains, small grains, served with meat, served with fish, served as a sweet, etc.) as well as names.

2. The phrase /juuz qnaaṭər/ 'two hundredweights' uses the number /juuz/ 'two' in a counted noun construction rather than the grammatical dual (as in MSA /qinṭaaraan/. This phrase illustrates that SAA, like certain other varieties of spoken Arabic, no longer relies on the grammatical dual to express the "two". The dual still occurs in SAA. It is largely limited, however, to expressions of time (as in /saaʕteen/ 'two hours') and body parts (/ʕeeneen/ 'two eyes').

3. The male speaker consistently uses FS agreement with non-human plural nouns, as he does here in /uumuur uuxraa/ 'other things'. As mentioned in Selection 2, Note 6, agreement for verbs, adjectives, and pronouns with both human and non-human plurals in SAA is generally plural, as in /lmuuduun looxriin/ 'the other cities'. This speaker's use of FS agreement may be a marker of formal style. Note that he employs a number of words and phrases associated with MSA, such as /lkaaθaafa/ 'the capacity' and /wə-ɣeerhaa/ 'and so on, lit. and things other than them (fs)'.

4. The form /kiifiit/ 'procedures' in the phrase **/kiifiit** lʕərs / 'the procedures of the wedding' derives from /kiifiyya(t)/. In SAA, as in other varieties of spoken Arabic, the sequence /iyyat/ may reduce to /iit/. This occurs where the noun ending in the sequence /iyyat/ occurs in a construct phrase, as here, or takes a suffixed pronoun, as in /kiifiituu/ 'its procedures'. This reduction, when it occurs, occurs in rapid speech.

5. The male speaker uses French as well as Arabic in the phrase /soit bə-nnəsba lə-lʕaariis **wəllaa** lʕaaruus/ 'either for the bride or for the groom'. The result is the contruction /soit ... wəlla .../ 'either ... or ...". This mixed-code construction, appearing again in this selection (/**soit, soit** mən jiiht əlʕaaruusa **wəllaa** mən jiihət lʕaariis/ '*either, either* on the bride's side *or* on the groom's side'), does not seem to be a slip of the tongue. Later selections illustrate other ways in which speakers of SAA combine Arabic and French in speech.

6. The male speaker points out here that the bride's family as well as the groom's family prepares rfiss for the wedding feast. This is somewhat unusual. In other places, the groom's family takes responsibility for hosting the wedding feast.

Before We Start the Wedding There Are Local Customs

A: At the same time, when it get close ... there is little time left until the wedding. Of course, the ... we say the groom, we say ... the family of the groom and such, they prepare things for the ... for the wedding, which is ... we say, they roll the berboucha, we call it berboucha.

B: Yes.

A: They roll <u>berboucha</u> that they ... the region ....

B: <u>Berboucha</u> [xxx].

A: We ....

B: It's our <u>naʕma</u>.

A: The ... The <u>naʕma</u> that they call <u>ṭ̣ʕam</u> in our region.

B: <u>Ṭ̣ʕam</u>.

A: <u>Berboucha</u>, they prepare it according to the family. They prepare a hundredweight or two, whatever they are able to, depending on the ... the ... the capacity of the family. We mostly, ... There's not less than two hundredweights, because the family ... is large, and at a wedding, the ... the ... the ... the ... it comes. For us, it's our "people" as we call it in the region. We call it our people, our people are numerous. For that reason they prepare the ... a lot of <u>naʕma</u>, [burp] plus other things, sweets and other things. These are what they prepare. They prepare what is necessary. So on the day of the wedding it seems to me that, ah ... these things, ah ... will be ready [tongue click]. For example, let's start with the procedure for the wedding. First, ah ... before we start the wedding, ah ... there are local customs. What are these local customs? The ... first of all, we invite the family in an official way. For example, the ... the girl, the bride ... invites what we call her grandmother and all that. The groom, I mean, the mother of the groom does the inviting, saying, "So-and-so's family, we're going to have a wedding."

B: True.

A: So, so that everyone knows, I mean ....

B: Yes.

A: The people, all of our people should know. They will be present on the wedding day and everything, there .... Everything is official. This wedding of ours, how does it take place? First of all, ah ... we mostly, in the old days ... now it is cut short ... In the old days, our weddings lasted at least a week ... a week.

B: A week.

A: It has to be at least a week, I mean. Now I will explain to you how. This speech will be long but it doesn't matter, I will explain to you. That week ... we in the region, according to custom *either* for the bride or for the groom, what do we do during that week? Ah ... on the first day, the first day, we, there is a special dish that must, it must be made. The dish, I mean, we have to make it on that day. Ah ... there is something, ah ... we call it rfiss.

B: We do, too.

A: Rfiss.

B: We have rfiss.

A: Rfiss with bread, not with ... the other, not the ... not the sweet kind that is eaten ....

B: *No, no.* We also ....

191

A: From na͡ʕma, right.

B: From bread.

A: That's it, so we both understand it ....

B: Yesterday we ...

A: Yes ....

B: ... were making some.

A: Yes. Rfiss, this is on the first day of the wedding, right. *Either, either* on the bride's side or the groom's side, when ... they both make it.

B: Yes.

A: Rfiss, and they make ... a regular soup, we call it shorba. We mostly make it with frik. We call it dchicha in our region. We call it dchicha, but it is the dchicha, frik, as they say, depending on the name. At the same time, they make couscous, so that's three dishes that have to be there on the first day. Then, ah ... this ... rfiss, they will get sweet with it. I mean, so that, as we say, the wedding will be sweet and the bride will be sweet, I mean, according to custom and all ....

ənnhaar naqra?uu lfaatḥa

This is the final selection dealing with weddings in El Meghaier. Note that preparations and celebration include both family and community. Even the female speaker here is surprised to hear that neither the bride nor the groom attends the actual wedding.

A: haaðaa huwa ðaak ənnhaar[1] naqra?uu lfaatḥa.[2] lfaatḥa haaðii kiifaaʃ ndiiruuhaa ḥnaayaa? fə-lmanṭiqa w-maa ... haaðii maa zaalt ḥattaa[3] lyoom, əlfaatḥa waaʃ idiiruu? iijiibuu ḥnaa ʃʃeex ntaaʕ əljaaməʕ wə-?illaa lə ... laa, wə-lkuθra yədiiruuhaa aayma taaʕ əjjaaməʕ. maa kaaʃ mə ... *parce que* lfaatḥa laazəm yəqraahaa iimaam taaʕ jjaamaʕ yə ... taaʕ əlmanṭiiqa wəllaa taaʕ əlʕaarʃ wəllaa ʕlaa ḥsaab maa yʃuufuu huuma. iidiiruuhaa baʕd ṣlaat lʕaaṣər ḥattaa l-yuumnaa haaðaa maa zaal haakðaa, ḥattaa l-yuumnaa haaðaa maa zaalt baʕda ṣaalaat əlʕaaṣər iidiiruuhaa, iiṣalluu lʕaṣar. gaal lyoom lfaatḥa nnaas ma ... ʕaarfiin, iijiibuu ɣeer ṭṭaaləb bərk llii maḥsuub ʃɣul maʕruuḍ wəllaa. wə-lbaaqii mʕaaʃər moojuudiin səmmaa[4] raahum fə-lmaakaan maa yruuḥuuʃ ... iijuu l-daar lʕaariis, maa təqraaʃ[5] wə-yiijuu fii daar lʕaariis a .... muuhuuʃ fii ddaar wiin kaayn lʕaariis[6] haaðaak huwa llooxər, daar yaa immaa daar əlʕaariis iiðaa kaan ʕandhum lə ... llooxraa[7] aw daar xuu wəllaa ʕammuu, lmuuhəmm daar laqrab, laa xaaṭər wiin ... ʃkuun yəḥ̣ðər əlfaatḥa? iiḥaḍruu fiihaa nnaas ləkbaar, maa yḥaḍḍruuʃ lmṣaaɣar, iiḥaḍruu fiihaa nnaas ləkbaar ḥattaa lʕaariis maa yḥaḍḍruuhʃ.[8]

B: kiifaah?

A: iiḥaḍḍruu fiihaa lkuubaar taaʕ əl ... taaʕ əlʕaarʃ, nguuluu ḥnaa baabaat əṭṭfəl, lʕəmm wə ...

B: eeh.

النّهار نقرأوا الفاتحه

أ: هذا هو ذاك النّهار [1] نقرأوا الفاتحه. [2] الفاتحه هذي كيفاش نديروها احنايا؟ فـالمنطقه ومـا ... هذي مـا زالت حتّى [3] اليـوم، الفـاتحه واش يديروا؟ يجيبوا احنا الشّيخ نتـاع الجامع وإلاّ الـ ... لا، والكثره يديروها الأيمه تاع الجامع ما كاش مـ ... parce que الفاتحه لازم يقراها إمـام تاع الجامع يـ ... تاع المنطقه ولاّ تاع العارش ولاّ على حسـاب مـا يشوفـوا هومـا يديروهـا بعد صلاة العـاصر حتّى ليومنا هذا مـا زال هكذا، حتّى ليـومنا هذا مـا زالت بعد صلاة العـاصر يديروهـا، يصلّوا العـاصر. قـال اليـوم الفـاتحه النّـاس مـ ... عـارفين، يجيبـوا غيـر الطّالب برك اللّي محسب شغل معروض ولاّ. والبـاقي معـاشر موجودين سمّى [4] راهم في المكان مـا يروحوش ... يجـوا لدار لعاريس، مـا تقراش [5] ويجوا في دار العاريس ا ... موهوش في دار وين كاين العاريس [6] هذاك هو الأوخر، دار يا امّا دار العاريس إذا كان عندهم الـ ... الأوخرى [7] أو دار اخوه ولاّ عمّه، الموهمّ دار الاقرب، لا خـاطر وين ... شكون يحضر الفاتحه؟ يحضروا فيهـا النّـاس الكبار، مـا يحضّروش المصاغر، يحضروا فيهـا النّـاس الكبار حتّى العاريس مـا يحضّروهش. [8]

ب: كيفاه؟

أ: يحضّروا فيها الكبار تاع الـ... تاع العارش، نقولوا احنا بابات الطّفل، العمّ و....

ب: ايه.

A: maa yḥaḍḍruuʃ ... maa yḥaḍḍruuʃ ləmṣaayar, ləmkaars.

B: [xxx] maaʃii ləmṣaayar.

A: laa laa, maa yḥaḍḍruuʃ ləmkaars, ləmkaars kiimaa yḥa ... iiḥaḍḍruu
lbaʕḍ mən rəbaʕa lə-xəmsa iiwəzzʕuulhum ... mən baʕd wəʃ nquulləkum?
wəʃ iidiiruu fəl .... iiðan iiḥaḍḍruu fiihaa ləkbaar, haaðuuk əlkuubaar
ḥaawaalii θlaaθiin rəbʕiin xəmsiin waaḥəd llii yḥaḍruu. iijii ʃʃiix w-iijii
nguuluu ḥnaa abb əṭṭfal wə-buu ṭṭəfla wəllaa lmuukkəl ʕleeh wəllaa
kaðaa. ʕlaa ḥsaab maa yətfaahmuu. a ... ʃʃiix yəstəftəḥ, yəqraʔalhum
lfatḥa w-kull ʃii, lmuuhəmm xlaaṣ. baʕd maa yəqraaw lfaatḥa [sniff] a
... iikuunuu muujuudiin maʔkuulaat a ... ʃii ṭaabiiʕii ḥnaa maʔkuulaat a
... haaðii muujuuda ḥattaa l-yuumnaa haaðaa. laazəm iikuun fiihaa
ttəmər w-laazəm iikuun əlḥliib fə-lfaatḥa.[9] haaðii laazəm yə... ḥattaa
wə-luu maa ykuunʃ laazəm iidəbbruu, iidəbbruu raashum. lmuuhəmm
ttəmər wə-lḥliib yuʕaddiin[10] mə-lʕaadaat llii maa zaalt muujuuda, laazəm
iidiiruuhaa w-luu yəkuun maahuuʃ woqt əttəmər laazəm yə... yʃuufuu
kiifaaʃ yətṣərrfuu. ttəmər wə-lḥliib wə-djiib[11] baʕd lḥaalaawiyyaat llii
tuṣnaʕ fə-ddaar *le gâteau* ḥnaa lə ... məjmuuʕ anwaaʕ lḥaalaawiyyaat
laazəm tkuun waajda mʕa lməʃruubaat, əlgaazooz wə-kðaa, haaðiik m-baʕd
haaðaa, laakən laa, ttəmər wə-lḥliib yəf ... yəftḥuu biihum əlluwwəliin
jə ... jraat lʕaada haakðaa, baaqii iilaa yoomiinaa haaðaayaa. yaqraaw
lfaatḥa w-kull ʃii səmmaa, maa bqaawluu ... laazəm lʕaaʃiyya haaðiik
nnhaar yəqraaw lfaatḥa, laazəm lʕaaʃiyya haaðiik laazəm lʕaaruusa djii
l-daar zoojhaa, l-daar lʕaariis naguuluu ḥnaa, laazəm fə-lʕaaʃiyya haaðiik
baʕd maa yruuḥuu w-kullʃ. fə-lʕaaʃiyya haaðiik iijiibuu lʕaaruusa ṭabʕan
ḥnaa kii ijiibuu lʕaaruusa iiðaa qriiba w-ḥaabbiin iijiibuuhaa təmʃii
liiʔanna lə ... lʕaarʃ kbiira.

أ: ما يحضّروش ... ما يحضّروش المصاغر، المكارس.

ب: ماشي المصاغر.

أ: لا لا، ما يحضّروش المكارس، المكارس كيما يحـ ... يحضّروا البعض من اربعه لخمسه يوزعولهم ... من بعد واش نقوللكم؟ واش يديروا فلـ ... إذًا يحضّروا فيها الكبار، هذوك الكبار حوالي ثلاثين اربعين خمسين واحد اللي يحضروا. يجي الشّيخ ويجي نقولوا احنا ابّ الطّفل وابو الطّفله ولّا الموكّل عليه ولّا كذا. على حساب ما يتفاهموا. ا ... الشّيخ يستفتح، يقرألهم الفاتحه وكلّ شي، الموهمّ خلاص. بعد ما يقراوا الفاتحه [sniff] ا ... ا ... يكونوا موجودين مأكولات ا ... شي طبيعي احنا مأكولات ا ... هذي موجوده حتّى ليومنا هذا. لازم يكون فيها التّمر ولازم يكون فيها الحليب[9] في الفاتحه. هذي لازم يـ ... حتّى ولو ما يكونش لازم يديروا، يدبّروا راسهم. الموهمّ التّمر والحليب يعدّين[10] مالعادات اللّي ما زالت موجوده، لازم يديروها ولو يكون ماهوش وقت التّمر لازم يـ ... يشوفوا كيفاش يتصرّفوا. التّمر والحليب وتجيب[11] بعض الحلويّات اللّي تُصنع في الدّار le gâteau احنا الـ ... مجموع انواع الحلويّات لازم تكون واجده مع المشروبات، القازوز وكذا. هذيك مبعد هذا، لكن لا، التّمر والحليب يفـ ... يفتحوا بهم هم الأوّلين جـ ... جرات العاده هكذا باقي إلى يومنا هذايا. يقراوا الفاتحه وكل شي سمّى ،ما بقاوله ... لازم العاشيّه هذيك النّهار يقراوا الفاتحه، لازم العاشيّه هذيك لازم العاروسه تجي لدار زوجها، لدار العاريس نقولوا احنا، لازم فالعاشيّه هذيك بعد ما يروحوا وكلش. فالعاشيّه هذيك يجيبوا العاروسه طبعًا كي احنا يجيبوا العاروسه إذا قريبه وحابّين يجيبوها تمشي لأنّ الـ ... العارش كبيره.

197

iijiibuuhaa təmʃii iiðaa maa kaaʃ laazəm yə... ssiyyaaraat. wə-ḥnaa ssiyyaaraat laazəm tkuun qaafiila liiʔanna lʕaaylaat kθiira bə-ḥayθu maa təkfiiʃ kraars. ḥattaa yjiibuu lkaamyuwwaat ...

B: [xxx].

A: yiijiibuu lkiiraan, lmuuhəmm lqaṭ ...

B: ʃuuf.

A: eeh, lʕaaylaat kbiira, lʕaaylaat kbiira wə-kii tʕuud ʕaayla kbiira tkuun kaayn waasaayəl ənnaqəl bəzzaaf, yaʕnii lkraasii ykuunuu bəzzaaf.

B: iih.

A: duuk humma laa ... ʕlaa xaaṭər ḥattaa blaa ʕarða səmmaa fə-nnhaar kiimaa haaðaak ....

B: ṣaḥḥ.

A: yaʕnii lə ... llii lə ... fə-lʕaayla llii kaayn kaaməl ... illii ʕanduu kurruusa wəllaa ʕanduu kaamya blaa maa yguuluuluu laazəm iijiibhaa. maa daam raahuu yaakul əmmaa laazəm iijiibhaa wə-yiijiibhaa [xxx] yəfham *parce que* lmaasaafa maaʃii bʕiida w-laazm ənnaas kull taḥðar,[12] maa fiihaa ḥattaa muʃkəl.

يجيبوها تمشي إذا ما كاش لازم يـ ... السيّارات. واحنا السّيارات لازم
تكون قافيله لإنّ العايلات كثيره بحيث ما تكفيش كرارس، حتّى
يجيبوا الكاميوات ...

ب: [xxx].

أ: يجيبوا الكيران، الموهمّ القط ....

ب: شوف.

أ: ايه، العايلات كبيره، العايلات كبيره وكي تعود عايله كبيره تكون كاين
وسايل النّقل بزّاف، يعني الكراسي يكونوا بزّاف.

ب: ايه.

أ: دوك همّ لا ... على خاطر حتّى بلا عرضه سمّى في النّهار كيما هذاك ....

ب: صحّ.

أ: يعني الـ ... اللّي الـ ... فالعايله اللّي كاين كامل ... اللّي عنده كورّوسه
ولاً عنده كاميا بلا ما يقولوله لازم يجيبها. ما دام راه ياكل إمّا لازم
يجيبها ويجيبها [xxx] يفهم *parce que* المسافه ماشي بعيده ولازم النّاس
كلّ[12] تحضر، ما فيها حتّى مشكل.

Vocabulary:

faatḥa فاتحه *prop* the Fatiha (first sura of the Qur'an, recited on formal occasions)

ḥnaayaa حنايا [*also* ḥnaa; ḥanaa] *pro* we (1P)

ʃeex شيخ *nms* religious scholar or leader; chief, headman; holy man {*pl:* ʃyuux, *pl:* ʃyaax}

iimaam ايمام *nms* imam {*pl:* ayma}

parce que *conj* because

ʕaaṣər عاصر *nms* afternoon prayer (Islamic); afternoon {*pl:* ʕaṣaarii}

ṭaaləb طالب *nms* person with Islamic religious education, religious scholar {*pl:*

199

ṭəlba}

bərk برك [*also* bark] *adv* only, just

maḥsuub محسوب *disc* that is to say, I mean (lit. considered to be)

maʕruuḍ معروض *adj* invited {*fs:* maʕruuḍa, *pl:* maʕruuḍiin}

baaqii باقي *adj* rest, what stays, what remains; resting, staying, remaining

maʕʃər معشر *nms* kinfolk; group; community {*pl:* mʕaaʃər}

səmmaa سمّا [*also* təmmaa; tsəmmaa; θəmmaa] *adv* there, over there

xuu أخو *nms* brother {*pl:* xwaat, *pl:* xwaan}

qriib قريب *nms* close relative {*pl:* qraab}

laa xaaṭər لا خاطر [*also* ʕlaa xaaṭər; laa xaatʃ; laa xaatʃii] *conj* because, due to the fact that

ḥaḍḍər حضّر *v* to make, cause to appear, attend {*imperf:* iiḥaḍḍər}

kbiir كبير *nms* adult, grownup; large {*fs:* kbiira, *pl:* kuubaar}

məkruus مكروس *nms* young adolescent, young teenager {*pl:* mkaars}

θlaaθiin ثلاثين [*also* tlaatiin] *nms* thirty

rəbʕiin ربعين *nms* forty

xəmsiin خمسين *nms* fifty

abb اب *nms* father {*pl:* abawaat}

buu بو *nms* father {*pl:* bwaat}

muukkəl ʕlaa موكّل على representative of, for {*fs:* muukkla ʕlaa, *pl:* muukkliin ʕlaa}

ʃiix شيخ [*also* ʃeex] *nms* religious scholar or leader; chief, headman; holy man {*pl:* ʃyuux, *pl:* ʃyaax}

stəftaḥ استفتح *v* to open (a ceremony); to start {*imperf:* yəstəftaḥ}

dəbbər دبّر *v* to conduct, direct, take care of {*imperf:* iidəbbər }

raas + suffixed pronoun راس self

dəbbər raas- + suffixed pronoun دبّر راس to manage, work out; to do one's best {*imperf:* iidəbbər raas}

gâteau *nms* cake

gaazooz قازوز *nms* carbonated soft drink

ftəḥ فتح *v* to start, begin; to open {*imperf:* yəftəḥ}

haaðaay هـذاي [*also* haadaa; haadaayaa; haaðaa] *pro* this (MS near demonstrative) {*fs*: haadiyyaa}

zooj زوج *nms* husband, spouse {*pl*: zwaaj}

siyyaara سـيّاره *nfs* car, automobile {*pl*: siyyaaraat}

qaafiila قـافـيـلـه *nfs* caravan {*pl*: qwaafəl, *pl*: qfuul}

kurruusa كرّوسـه *nfs* car; horse-drawn cart {*pl*: kraars}

kaamyuu كـامـيـو [*also* kaamyaa] *nms* truck {*pl*: kaamyuwwaat}

kaar كار *nms* bus {*pl*: kiiraan}

wsiila وسـيـلـه *nfs* means, way {*pl*: wsaayəl}

ſlaa xaatʃər علـى خـاطـر [*also* laa xaatər; laa xaatʃii; laa xaats] *conj* because, due to the fact that

blaa بلا *prep* without

ſarða عـرضـه *nfs* invitation {*pl*: ſarðaat}

kaaməl كـامـل *adj* all, entire ; invariable {*fs*: kaamla, *pl*: kaamliin}

kaamyaa كـامـيـا [*also* kaamyuu] *nms* truck {*pl*: kaamyuwwaat}

maa daam مـــا دام *v; invariable, also conjugated, also takes suffixed pronoun* as long as

ḥuwwəs حـوّس *v* to take a walk; to make, take a tour {*imperf*: iiḥuwwəs}

Notes:

1. The form /ðaak/ as in /**ðaak** ənnhaar/ 'that night' first occurred in Selection 16. It is a version of the far demonstrative /haaðaak/ and its variants. It has the FS form /ðiik/ and P form /ðuuk/. The form /ðaak/ also occurs invariably.

2. The phrase /nəqraʔuu lfaatħa/ 'we recite the Fatiha' describes the simple legal process that is the actual marriage ceremony. The social events that accompany the legal process in Algeria, as elsewhere, are more complex. Note that it is common in Islamic societies to seal agreements and contracts of all kinds with a recitation of the Fatiha.

3. The male speaker uses /ħattaa/ in its MSA sense in the phrase /**ħattaa** lyoom/ 'up to today'. He also uses /ħattaa/ in the specifically North African sense of 'even'. The North African usage occurs at the end of this stretch of

speech, in /ḥattaa lʕaaruus maa yḥaḍḍruuʃ/ 'they don't even bring in the groom'. Context is the best guide to distinguishing between these two usages, which are both common.

4. The form /səmmaa/ 'I mean, that is, lit. it is called' has several variants in SAA. These variants include /tsəmmaa/ and /təmmaa/. Of the three variants that appear in our data, /səmmaa/ occurs least frequently. Note, too, that this form has a homophone. It is /səmmaa/ (and its variants) 'there, over there'.

5. The phrase /maa təqraaʃ/ 'she does not recite' appears to refer to the bride. She does not attend the wedding and, thus, does not recite the Fatiha with the other participants in the ceremony. Instead, as may occur in certain traditional settings, a /muukkəl ʕleehaa/ 'her legal proxy' represents her. The proxy may be her father, paternal uncle, or her brother.

6. The male speaker points out that where the wedding guests gather is /muuhuuʃ fii ddaar wiin kaayən lʕaariis/ 'it's not at the house where the groom is'. The groom is in a house that has been set aside for his use. According to custom, he spends the period before the wedding in a kind of seclusion, cared for by male relatives and friends. This appears to be a local custom.

7. The FS form /llooxraa/ 'the other' agrees with /daar/ 'house' in the clause /yaa ʔimmaa daar əlʕaariis ʔiiðaa kaan ʕandhum lə ... llooxraa/ 'either the groom's house if they have ... the other'. This agreement is conventional. In SAA as in MSA, /daar/ is grammatically feminine even though it lacks a feminine marker (such as the final /a/ or taaʔ marbuuta).

8. As the male speaker notes /ḥattaa lʕaariis maa yḥaððruuʃ/ 'they don't even bring in the bridegroom'. He and the bride, according to custom, are represented by a /muukkəl/ 'legal proxy'. This process illustrates a view of marriages that links families in a negotiated legal contract. It differs from the conventional Western ideal of a love match between two individuals. Note, however, that life in an arranged marriage can be as satisfying as in a love match.

9. Wedding and certain other formal occasions can be described with the phrase /laazəm yəkuun fiihaa ttəmər w-laazəm yəkuun əlḥliib/ 'there must be dates there and there must be milk'. In this, people follow custom. As the speaker indicates, /yəfthuu biihum əlluwwəliin/ 'people in the old days began with them'.

10. The form /yuʕaddiin/, translated here as '[they] are considered' appears to be a slip of the tongue. The stem of the verb /yuʕaddiin/ is /yuʕadd/ 'it (ms) is considered'. This verb is the true or ablaut, MSA-style passive of the verb

/ʕadd/ - /iiʕadd/ 'to consider; to see'. The use of the true passive in SAA is, however, unusual (see Selection 4, note 5; Selection 7, note 10; Selection 12, note 4). Furthermore, the suffix /iin/ in /yuʕaddiin/ is not a conventional suffix of the imperfect in either SAA or MSA. Context, however, helps comprehension here.

11. The subject of the verb /djiib/ 'they (fs) bring' is not explicit in the phrase /wə-djiib baʕd lhaalaawiyyaat/ 'they (fs) bring some sweets'. Context makes it likely that the subject is /nnaas/ 'people, the people'. This form may take P agreement, as occurs in this selection in /nnaas ma ... ʕaarfiin/ 'people know'. The same form also takes FS agreement, as occurs in this selection in /laazm ənnaas kull taḥḍar/ 'everyone has to come'.

12. The use of /kull/ 'all' in the phrase /laazm ənnaas kull taḥḍar,/ 'everyone has to come' is not conventional in SAA. More typical usage includes a pronoun suffix to link /kull/ to /nnaas/. The conventional result would be /nnaas kullhum/ or /nnaas kullhaa/ (see previous note on agreement). Alternatively, /kull/ precedes /nnaas/ in the construct phrase /kull ənnaas/.

The Day on Which We Recite the Fatiha

A: This would be on the day we recite the Fatiha. This Fatiha, how do we do it? In our region and not .... This continues up to today. The Fatiha, what do they do? We, they bring the sheikh of the mosque or ... No, mostly the imams of the mosque do it, there is no ... Because the Fatiha must be recited by an imam from a mosque ... from the region or from the tribe or and according to what they think. They do it after the afternoon prayer. Up to the present day it's like this. Up to the present day it's still after the afternoon prayer that they do it, they pray the afternoon prayer. It's been said that today is the Fatiha, people ... they know. They just bring only a religious scholar who is supposed to be kind of invited or whatever. The rest are kinfolk who are there. They are in the place, that is, they don't go ... They come to the groom's house, she doesn't recite, they come to the groom's house, ah .... It's not at the house where the groom is, that's another one. A house, either the groom's house if they have ... the other ... or his brother's or his paternal uncle's. The point is it's a house belonging to some relatives because it's where ... Who attends the Fatiha? The adults attend it. They don't bring in the youngsters. The adults attend it. They don't even bring in the groom.

B: How is that?

A: They bring in the adults of ... of the tribe. We call them the child's baabaat, the paternal uncle and ...

B: Yes.

A: They don't bring in ... they don't bring in the young people, the youngsters.

B: [xxx] Not the youngsters.

A: No, no, they don't bring in the youngsters, the youngsters as .... They bring in some, from four to five, they spread them out .... After that, what should I tell you they do at the .... So, they bring in adults to attend it. These older people are about thirty, forty, fifty people who attend. The sheikh comes and, we say, the father of the boy and the father of the girl or his proxy or whatever, according to whatever they have agreed. Ah ... the sheikh begins, he recites the <u>Fatiha</u> for them and everything. The point is, that's it. After they recite the <u>Fatiha</u> [sniff] ah ... foods should be present, ah ... It's a natural thing, we, foods, ah .... This is present up to today. There must be dates there and there must be milk at the <u>Fatiha</u>. This is necessary ... even if there isn't any, they have to handle ... they manage. The point is, dates and milk are considered to be among the customs that are still present, they must do them, even if it is not date season, they have to ... to see how to behave. Dates and milk and they bring some sweets that are made at home, *cake*, we .... A whole variety of sweets must be ready with beverages, soft drinks and such. This is after that, but no, dates and milk ... people in the old days began with them.... The custom continues this way, it continues up to today. They recite the <u>Fatiha</u> and everything, that is, he has no .... In the evening, on this day they have to, they recite the <u>Fatiha</u>, in the evening the bride must go to her husband's house, to the groom's house, we say. They have to, in the evening after they go and all that. In the evening they bring the bride, ah ... of course, we, when they bring the bride, ah ... if she is nearby they want to bring her on foot because ... the tribe is large. They bring her on foot if cars ... are not needed. We, the cars have to make up a caravan because the families are numerous, such that carts are not enough, to the point that they bring trucks ....

B: [xxx].

A: Or they bring buses. The point is ...

B: Really.

A: Yes. Families are big, families are big. When a family gets big there has to be a lot of transportation. I mean, there must be a lot of seats.

B: Yes.

A: Now they don't ... because even without an invitation, that is, on a day like this ....

B: Right.

A: I mean ... whoever ... in the family there is are all ... whoever has a cart or has a truck without them telling him he has to bring it. As long as he is there eating, either he has to bring it and he brings it [xxx]. He understands *because* the distance is not great and everyone has to attend; there is no problem.

ləʕʃaa c'est ṭṭʕaam

Another selection from a non-urban, desert community, this one describes the
daily menu of herders, where couscous is a staple food.

A: ʕandək a ... fiimaa yxuṣṣ ələ ... ləmaakla a ... lmaakla ʕandək fə ... a
... maa kaanʃ a ... əs ... mən bəʃʃaar wəllə ... w-ruuḥii l-heeh, tsəmmaa
lə ... ljaanuub, maa kaaʃ llii yətʕaʃʃaa bə ... maḥsuub maa ydiirʃ
ṭṭʕaam.

B: eeh.

A: ṭṭʕaam *c'est* a ... tsəmmaa lə ... lʔakəl, lʔookla lʔasaasiyya.

C: ah, *c'est ça.*

A: ilaa[1] maa daaruuʃ ṭṭʕaam fə-laʕʃaa b-ḥaal ilaa maa ... nnaas maa tʕaʃʃaatʃ,
haaðaa huwa.

B: ʃuuf.

A: ələ ...

B: kull yoom? kull yoom?

A: kull yoom, kull yoom, *alors,* haaðaa xlaaṣ.

B: iidiiruu ṭṭʕaam?

A: ʕandək fələ ... ʕand əṭṭnaaʃ maʕliiʃ nnaas ddiir lmərqa wə-ddiir kðaa,
mais lə ... ləʕʃaa c'est ṭṭʕaam, lkusksii lə .... nnaas ʕaawəd taanii *c'est*
des murabbiyyiin, əlxruuf wələ ... wəllaa jjəmal wəllaa, mʕa ṭṭʕaam
w-haaðaa huwa lə .... *alors,* ʕandək a ... ṣṣbaaḥ a ... alkuθra yədiruu
b-ḥaal lmɣaarba[2] lḥariira.[3]

الطّعام c'est العشا

أ: عندك اه ... فيما يخصّ الـ ... الماكله اه .... الماكله عندك فـ ... ا ... مكانش
اه ... اسـ... من بشّار ولـ ... وروحي لهيه، تسمّى الـ ... الجنوب، ما
كاش اللّي يتعشّى بـ ... محسوب ما يديرش الطّعام.

ب: ايه.

أ: الطّعام c'est ا ... تسمّى الـ ... الأكل، الأوكله الأساسيّه.

ب: اه، c'est ça.

أ: الا[1] ما داروش الطّعام في العشا بحال الا ما ... النّاس ما تعشّاتش، هذا
هو.

ب: شوف.

أ: الـ....

ب: كلّ يوم؟ كلّ يوم؟

أ: كلّ يوم، كلّ يوم، alors، هذا خلاص.

ب: يديروا الطّعام؟

أ: عندك فـ ... عند الطّناش، معليش النّاس تدير المرقه وتدير كذا، mais الـ
... العشا c'est الطّعام، الكسكسي الـ .... النّاس عاود تاني c'est des
مربيّين، الخروف ولـ ... ولاّ الجّمل ولاّ. مع الطّعام وهذا هو الـ ....، alors،
عندك ا ... الصّباح ا ... الكثره يديروا بحال[2] المغاربه الحريره.[3]

B: ʃuuf.

A: *C'est de la soupe faite à partir d'*dʃiiʃa wəllaa faariina maʕa lxmiira wəllaa ... *des bouts de viande* wəllaa ntaaʕ *la graisse.* haadii ʕaawəd taanii ṣṣbaaḥ, ʕa-ṣṣbaaḥ daaymən, daaymən əlḥriira.

ب: شـوف.

أ: دشـيـشـه ولاّ فـارينـه مـع الخـميـره ولاّ des *C'est de la soupe faite à partir d'*
bouts de viande ولاّ نتـاع *la graisse.* هذي عـاود تانـي الصّـبـاح، عـالصّـبـاح
دايمـاً دايمـاً الحريره.

Vocabulary:

c'est it is

bəʃʃaar بـشّـار *prop* Béchar (city in southernAlgeria)

heeh هيـه *adv* there, over there

tsəmmaa تـسـمّـا [*also* təmma; θəmma; səmmaa] *adv* there, over there

jaanuub جـانـوب *nms* south

c'est it is

c'est ça that's it

b-ḥaal بـحـال *prep* like, as

ilaa إلاّ *part.* if

alors *adv* so, then

mərqa مــرقـه *nfs* stew (any dish that has a sauce or gravy); sauce, gravy {*pl:* mərgaat}

c'est it is

kusksii كسكسـي *nms* couscous

ʕaawəd taanii عـاود تانـي *also,* too, as well

c'est des there are some; lit. it is some

mrabbii مـربّـي *nms* breeder, raiser (of livestock) {*pl:* mrabbiyyiin}

alors *adv* so, then

maɣrəbii مـغربـي *adj* Moroccan {*fs:* maɣrəbiyya, *pl:* mɣaarba}

ḥariira حريره *nfs* hariira (kind of North African soup)

c'est de la soupe faite à partir it is soup made from

dʃiiʃa تـشـيـشـه [*also* tʃiiʃa] *nfs* dchica (kind of coarse-ground barley or wheat)

xmiira خمـيره *nfs* leavening; baker's yeast

des bouts de viande pieces of meat

la graisse nfs fat

Notes:

1. The particle /ilaa/ in /**ilaa** maa daaruuʃ ṭṭʕaam fə-laʕʃaa bḥaal ilaa maa ... nnaas maa tʕaʃʃaatʃ/ 'if they don't make couscous for dinner, it's as if no ... people don't eat anything at all' is one of several conditional particles in SAA. Others are /iðaa/ (also /idaa/), /luu/ (also /loo/) and, rarely, /kuun/. Where the particle /ilaa/ marks the if-clause of a conditional sentence and the verb of the clause is perfect or imperfect, the condition is usually real or predictive. Where, however, /ilaa/ marks the if-clause and the verb of that clause is compound past (past perfect or past imperfect) the condition is usually unreal or contrary to fact.

2. The form /bḥaal/, as in /bḥaal lmɣaarba/ 'like the Moroccans', is not usually associated with SAA. It is considered more typical of Arabic as spoken in Morocco. Note, however, that male speaker is describing his home region, near Béchar on the Algerian-Moroccan border. Because language use does not always follow political borders, his use of /bḥaal/ is not unusual.

3. The soup known as /ḥariira/ takes a variety of forms, as the male speaker says. It is based on broth made from /des bouts de viande wəllaa ntaaʕ la graisse/ 'pieces of meat or of fat'. It usually includes a grain or grain-based product, such as /dʃiiʃa wəllaa faariina maʕa lxmiira wəllaa/ 'dchicha or flour with leavening or whatever'. Vegetables, especially tomatoes, may also be included.

At Dinner, It's Couscous

A: You have ... as far as ... food is concerned, ah ... food you have in ... there is no, ah ... from Béchar and the ... Go there, that is, in the ... the south, nobody eats dinner with ... that is, he doesn't make couscous.

B: Yes.

A: Couscous, *that's*, ah ... there it's the ... the food, the basic dish.

B: Yes, *that's right*.

A: If they don't make couscous for dinner, it's as if no ... people don't eat anything for dinner, that's it.

B: Really.

A: The ...

B: Every day? Every single day?

A: Every day, every single day. So, that's that.

B: They make couscous?

A: You have ... at noon, it doesn't matter. People make stew and they make whatever, *but* ... at dinner, *it's* couscous, couscous for ... Besides, the people, *they are* livestock breeders. Sheep ... or camels or whatever. With couscous and that's that ... So, you have ... in the morning, ah ... mostly they make <u>harira</u> like the Moroccans.

B: Really.

A: It's *soup made from* <u>dchicha</u> or flour with leavening or whatever, and *pieces of meat* or *of fat*. This is also in the morning, in the morning, always, always it's <u>harira</u>.

213

bəʃʃaar zdahrət f-woqt ləstiʕmaar

The economic ups and downs of the region of Béchar in southern Algeria are the subject of this selection. This speaker's usage also shows markers of non-urban SAA.

A: bəʃʃaar, wəʃ nguullək? bəʃʃaar zdahrət a ... lkuθra f-woqt ləstəʕmaar llii ... kii kaan lməʃruuʕ ntaaʕ riiggan[1] kii kaanuu a ... lfiiraansaawiyyiin iidiiruu lə ... ttaajaarəb ntaaʕ a ... lquunbuula haaðiik a ... ddərriyya fii riiggaan. xəddmuu bəzzaaf nnaas *surtout* fələ ... nnaqəl, *les transports.* kaanuu yəddiihum mən təmmaa, mən bəʃʃaar a ... *alors* kaant a ... gaaʕ əl ... l*budget* ntaaʕ a ... haaðaak kaanuu yəvarsiyuuh fii bəʃʃaar. *alors* bəʃʃaar zdahrət *un peu mais* baaʃ a ... tguul fiihaaʃ[2] a ... maḥsuub a ... aʃɣaal a ... ṣiinaaʕiyya maa kaanʃ.

B: maa kaanʃ.

A: kaayna, kaanət bəkrii . ...

C: taqliidiyya.

A: eeh, kaanət bəkrii fii knaadsa. kaant a ... maanaajəm ntaaʕ əlfaḥm, *charbon.* a ... druuk xlaaṣt, *donc* maa kaayn waaluu. a ... lfiilaaḥaa maa kaayna waaluu, tsəmmaa fii *les environs* ntaaʕ a ... bəʃʃaar kaaynət[3] ʃwiyya, yədiiruu xuḍra, *mais* lʔaaɣlabiyya ntaaʕ lxuḍra truuḥ mə-ʃʃaamaal, truuḥ lə ... llaaxər.[4] *même* daaruu *barrage*, sədd kbiir.

B: ʃuuf.

A: sədd kbiir fii, fii jərf əttarba, anaa nḏ̣ənn huwwa akbar sədd fə-llaaxər. a ... maa thallaawʃ fiih lʔaaraadii llii stəṣləḥuuhaa, ʕaawəd taanii ɣmarhaa lə ... ɣamrathaa rrməl. w-ʕandhum maaʃaakiil kbiira fiimaa yxuṣṣ a ... baaʃ iiḥadduu rrməl wə ...

بشّار ازدهرت في وقت الاستعمار

أ: بشّار، واش نقولّك؟ بشّار ازدهرت ا ... الكثره في وقت الاستعمار اللّي
... كي كان المشروع نتاع رقّان¹ كي كانوا ا ... الفيرانساويّين يديروا الـ
... التّجارب نتاع القونبوله هذيك ا ... الدّريّه في رقّان، خدّموا بزّاف
النّاس surtout فلـ ... النّقل، les transports، كانوا يدّيوا من تمّا، من بشّار ا
... alors كانت ا ... قاع الـ ... الـbudget نتاع ا ... هذك كانوا يڤرسيوه
في بشّار. Alors بشّار ازدهرت un peu mais باش ... تقول فيهاش² ا ...
محسوب ا ... اشغال ا ... صناعيّه ما كاهش.

ب: ما كانش.

أ: كاينه، كانت بكري ....

ج: تقليديّه.

أ: ايه، كانت بكري في كنادسه. كانت ا ... ماناجم نتاع الفحم، charbon. ا
... دروك خلاصت، donc ما كاين والو. ا ... الفيلاحه ما كاينه والو،
تسمّى في les environs نتاع ا، ... بشّار كاينت³ شويّه، يديروا خضره،
الأغلبيّه mais نتاع الخضره تروح من الشّمال تروح الـ ... الآخر.⁴ même
داروا barrage، سدّ كبير.

ب: شوف.

أ: سدّ كبير في، في جرف التّربه، انا نظنّ هوّ اكبر سدّ فالآخر. ا ... ما
تهلاوش فيه الأراضي اللّي استصلحوها. عاود تاني غمرها الـ ... غمرتها
الرّمل. وعندهم مشاكيل كبيره فيما يخصّ ا ... باش يحدّوا الرّمل و ....

215

C: baaʃ maa yziidʃ.

A: eeh, wə-nnaas maahuumʃ fəllaaḥiin ntaaʕ əṣṣaḥraa, ḍṭarruu baaʃ jaabuu
mən mʕaaskar wə-kðaa wə.... bə-ṣṣaḥḥ ṣḥaab mʕaaskar kii maa yəgʕudʃ
llaaxər maaʃii ... əlfəllaaḥ mʕa a ... tsəmmaa ʕaam, ʕaameen, tlət sniin
iiʕaawəd yərjaʕ blaaduu. iiðan maa ʕṭaatʃ nataayəj a ... laabas biihaa.

ب: باش ما يزيدش.

أ: ايه، والنّاس ما هومش فلّاحين نتاع الصّحرا، اضطرّوا باش جابوا من معاسكر وكذا و.... بالصّحّ اصحاب معاسكر كي ما يقعدش الآخر ماشي ... الفلّاح مع ا ... تسمّى عام، عامين، تلت سنين يعاود يرجع بلاده، اذًا ما اعطاتش نتايج ا ... لا بس بيها.

Vocabulary:

riiggaan رقّان *prop* Reggane (city in south central Algeria)

taajriiba تاجيبه *nfs* experiment, trial {*pl:* taajaariib}

quunbuula قونبوله *nfs* bomb, explosive device {*pl:* qaanaabəl}

dərrii درّي *adj* atomic, nuclear {*fs:* dərriyya}

xəddəm خدّم *v* to employ, put to work {*imperf:* iixəddəm}

surtout *adv* especially

les transports *nmp* transportation

təmmaa تمّا [*also* θəmma; tsəmma; səmmaa] *adv* there, over there

alors *adv* so, then

budget *nms* budget

varsaa ڤرسى *v* to put; to pour {*imperf:* iivarsii}

un peu mais a little bit but

knaadsa كنادسه *prop* Kanadsa (city near Béchar in western Algeria)

mənjəm منجم *nms* mine, pit {*pl:* maanaajəm}

charbon *nms* coal

druuk دروك [*also* daaruuk] *adv* now

donc *conj* then, so

fiilaaḥa فيلاحه *nfs* agriculture, farming

les environs *nmp* the surrounding area

xuḍra خضره [*also* xuṭra] *nfs; collective* vegetables

mais *conj* but, however

ʃaamaal شامال *nms* north

même *adv* even

barrage *nms* dam

jərf əttarba جــرف الـتـربـه *prop* Djorf Torba (village near Béchar in western Algeria)

ɣmar غمر *v* to cover, bury; to flood, inundate {*imperf:* yəɣmar}

tlət تلت [*also* θəlθ; θlaaθa; tlaata] *nms* three

laa baas لا بـاس *interj* fine, all right (general response to "how is s.o. or s.t.?"); rich, well-off ; *invariable*

laa baas bii + noun or suffixed pronoun لا بـاس بـ s.o. or s.t. is fine, all right (general response to "how is s.o. or s.t.?"); rich, well-off

Notes:

1. What the male speaker calls /lməʃruuʕ ntaaʕ riiggan/ 'the Reggane project' began in 1960. Reggane was the site of the first French nuclear weapons test. Testing continued at several sites in Algeria until 1965.

2. The male speaker omits the negative /maa/ in the phrase /tguul fiihaaʃ ʔa .../ 'you can say that it (fs) has no ...'. This is not typical of SAA. Negation in SAA usually includes /maa/ as well as /ʃ/ (or /ʃii/), as in /**maa** fiihaaʃ/. The use of /ʃ/ alone, omitting /maa/, occurs in certain other varieties of Arabic.

3. The form /kaaynət/ is unusual in the clause /fii les environs ntaaʕ ʔa ... bəʃʃaar **kaaynət** ʃwiyya/ 'in the area there, surrounding ah ... Béchar there is a little'. The form /kaayən/ 'there is, there are' is usually, but not necessarily, invariable in SAA. Where this form takes the feminine ending /a/, the result is typically /kaayna/, as in /fiilaaha maa **kaayna** waaluu/ 'there is no agriculture at all'. The form /kaaynət/ here appears to be a slip of the tongue.

4. The male speaker appears to use the form /llaaxər/ 'the other one' as an all-purpose filler, as in /lʔaaɣlabiyya ntaaʕ lxuḍra truuh mə-ʃʃaamaal truuh li ... **llaaxər**/ 'the majority of vegetables come from the north, it comes from ... the other one'. That is, it seems to function as "what do you call it" does in English.

218

Béchar Flourished Under Colonialism

A: Béchar, what can I tell you? Béchar flourished ... mostly at the time of colonialism, which ... when the Reggane project took place, when they were, ah ... the French were doing, ah ... atomic ... bomb... experiments at Reggane. They hired a lot of people *especially* for the ... for *transportation, transportation*. They brought them there, from Béchar. *So* it was ... all of the ... the *budget* for ... They poured it into Béchar. *So* Béchar flourished *a little but* to ... you can say that it has no ... that is ... there are not types ... of industry.

B: Nothing.

A: There is, there was in the old days ....

C: The traditional kind.

A: Yes. There was in the old days in Kenadsa. There were, ah ... coal, *coal* mines. Ah ... now it's all over, so there is nothing. Ah ... there is no agriculture at all. That is, surrounding, ah ... Béchar there is a little, they grow vegetables, *but* the majority of vegetables come from the north, they come from ... the other one. They *even* built *a dam*, a big dam.

B: Really.

A: A big dam at, at Djorf Torba I think it is the biggest dam in the other one. Ah ... they didn't maintain the land that they reclaimed. It was covered up again by ... The sand covered it up. They have a real problem with what concerns ... to keep back the sand and ....

B: From coming back.

A: Yes. And the people are not farmers, the people in the desert. They were forced to bring them in from Mascara and such and .... But when the people from Mascara didn't stay in the other one, it isn't .... A farmer, that is, a year or two or three, he goes back home. So it didn't give a yield that was ... good.

219

llii yḥabb les dattes

*The Algerian date industry, the topic of this selection, once led the world. It is
still important in the oases of Algeria. Note that the speaker relies more heavily
on French here, although his usage is not always standard.*

A: w-wilaayat a ... biiskra haaðii maʕruufa bii-ṭoolga. ṭoolga *parce que
c'est la production*[1] taaʕ əttmar, *les dattes.*

B: eeh naʕam.

A: ʕandhum ... ʕandhum təmmaa ɣeer əttmar. ttmar haadiik əlxədma taaʕhum
llii duuka ʕandhum taqriiban waaḥd ʕaameen wəllaa tlaaθa llii bdaat
l'exportation taaʕ ttmar l-lxaarəj. nnaas wullaaw yəksporṭyuuh l-lxaarəj,
mən duuka ṭoolga wullaat a ... maʕruufa. maʕruufa fii *Marseille,* maʕruufa
fələ ... *même* fii *Canada.* ham daaruu ʕleehaa *publicité* waaḥd əlwoqt.
même θəmmaa, kii kunt θəmmaa, jaat *TF1* daarət ruu ... daarət *un
reportage* ʕlaa ... ʕlaa *les gens qui produi[s]ent les dattes*[2] a ... təmmaa
laa ... kiifaaʃ iixədmuu w-kiifaaʃ *les palmiers,* kiifaaʃ mənnaa. baaʃ a ...
baaʃ iidiiru waaqiil *la pub* ... *la publicité* taaʕhum, taaʕ *les dattes* haay
... təmmaa. *tellement* duuk wullaat ṭoolga maʕruufa, ktar mən biiskra,
ṭoolga hiya llii ṭəllʕat a ... biiskra. maaniiʃ zə ... zaʕmaa nguullək bəllii
ṭoolga hiya xeer mən biiskra *mais* b-ṣaḥḥ ṭoolga llii raahii ʕandhaa *la
production* taaʕ *les dattes, c'est des meilleures* fə *le monde entier.* lʕiiraaq
ʕandhum *la quantité,* ddzaayər ʕandhaa *la qu* ... ʕandhaa *la qualité, la
qualité* llii maa təlgaayhaaʃ a ... gaaʕiitiik. w-mən duuka fə-ṣṣaḥraa
maa wulluuʃ[3] ɣeer iixədmuu ɣeer a ... nnxal. wullaaw iixədmuu buyuut
plastiikiyya, wullaaw iixədmuu gaaʕiitiik lə ... gaaʕiitiik əlfə ... gaaʕiitiik
ləflaaḥa. *parce que* nnaas θəmmaa wullaaw yaanvastiyuu[4] θəmmaa
fə-nnxal. wullaaw iijiibuu *les poclains,* wullaaw iidiiruu *les puits de
forage,* wullaaw a ... yəɣrasuu w-kulləʃ.

للّي يـحـبّ les dattes

أ: وولاية ا ... بسكره هذي مـعـروفـه بطولقـه. طـولقـه *parce que c'est la*
production[1] تـاع الـتّـمـر، *les dattes*.

ب: ايه نـعم.

أ: عندهم ... عندهم تمّا غير الـتّـمـر. الـتّـمـر هذيك الخدمـه تاعـهم اللّي دوك
عندهم تقريبًا واحد عامـين ولّ ثلاثـه اللّي بدات *l'exportation* تـاع التمار
للخـارج. النّـاس ولّوا يكسپـرطيـوه للخـارج، من دوك طـولقـه ولّت ا ...
مـعـروفـه. مـعـروفـه فـي *Marseille*، مـعـروفـه فـال ... *même* فـي *Canada* هم
داروا عليهـا *publicité* واحد الوقت. *Même* ثـمّـا، كي كنت ثـمّـا، جات *TF1*
دارت رو ... *un reportage* على ... على *les gens qui produi[s]ent les*
dattes[2] ا ... تمّـا لا ... كيفـاش يخدمـوا وكيـفـاش *les palmiers*، كيفـاش منـأ.
بـاش ا ... بـاش يديروا وقـيـل *la publicité* ... *la pub* تاعـهم تـاع *les dattes*
هايـ ... تمّـا. *Tellement* دوك ولّت طـولقـه مـعـروفـه، اكـثـر من بسكره،
طـولقـه هـي اللّي طـلّعت ا ... بسكره. مـانيش ز ... زعمـا نقـولك باللّي
طـولقـه هـي خـيـر من بـسكره *mais* بصـحّ طـولقـه اللي راهي عنـدهـا la
production تـاع *les dattes, c'est des meilleures* فـي *le monde entier*.
الـعـراق عندهم *la quantité*، الـدّزايرعندهـا ... *la qu* عندهـا *la qualité, la*
qualité اللّي مـا تلقايهـاش ا ... قـعيتيك. ومن دوك في الصّـحـرا مـا
ولاوش[3] غير يخدمـوا غيـر ا ... النخل. ولّوا يخدمـوا بـيـوت پلاستيكيـه،
ولّوا يخدمـوا قـاعيتيك ال ... قـاعيتيك الفلاحـه. *parce que.* النّـاس ثـمّـا
ولّوا ينافـسـتيـوا[4] ثـمّـا في النّـخل.

même lbanaanaa kaayən waaḥəd təmmaa *il a essayé de faire la production*
taaʕ *les bananes, même* kaayən a ... yəxdmuu təmmaa lbaṭṭiix, lə ...
ṭṭoomaaṭiiʃ, a ... lfəlfəl, a ... lbaaṭaaṭaa, əlgaməḥ. ham bdaaw ya ...
yəɣarsuu ʕleeh *parce que* θəmmaa kaayən l'*espace* kbiir. daaruu θəmmaa
lii ... gaaʕiitiik, gaaʕət əlwasaaʔəl llii ddawla taaʕnaa ... llii aʕṭaatuulhum
w-kaayən nnaas llii aañvastyaaw məd ... məd ... mə-ddraaham. daaruu
θəmmaa lə ... lalgaməḥ wə ... lḥaaja təmmaa llii ... lḥaaja llii
ydoomaandee *beaucoup d'espace* xədm ... xədmuuhaa. w-kaayən taanii
fələ ... *les dattes, les dattes* yətnuuwʕuu, kaayən taqriiban waaḥd əlmya
w-waaʃ mə-nnawʕ taaʕ *les dattes.* kaayən diiglat nuur, kaayən girbaaʕii.
kaan kə ... kaayn əlgirbaaʕii, kaayən ənnaas iiʕayyṭuuluu maaʃii digla,
kaayən naas iiʕayyṭuuluu waaqiilatan a ... tmuuʃənt. kaayna ɣarsaaya,
haadii yəxdmuu biihaa ɣeer a ... lɣars, lɣars haad ənnaas iidiiruu biih
les gâteaux w-iidiiruu biih lmaqruuṭ. w-nnaxla, nnaxla təbdaa taɣrəshaa,
taɣrəshaa ṣɣiira, triyyəḥ *quinze ans* baaʃ twullii tməddlək *la récolte*
taaʕhaa. *quinze ans* wə-nta təxdəm ʕleehaa baaʃ təbdaa tməddlək. wə-
ləxədma[5] taaʕ ənnaxla maahiiʃ sahla, xədmat ənnaa ... xədmat ənnaxla
ddoomaandee bəzzaaf lxəddaamiin. kaayən a ... əttəlgaaḥ. duuka lwoqt
əllii raanaa fiih duuka xalleethum liġḥuuh. w-duuka raahum f-woqt
əttaʕdaal, ttaʕdaal haaðaa yʕaddluu lə ... lʕarjoon. qbəl ... qbəl maa yjii
yuxrəj, iiʕaddluuh. w-m-baʕda yʕaawduu m-baʕda yʕaawduu ... iirabṭuuh,
yərabṭuuh fələ ... fə-ljiðiʕ taaʕ ənnaxla baaʃ kii ydərbuuh rriiḥ maa
ykassruuʃ. [background talk] w-m-baʕda,

ولّوا يجيبوا les poclains، ولّوا يديروا les puits de forage، ولّوا

il a essayé de faire la تمّا واحد كاين البنانا Même. يغرسوا وكلّش.

production تاع les bananes, même ... كاين ... يخدموا تمّا البطّيخ، الـ ...

الطوماطيش، ا... الفلفل، ا ... البطاطا، القمح. هم بداوا يـ ... يغرسوا

عليه parce que كاين تمّا l'espace كبير. داروا تمّا اللّي ... قاعيتيك،

قاعت الوسائل اللّي الدوله تاعنا ... اللّي اعطاتلهم وكاين النّاس اللّي

أنقستياوا مد ... مد ... من الدراهم. داروا تمّا ال ... القمح و ... الحاجه

تمّا اللّي ... الحاجه اللّي يدوماندي beaucoup d'espace خد ... خدموها. و

كاين تاني فالـ ... les dattes, les dattes يتنوّعوا، كاين تقريبًا واحد الميه

وواش من النّوع تاع les dattes. كاين دجلة نور، كاين قرباعي.كاين كـ

... كاين القرباعي، كاين ناس يعيّطولوله ماشي دجله. كاين النّاس

يعيّطولوا وقيلة ا ... تموشنت، كاين الغرسايه وهذي يخدموا بيها غير

ا ... الغرس، الغرس هذا النّاس يديروا بـ les gâteaux ويديروا بـ

المقروط. والنّخله، النّخله تبدا تغرسها، تغرسها صغيره، تريّح quinze

ans باش تولّي تمدلك la récolte تاعها. Quinze ans وانت تخدم عليها

باش تبدا تمدلك. والخدمه[5] تاع النّخله ماهيش سهله، خدمة النّـ... خدمة

النّخلة تدوماندي بزّاف الخدّامين. كاين ا ... التّلقاح، دوك الوقت اللّي

رانا فيه دوك خلّيتهم لقحوه. ودوك راهم في وقت التّعدال، التّعدال هذا

يعدّلوا الـ ... العرجون. قبل... قبل ما يجي يخرج، يعدّلوه. ومبعد

يعاودوا، مبعد يعاودوا يربطوه، يربطوه فالـ ... في الجذع تاع النّخله

باش كي يضربه الرّيح ما يكسّرهش. [background talk] ومبعد،

223

duuka ʃɣul haadii, *c'est une technique* jdiida, bdaawhaa f-*les années quarante-vingt*, wullaaw iidiiruuluuh *le nylon* baaʃ kii tṣəbb ʃʃtaa,[6] maa tfəssədʃ a ...

B: eeh.

A: ... *les dattes.* wullaaw iidiiruulhum *des nylons* baaʃ maa təfəssədʃ *les dattes.* w-m-baʕda yjii woqt əlgəṭṭaaʕ w-θəmmaa fii *la période* təmmaa taaʕ a ... ttmar. *c'est la période* taaʕ əlxriif. laxriif llii ... llii təbdaa *la récolte* taaʕ *les dattes* w-təmmaa wiin biiskra, twullii fiihaa lə ... lxədma, twullii fiihaa lə ... twullii fiihaa *le mouvement* taaʕ *le va et vient que* ... *le commerce. même les gens* iijuu mə-lxaarəj, iijuu ɣeer f-*la période* taaʕ əlxriif baaʃ yə ... baaʃ iixədmuu. w-biiskra *c'est intéressant de venir* ɣeer fii ... fə-lxriif lə-llii yḥabb a ... *les dattes.*

les années في هـذي، بـداوهـا جـــديده، c'est une technique، دوك شـــغل
quarante-vingt، ولّوا يديروله le nylon بـاش كـي تصبّ الشّتـا⁶ مـا تفسّدش

... ا

ب: ايه.

أ: Les dattes ولّوا يديرولهـم des nylons بـاش مـا تفسّدش les dattes. ومبعد
c'est la التّــمــر ... الـ تاع تمّا في la période وثمّـا وقت القّطّـاع يـجي
les dattes تـاع la récolte اللّي تبدا اللّي ... الخريف. الخريف اللّي، période
le تولّي فيهـا الـ ... الـ فيهـا تولّي الخدمه، الـ فيهـا تولّي بسكره ويـن وتمّا
mouvement تـاع le va et vient que ... le commerce. même les gens يـجـوا
بـاش ... ـي بـاش الخـريف تـاع la période في غـيـر يـجـوا الخـارج، مـن
اللّي الخريف في ... في غير c'est intéressant de venir وبسكره يخدمـوا.
.les dattes يحبّ

Vocabulary:

biiskra بـسكره prop Biskra (town in south central Algeria)

ʈoolga طـولقه prop Tolga (town in southeastern Algeria)

parce que c'est la production because it is the production

les dattes nfp dates

l'exportation nfs the export

əkspoRʈaa اكسيـرطـى v to export {imperf: yəkspoRʈii}

Marseille prop Marseille (city in southern France)

même adv even

Canada prop Canada

ham هـم [also huuma; humm(a); hum] pro they (3P)

publicité nfs commercial, advertisement

même adv even

TF1 prop TF1 (French television channel)

un reportage nms a news report

225

les gens qui produi[s]ent les dattes the one who produce dates

les palmiers *nmp* the palm trees

w-kiifaaʃ mənnaa وكيفاش منّا and so on (lit. and how from here)

waaqiil واقيل [*also* waaqiilaatən] *disc* maybe, perhaps; apparently

la publicité *nfs* commercial, advertising

les dattes *nfp* dates

tellement *adv* so much

ṭəlləʕ طلّع *v* to promote, elevate {*imperf:* iiṭəlləʕ}

zaʕmaa زعما *disc* that is to say, I mean, that is to say; so, then; really

mais *conj* but, however

la production *nfs* the production

les dattes, c'est les meilleures the dates, they are the best ones

le monde entier the whole world

lʕiiraaq العراق *prop* Iraq

la quantité *nfs* the quantity

la qualité, la qualité the quality, the quality

lgaa لقى *v* to find, encounter {*imperf:* yəlgaa}

gaaʕiitiik قاعيتيك [*also* gaaʕətiik] *adv* not at all, never (with negative); all; every, each

nxal نخل *nms; collective* palm trees {*fs:* nəxla, *pl:* nəxlaat}

xdəm خدم *v* to plant, cultivate, grow; to weave; to do, make {*imperf:* yəxdəm}

plaastiikii پلاستيكي *adj* plastic, made from plastic {*fs:* plaastiikiyya, *pl:* plaastiikiyyiin}

parce que *conj* because

aanvastaa انڤاستى [*also* aañvastaa] *v* to invest in, put money into {*imperf:* yaanvastii}

les poclains *nmp* the bulldozers (Fr. brand name)

les puits de forage drilled wells

ɣras غرس *v* to plant, sow {*imperf:* yəɣras}

même *adv* even

baanaanaa بانانا [*also* baanaan] *nms* banana

il a essayé de faire la production he tried to produce

les bananes, même bananas, even

baṭṭiix بطّيخ *nms* melon {*ms:* baṭṭiixa, *pl:* baṭṭiixaat}

ṭoomaaṭiiʃ طوماطيش *nms; collective* tomatoes {*fs:* ṭoomaaṭiiʃa, *pl:* ṭoomaaṭiiʃaat}

fəlfəl فـلـفـل *nms; collective* pepper (spice and vegetable) {*fs:* fəlfla, *pl:* fəlflaat}

baaṭaaṭa بـاطـاطـه *nfs* potato

gaməḥ قـمـح *nms* wheat

parce que *conj* because

l'espace *nms* space

gaaʕət قـاعـت *adv* all; every, each; not at all, never (with negative constructions)

aañvastaa انـڧـاسـتـى [*also* aanvastaa] *v* to invest in, put money into {*imperf:* yaaɲvastii}

doomaandaa دومـانـدى *v* to require; to ask for {*imperf:* iidoomandee}

beaucoup d'espace a lot of space

mya مـيـه *nfs* hundred {*pl:* miyaat}

les dattes, les dattes dates, dates

les dattes *nfp* the dates

tmuuʃənt تمـوشـنـت *prop* Temouchent (variety of date); Temouchent (city in western Algeria)

ɣars غـرس *prop* ghars (variety of date)

les gâteaux *nmp* cakes

maqruuṭ مـقـروط *nms* maqrout (kind of confection made with dates, also pastry filled with this confection)

riyyəḥ ريّـح *v* to be left to rest, left fallow; to rest, relax {*imperf:* iiriyyiḥ}

quinze ans 15 years

mədd مـدّ *v* to give {*imperf:* iimədd}

la récolte *nfs* the harvest

quinze ans 15 years

təlgaaḥ تلـقـاح *nms* pollination

lgaḥ لقـح *v* to pollinate {*imperf:* yəlgəḥ}

taʕdaal تعـدال *nms* straightening; pruning

ʕaddəl عـدّل *v* to straighten, make s.t. straight; to prune {*imperf:* iiʕaddəl}

ʕarjoon عـرجون *nms* date palm branch with date cluster {*pl:* ʕaaraajən}

rbaṭ ربـط *v* to tie, tie up {*imperf:* yərbaṭ}

c'est une technique it is a technique

les années quarante-vingt the eighties

le nylon *nms* nylon (as in cording); plastic bag

şəbb ‎صِبْ‎ v to fall (rain) {imperf: iişəbb}
les dattes nfp the dates
des nylons nylons; plastic bags
les dattes nfp the dates
gəţţaaʕ ‎قَطّاع‎ nms cutter, person who cuts {fs: gəţţaaʕa, pl: gəţţaaʕiin}
la période nfs the time
c'est la période it is the time
la récolte nfs the harvest
les dattes nfp dates
le mouvement nms the movement
le va et vient que ... le commerce, même les gens the coming-and-going that
    ... commerce, even people
la période nfs the time
c'est intéressant de venir it is interesting to come
les dattes nfp dates

Notes:

1. The male speaker here uses the French c'est 'that is' in a non-standard way
    in /parce que c'est la production taaʕ əttmar/ 'because there is [lit. that is]
    the production of dates'. His usage of the same form is again non-standard in
    the phrase /les dattes, c'est les meilleurs fə le monde entier/ 'the dates,
    they are [lit. that is] the best in the whole world". These and other non-standard
    uses are not limited to Algeria. They occur among speakers of French
    everywhere.

2. The male speaker's usage in the phrase /ils produi[s]ent les dattes/ 'they
    produce the dates' is not that of an educated speaker of French. The standard
    French version would be /ils produisent des dattes/ 'they produce dates'.

3. The form /maa wulluuʃ/ 'they did not start', with a long /uu/ in the final
    syllable, occurs most often in some sub-varieties of SAA. Other varieties of
    SAA have the diphthong /aaw/ in the final syllable of this and other
    finally-weak verbs, as in /wullaawʃ/.

4. Note that the male speaker's pronunciation of the form /yaanvastiyuu/ 'they
    invest' differs from his pronunciation of the same word later in this selection.
    The second occurrence is /yaaɲvatiyuu/ 'they invest', with a nasalized
    vowel ending the first syllable. The second occurrence resembles the French

word <u>investir</u>. The reason for variation here is not clear. On one hand, it may indicate that the borrowed verb is not fully integrated into SAA. On the other hand, it may be a slip of the tongue.

5. The additional short /ə/ that follows the definite article in the phrase /wə-ləxədma/ 'the work' is not typical of SAA. A more usual form is /wə-lxədma/, with no vowel after the article. The inserted short /ə/ in /wə-ləxədma/ results from speaker hesitation, not from a regular sound change.

6. The phrase /kii tṣəbb ʃʃtaa/ 'when it rains, lit. when rain falls' is grammatically correct. The verb /tṣəbb/ 'it (fs) falls' takes the 3FS imperfect prefix /t/. The subject of that verb is /ʃʃtaa/ 'rain', a grammatically feminine noun. It derives from the MSA ʃitaaʔ 'rainy season; winter'. As the MSA noun is grammatically feminine (because the final sequence aaʔ is not part of the word root), so is its SAA counterpart.

For Those Who Like Dates

A: And the province of ah ... Biskra is known because of Tolga. Tolga because *there is the production* of dates, *dates.*

B: Yes.

A: They have ..., they only have, I mean, dates. These dates are their work, which they have had now for about two or three years, when *the export* of dates overseas began. People started exporting them overseas. From that point, Tolga became, ah ... well-known, well-known in *Marseille*, well-known ... *even* in Canada. They made a *commercial* about it one time. *Even*, I mean, when I was there, *TF1* ... did ... *a news report* on ... on... *the people who produce the dates*, there ... how they work and how the *date palms*, how, and so on. This is so ah ... maybe to do ... *publicity* ah ... for themselves, for the dates ... there. Now Tolga has become so well known, more than Biskra, that Tolga is what promoted ah ... Biskra. I'm not ... that is, I'm not telling you that Tolga is better than Biskra, *but* Tolga really has *the production of dates. It is the best* in *the whole world.* Iraq has *quantity*, Algeria has ... it has *the quality, the quality* that you won't find ... elsewhere. Since then in the Sahara they didn't just ... just start growing date palms, they started putting up green houses. They started working in all ... all ... on all kinds of agriculture, because people there started investing in date palms. They started bringing in *bulldozers*, they started making *drilled wells*, they started, ah ... planting and everything. *Even* bananas, there is one person there, *he tried to produce bananas.* There are even ... they are growing melons ... tomatoes ... peppers ... potatoes, wheat. They started growing them *because* there is a lot of *space* there. They did it there..., all, all of the means that our country ... that it gave them. There are also people who invested ... money. They grew ... wheat there and ... things there, that are things that require *a lot of space* ... they grow them. There are also ... *dates*, *dates* that come in many varieties. There are about a hundred and some odd kinds of dates. There is the deglat nour, there is the girba'i, there was ... There is the girba'i, people call it "not degla", there are people who call it, ah ... maybe Temouchent. There is the gharsaya that they grow only for, ah ... ghars. The ghars, people make *cakes* with them and they make maqrout with them. Date palms, date palms, you start planting them, you plant them young. They rest for 15 years to start giving you *a harvest*, 15 years while you cultivate them so that they start giving you something. Work on ... date palms is not easy. Work ... work on date palms requires a lot of workers. There is, ah ... pollination. Now is the time, that we're in now, I left them pollinating, and now they are in the time of straightening out. This straightening out is when they straighten the branches before ... before they start to emerge. They straighten them out. Later they go back ... later they go back and tie them, they tie them to the ... to the trunk of the date palm so that when the wind blows, it won't break them. [background talk]. After that there is, like, this, *it is a* new *technique*. They started it in *the eighties*. They started putting *plastic bags* on them so that when it rains it won't ruin ...

B: Yes.

A: ... the dates, they started putting *plastic bags* on them so that it would not ruin the *dates*. Later comes the time for person who does the cutting and, that is, in the *time*, that is ... for the dates, *it's the time* of the fall, the fall that ... that starts the *harvest* of the dates. There, where Biskra is, the work ... it begins there, it begins ..., *the action of back and forth...* , *business* begins, *people even* come from away. They come only in the *time* of the fall to ... to work. Biskra, *it's interesting to* visit only in ... in the fall ... for those who like, ah ... *dates*.

231

nnaas ṭṭwaarəg

The Tuareg people are a minority group in Algeria, as well as in Burkina Faso, Libya, Mayli, Niger, and elsewhere. As described here by a non-Tuareg, they seem both primitive and exotic.

A: wə-nnaas ṭṭwaarəg[1] təmmaa maa zaalhum[2] ʕaayʃiin kiimaa zmaan, *le temps* ʕandhum ḥaabəs, *le temps* təmmaa ʕandhum ḥaabəs. kii truuḥii tʃuufiihum *le temps* ḥaabəs, kii tʃuufiihum tguulii ḥnaa ... maanaaʃ fii ... f-*l'an 2000*, maa zaalhum ...*le temps* taaḥḥum ḥaabəs wəllaa hum ʕaayʃiin fə-zzmaan taaʕ bəkrii f-woqt jjaahiliyya.

B: ʃuuf.

A: maaʃii fə-woqt əljaahiliyya səmmaa maa ʕandhumʃ əl ... lʔaxlaaq wəllaa looxriin, *les traditions* taaḥḥum maa zaalhum ʕaayʃiin fil ... ləxyəm, maa zaal ʕaayʃiin a ... bilə ... əlmʕiiz, maa zaal ʕaayʃiin ʃɣul a ... haakðaak, bərk *à la* ... *à la nature*. w-kii truuḥii tgaṣṣrii mʕaah yə... iiraḥḥab biik, iðayyfak ʕanduu w-iiṭayyblək llaataay, iiṭayyblək *même la* ta ... *la taguela* taaḥḥum *c'est la sa* ... *la specialité* taaḥḥum.

B: waaʃ hii *la taguela*?

A: *La ta* ... *la taguela c'est* ʃɣul lkəsra yṭayybuuhaa fə-ṛṛaməl w-iiʕaawduu yəfittuuhaa[3] w-iidiruulhaa *la sauce* taaḥḥaa bəl ... bə-lḥam jjməl wəllaa yə... w-iidiiruulhaa ddhaan, ddhaan iixarrjuuh milə ... milə ... lḥliib taaʕ əlmʕiiz wəllaa mə-lḥliib taaʕ ... taaʕ ... taaʕ ənnaaga, nnaaga *c'est la femelle* taaʕ jjməl. uwa ... a ... yidiiru haaðaak əl ... *les* ... *les produits* taaʕhum baaʃ idiiruu *la taguela*. wə-huwwa raa ... raahii *la taguela c'est la specialité* taaʕ nnaas taaʕ ... taaʕ tamanraasət w-taaʕ ṭṭwaarəg.

النّاس الطوارق

أ: والنّاس الطوارق[1] تمّى ما زالهم[2] عـايشـين كيـما زمـان، *le temps* عندهم
حابـس، *le temps* تمّى عندهم حابس. كي تروحي تشوفيهم *le temps* حابس،
كي تـشـوفيهم تقولي احنـا ... مـاناش في *l'an 2000*، مـا زالهـم ... *le temps*
تاعهم حابـس ولاّ هم عايشين في الزّمـان تـاع بكري في وقـت الجاهليّه.

ب: شوف.

أ: مـاشي في وقت الجاهليّه سمّى مـا عندهمش الـ ... الأخلاق ولاّ الاوخرين
تاعهم ... مـا زالهم عـايشين فلـ ... في الخيم، مـا زال عـايشين *les traditions*
ا ... بلـ ... المعيـز، مـا زال عـايشين شغل ا ... هكذاك، برك *la* ... *à la* .
nature وكي تـروحي تقصّـري مـعـه يـ ... يرحّب بيك، يضـيّفك عنده
ويطيّبلك التّاي. يطيّبلك *la taguela* ... *la ta* ... *même la ta* ... تاعهم *la sa* ... *c'est la sa*
specialité تاعهم.

ب: واش هي *la taguela*؟

أ: *La ta* ... *la taguela, c'est* شـغل الكسره يطيّبـوها في الرّمل ويعـاودوا
يفتّـوها[3] ويديرولها *la sauce* تاعهـا بالـ ... بلحم الجّمـل ولاّ ... يـ ...
ويديرولها الدّهان. الدّهـان يخرّجوه ملـ ... ملـ ... الحليب تـاع المعيـز ولاّ
مالحليب تـاع ... تـاع ... تـاع النّاقه. النّاقه *c'est la femelle* تـاع الجّمـل. او
... ا ... يديروا هذاك الـ ... *les produits* ... *les* ... تاعهـم باش يديروا *la*
taguela وهوّ را ... راهي *la taguela c'est la specialité* تـاع النّـاس تـاع ...
تاع تمنراست وتاع الطّوارق.

Vocabulary:

ţərgii طرقي *adj* Tuareg (Berber-speaking nomadic peoples of the southern Sahara)
{*pl:* ţərgiyya, *pl:* ţwaarəg}

le temps *nms* time

ḥaabəs حابس *adj* stopped, not moving {*fs:* ḥaabsa, *pl:* ḥaabsiin}

le temps *nms* time

le temps *nms* time

maanaaʃ ماناش we are not

l'an *2000* the year 2000

jaahiliyya جاهليّه *prop* the Jahiliyya, pre-Islamic Arabia: ignorance. barbarism

les traditions *nfp* the traditions

xiima خيمه *nfs* tent {*pl:* xyəm}

mʕaz معز *nms* goat {*pl:* mʕiiz}

à la ... à la nature in the style of ... naturally

gaşşər قصّر *v* to talk, chat; to pass, spend the evening {*imperf:* iigaşşər}

ðayyəf ظيّف *v* to host, treat as a guest {*imperf:* iiðayyəf}

laataay لاتاي *nms* tea

même la ta ... la taguela even the ... the *taguela*

c'est la sa ... c'est la spécialité it is the specialty

la taguela *nfs* *taguela* (kind of bread cooked in hot ash)

la ta ... la taguela the ... *taguela*

raməl رمل *nms* sand

fəttət فتّت *v* to break into small pieces, crumble {*imperf:* iifəttət}

la sauce *nfs* the sauce

dhaan دهان *nms* butter; cooking oil, fat

naaga ناقه *nfs* female camel {*pl:* nyaag, *pl:* nuug}

c'est la femelle it is the female

les, les produits the, the products

la taguela *nfs* the *taguela* (kind of bread cooked in hot ash)

la taguela c'est la spécialité *nfs* *taguela*, it's the speciality

tamanraasət تمنراست *prop* Tamanrasset (city in southern Algeria)

Notes:

1. Speaking about /nnaas ṭṭwaarəg/ 'the Tuareg people', the speaker describes a group to which he does not belong and may not actually know. In Algeria, the Tuareg live in the far south. Tamanrasset is the main urban center of the region. Tuareg also live in the Saharan regions of Burkina Faso, Libya, Mali, and Niger. They form a minority group in each of these countries. Historically, the Tuareg are nomads who traditionally live by herding and the caravan trade. They speak a variety of Berber called Tamahaq or Tamashek, and their practice of Islam retains non-Islamic elements. All of these factors help explain by the speaker describes the Tuareg as strange, primitive, and even immoral. The Tuareg as a group are none of these things, although theirs is different from the majority culture of Algeria.

2. The speaker's use of /maa zaal/ 'to still be, do' here contrasts with his use of the same structure later in this selection. The first occurrence is /**nnaas ṭṭwaarəg** təmmaa maa zaalhum ʕaayʃiin ? ... kiimaa zmaan/ 'the Tuareg people there still live ... like the old days'. Here, the 3P suffixed pronoun /hum/ of /maa zaalhum/ 'they still' shows agreement with the grammatical subject of the clause /nnaas ṭṭwaarəg/ 'the Tuareg people'. The structure /maa zaal/ occurs again in the phrase /**maa zaal** ʕaayʃiin/ 'they still live'. In this second occurrence, /maa zaal/ is invariable, showing no agreement with the 3P subject. A third structure also occurs in SAA. It resembles MSA usage. In this third structure, /maa zaal/ inflects as a perfect verb to agree with its subject, as in /lʕaadaat llii **maa zaalt** muujuuda/ 'the customs that are still present' (Selection 18). All three forms occur in SAA. They appear to be associated with regional variation.

3. The form /yfiṭṭuuhaa/ 'they break it (fs) up' with a doubled /ṭ/ and no apparently third consonant to complete the three-consonant root, derives from the Form II verb /fəṭṭəṭ/ 'to break s.t. into pieces'. A Form II verb with a strong or three-consonant root has a 3P imperfect like that of /iiḥaggruu/ 'they despise'. The strong root verb has loss of the unstressed short vowel before C₃, the short /ə/ vowel of the 3MS imperfect /iiḥaggər/ 'he despises'. As a result, the strong root verb has a cluster of three consonants in the 3P imperfect. The form /yfiṭṭuu/ has also lost the unstressed short vowel that is apparent in the 3MS form /iifəṭṭəḥ/. The form, however, has no three-consonant cluster because SAA does not have clusters of three identical consonants. Thus, /yfiṭṭuu/ loses the third /ṭ/.

The Tuareg People

A: The Tuareg people, that is, still live ah... like in the old days. *Time* has stopped for them, *time*, that is, has stopped for them. When you go to see them *time* stopped. When you see them, you'll say we ... We're not in ... in *the year 2000*. They are still ... *time* for them has stopped. Or they are living in the past, in the old days, in pre-Islamic Arabia.

B: Really.

A: Not in the time of pre-Islamic Arabia, that is, they don't have ... morals or other things. Their *traditions* ... they are still living in ... in tents. They still live, ah .... off ... off of sheep. They still live a kind of ... that way, just ... *naturally*. When you go and talk to one of them ... he will welcome you, treat you as his guest, and make you tea. He'll *even* make you their <u>taguela</u>. It's ... their *specialty*.

B: What is <u>taguela</u>?

A: It ... <u>taguela</u> is like bread. They cook it in the sand, and take it out and tear it into pieces, and make a *sauce* for it with ... with camel meat or they ... and they put fat in it, the butter they get from ... from goat milk or from the milk of ... of ... of the <u>naaga</u>. The <u>naaga</u>, *that's the female* camel. This way they use *the ... the products* they have to make <u>taguela</u>. And it is ..., <u>taguela</u> is *the specialty* among the people of ... of Tamanrasset and among the Tuareg.

ttaaqaaliid ntaaʕ laataay

Small glasses of heavily sweetened tea are the basis of hospitality in Algeria as elsewhere. This selection details the importance of tea and the customs associated with it. Note that, in the south, men prepare and serve tea to their male guests.

A: ʕandak a ... ḥaaja ooxraa, laataay.[1] maa kaanʃ əddaar ... l*budget* ntaaʕhum fii laataay w-ssukkur.

B: ṣaḥḥ.

A: laataay, maaʃii laataay llii nʃruuhaa ḥnaa. laataay ɣaalii, laataay daaymən *c'est le* waaḥd w-səbʕiin haaðaak.

C: aah.

A: w-loo kaan iiruuḥ ʕleeh l-bəʃʃaar,[2] loo kaan iixallii əl ... ʕleeh lxulṣa ntaaʕuu, iixallii lə ... lʕuula ntaaʕ a ... lgamiḥ wəllaa ntaaʕ əlfaariina w-iiʃrii *d'abord* laataay. laataay wə-ssukkur haaðii maa kaanʃ əddaar llii mənnuu.

B: [laugh]

C: [xxx].

A: *Alors* ʕandək a ... ttaaqaaliid ndaaʕuu[3] daaruuk, loo kaan kii sii ʕabd əlqaadir gaal, tʃarbuu laataay? w-kaan nruuḥ l-ʕandhum[4] anaa ysuuwluunii, yguullii, 'tʃarb[5] laataay?' nguul. 'eeh.' b-ḥaal ilaa tsəmmaa *je me suis engagé* ʕalaa a ... *trois verres*, kii yguullək tʃarb laataay? laataay huuma ʕandhum barraad, lluwwəl wə-zzawj wə-ttaalət. maa ysuwwələkʃ qbəl ... waaʃ tziid qbəl *le quatrième*.

C: *Quatrième.*

التّاقاليد نتاع لاتاي

أ: عندك ا ... حاجـه اوخرى، لاتاي.[1] مـا كـانش الدّار الـ budget نتـاعـهم في
لاتاي والسّكر.

ب: صحّ.

أ: لاتاي، مـاشي لاتاي اللّي نشـروهـا احنـا. لاتاي غـالي، لاتاي دايمًا le est'c
واحد وسبعين هذاك.

ج: اه.

أ: ولو كان يروح عليه لبشّار،[2] لو كان يخلّي الـ ... عليه الخلصـه نتـاعـه،
يخلّي الـ ... العوله نتـاع ا ... القمح ولاّ نتـاع الفـارينه ويشـري d'abord
لاتاي، لاتاي والسّكر هذي ما كانش الدّار اللّي منّه.

ب: [laugh].

ج: [xxx].

أ: Alors عندك ا ... التأقاليد نتاعه[3] داروك، لو كان كي سي عبد القادر قال،
«تشـربوا لاتي؟» وكان نروح لعندهم[4] انا يسـوّلوني يقولّي، «تشرب[5]
لاتاي؟ نقول، «ايـه.» بحـال الى تسـمّى je me suis engagé على ا ... trois
verres كي يقــولّك، «تشــرب لاتاي؟» لاتاي هـوم عندهم برّاد، اللاّوّل
والزّوج والتّالت. مـا يسوّلكش قبل ... «واش تزيد؟» قـبل le quatrième.

ج: Quatrième.

A: w-ʕandhum loo kaan a ... maḥsuub a ... maa tguulluu, 'tʃarb laataay?'
    w-b-ḥaal ilaa səbbeetuu ilaa maa ... ilaa maa tʃarbʃ laataay xaaṭər yə
    ... yəxxədmuuh b-waahəd a ... tsəmmaa maaḥabba w-waaḥəd *l'affection*
    w-waaḥəd a ... waaḥəd *protocole* iiḥəṭṭ llaaxuur w-iiḥaṭṭuu ḥdaamuu
    haaðaak w-haaðaa wə-nnaas ... loo kaanuu iijiibuu a ... lmaθal a ...
    tkuunuu ʕaayla kiimaa haak ö̞yaaf w-iijiibuu lə ... laataay yəndaar
    kiimaa yguuluu huuma ʕand ənnsaa, iigəlbuuh xlaaṣ. laataay yəndaar
    ʕand ərrjaal w-iidiiruuh rrjaal, tsəmmaa nnsaa maa ... [laugh], maa
    yʃərbuuhʃ.

B: ṣaḥḥ.

A: *Ah, ça c'est* xlaaṣ a ....

B: həm.

A: *Alors le ... même* əlmaa, iixəṣṣ lmaa yṭiib w-luu kaan maḥsuub maa
    ykuunʃ waaṣəl l-waaḥəd əddaraja ntaaʕhaa, ssxaana, maa ydiiruuʃ
    tsəmmaa lə ... gaaʕ ... *c'est tout un protocole* baaʃ ii ...

B: ṣaḥḥ, ṣaḥḥ.

C: [xxx].

A: ... baaʃ iidiiru laataay.

240

أ: وعندهم لو كان... مـحـسـوب ا ... مـا تقولّه، «تشرب لاتاي؟» بـحـال لى
سبّيـتـه، الا مـا ... الا مـا تشربـش لاتاي خـاطر يـ... يخّدمـوه بـواحد ا ...
تسمّى الماحبّه وواحد l'affection وواحد ا ... واحد protocole يـحطّ اللاّخر
ويـحطّه حدامـه هذاك وهذا والنّـاس ... لو كان يـجـيـبـوا ا ...المثل ا ...
تكونوا عايله كيما هاك ضياف ويجيبوا الـ ... لاتاي يندار كيما يقولوا
هوم عند النّسـا، يقلبـوه خـلاص. لاتاي يندار عند الرّجـال ويديروه
الرّجال، تسمّى النّسا مـا [laugh] ... مـا يشربوهش.

ب: صحّ.

أ: .... ا خلاص Ah, ça c'est

ب: هم.

أ: Alors le ... même المـا، يخصّ المـا يطيب ولو كان مـحـسـوب مـا يكونش
واصل لواحد الدّرجه نتاعها، السّخانـه، مـا يديروش تسمّى الـ... قاع ...
باش يـ.... c'est tout un protocole

ب: صحّ، صحّ.

ج: [xxx].

أ: ... بـاش يديروا لاتاي.

Vocabulary:

le budget *nms* the budget
c'est le it is the
waaḥd w-səbſiin واحد وسبعين 71 (kind of tea)
xulṣa خلصه *nfs* salary {*pl:* xulṣaat}
ſuula عوله *nfs* provisions, supplies
d'abord *adv* first, at first, first of all
daaruuk داروك [*also* druuk] *adv* now

je me suis engagé I have committed myself

trois   verres three glasses

barraad برّاد *nms* tea pot {*pl:* braarəd}

zawj زوج [*also* zooj; zuuj; juuz] *nms* two

suwwəl سوّل *v* to ask, inquire {*imperf:* iisəwwəl}

taalət تالت *adj* third {*fs:* taalta}

zaad زاد *v; pre-verb* to do again (action of main verb); to continue to do (action of main verb); to be born {*imperf:* iiziid}

səbb سبّ *v* to insult, call s.o. a name {*imperf:* iisəbb}

le quatrième *adj* the fourth

xaaṭər خاطر [*also* xaaṭʃ; xaaṭʃii; xaaṭ] *conj* because, due to the fact that

quatrième *adj* fourth

maaḥabba ماحبّه *nfs* affection, love

l'affection affection

protocole *nms* formalities

ḥdaam حدام *prep* next to

ȡiif ظيف *nms* guest {*pl:* ȡyaaf, *pl:* ȡyuuf}

gləb قلب *v* to reverse, turn upside down {*imperf:* yəgləb}

ça c'est that is

alors le ... même so, the ... even

xəṣṣ خصّ *v; pre-verb* to be necessary (for s.o. or s.t. to do action of the main verb) {*imperf:* iixəṣṣ}

ṭaab طاب *v* to boil, be on the boil; to cook, to be cooking; to ripen, be ripe {*imperf:* iiṭiib}

c'est tout un protocole it is all formalities

Notes:

1. Note the form /laataay/ 'tea' in SAA. The initial /l/ is not that of the definite article. The SAA usage of this word differs from, for example, that of Spoken Moroccan Arabic (SMA). The form in SMA is /aataay/, without an initial /l/. Note that both forms are invariable and do not take the definite article /əl/.

2. The male speaker here uses the form /bəʃʃar/ 'Béchar', with stress on the

first syllable and a short vowel /a/ in the second. More usually in SAA, the city is /bəʃʃaar/, with a long vowel in the second syllable that therefore takes stress.

3. The male speaker's use of the form /ndaaʕuu/ 'belonging to it (ms)', with /d/ following /n/, appears to be a slip of the tongue. The more usual SAA form is /ntaaʕuu/, with /t/ following /n/.

4. The male speaker's use of /kaan/ as a conditional particle, as in /**kaan** nruuḥ l-ʕandhum/ 'if we went to visit them' is associated with regional variation. Some regional sub-varieties of SAA have the paired conditional particles /loo kaan/ and /kaan/. The particle /loo kaan/, as in other sub-varieties of SAA, tends to mark unreal or contrary-to-fact conditionals, as in /**loo kaan** yruuḥ ʕlaah l-bəʃʃar/ 'even if he were to go to Béchar for it' (this selection). The particle /kaan/, in contrast, marks real or predictive conditionals, as it does here.

5. The form /tʃarb/ 'you (ms) drink' is a variant form of /tʃrab/.

The Traditions of Tea

A: You've got ah ... something else, tea. There is no house ... its budget is for tea and sugar.

B: Right.

A: Tea, it's not the tea that we buy. Tea is expensive. That tea there *it is* always "Number 71".

C: Yes.

A: Even if someone goes to Béchar for tea, even if he sets aside something for it from his salary, he leaves out ... provisions of ... wheat or flour, and he buys tea *first*. Tea and sugar, no house is without them.

B: [laugh].

C: [xxx].

A: So now you have ah ... the traditions of tea. If Mr. Abdelkader says, "Will you have tea?" And if I went to their place, he'd ask me, he'd say, "Will you have tea?" I say, "Yes." It's as if, that is, *I have committed myself* to, ah ... *three glasses* when they say, "Will you have tea?" Tea for them is, they have a pot of tea, the first glass, the second glass, and the third glass. They don't ask you want more until ... "Would you like another?" until the *fourth*.

C: *The fourth.*

A: For them, if ah ... that is, ah ... you don't say to him, "Will you have tea?" It would be as if you had insulted him if ... if you don't drink tea, because ... they make it with ah ... that is, love and a certain *affection* and a certain ah ... *protocol*. He puts this and he puts it next to that one ... That and people, if they brought ah ... the example is ah ... you are a family like that, guests, and they bring the ... tea made, as they say, among women, they would pour it right out. Tea is made among men and men make it. That is, women don't ... [laugh] they don't drink it.

B: True.

A: *Ah, that is*, that's it, ah ....

B: Hum.

A: *So the ... even* the water, the water has to boil, and if it hasn't reached a particular degree of it, of heat, they don't make it. That is, the ... all ... *there is an entire protocol* for ....

B: Right, right.

C: [xxx].

A: ... for making tea.

245

rrdiim haaðaa yərdmuuh bə-rrəməl

As previous selections indicate, life in Algeria differs differs from place to place. The traditional remedy described here is another example of these differences.

A: w-kaayən taanii *un autre remède* iidiiruuh təmmaa fə-ṣṣaḥraa, rrdiim. rrdiim haaðaa yərdmuuh bələ ... bə-rrəməl, *parce que* θəmmaa huuma yjuu f-*la période* taaʕ *août*[1] wiin tkuun ssxaana.

B: wəs ... wə-smuu kiifaah?

A: rrdiim.

B: rrədiim.

A: rrdiim, haaðaa rrdiim jaa mən kilmət yə ... yərdim waaḥəd bə-rraməl. hiyya kii llii waaḥəd raahuu llii kii fə-*la plage* yaḥfər ḥafra, yədxul daaxəl w-iiɣaṭṭii ruuḥuu. iiɣaṭṭii ruuḥuu haaðaak w-yəmsaḥuu. w-θəmmaa ssxaana taaʕ əṣṣaḥraa wə-ssxana taaʕ *la plage* maaʃii kiif kiif.

B: eeh.

A: ssxaana haaðiik ... w-taanii yruuḥuulhaa fii *août*, ssxaana llii ḍḍarbak fə-ssəmʃ mən foog ərraas, *la température* taaḥḥaa təlḥag aḷḷaah aʕlam waaqiil waaḥəd[2] *cinquante* wəllaa *cinquante-cinq degrés.*[3] immaalaa ssxaana haaðiik llii fə-rrəməl, ərrməl raahuu θaanii sxuun kii yədxul waaḥəd θəmmaa, əssxaana haaðiika təjbədluu gaaʕiitiik ələ ... lmaa llii raahuu fələ ... rkaaybuu wəllaa, haaðaa *le rhumatisme* gaaʕiitiik təjbədluu, səmmaa rrəməl haaðaa yməṣṣluu lʕaraq taaʕuu.

B: eeh.

الرديم هذا يردموه بالرمل

أ: وكـايـن تـانـي *un autre remède* يديروه تمّا في الصّحرا، الرديم. الرديم هذا يـردمـوخ بـالـ ... بـالـرمـل، *parce que*، ثمّى هـوم يجـوا فـي *la période* تـاع *août*[1]وين تكون السّخانه.

ب: وسـ ... واسمه كيفاه؟

أ: الرّديم.

ب: الرّديم.

أ: الرّديم، هذا الرّديم جا من كلمة يـ... يردم واحد بالرّمل. هيّ كي اللّي واحد راه اللّي كي في *la plage* يـحـفـر حفـره يدخل داخل ويغطّي روحه. يغطّي روحه هذاك ويمسحه. وثمّى السخانه تاع الصّحرا والسّخانه تاع *la plage* مـاشي كيف كيف.

ب: ايه.

أ: السّخانه هذيك ... وتانـي يـروحـولها في *août*، السّخانه اللّي تضربك في السّـمـش مـن فـوق الـراس، *la température* تـاعـهـا تلحـق اللّه اعلم وقـيـل واحـد[2]*cinquante* و لاّ[3] *cinquante-cinq degrés*. مّـالا السّخانه هذك اللّي في الرّمل، الرّمل راه ثانـي سـخـون كي يدخل واحد ثمّى السّخانه هذيك تجبدله قاعيتيك الـ ... المـا اللّي راه فلـ ... ركـايـب و لاّ. هذا *le rhumatisme* قاعيتيك تجبدله، تسمّى الرمل هذا يمصّله العرق تاعه.

ب: اسه.

A: wə-m-baʕda kii ybrəd ʕleeh, iiziid iiʕaawəd yədxul fii ḥafra waaḥd uuxra w-iiziid iiʕaawəd iiɣaṭṭii ruuḥuu. *en même temps* huwwa kii yʃrab fə-laataay[4] w-yəʃrab əzziit ziituun[5] baaʃ maa yənʃəfʃ.

B: iih. ṣaḥḥ.

A: *Parce que* huwwa kii yədxul daaxəl yaʕrag, *tellement* yaʕrag laazəmluu, laazəmluu yəʃrab w-baaʃ yəʃrab əlmaa *sec*[6] uu ... waaḥduu, *peut-être* yəṣraaluu *d'autres problèmes*[7] wəllaa maa ʕlaa baalii, iiʃarrbuuluu laa ... yʃarrbuuluu laataay wəllaa zziit ziituun. haaðaa kaayən naas llii raahum kii yjuu *même* θaanii mə-lxaarəj baaʃ iidiiruu *le traitement* haaðiyyaa. *même* taanii kaayən, kaayən *des médecins* llii yaʕjəbhum, kaayən *des médecins* llii *conseillent ma* ... *les* ... *les gens* baaʃ iiruuḥuu yədiiruu *le remède* haaðaa.

أ: ومبعد كي يبرد عليه يزيد يعاود يدخل في حفره واحد اوخرى ويزيد
يعود يغطّي روحه. *en même temps.* هو كي يشرب في لاتاي⁴ ويشرب
الزّيت زّيتون⁵ باش ما ينشفش.

ب: ايه.، صحّ.

أ: *Parce que* هوّ كي يدخل داخل يعرق، *tellement* يعرق لازمله، لازمله
يشرب وباش يشرب الما *sec*⁶ و... وحده، *peut-être* يصراله *d'autres*
*problèmes*⁶ ولا ما على بالي يشّربوله لا ... يشّربوله لاتاي ولا الزّيت
الزّيتون. هذا كاين النّاس اللّي راهم كي يجوا *même* تاني مالخارج باش
يديروا *le traitement* هذيا تاني *même* كاين، كاين *des médecins* اللّي
يعجبهم، كاين *des médecins* اللّى *les gens les* ... *les* ... *conseillent ma* باش
يروحوا يديروا *le remède* هذا.

Vocabulary:

rdiim رديم *nms* burial (in sand, debris, etc.)

rdəm ردم *v* to bury, cover with (sand, debris, etc.); to fill up with earth (hole, etc.)
{*imperf:* yərdəm}

un autre remède another remedy

parce que *conj* because

la période *nfs* the time

août *nms* August

sm- + suffixed pronoun + kiifaah اسم ... كيفاش *nms* what is s.o.'s name

la plage *nfs* the beach

ɣaṭṭaa غطّى *v* to cover, conceal {*imperf:* iiɣaṭṭii}

msaḥ مسح *v* to wipe, wipe off {*imperf:* yəmsaḥ}

août *nms* August

səmʃ سمش [*also* ʃəms; ʃəmʃ] *nfs* sun

la température *nfs* the temperature

aḷḷaa aʕlam الله اعلم God only knows (lit. God is the most knowing; said of uncertain or undesirable outcome)

lḥag لحق *v* to catch up with, overtake; to reach, arrive at {*imperf:* yəlḥag}

cinquante 50

rəkba ركبه *nfs* knee {*pl:* rkaayəb}

cinquante-cinq degrés 55 degrees

le rhumatisme *nms* rheumatism

məṣṣ مصّ *v* to absorb, suck up {*imperf:* iiməṣṣ}

en même temps at the same time

ziit ziituun زيت زيتون olive oil

nʃəf نشف *v* to dry up, become dry {*imperf:* yənʃəf}

parce que *conj* because

ʕraq عرق *v* to sweat, perspire {*imperf:* yaʕraq}

tellement *adv* so much

laazəm 1 + suffixed pronoun لازم لـ *adj; pre-verb; invariable* it is necessary for (s.o. to do action of main verb)

sec *adj* alone, with nothing else

peut-être *adv* maybe

ʃarrəb شرّب *v* to give s.o. to drink, make s.o. drink {*imperf:* iiʃa rrəb}

d'autres problèmes other problems

même *adv* even

le traitement *nms* the treatment

des médecins some doctors

conseillent ma ... les ... les gens advise [3p] ... people

le remède *nms* the remedy

Notes:

1. The male speaker uses the French <u>août</u> or the SAA borrowing from French /uut/ to name the month of August. Speakers of Arabic in North Africa mostly use the month names used by their former colonizers for the months of the secular calendar. The months of the Islamic or hijri calendar, of course, have their Arabic names.

2. The phrase /**waaḥəd** cinquante wəllaa cinquante-cinq degrés/ 'about 50 or 55 degrees' uses the form /waaḥəd/ as an indefinite article (see Selection 1, note 11). Here, /waaḥəd/ is best translated as 'about, around'. As an indefinite article in a counted-noun construction, /waaḥəd/ precedes the

counted-noun construction that is also definite.

3. A temperature of /waaḥəd *cinquante* wəllaa *cinquante-cinq degrés*/ 'about 50 or 55 degrees' does not sound extreme on the centigrade scale. The fahrenheit equivalent, however, is 120 - 130 degrees.

4. The clause /yʃrab **fə-laataay**/ 'he keeps on drinking tea' has an indirect object /laataay/ marked with the preposition /fə-/. The verb /ʃrab/ - /yəʃrab/ usually takes a direct object, as in /yəʃrab **əlmaa** sec/ 'he drinks water by itself' in this selection. The use of the indirect object here suggests that the action of the verb takes place over a period of time.

5. The phrase /**əz**ziit ziituun/ 'olive oil', with the definite article on the word /ziit/ 'oil', is unusual in SAA. This phrase occurs more usually as the construct phrase /ziit **əz**ziituun/, where the second noun of the construct /ziituun/ 'olives' takes the definite article.

6. The male speaker's use of the form *sec* in the clause /yəʃrab əlmaa *sec*/ 'he drinks water *alone*' is not clear. The French form *sec* means 'dry, without dampness', but also 'alone, by itself' and 'in one go, all at once'. The speaker's use of the word here apparently comes from a second meaning of *sec*, 'by itself, without water (usually used of liquor)'.

7. The male speaker describes the results of drinking plain water during <u>rdiim</u> by saying /*peut-être* yəṣraaluu *d'autres problèmes*/ 'it might cause him other problems'. It is not clear what kinds of problems he means by that statement. The following phrase /wəllaa maa ʕalaa baalii/ 'or whatever, I don't know' suggests that these problems are not clear to the speaker, either.

This <u>Rdim</u>, They Bury Him in the Sand

A: There is also *another cure*. They do it there in the Sahara, it is <u>rdim</u>. This <u>rdim</u>, they bury him in the sand, *because*, that is, they come there in the *time* of *August* when it is hot.

B: Wha ... what is it called?

A: <u>Rdim</u>.

B: <u>Rdim</u>.

A: <u>Rdim</u>, this <u>rdim</u> comes from the word ... <u>yirdim</u>, to cover someone with sand. It's like when someone who, when he goes to *the beach*, digs a hole and gets inside and covers himself up. He covers himself up and smoothes it down. But, that is, the heat of the desert and the heat of *the beach* are not the same.

B: Yes.

A: Such heat. In addition, they go there in *August*. The heat that beats down on your head from the sun, its temperature reaches, God knows, maybe *50* or *55 degrees*. So this heat, which is in the sand, the sand itself is also hot. When a person gets in it there, this heat takes out all the ... the water that is in the ... his knees or whatever. *The rheumatism*, it takes it all out. That is, this sand sucks up all of his sweat.

B: Yes.

A: Later, when it cools down, he gets into another hole and covers himself up again. *At the same time* as he keeps on drinking tea or olive oil so he does not get dehydrated.

B: Yes, right.

A: *Because*, when he gets inside, he sweats, he sweats *so much* he has to, he has to drink something. For him to drink water *alone*, by itself *might* cause him *other problems* or whatever, I don't know. They have him drink, they have him drink tea or olive oil. All that, and there are people who also come from abroad to have this *treatment*. Also there are even, there are *doctors* who like it, who advise ... people to go and have this *remedy*.

l'histoire ntaaʕ ə aars

An argument over a date palm turns violent in this selection. Like many family stores, however, an unfortunate incident has a reasonably happy ending.

A: baabaa ḷḷaah yərḥamuu kaan a ... wuqʕətluu ḥaadəθa, wuqʕatluu ḥaadəθa fələ ... fələ... haaðaa fə-luujaah lbayyəð, ʕannaa nxal wə-ʕannaa kəðaa wələ ... w-iijii ... kaayna θəmmaa ...ʕannaa zzwii,[1] haaðuu zzwii θəmmaa huuma ... .

B: wəʃ hiya[2] zzwii?

A: ʃurf ... zzwii *c'est* ʃərfaa, ʃərwə ... .

B: wəʃ hiya ʃʃərfaa, *pardon*?

A: ʃʃərfaa *c'est les descendants du prophète*, ay.

B: aah [xxx].

A: ay *et alors* lə ... llooxriin llii maaʃii ʃərfaa yxəddmuuhum, maḥsuub yaʕṭiiw ṣadaqa *et caetera. Bon, ah ... pratiquement c'est, c'est des seigneurs. Alors* jaa xaṭra gaal lə ... lə ... lə ... lə ... lə-ʃʃeex gaalluu,[3] haað ləs ... kaat ʕannaa waaḥd ənnəxla taʕṭii waaḥd əttmar *extraordinaire*. gaalluu, 'jjiiha haaðii xalliihaa, maa tə ... xaaṭiikum haaðii, maa tziidʃ dduur biihaa.' naaḍ jəddii ḷḷaah yərḥamuu, gaalluu, 'xalliihaaluu, mneen ḥaabb ṭṭmaʕ fiihaa? maaʕliiʃ w-haaðuu, tsəmmaa ʃʃərfaa [xxx].' lə ... ʃʃiibaanii maa ḥabbʃ, gaalluu, 'laa, ʕlaah kiifaaʃ hiyya?' *Bon*, tnawwḍuu ʕliihaa, lgaah xaṭra yənquʃhaa, jraa m-wraah. məm-baʕdiin mərra ooxraa ʕaawəd taanii lgaah yənquʃhaa, byaa yəjrii m-wraah, jraa m-wraah bə-xudmii, *avec un poignard*. lə ... ʃʃiibaanii ḷḷaah yərḥamuu kaan ʕanduu waaḥəd lxəddiimii kiimaa haak, ḥrab, mniin ʃaafuu garrab leeh, jbəd lxədmii haaðaak w-ɣeer mən taḥt l-taḥt aʕṭaah mən hnaa lə-hnaayaa, fətḥ ... fətḥuu. fətḥuu wə-jraa m-wraah, mə ... mə ... raɣəm maḥsuub a ... mbliisii.[4]

نتاع الثار l'histoire

أ: بابا اللّه يرحمه كان ا ... وقعتله حادثه، وقعتله حادثه فـ ... فلـ ... هذا فالوجاه البيّض، عندنا نخل وعندنا كذا والـ ... ويجي... كاينه تسمّى ... عندنا الزّوي،[1] هذو الزّوي ثمّا هوم ....

ب: واش هي[2] الزّوى؟

أ: شرفـ ... الزّوي c'est شرفا، شرفا و ....

ب: واش هي الشّرفا، pardon؟

أ: الشّرفا c'est les descendants du Prophète، اي.

ب: اه [xxx].

أ: ايه. Et alors الـ ... الأوخرين اللّي ماشي شرفا يخدّموهم، محسوب يعطيوا صدقه et caetera. Bon, ah ... pratiquement c'est, c'est des seigneurs. Alors جا خطره قال الـ ... الـ ... الـ ... الشّيخ قالّه[3] هاز السـ ... كات عندنا واحد النّخله تعطي واحد التّمر extraordinaire. قالّه، «الجّيهه هذي خلّيها، ما تـ ... خاطيكم هذي، ما تزيدش تدوّر بيها.» ناض جدّي اللّه يرحمه، قالّه، «خلّيهاله، منين حابّ تطمع فيها؟ معليش وهذو. تسمّى الشّرفا [xxx].» الـ ... الشّيباني ما حبّش، قالّه، «لا، علاه كيفاش هي؟ Bon، » تناوضوا عليها، لقاه خطره ينقشها، جرى موراه، من بعدين مرّه اوخرى عاود تاني لقاه ينقشها، بغى يجري موراه، جرى موراه بخدمي، avec un poignard الـ ... الشّيباني اللّه يرحمه كان عنده واحد الخدّيمي كيماه هاك، هرب، منين شافه قرّب ليه، جبد الخدمي هذاك وغير من تحت لتحت اعطاه من هنا لهنايا، فتحـ ... فتحه. فتحه وجرى موراه، مـ ... ممـ ... رغم محسوب ا ... مبليسي.[4]

255

C: [xxx].

A: jraa m-wraah w-bdaa yxaaf ʃʃiibaanii, gaal xlaaṣ. lḥag ʕleeh wə-laa …
nsiit baaʃ nquul bəllii ssiid haaðaa,[5] kaan tbaark aḷḷaah a … insaan a
… .

C: gaadər.

A: gaadər w-kəðaa w-gaaʕ nnaas txaaf mənnuu, gaaʕ nnaas txaaf mənnuu.
maḥsuub kaan … *alors* kii jraa m-wraah *à un certain moment* jaa lə …
kaan lgaa … tlaagaaw tsəmmaa ḥeeṭ. ʃʃiibaanii ḷḷaah yərḥamuu daar
iiduu kiimaa haak w-nəggəz … wə-llaaxər *carrément* … .

B: yuuh!

A: *Il l'a enjambé.* tsəmmaa nəggzuu blaa maa ydiir iideeh. bə-ṣṣaḥḥ haaðiik
ttəngiiza lə … tsəmmaa lə … fwaaduu xrəj.

B: aah.

A: fwaaduu xrəj bdaa yʃəmm ərriiḥa, bdaa yduux, ʕaad tsəmmaa bdaa yə…
yaʕyaa wə … wə-ʃʃiibaanii raaḥ. mziyya jaaw lə … nnass *juste* məm-baʕd,
lgaawuu haakðaak θəmmaa a … raayaḥ [xxx], ɣaadii ymuut. w-gaallhum
b-fummuu, gaal, 'yaa wuddii jiitluu anaayaa wə-tsəmmaa hnaayaa kutt
baaɣii nə … haaðaak tsəmmaa rabbii maa ʕṭaaniiʃ fiih.' haaðaa llii
səllək ʃʃiibaanii *devant le tribunal* … *acquitté, mais* raak ʃaayəf ələ …
tsəmmaa *l'histoire* ntaaʕ ə aar,[6] ʕannaa maḥsuub əl … kii yuktəl haaðaak
laazəm llaaxər yuktəl wəllaa yəhjar. llii yuktəl yəhjar.

B: *Ah, bon.*

A: waaʃ daar ʃʃiibaanii? hjaṛ, hjaṛ, raaḥ bʕiid haaðiik hiyya də … bəʃʃaar
w-m-baʕd l-taabəlbaala, *c'est là où il a* maḥsuub a … zzəwwəj bə …
yəmmaa.

B: tzəwwəj təmmaa?

A: yəmmaa mən taabəlbaala.

256

ب: [xxx].

أ: جرى مـوراه وبـدا يخـاف الشّيبـانى، قـال خـلاص. لحق عليـه ولا ... نسيت بـاش نقول بللّي السّيد هذا،[5] كان تبـارك اللّه ا ... انسـان ا ...

ب: قادر.

أ: قـادر وكذا وقـاع النّـاس تخـاف منّه، قاع النّـاس تخـاف منّه. محـسوب كـان .... Alors كي جرى مـوراه à un certain moment جـا الـ ... كان لقى ... تلا قـاوا تسمّى حيط، الشّيبـاني اللّه يرحمـه دار ايده كيمـا هـاك ونقّز ... والاخر carrément ....

ب: يوه!

أ: Il l'a enjambé، تسمّى نقّزه بلا مـا يدير ايديه. بالصّـحّ هذيك التّنقيزه الـ ... تسمّى الـ ... فواده خرج.

ب: اه.

أ: فواده خرج، بدا يشمّ الرّيحـه، بدا يدوخ، عـاد تسمّى بدا يـ ... يعيى و ... والشّيبـاني راح. مزيّه جاوا الـ ... النّـاس juste ممبعد، لقاوه هكذاك ثمّى ا ... رايح [xxx]، غـادي يموت. وقـالّهم بفمّـه، قـال، «يا ودّي جيتله انـايا وتسمّى هنـايا كنت باغي نـ ... هذاك تسمّى ربّي مـا اعطانيش فيه.» هذا اللّي سلّك الشّيبـاني acquitté mais ... devant le tribunal، راك شـايف الـ ... تسمّى l'histoire نتـاع الثّـار،[6] عندنا محـسوب الـ ... كي يكتل هذاك لازم الاخر يكتل، ولاّ يهجر، اللّي يكتل يهجر.

ب: Ah, bon.

أ: واش دار الشّيبـاني؟ هجر، هجر، راح بعيد هذيك هيّـد ... بشّار ومبعد لتاب البـاله. c'est là où il a محـسوب ا ... تزوّج بـ ... يمّا.

ب: تزوّح تمّا؟

أ: يمّا من تاب البـاله.

257

Vocabulary:

l'histoire   *nfs* the story

θaar ثار *nms* revenge, vengeance

ḷḷaah yarḥam + **suffixed pronoun** يرحم الله God rest s.o.'s soul, (lit, may God have mercy on s.o.; said after mention of deceased's name)

wjaah وجاه *nms* region, area

lbayyəṍ البيّض *prop* El Bayadh (town in southwest Algeria)

zaawii زاوي *nms* descendant of the Prophet Muhammad {*pl:* zwii}

c'est they are, lit. it is

ʃriif شريف *nms* descendant of the Prophet Muhammad; noble {*pl:* ʃərfaa}

pardon   *nms* excuse me

c'est les descendants du prophète they are the descendants of the Prophet

et alors and so

ṣadaqa صدقه *nfs* charity, alms

et caetera. Bon ah ... pratiquement c'est, c'est des seigneurs. Alors
and such. Right, practically speaking, it is, they are the lords. So,

xaṭra خطره *nfs* time, moment {*pl:* xaṭraat}

extraordinaire   *adj* extraordinary

daar b- دار بـ *v* to care for, tend {*imperf:* iiduur bi-}

jədd جدّ *nms* grandfather {*pl:* jduud, *pl:* jdaad}

ṭmaʕ fii طمع في *v* to desire, covet {*imperf:* yəṭmaʕ fii}

ʃiibaanii شيباني *nms* elderly man {*pl:* ʃiibaaniyyiin, *pl:* ʃyaab, *pl:* ʃwaabiin}

bon   *interj* then; all right

tnawwəḍ تنوّض *v* to quarrel with one another {*imperf:* yətnawwəḍ}

nqəʃ نقش *v* to hoe; to chisel, engrave {*imperf:* yənqəʃ}

bɣaa بغى *v* to want; to like, love {*imperf:* yəbɣii}

xudmii خدمي *nms* knife, dagger {*pl:* xdaamaa}

avec un poignard with a dagger

xəddiimii خديمي *nms* small knife, dagger (diminutive of /xudmii/) {*pl:* xdaamaa}

haak هاك [*also* hakkaa; hakkaak] *pro* thus, in this way

hrab هرب *v* to run away; to escape {*imperf:* yəhrab}

mniin منـين *interrog* when; from where, whence

mən taḥt l-taḥt مـن تحت لتــحـت secretly, furtively, (lit. from underneath to underneath)

mən hnaa l-hnaayaa مـن هنـا لهنـايا from here to there

mbliisii مـبـليـسـي *adj* hurt, wounded {*fs:* mbliisiyya, *pl:* mbliisiyyiin}

tbaark aḷḷaah تبـارك الله God bless s.o. (lit. God be blessed; said in admiration or irony, also against the evil eye)

gaadər قـادر *adj* strong, powerful; able {*fs:* gaadra, *pl:* gaadriin}

alors *adv* so, then

à un certain moment at a certain point in time

ḥeeṭ حـيـط *nms* wall {*pl:* ḥyuuṭ}

nəggəz نقّز *v* to hop, leap {*imperf:* iinəggəz}

carrément *adv* straight out

il l'a enjambé he jumped over it

təngiiza تـنقـيـزه *nfs* jump, leap {*pl:* təngiizaat}

fwaad فـواد *nms* internal organs, entrails, guts {*pl:* fwaadaat}

riiḥa ريـحـه *nfs* smell, odor {*pl:* riiḥaat}

daax د اخ *v* to become dizzy; to feel ill {*imperf:* iiduux}

ʕyaa عيـى *v* to be or become tired, ill {*imperf:* yaʕyaa}

mziyya مـزيّه *adj* thankfully, fortunately; merit, superiority

juste *adv* right, just

ɣaadii غـادي *part.; pre-verb; invariable* will (expresses future)

fumm فـمّ *nms* mouth {*pl:* fwaam}

wuddii ودّي *nms* my friend, pal, buddy (ms)

ʕṭaa fii في اعطى *v* to give s.o. victory over (of the deity) {*imperf:* yaʕṭii fii}

səllək سلّك *v* to acquit, clear of an accusation {*imperf:* iisəllək}

devant le tribunal ... acquitté, mais in court ... acquitted, but

ktəl قتـل *v* to kill, murder {*imperf:* yuktəl}

Ah, bon. Oh, right.

c'est là où il a it is there that he has

taabəlbaala تابلبـاله *prop* Tabelbala (town in west central Algeria)

zzəwwəj تزوّج [*also* tzəwwəj] *v* to get married to s.o. {*imperf:* yəzzəwwəj}

Notes:

1. The form /zwii/ '<u>zwii</u>, descendents of the Prophet" is uncommon in urban varieties of SAA, as the female speaker's question indicates. More common then /zwii/ i urban varieties is /ʃərfaa/, with the same meaning. Note that the singular of /zwii/ is /zaawii/. This term also occurs in Hassaniyya, the spoken Arabic of Mauritania.

   In traditional communities in Algeria, as in other Arabic-speaking and Islamic communities, descendents of the Prophet Muhammad have a special status. They may also get special treatment from others. The behavior of the <u>zaawii</u> in this selection and the reaction of the male speaker's father are, however, exceptional.

2. The form /hiya/ 'she; it (fs); they (fp)' in the female speaker's question /wəʃ hiya zzwii?/ 'What is a <u>zwii</u>?' has two possible referents. It may be that /hiya/ refers to the word /kəlma/ 'word' as implied even if it does not occur here. It may also be that /hiya/ has no specific referent. Instead, as in MSA and other varieties of spoken Arabic, /hiya/ refers to someone or something whose identity (and thus gender) is unknown or unclear.

3. From this point to nearly the end of the selection, pronoun reference is unclear and may be confusing. The form /huwa/ 'he; it (ms)' refers to three persons. They are the speaker's father or /ʃʃiibaanii/ 'my old man' and his opponent /ʃʃiix/ 'the gentleman'. The speaker's grandfather or /jəddii/ also makes a brief appearance. Careful reading and listening will clarify matters.

4. The form /mbliisii/ 'hurt, wounded' combines a French stem with an Arabic derivation. The stem derives in the end from the French <u>blesser</u> 'to hurt, injure, wound'. The SAA derivation, however, treats it as a finally-weak stem. The resulting participle /mbliisii/ resembles a finally-weak participle, such as /mɣəṭṭii/ 'covered'.

   This combination of a French (or other non-Arabic) stem and an Arabic derivation is not unusual in SAA.

5. Two conjunctions occur in the clause that begins /nsiit **baaʃ** nquul **bəllii** ssiid haaðaa .../ 'I forgot to say that this gentleman ....' The conjunction /baaʃ/ means 'in order to' and links two verbs. The conjunction /bəllii/ 'that' links a verb of saying, knowing, or sensing to a following clause, as in /nʕarrfək **bəllii** kənt l-*manager*/ 'I should inform you that I was the

manager (u.d.)'.

6. Concepts of honor and revenge, summarized here as /l'*histoire* ntaaʕ əθθaar/ 'the business of revenge', play key roles in certain Algerian communities, as they do elsewhere. Honor requires that revenge wipe out the shame of a serious insult. It may be, as in this story, that the insult (the killing of the zaawii) is an accident. The accident may even be regretted by the person who committed it. Fortunately for the male speaker, his father was able to avoid the revenge of the zaawii's family by leaving town.

The Business of Vengeance

A: My father, God rest his soul, was, ah …. He was involved in an incident, he was involved in an incident in the … in the … This was in the region of El Bayadh. We have date palm trees and we have such, and the … he comes … there is, that is… we have <u>zwi</u>. These <u>zwi</u>, that is, they are …

B: What is <u>zwi</u>?

A: ˙ <u>Zwi</u>, it's <u>shurfa</u>, <u>shurfa</u> and …

B: What is <u>shurfa</u>? Excuse me.

A: <u>Shurfa</u>, they are the descendants of the Prophet, right.

B: Oh [xxx].

A: Yes. And so the … the others who are not <u>shorfa</u>, they employ them, that's to say, they give them charity *and so on. Right, practically speaking, they are, they are the masters.* So, he came one time and said to … to … to … to my old man he said to him, this …. We had one palm tree that gave *extraordinary* dates. He told him, "This side, leave it alone, don't …. Leave it alone, don't take care of it again". My grandfather, God rest his soul, got up and aid to him, "Leave it for him, why do you want to get greedy about it? It doesn't matter, and they are, that is, <u>shorfa</u> [xxx]. The … the old man didn't want to, he told him, "No, why?" *OK*, they argued about it. One day, he found him hoeing it. He ran after him. Later, another time, he found him again hoeing the date palm. He started to run after him. He ran after him with a knife, *with a dagger*. The old man, God rest his soul, had a little knife like this. He ran away, when he saw him getting close, he pulled out that knife and just he gave it to him, from here to there. He opened … he opened him right up and he ran after him, … even though, I mean, he was hurt.

B: [xxx].

A: He ran after him and the old man started to get scared. He said, this is it. He caught up with him and .... I forgot to say that this gentleman, God bless him, was a ... person, ah ....

C: Strong.

A: Strong and all that. Everyone was scared of him, everyone was scared of him, I mean, he was .... So, when he ran after him, *at one point*, he had gotten to ... he got to ... they met up at, that is, a wall. The old man, God rest his soul, put his hand like this and jumped ... and the other man, *straight ahead* ....

B: Wow.

A: *He jumped right over it*, that is, he jumped over it without using his hands but the jump, the ... that is, ... his entrails came out.

B: Oh.

A: His entrails came out, he started to smell it, he started to get dizzy, he started, that is, to ... to feel weak ... and the old man left .... Luckily, some people came ... *right* after. They found him like that, that is .... He was going [xxx]... he was going to die. He told them with his own mouth. He said, "Man, I came to him, that is, I was, right here, I wanted to .... That guy, that is, God did not give him over to me." That's what saved the old man. *In court ...found not guilty, but* .... You see the ... that I, it is the *business* of revenge. We have, I mean, the ... when someone kills someone else, the other person has to kill or he goes away. The one who did the killing goes away.

B: Oh, right.

A: What did the old man do? He went away, he went away, he went far away, his is ... Béchar and later to Tabalbala. *That's where he*, I mean ... he got married to ... my mother.

B: He got married there?

A: My mother is from Tabalbala.

mniin nzəwwjuu lbənt

Another, female view of wedding preparations is the topic of this selection. It also illustrates the distinctive sub-variety of Arabic spoken in Tlemcen. It is characterized by the use of /ʔ/ for the Arabic letter q. *Some but not all speakers have a uvular /ʁ/* rather than the more familiar apical /r/.

A: ah, ḥnaa fə-tləmsaan lə-lʔaan lʕaaʁuusa[1] tə ... tə ... nhaar lʕərs taaḥḥaa
    təlbəs lləbsa kii taaʕ ... kii ... kiifaaʃ iiʔuuluu? kiifaaʃ iiʔuuluu? kii
    taaḥ- ḥənnaa,[2] kii mwaahaa w-kii ḥənnaahaa w-kii mwaa dii ḥənnaa
    ḥənnaa ḥənnaa ḥənnaahaa. maa zaal, maa zaal iiləbsuu lʔafṭaan, ʔafṭaan
    a ... taaʕ lə ... ʔafṭaan ṣṣdəʁ, ʔafṭaan ṣṣdəʁ nəlbsuu ʕala ... kaayən
    bluuza taaʕ əlmənsuuj w-kaayən maa zaal yənsəj ... waaḥəd yənsəjhaa
    w-yəs ... yəsnəj.

B: yənsəjhaa.

A: yənsəjhaa fə-tləmsaan, bə-lbluuza taaʕ əlmənsuuj *c'est une* ...

B: iih.

A: ... *une robe de* ... *brodée*, a ... *tissée en fil d'or, d'accord?* w-baʕda ʕlaa
    haadiik ləbluuza yəlbsuu lʔaf ... ʔafṭaan əṣṣdəʁ, ʔafṭaan əṣṣdəʁ ijii ...
    yuuṣəl ḥattaa lʁəkba wə ... taaʕ əlʔaaḍiifa məxduum bə-lməjbuud w-fiih
    ləkmaam bə ... bə-lʕaʔiiʔ.

B: aywa.

A: w-yaʕamluu ʃaaʃiya, ʃʃaaʃiya w-haadiik ʃə ... wə-ʃʃaaʃiya yʃədduu ʕleehaa
    bə-zzʁaaʁəf, zzʁaaʁəf. *alors* ʕlaa ʁʁaas yaʕamluu ljbiin wə-zzʁaaʁəf
    w-yaʕamluu ... fə-lwədniin yaʕamluu lxooṣa, *large earrings, very large
    earrings.*

B: iih.

A: hiya lxooṣa. wə-ṣṣdəʁ yaʕamluu fiih ljoohaʁ wə-zzʁaaʁəf.

منين نزوّجوا البنت

أ: اه، احنا في تلمسان للآن العاروسه[1] تــ ... تــ ... تــ ... نهار العرس تاعها تلبس
اللّبسه كي تاع ... كي ... كيفاش يقولوا؟ كيفاش يقولوا؟ كي تاع حنّا،[2]
كي مواها وكي حنّاها وكي موا دي حنّا حنّا حنّاها. ما زال ... ما زال
يلبسوا القفطان، قفطان آ ... تاع قفطان الصّدر، قفطان الصّدر نلبسوه
على ... كاين بلوزه تاع المنسوج وكاين ما زال ينسج ... واحد ينسجها
ويـــ ... ينسج.

ب: ينسجها.

أ: ينسجها في تلمسان، بالبلوزه تاع المنسوج .... *c'est une*

ب: ايه.

أ: ... *une robe de ... brodée, euh ... tissée en fil d'or, d'accord?* وبعد على
هذيك البلوزه يلبسوا الأفـ ... قفطان الصّدر، قفطان الصّدر يجي ...
يوصل حتّى الركبه و... تاع القضيفه مخدوم بالمجبود وفيه الكيمام بـ ...
بالعقيق.

ب: ايوه.

أ: ويعملوا شاشيّه، الشّاشيّه وهذيك شــ ... والشّاشيّه يشدّوا عليها
بالزّرارف، الزّرارف. *Alors,* على الرّاس يعملوا الجبين والزّرارف
ويعملوا ... في الودنين يعملوا الخوصه، *large earrings, very large*
earrings.

ب: ايه

أ: هي الخوصه، والصّدر يعملوا فيه الجوهر والزّرارف.

B: ʃuufii.

A: w-maa zaal lʔaan a ... mniin nzəwwjuu lbənt, nəxədmuul(h)aa[3] lʔafṭaan
ʕand lə ... ʕlaa ḥsaab ṭṭaʁz taaʕ ḥinn ... taaʕ yəmm ... taaʕ a ... taaʕ
əlʔafṭaan taaʕ yəmmaahaa wəllaa taaʕ ḥənnaahaa ilaa lʔaan.

B: ʃuufii.

A: mahmaa kaanət ... mahmaa haadaak ... maa ... maa yəm ... maa
yəmkənʃ lbənt ttzəwwəj blaa, blaa maa yʃədduulhaa lʔafṭaan ṣṣdəʁ
wə-nhaaʁ ... nhaaʁ lʕərs təlbəs ʕafṭaan ṣṣidiʁ. maa tbəddəl maa waaluu,
maa tṣəḍḍəʁʃ b-ḥaal ʕandkum.[4]

B: ḥnaa nəṣaddruu.

A: laa, ḥnaa maa nṣaddəʁuuʃ. laa, ḥnaa yʃədduulhaa ....

B: ʃuufii.

A: haadaa nhaaʁ lʕərs xaaṣṣ bə ...

B: eeh, w-maa tbəddəlʃ yaʕnii wə ...

A: nhaaʁ lʕərs maa tbəddəlʃ, nhaaʁ lʕərs maa tbəddəlʃ.

B: wə ... wə-llawn taaʕ əlqəfṭaan haadaa?

A: ʕalaa ḥsa ... ʕalaa ḥsaab a ... ʕalaa ʕlaa ḥsaab a ... ʕlaa ḥsaab lbənt
ilaa, ilaa, ilaa ṣamʁaa wəllaa beeḍaa wəllaa a ... lloon taaʕ ʕayneehaa.
iiʃuu ... iiʃuufuu lloon əllii, llii ywaaləməlhaa.

B: iiwaaləməlhaa.

A: ahaa.

ب: شوفي.

أ: وما زال الآن ا ... منين نزوّجوا البنت، نخدمولها[3] القفطان عند الـ ... على حساب الطّرز تاع حنّ ... تاع يمّـ ... تاع ا ... تاع القفطان تاع يمّاها ولاّ تاع حنّاها الى الآن.

ب: شوفي.

أ: مهما كانت ... مهما هداك ... ما ... ما يمـ ... يمكنش البنت تتزوج بلا ... بلا ما يشدّولها قـفطان الصّدر ونهار ... نهار العرس تلبس قفطان الصّدر. ما تبدّل ما والو، ما تصدّرش بحال عندكم.[4]

ب: احنا نصدّروا

أ: لا، واحنا ما نصدّروش. لا، احنا يشدّولها ....

ب: شوفي.

أ: هذا نهار العرس خاصّ بــ...

ب: ايه، وما تبدّلش يعني و ....

أ: نهار العرس ما تبدّلش، نهار العرس ما تبدّلش.

ب: و , ... واللّون تاع القفطان هذا؟

أ: على حسـ ... على حساب ا ... على حساب ا ... على حساب البنت الاّ ... الاّ ... الاّ سمرا ولاّ بيضا ولاّ ا ... اللّون تاع عينيها، يشـو ... يشوفوا اللّون اللّي، اللّي يوالمها.

ب: يوالمها

أ: اها.

Vocabulary:

ʔafṭaan قفطان [*also* qafṭaan] *nms* caftan {*pl:* ʔafaaṭən}

ʔafṭaan ṣdər قــفطان صــدر [*also* qafṭaan ṣdər] caftan (worn as an underlayer) {*pl:* ʔafaaṭən ṣdər}

ləbsa لبسه *nfs* piece of clothing; costume {*pl:* ləbsaat}

ʔaal قال [*also* qaal; gaal] *v* to speak, talk {*imperf:* iiʔuul}

mwaa مواI *nfs* mother {*pl:* maawaat}

bluuza بــلوزه *nfs* blouse, woman's shirt {*pl:* bluuyəz, *pl:* bluuzaat}

mənsuuj مــنسوج *adj* woven (fabric) {*fs:* mənsuuja, *pl:* mənsuujiin}

nsəj نــسج *v* to weave {*imperf:* yənsəj}

c'est une it is a

une robe de ...   brodée, a ...   tissée en fil d'or, d'accord a dress of ... embroidered ... woven with gold thread, right?

wṣəl وصل *v* to reach, arrive at {*imperf:* yuuṣəl}

ʔaaḍiifa قضيفه *nfs* velvet

məxduum مــخدوم *adj* made, done; woven {*fs:* məxduuma, *pl:* məxduumiin}

məjbuud مــجبود *nms* gold thread; thread

kəmm كمّ *nms* sleeve {*pl:* kmaam}

ʕaʔiiʔ عقيق [*also* ʕaqiiq] *nms* beading, beads

ʃaaʃiya شــاشيه *nfs* cap, skullcap {*pl:* ʃaaʃiyaat}

ʃədd ʕlaa شـــدّ علــى [*also* ʃədd l-] *v* to dress s.o., put on s.o.'s clothing or headgear {*imperf:* iiʃədd ʕlaa}

zruuf زروف *nms* *zrouf* (kind of jewelry worn on the head) {*pl:* zraarəf}

ʁaas راس [*also* raas] *nms* head {*pl:* ʁuus}

jbiin جــبين *nms* forehead {*pl:* jbiinaat, *pl:* jbən}

wdən ودن *nfs* ear {*pl:* wədniin}

xooṣa خــوصه *nfs* earrings, large earrings {*pl:* ? }

joohar جوهـر *nms* jewel, gem {*pl:* jwaahər}

·ṭarz طـرز *nms* style, design {*pl:* ṭruuz}

270

ʃədd l- ﺷَﺪّ ﻟ [also ʃədd ʕlaa]   v to dress s.o., put on s.o.'s clothing or headgear {imperf: iiʃədd l-}

tbəddəl ﺗَﺒَﺪّل   v to change (o.s. or one's clothing) {imperf: yətbəddəl}

ṣəddər ﺻَﺪّر   v to seat in the place of honor, place up front {imperf: iiṣəddər}

qafṭaan ﻗﻔﻄﺎن [also ʔafṭaan] nms caftan ({pl: qfaaṭən}

ṣmaʁ اﺻﻤﺮ [also ṣmar] adj dark-skinned, dark {fpl: ṣamʁaa, pl: ṣamaʁ}

ṣmar اﺻﻤﺮ [also ṣmaʁ] adj dark-skinned, dark {fs: ṣamraa, pl: ṣamar}

byaḍ اﺑﻴﺾ adj fair-skinned; white {fs: beeḍaa, pl: biiḍ}

waaləm واﻟﻢ v to be flattering, suitable {imperf: iiwaaləm}

Notes:

1. The main female speaker in this selection is from Tlemcen in northwestern Algeria. Her speech shows the characteristic features of Tlemceni Arabic. She has a voiced uvular fricative /ʁ/ rather than an apical trilled /r/. Note, however, that the uvular /ʁ/ does not completely replace /r/. In another case, however, one sound replaces another. That sound is the hamza or /ʔ/ that replaces the ق of MSA, as it does in /iiʔuuluu/ 'they say'.

    The uvular /ʁ/ occurs in Tlemcen and other older urban centers in North Africa. These include Fez in Morocco and Kairouan in Tunisia. It may also occur among speakers of Iraqi Arabic. The uvular /ʁ/ is not always a dialect feature. Some speakers substitute /ʁ/ for the apical /r/ that they cannot pronounce.

2. The phrase /taah- ḥənnaa/ 'belonging to her grandmother' derives from /taaʕ ḥənnaa/. Assimilation of the /ʕ/ in /taaʕ/ is common in SAA. It occurs in this selection /lʕərs taaḥḥaa/ 'her wedding'. This kind of assimilation usually takes place within a single word.

3. The form /nəxdəmuul(h)aa/ 'we make for her' illustrates how SA treats an indirect object. The indirect object marker /l-/ follows the verb. The suffixed pronoun that is the indirect object follows /l/. When the verb has both an indirect object suffixed pronoun and a direct object that is a noun phrase, the noun phrase follows the complex of verb, indirect object marker, and indirect object, as in /nəxdəmuul(h)aa lʔafṭaan/ 'we make the caftan for her'. In contrast, the order of direct and indirect object is reversed when the direct

object is a suffixed pronoun, as in /aʕṭaaṭuulhum/ 'she gives it (ms) to them'.

4. Some discussion follows the main speaker's statement about the bride: /maa tṣəddərʃ bḥaal ʕandkum/ 'she does get up in front of people like you do'. It is clear that wedding customs differ. In other urban centers in Algeria, the bride /tbəddəl/ 'she changes clothes' and /tṣəddər/ 'she gets up in front of people'. That is, she models the clothing from her dowry for the women guests. The speaker, however, does not make clear what, if anything, the bride does in Tlemcen.

272

When We Marry off a Girl

A: Ah, up to now we, in Tlemcen, the bride ... on her wedding day she dresses like ... like ... How do they say it? How do they say it? Like her grandmother, like her mother, like her grandmother, and like the mother of her grandmother's grandmother's grandmother's grandmother. They still, still wear the caftan, the caftan, ah .... of ... the sadr caftan. The sadr caftan, we wear .... There is a blouse of woven fabric, and he still weaves ... Someone weaves it or ... weaves ...

B: Weaves it.

A: Someone in Tlemcen weaves it, with a blouse of woven fabric. *It's a ....*

B: Yes.

A: *... a gown of ... embroidered, ah ... woven with gold thread, right?* And then, after that, over that blouse, they wear the ... the sadr caftan. The sadr caftan comes ... it goes down to the knees ... made from velvet, worked in gold thread. It has sleeves with ... with beads.

B: Yes.

A: They put on the shashia, the shashia. This ... the shashia, they put it on her with the zraref, the zraref. *Then* they put the jbin on her head, and the zraref. They put ... they put khosa in her ears, *large earrings, very large earrings.*

B: Yes.

A: There are the khosa, and on her chest they put gems and the zraref.

B: Really.

A: Still, even now ... when we marry a girl off, we make her a caftan at the ... according to the design that belonged to her ... her ... her, ah ... oof the

273

caftan that belonged to her mother or her grandmother, up to today.

B: Really.

A: Whoever she may be ... whoever this ... a girl can't get married without, without them putting the sadr caftan on her. On the day ... the day of her wedding she wears the sadr caftan. She doesn't change clothes or anything. She doesn't get up in front of people the way you you.

B: We get up in front of people

A: No, we don't get up in front of people, no. We dress her up ....

B: Really.

A: The wedding day is reserved for ....

B: Yes, and she doesn't change clothes, I mean, and ....

A: The wedding day she doesn't change clothes. The wedding day she doesn't change clothes.

B: And ... and the color of this caftan?

A: It ... it depends on, ... it depends on, ah ... on the girl, whether, whether, whether she is olive-skinned or fair or, ah .... The color of her eyes, ... they look for the color that, that suits her.

B: It suits her.

A: Exactly.

rraay tɣayyər ʃwiyya mʕa lwaqt

This selection gives a brief summary of the development of raï, a kind of Algerian popular music. Raï first appeared on the world music scene in the 90s. Its origins, however, date to Oran in the 30s.

A: wa-rraay[1] ʕanduu ... *bon*, baalaak maa, maaniiʃ *expert* f-*la musique mais* a ... lmuusiiqaa hiya qdiima məl ... lbiidaaya taaʕ əl *nineteen hundreds* haaduu wə-l *eighteen hundreds plutôt*. a ... w-laakən rraay tɣayyər ʃwiyya mʕa lwaqt. bəkrii kaan bə-lgəṣba wə-lgəlluuz wə ... w-kiiʃ ... iiguuluu? w-daaruuk tbəddəl wəllaa b-ssantitiizaar *synthétiseur*, w-*guitar éléctrique* w-haadii. *et aussi* fə-nafs əlwaqt lka ... lklaam tbəddəl ʃwiyya. bəkrii *c'était* a ... *du dialecte littéraire* səmmaa maaniiʃ ʕaarf kii ... iiguulhaa bə-lʕarbiyya. fhamtii? kiimaa maṣṭfa bəm- braahiim,[2] lxaaldii,[3] haaduu *c'étaient des poetes de dialecte*. lklaam jaaybiinhaa mrassəm. b-ṣaḥḥ məʃii klaam taaʕ əʃʃiʕr, matalan taaʕ əʃʃarq lʔawṣaṭ[4] wəlla, maʕṛuuf a ... wə ... w-kaðaalik a ... wəllaa, wəllaa ... bdaa ʃwiyya rraay *un peu vulgaire au début*,[5] fhamtii? kaan ...

B: [xxx].

A: ʃwiyya ... eeh, lklaam kaan ʃwiyya *uncomfortable even*, fhamti? w-laakən ʕaawəd mʕa lwaqt a ... saawuu lklaam wəllaa [xxx] klaam mliiḥ, fhamtii? kiimaa məʃ ʕaarəf anaa ṣḥaab lbaaruud[6] wəllaa ʃʃaabb xaald iiɣanniilək taaʕ ṣaḥraa haadiik wəllaa taaʕ yaa jaazaaʔriyya, haadaa kull ʃii.

الرّاي تغيّر شويّه مع الوقت

أ: والرّاي¹ عنده ... bon بالاك ما، مانيش expert في la musique mais ا ...
الموسيقى هي قديمه مـ ... البدايه تاع 1900s هذو والـ 1800s plutôt ا ...
ولكن الرّاي تغيّر شويّه مع الوقت. بكري كان بالقصبـه والقلّوز ...
وكيش يقولوا؟ وداروك تبدّل ولّى بالسانتتيزار، synthétiseur و guitar
éléctrique وهذي. et aussi في نفس الوقت الكـ ... الكلام تبدّل شـويّه.
بكري du dialecte littéraire ... c'etait a سمّى مانيش عارف كيـ ... يقوله
بالعربيـه. فهمتي؟ كيمـا مصطفى بن براهيم،² الخالدي،³ هذو c'étaient
des poetes de dialect. الكلام جايبينها مرسّم بصحّ ماشي كلام تاع الشّعر،
مثلاً تاع الشّرق الاوسط⁴ ولاّ، معروف ا ... و ... وكذلك ا ... ولّى، ولّى
... بدا شويّه الرّاي un peu vulgaire au début⁵، فهمتي؟ كان ....

ب: [xxx].

أ: شويّه ... آيه، كان الكلام شويّه uncomfortable even، فهمتي؟ ولكن عاود
مع الوقت ا ... ساووا الكلام ولّى [xxx] كلام مليح فهمتي؟ كيمـا مش
عارف انا، اصحاب البارود ولاّ الشّاب خالد يغنّيلك تاع صحرا⁶ هديك ولاّ
يا جزايريـه .... هدا كلّ شي.

Vocabulary:

raay راي *nms* raï (kind of Algerian popular music originating in Oran)
bon *interj* then; all right
expert *nms* expert
la musique, mais music, but
plutôt *adv* instead, rather
gəşba قصبه *nfs* gesba (kind of reed flute) {*pl:* gəşbaat}
gəlluuz قلّوز *nms* guellouz (kind of drum)
santitiizaar سنتيزار *nms* synthesizer {*pl:* santitiizaaraat}
synthétiseur *nms* synthesizer
guitare éléctrique electric guitar
et aussi and also
c'était, a ... du dialecte littéraire it was ah ... in the literary language
maştfaa bəm- braahiim مصطفى بن براهيم *prop* Mustafa Ben Brahim (19th century Algerian poet whose work is considered an early source of raï music)
lxaaldii الخالدي *prop* Abdelkader El Khaldi (Algerian poet whose lyrics continue to influence raï music)
c'étaient des poetes de dialecte. they were poets of the dialect
mrassəm مرسّم *adj* composed; appointed {*fs:* mrassma, *pl:* mrassmiin}
un peu vulgaire au début a little vulgar at the start
ʕaawəd عاود *v ; pre-verb* to begin, start (to do the action of the following imperfect verb); to re-do, replace; to do again (action of following imperfect verb)
saawaa ساوى *v* to form, put together, make up; to do, make {*imperf:* iisaawii}
ʃaabb xaald شابّ خالد *prop* Cheb Khaled, Khaled (star of raï music)

278

Notes:

1. The term /rraay/ means 'opinion', but also names the musical genre known as raï in the west. Raï originated in western Algeria, but first became popular in Oran in the 1930s. It appeared on the world music scene in the early 90s. Raï combines linguistic and musical influences from Algeria, Spain, and France. Today, it relies on Western instruments, simple lyrics, and danceable rhythms.

2. The influence of /maṣṭfaa bəm- braahiim/ Mustafa Ben Brahim (1800? - 1867) is still evident in Algerian folk and popular music. He is perhaps the most famous Algerian composer of <u>melhoun</u> poetry, a genre composed in SAA rather than MSA. He is also remembered for having fought with Emir Abdelkader against the French colonial forces.

3. The poet /lxaaldii/ Abdelkader El Khaldi was another 19th-century composer of <u>melhoun</u>. He was born in Mascara but flourished in Oran. Like that of Mustafa Ben Brahim, the influence of Abdelkader El Khaldi can still be heard in Algerian poetry and music.

4. The speaker's reference to /klaam taaʕ əʃʃiʕr, matalan taaʕ ʃʃarq lʔawsaṭ/ 'the words of a poems, for example, of the Middle East' is not clear. It may refer to well-known vocalists such as the Egyptian Umm Kulthoum. Some of the greatest poets of her time wrote poems for her that were set to music. In contrast, the lyrics of raï are usually improvised. The singer may begin singing from a composed text of some kind. That text, however, provides only a theme or chorus for the song.

5. Raï did, in fact, /bdaa ʃwiyya ... *un peu vulgaire au début*/ 'it started out a little ..., *a little vulgar at the beginning*". From the earliest times, raï has celebrated freedom and pleasure in frank terms. It has been equally open about personal, social, and political problems. In the mid-80s, however, the market for this music began to open up. Blunt expression and questionable topics were toned down or disappeared entirely. The result is a focus on romance and love, sometimes called "clean raï."

6. The singer /ʃʃaab xaald/ Cheb Khaled is perhaps the best-known raï musician. Two of his albums are /ṣhaab lbaaruud/ or <u>S'hab El Baroud</u> (1992) and /ṣaḥraa/ or <u>Sahra</u> (1996).

Raï Has Changed a Bit Over Time

A: And raï has ... *well*, maybe, not, I am no *expert* on *music but*, ah ... the music is old, from ... the beginning of the *nineteen hundreds* and the *eighteen hundreds rather*. Ah .... but raï has changed a bit over time. In the old days it was with a <u>gasba</u> and <u>guellouz</u> and what do they say? Now it has changed, it is with a synthesizer, *synthesizer*, and *electric* guitar and such. *Also*, at the same time, the ... the words have changed a little. In the old days, *it was*, ah ... *in the literary dialect*, that is, I don't know ... what they call it in Arabic. You know? Like Mustafa Bin Brahim and al-Khaldi. Those, *they were poets in the dialect*. The words they brought in were composed. But they're not the words of a poem, for example, in the Middle East, or whatever. Everyone knows ah ... and, and therefore, ah ... or, or .... Raï was, was, it started out a little, *a little vulgar at the start*, you know? It was ....

B: [xxx].

A: A little .... Yes, the words were a little uncomfortable even, you know? But with time ... they went back and fixed the words, [xxx] good lyrics, you know? Like, I don't know, <u>S'hab al-Barud</u> or Cheb Khaled singing <u>Sahra</u> or the one "<u>yaa jaazaaʔriyya</u>". That's it.

raayii fə-lḥaala haaðii

The male speaker's view of the Algerian situation is not optimistic. He does,
however, try to lighten the tone of his opinion with the use of a French borrowing.

A: wəʃ raayii fə-lḥaala haaðii?[1] eeh, lḥaala haaðii sʕiiba. ḷḷaah yəhdiihəm,
ḥnaa nguuluu aḷḷaah yəhdiihəm. eeh, laa xaaṭʃii haaðii maa kaaʃ llii
raah yərbaḥ mənhaa. a ... ləblaad raayḥa təðð̣arr w-wlaad jjazaayər
raayḥiin yəðð̣ərruu. a ... anaa ʃaxṣiyyən maa nʃuufʃ ʃkuun llii raah
yərbaḥ fiihaa, a ... laa xaaṭʃii ʃkuun a ... *déjà* dərnaa *guerre* sʕiiba mʕa
faaraansaa[2] w-wəddərnaa wlaatnaa[3] uu ... w-la-haaðii wiin lḥaqnaa,
maḥsuub *c'est ... c'est pas la peine.* nnaas laazəm yaʕqaluu ʃwiyya,
yəgʕaduu yahdruu a ... mʕa baʕðhum baʕð̣ w-yəlgaaw ləḥall a ...

B: iih.

A: haadii ʃkuun llii raah yəstfaad mənhaa? ḥattaa waaḥəd maa raah yəstfaad.

B: w-aḷḷah.

A: aywa, ḥattaa waaḥəd muʃ yəs ... haaðaa lə ... ʃaxṣiyyən anaa haaðaa lə
... laa xaaṭʃ ... *et la violence, elle va rien résoudre. C'est-à-dire* maa
ʕandhaa, maa, maa thall ḥattaa məʃkəl, ʃʃtaat jaaya mən ʕand *les*
groupes haaðuuk[4] wəllaa mən ʕand *le gouvernement.*

B: ṣaḥḥ.

رايي في الحاله هذي

أ: واش رايي في الحاله هذي؟[1] ايه، الحاله هذي صعيبه. اللّه يهديهم، احنا نقولوا اللّه يهديهم. ايه، لا خاطشي هذي ما كاش اللّي راه يربح منها. ا ... البلاد رايحه تضرّ، وولاد الجزاير رايحين يضرّوا. ا ... انا شخصيًّا ما نشوفش شكون اللّي راه يربح فيها، ا ... لا خاطشي شكون ا ... déjà درنا guerre صعيبه مع فرنسا. وودّرنا ولاتنا[3] و ... ولهذي لحقنا، محسوب c'est ... c'est pas la peine. النّاس لازم يعقلوا شويّه، يقعدوا يهدروا ا ا ... مع بعضهم بعض ويلقاوا الحلّ.

ب: ايه.

أ: هذي شكون اللّي راه يستفاد منها؟ حتّى واحد ما راه يستفاد.

ب: واللّه.

أ: ايوه، حتّى واحد مش يس.... هذا الـ ... شخصيًّا انا هذا الـ ... لا خاطشي et la violence elle va rien résoudre. c'es- à-dire ... ما عندها، ما، ما، ما تحلّ حتّى مشكل، الشّتات جايّه من عند les groupes هذوك[4] ولا من عند le gouvernement.

ب: صحّ.

283

A: *Ça va rien résoudre, ça va aggraver les problèmes.* laa xaatʃ ənnaas raayḥiin a ... ywəddruu a ... naas mən ʕaaylaathəm w-haakðaaka w-iiziid lḥugd yəkθər yəkθər ḥattaa nəlḥəgu baalaak *un certain point* maa nənjmuuʃ nərjəʕuu [xxx]. nnaas haadii rubbamaa maa yxammuuʃ fiihaa. bə-ṣṣaḥḥ *parfois* kaayən bəldaan hakkaa nʃuuf fiihum fii, fii friiqyaa w-ʔaazyaa⁵ yəlḥəguu l-haaðaak *le point* w-kii yəlḥəguu *un point de non retour* wiin ləblaad maa tənjəmʃ tə ... tarjaʕ *ensemble* mən baʕd, təqdər təklaaṭii.⁶

B: ṣaḥḥ.

A: [xxx] lklaam taaʕnaa, 'təklaaṭii.'

A, B: [laugh].

أ: النّاس خــاطشي لا، *ça va rien résoudre, ça va aggraver les problèmes*

رايحــين ا ... يودّروا ا ا ... نـاس مـن عـايـلاتهم وهكذاك ويـزيد الحـقد يكثر

يكثر حتّى نلحـقوا بـالاك *un certain point* مـا ننجـمـوش نـرجعوا [xxx].

النّاس هذي ربّمـا مـا يخمّوش فيها، بـالصّحّ *parfois* كايـن بـلدان هكّا نشـوف

فيهم فـي، فـي افريـقيـا وازيا⁵ يلحـقوا لهذاك *le point* وكي يلحقوا *un point*

de non retour ويـن البـلاد مـا تنجـمـش تـ ... ترجـع *ensemble* مـن بـعد، تقدر

تكلاطي.⁶

ب: صحّ.

أ: [xxx] الكلام تـاعنـا « تكلاطي ».

أ، ب: [laugh].

Vocabulary:

aḷḷaah yǝhdii + suffixed pronoun الله يهـدي God guide s.o. (i.e. to the right path, often said in criticism)

ḏ̣ḏ̣ǝrr اظرّ *v* to be forced to, compelled to {*imperf:* yǝḏ̣ḏ̣ǝrr}

déjà adv already

guerre nfs war

wǝddǝr ودّر *v* to lose, misplace {*imperf:* iiwǝddǝr}

c'est ... c'est pas la peine it is ... it is not worth it

ʕqal اعقل *v* to recall, remember {*imperf:* yǝʕqal}

hdǝr هدر *v* to speak, talk {*imperf:* yǝhdǝr}

maʕa baʕḏ̣ + plural suffixed pronoun + baʕḏ̣ مـع بـعض ... بـعض with one other, together

et la violence, elle va rien résoudre c'est à dire and violence, it will not solve anything, that is

ʃtaa شتـاة many, numerous; dispersed, separate {*fs:* ʃtaat}

les groupes nmp the groups

le gouvernement nms the government

ça va rien résoudre, ça va aggraver les problèmes it is not going to

285

solve anything. it's going to make the problems worse

ḥuqd حقد *nms* hatred, malice

un certain point a certain point

njəm نجم *v; pre-verb* to be able to {*imperf:* yənjəm}

xamm fii- خمّ في *v* to think about, reflect on {*imperf:* iixamm fii-}

parfois *adv* sometimes

le point *nms* the point

un point de non-retour a point of no return

ensemble *adv* together

klaaṭaa كلاطى *v* to explode, blow up {*imperf:* yəklaaṭii}

Notes:

1. The male speaker refers to /lḥaala haaðii/ 'this situation' with no more detail. The situation, of course, is the civil war in Algeria that began in 1992. Other speakers also refer the cycle of violence, murder, and political unrest indirectly. They call it /lḥaala/ or /lwəḍʕiyya/.

2. The /guerre ṣʕiiba mʕa faaraansaa/ 'the difficult war with France' is the Algerian war of independence. That war lasted from 1954 to 1962. It killed hundreds of thousands of people, Algerian and French, military and civilian, in Algeria and in France.

3. The form /wlaatnaa/ appears to be a slip of the tongue for /wlaadnaa/ 'our children'.

4. By /les groupes haaðuuk/ 'those groups', the male speaker means the armed groups affiliated with Algerian Islamist parties. The best-known of these is the GIA or Groupe islamique armé (Armed Islamic Group). Other groups, however, some small and regional, have operated in Algeria.

5. The form /azyaa/ is a variant form of /aasya/ 'Asia'.

6. The form /təklaaṭii/ 'it (fs) explodes' derives from the French éclater 'to explode'. This kind of borrowing is not unusual in SAA (see Selection 11, note 5). In this instance, however, the male speaker uses it to lighten up his pessismistic view of Algerian politics.

What I Think about This Situation

A: What do I think about this situation? Well, this situation is very difficult. God guide them, as we say, God guide them. Yes, because there is no one who profits from this. Ah ... the country will be hurt, and the children of Algeria will be hurt. Ah ... I personally don't see who on earth profits from it, ah ... because who, ah .... We have *already* fought a difficult war with France and lost our children. And ... because of this, wherever we end up, I mean, *it's, it's not worth it*. People have to be a little reasonable and keep talking, ah ... with each other and find the solution ....

B: Yes.

A: Who benefits from this? No one benefits.

B: Absolutely.

A: Yes. No one ... this ... personally I ... because ... *And violence, it's not going to solve anything, that is,* it doesn't have, it doesn't, it doesn't solve any problems, whether it comes from those groups or from the *government*.

B: Right.

A: *It's not going to solve anything. It's only going to make the problems worse* because people are going to ... lose ... members of their families and so on. Hatred increases, it grows and grows until we maybe reach *a certain point* where we can't go back [xxx]. These people may not think about it, but *sometimes* there are countries like this. We see them in, in Africa and Asia. They reach *that point* and when they reach *the point of no return*, where the country can't ... come back *together* afterwards, it can explode.

B: Right.

A: We say, "it explodes."

A, B: [laugh].

287

haaðiik llii ḥayyratnii anaayaa

This view of the Algerian situation comes from the same speaker as the previous selection but is more optimistic. It describes a visit to Algeria and details both his reactions and the continuing difficulties he experienced.

A: lḥaala mliiḥa. twaḥḥəʃnaa ʃwiyya w-ruḥnaa ʃufnaa lʕaayla w-aṣdiiqaa.

B: ṣaḥḥ, wəl ... yaʕnii wəl ... haaðaa lʔirhaab llii fə-ljazaayər, waaʃ yaʕnii ʃəftuuh ntuumaa?

A: anaa maa ʃəftʃ waaluu,[1] anaa maa ʃəft waaluu. maa ʃəft waaluu, sməʕnaa w-laakən kii ruḥt, a ... lḥaala məʃ kiimaa nə ... nəqraawhaa fəl ... hnaayaa fə-jjaraayəd wəllaa nʃuufuuhaa fə-t-*télévision*. nnaas θəmmaa ysəmmaa waalfuu, waalfuu w-nnaas yəxxədmuu yə ... yəvwaayaajuu yə ... iiruuḥuu yuxrujuu, iiruuḥuu *les plages*, lḥaala ʃwiyya mʕammra. haaðiik llii ḥayyratnii anaayaa, kənt nəḥsəb nəlqaa lə ... nnaas xaayfiin wə-məddarrgiin wə... w-laakən waaluu. nnaas gaaʕ llii naʕrafhum anaa yəmʃuu fə-ʃʃaarəʕ w-haakðaa, nnaas fii ḥaala kiimaa bəkrii.

B: mliiḥ.

A: [xxx].

B: xeer. wə-mʃiit lə-jjəlfa? nta, nta mən jjəlfa ....

A: eeh, mən jjəlfa.

B: ... sii ʕlii?

A: eeh, ṭabʕan mʃiit lə-jjəlfa, eeh.

B: w-kiifaah lgiit a ... jjəlfa?

A: laa, jjəlfa, jjəlfa ḥsan laa xaatʃii jjəlfa maa fiihaaʃ lə ... lʔirhaab wə-t-*terrorism* haaðaa llii nəsməʕuu biih hakkaa. daaruuh marra wəllaa zuuj fə-ssniin haaðum gaaʕ, b-ṣaḥḥ *pas plus* a ...

288

هذيك اللّي حيّرتني انايا

أ: الحاله مليحه. توحّشنا شويّه ورحنا شفنا العايله والاصدقا.

ب: صحّ، والـ ... يعني والـ ... هذا الإرهاب اللّي في الجـزاير، واش يعني شفتوه انتما؟

أ: انا مـا شفتش والو،[1] انا مـا شفت والو. مـا شفت والو، سمعنـا ولكن كي رحت، ا ... الحاله مـاش كيمـا نـ ... نقراوهـا فالـ ... هنايا في الجرايد ولّ نشوفوهـا في الـ télévision. النّاس ثمّا يسمّى والفوا، والفوا والنّاس يخّدمـوا يـ ... يقواياجوا يـ ... يروحوا يخرجوا، يروحوا les plages، الحاله شويّه معمّره. هذيك اللّي حيّرتني انايا، كنت نحسب نلقى الـ ... النّاس خايفين ومـدّرّقين و ... ولكن والو. النّاس قاع اللّي نعرفهم انا يمشوا في الشّارع وهكذاك، النّاس في حاله كيمـا بكري.

ب: مليح.

أ: [xxx].

ب: خير. ومشيت للجلفه؟ انت، انت من الجلفه ....

أ: ايه، من الجلفه.

ب: ... سي علي؟

أ: ايه، طبعًا مشيت الجلفه، ايه.

ب: وكيفاه لقيت ا ... الجلفه؟

أ: لا، الجلفه، الجلفه احسن لا خاطشي الجلفه مـا فيهـاش الـ ... الإرهاب والـterrorisme هذا اللّي نسمعوا بيه هكّا. داروه مرّه ولّا زوج في السّنين هذم قاع، بصحّ pas plus | ....

B: xeer.

A: *Le voyage* ʃwiyya ṣʕiib, *le voyage* ʃwiyya ṣʕiib laa xaaṭʃii *il y a les barrages*, baaʃ lwaaḥəd yəlḥaq griib waaḥəd ʕəʃriin uu-θlaaθiin *barrages* wə-nnaas iixawwfuuk. iiguullək maa taʕrafʃ, *même* tʃuufhum laabsiin w-*les camions* w-*les uniformes*, maa təʕrafʃ illaa, illaa *barrage* haakðaa wəllaa *barrage* haakðaak.[2] eeh, iilaa ḥaaðiik ... kaayn əlxoof, nnaas durka maa yəmʃuuʃ fə-lliil, yəmʃuu fə-nnhaar bərk. bə-ṣṣaḥḥ haakðaa w-kaayn əlxoof laa xaaṭʃii kaayən saaʕa w-iiguuluu kaayn *les barrages*.

B: ṣaḥḥ, nta a ... dərt *voyage* mən jjəlfa lə-ddzaayər lʕaaṣma?

A: eeh, eeh, eeh, ṣʕiib. waaḥd lxams swaayəʕ[3] wəllaa haak, hiyya *normalement même pas, même pas trois heures.*

B: eeh.

A: kii tʕuud ṭṭriig mliiḥaa w-kiimaa bəkrii [xxx], *même pas trois heures.* lwaaḥəd ilaa ... xaaṭʃii kaayən *les barrages*, kii yjii lwaaḥəd daaxəl *les villes.*

B: ṣaḥḥ.

A: eeh, w-kaayən *barrages* ddaxla, lxarja, *parfois* ...

B: iih.

A: ... ḥattaa fə-lwuṣṭ.

B: ʃuuf.

A: eeh, haaðiik llii ṣʕiiba, w-iiḥəbsuuk w-iisəqsuuk w-iifarktuuk w-haaðii hiya.

ب: خير.

أ: *le voyage* شويّة صعيب، *le voyage* شويّة صعيب لا خاطشي *il y a les barrages* باش الواحد يلحق قريب واحد عشرين اوثلاثين *barrages* والنّاس يخوّفوك. يقولّك ما تعرفش، *même* تشوفهم لابسين و*les camions* و*les uniformes*. ما تعـرفش الآ، الآ *barrage* هكذا ولآ *barrage* هكذاك.[2] ايه، الى هذيك كاين الخوف. النّاس درك ما يمشوش في اللّيل، يمشوا في النّهار برك. بالصّحّ هكذا وكاين الخوف لا خاطشي كاين ساعه وويقولوا كاين *les barrages*.

ب: صحّ، انت ا ... درت *voyage* من الجلفه للدّزاير العاصمه؟

أ: ايه، ايه، ايه، صعيب. واحد الخمس سوايع[3] ولآ هاك، هيّ *normalement même pas, même pas trois heures*.

ب: ايه.

أ: كي تعود الطّريق مليحه وكيما بكري [xxx]، *même pas trois heures*. الواحد الا ... خاطشي كاين *les barrages*، كي يجي الواحد داخل *les villes*.

ب: صحّ.

أ: ايه، وكاين *barrages* الدّخله، الخرجه *parfois* ...

ب: ايه.

أ: ... حتّى في الوسط.

ب: شوف.

أ: ايه، هذيك اللّي صعيبه. ويحبّسوك ويسقسوك ويفركتوك وهذي هيّ.

Vocabulary:

même *adv* even

twaḥḥaʃ توحّش *v* to miss, long for {*imperf:* yətwaḥḥaʃ}

ntuumaa انتوما *pro* you (2P)

télévision *nfs* television

vwaayaajaa فوايا جى *v* to travel {*imperf:* iivwaayaajii}

les plages *nfp* the beaches

mʕammar معمّر *adj* full, filled up {*fs:* mʕammra, *pl:* mʕammriin}

məddarrəg مـــدّرّق *adj* having hidden, concealed o.s. {*fs:* məddərrga, *pl:* məddərrgiin}

haakðaa هكذا [*also* haakdaa] *pro* thus, in this way

jjəlfa الجلفه *prop* Djelfa (city and province in central Algeria)

haakdaa هكدا [*also* haakðaa] *adv* thus, in this way

haaðum هذم [*also* haaduu; haaðuu; haadum] *pro* these (P near demonstrative)

pas *plus* no more

le voyage *nms* the trip

il y a les barrages there are roadblocks

griib قريب *adv* nearly, approximately

barrages *nmp* roadblocks

les camions *nmp* the trucks

les uniformes *nmp* the uniforms

durka درك [*also* durk; duuk; duuka] *adv* now

les barrages *nmp* the roadblocks

saaʕa ساعه *nfs* hour {*pl:* swaayəʕ, *pl:* saaʕaat}

normalement même pas, même pas trois heures normally, not even, not even three hours

même pas trois heures not even three hours

les barrages *nmp* the roadblocks

les villes *nfp* the cities

parfois *adv* sometimes

ḥbəs حبس *v* to make stop; to stop o.s. {*imperf:* yəḥbəs}

saqsaa سقسى *v* to ask, inquire {*imperf:* iisaqsii}

farkət فركت *v* to search (violently or roughly) {*imperf:* iifarkət}

Notes:

1. The male speaker's statement /maa ʃəftʃ **waaluu**/ 'I didn't see anything' contains three negative elements. They are /maa/, /ʃ/, and /waaluu/. Negation in SAA usually relies on two negatives. One of the two is /maa/. The other is usually /ʃi/ or /ʃ/, although another negative may replace /ʃi/ (see Selection 2, note 4). The use of three negtive elements here adds greater force or emphasis to the statement.

2. The male speaker alludes to the worst period of violence in Algeria when he says /illaa barrage haakðaa wəllaa *barrage* haakðaak/ 'if it's this kind of *roadblock* or that kind of *roadblock*'. At the height of the violence, roadblocks were dangerous places. Government forces maintained roadblocks on highways and in cities for security purposes. At the same time, militia forces disguised themselves in military uniforms to set up their own roadblocks. As the speaker points out, travellers had no way of knowing who stopped them.

3. The form /swaayəʕ/ 'hours' is a plural. The singular is /saaʕa/. The plural /swaayəʕ/ is an alternative form that occurs in SAA and certain other varieties of spoken Arabic. The more regular plural is /saaʕaat/.

That's What Confused Me

A: The situation is good. We were a little homesick and we went to see family and friends.

B: Right, and the ... I mean, the ... this terrorism in Algeria, did you, I mean, see it?

A: I didn't see anything. I didn't see anything. I didn't see anything, we had heard, but when I went, ah ... the situation is not like ... what we read in the ... in the papers here or see on *television*. People there are, I mean, used to it, they are used to it. People work ... they travel ... they go out, they go to the *beach*. It's kind of crowded. That's what confused me. I was expecting to find ... people scared and hiding out, and ... but nothing. Everyone I know walks in the street and things like that. People are like it was the old days.

B: Good.

A: [xxx].

B: Very good. Did you go to Djelfa? You, you are from Djelfa ...

A: Yes, from Djelfa.

B: ... Mr. Ali?

A: Yes, of course I went to Djelfa, yes.

B: And how did you find, ah ... Djelfa?

A: No, Djelfa, Djelfa is better because Djelfa doesn't have the ... the terrorism, this *terrorism* we heard about like that. They did it only once or twice in all these years. But *no more*, ah ....

B: Very good.

A: *The trip* was a little hard, the *trip* was a little hard because there are *roadblocks*, so that you hit something like 20 or 30 *roadblocks*. People scare you, that is, you don't know, you even see them dressed ... and *the trucks* and *the uniforms*. You don't know if it's this kind of *roadblock* or that kind of *roadblock*. Yes, and if it's this kind ... it's scary. Now people don't go out at night, they only go out during the day. But it's like that, and it's scary because sometimes they say there are *roadblocks*.

B: Right. You, ah ... made the *trip* from Djelfa to Algiers?

A: Yes, yes, yes, it's hard. It's about five hours or something like that. It's *normally not even, not even three hours.*

B: Yes.

A: When the road is good again and like before [xxx], not even three hours. A person ... because there are *roadblocks* as you go into the cities.

B: True.

A: Yes, and there are *roadblocks* as you enter and leave, *sometimes* ...

B: Yes

A: ... even in the middle of the city.

B: Really.

A: Yes. That's what's hard, they stop you and they ask you questions and they search you. And that's the way it is.

ḥanaa Ɛadnaa *dialecte différent*

The male speaker here describes how the Arabic of his hometown, Sidi Bel Abbès, differs from that of nearby Oran. He also touches on other topics. These include language variety in Algeria, the sources of SAA, and the speed of language change.

A: lloolaa *c'est* ... *c'est le* ... *le* ... kiimaa yguuluu lmooqəɛ taaɛ, taaɛ *la région* taaɛnaa, taaɛ əl ... lmdiina w-taaɛ ... ḥnaa jaayiin fə-lɣarb lə-jjazaayər, OK? a ... jaanuub wahraan, *au sud d'Oran*. maɛnaah kaayn ... *même* ḥnaa Ɛannaa a ... *même* ḥanaa Ɛadnaa *dialecte différent*, taaɛnaa, ʃwiyya Ɛlaa taaɛ wahraan.[1]

B: ʃuuf.

A: ʃwiyya *différent* Ɛlaa taaɛ wahraan, kaayən ʃii kəlmaat w-ʃii ... kiimaa yguuluu 'ʃii xaarjaat, ʃii daaxlaat'.

B: kiifaah haad əlkəlmaat?

A: dduuxii. maθalan iiguuluu huum ...

ahnaa nguuluu, 'ʃtaa hwaa?' fhəmtii?

huuma yguuluu 'ʃtaa hwaalaa?' OK?

ḥanaa nguuluu, kii nəlguu waaḥəd fə-ṭṭriig wəllaa, 'ʃḥaal raahaa ssaaɛa?'

nguuluu, ḥnaayaa nguuluu, 'xayyii, ʃḥaal raahaa ssaaɛa?'

huma yguuluu, 'ṣaaḥbii, ʃḥaal raahaa ssaaɛa?'

fhəmtii? haaðii biinnaa w-biin wahraan, aah?

B: eeh.

A: *Alors*, loo kaan nruuḥuu maa biinnaa w-biin *Alger* wəllaa biin a ... qṣanṭiina w-Ɛannaaba, maa fraatʃ.[2]

احنا عندنا dialecte différent

أ: اللاولى ... le ... c'est le ... c'est كيما يقولوا الموقع تاع، تاع la region تاعنا، تاع الـ ... المدينه وتاع ... احنا جاين في الغرب للجّزاير OK؟ ا ... جنوب وهران، au sud d'Oran. معناه كاين ا ... même احنا عندنا dialecte différent، تاعنا، شويه على تاع وهران.[1]

ب: شوف.

أ: شويه différent على تاع وهران، كاين شي كلمات وشي ... كيما يقولوا شي « خارجات شي داخلات ».

ب: كيفاه هاد كلمات؟

ب : تدوخي. مثلاً يقولوا هم ....

احنا نقولوا، «شتا هو؟ » فهمتي؟

هم يقولوا، «شتا هو لها؟ » OK؟

احنا نقولوا، كي نلقوا واحد في الطريق ولاّ، «شحال راها الساعه؟ »

نقولوا احنايا نقولوا، « خيّ، شحال راها الساعه؟ »

هم يقولوا، «صاحبي، شحال راهي الساعه؟ »

فهمتي؟ هذي بينّا وبين وهران، اه؟

ب: ايه.

أ: Alors, لو كان نروحوا ما بينّا وبين Alger ولا بين ا... قسنطينه وعنّابه، ما فراتش.[2]

297

B: [laugh].

A: fhəmtii? *donc* w-əḥnaa ʕannaa *un mélange* nxall … nxallṭuu fiihaa lʕarbiyya, nxallṭuu fiihaa baalaak ʃwiyya faaraansii hakkaa marra marra, ʃwiyya spaanyuuliyya. *et puis* llii wraθnaa mə … məʃ ʕaarf, mən jduudnaa, məʃ ʕaarəf tturk wəllaa. maaniiʃ ʕaarf mniin jaaybiinaa.³

B: [laugh].

A: [laugh], nda … mxallṭiin, [xxx] kiimaa yguuluu ddaʕwaa 'mxallṭa wə-mjallṭa'.

B: [laugh].

A: bə-ṣṣaḥḥ a … nfəhmuu, nfəhmu ṣḥaab wahraan a … yaʕnii *très bien.* *même Alger* nfəhamuu taanii , [xxx] nnaas llii ydiiruu məjhuud, *ceux qui font un effort.* bə-ṣṣaḥḥ *sinon* kaayn ʃii kəlmaat maa, maa nfəhmuuʃ. maθalan yəmmaa anaa, yəmmaa tə … təsmaʕ l-waaḥəd mən ʕannaaba wəllaa mən suuq ahraas *plutôt,* maa təfhamluuʃ baalaak *cent pour cent.*⁴ tquullək, 'ʃtaa raah iiguul?'

B: ʃuuf.

A: aah, liʔanna kaayən keef? kiimmaa ntuumaa tguuluu, 'ləwḥaayəd wə-llawṭa,' w-ḥnaa maa ʕannaaʃ haaduu ləwḥaayəd wəl …

B: kiifaah?

ب: [laugh].

أ: فهمتي؟ *donc* واحنا عندنا نخلّ ... نخلّطوا فيها العربيه، نخلّطوا فيها بالاك شويّه فارانسي هكّا مرّه مرّه، شويّه اسبانيوليّه. *Et puis* اللي ورثنا مـ ... مش عارف، من جدودنا، مش عارف التّرك ولاّ. ما نيش عارف منين جايبنها.[3]

ب: [laugh].

أ: [laugh]. ند ... مخلّطين، [xxx] كيما يقولوا الدعوى « مخلّطه ومجلّطه »

ب: [laugh].

أ: بالصّحّ ا ... نفهموا، نفهموا اصحاب وهران ا ... يعني *très bien, même* نفهموا ثاني، [xxx] الناس اللي يديروا مجهود، *Alger ceux qui font un effort*. بالصّحّ *sinon* كاين شي كلمات ما، ما نفهموش. مثلاً، يمّا انا، يمّا تـ ... تسمع لواحد من عنّابه ولاّ من سوق اهراس *plutôt*، ما تفهمهش بالاك *cent pour cent*[4]. تقولك « شتى راه يقول؟ »

ب: شوف.

أ: اه، لأنّه كاين كيف؟ كيما انتما تقولوا، « الوحايد واللوطا،» واحنا ما عندناش هذو الوحايد والـ....

ب: كيفاه؟

299

A: wḥaayəd w-kaʕba wə-llawṭaa w-ḥabba ʕḍam. ḥanaa nguuluu, 'ḥabba bayḍ' wə-nguuluu 'llawṭa.' matalan a … *downstairs*, nguuluu 'ltəḥt,' məʃ əllawṭ. əlwḥaayəd nguuluu … maa nguuluuʃ ləwḥaayəd [xxx], kaʕba nguuluu, 'waaḥda, zuuj, θlaaθa.' *les unités* maa nguuluuʃ, 'lkaʕba w-kaʕbateen.' ʃtaa llf? *et puis* məllii jiit lə-hnaa anaayaa *ça fait* ʕaʃra sniin wəllaa maaniiʃ ʕaarf ḥdaaʃən ʕaam, *even* d-*dialecte* haaðaak ʃwiyya tɣayyər. kaayn ʃii kəlmaat zaaduu fə-l … fə-l *dictionary* taaʕ, taaʕ haaðaak d-*dialect*, anaa *I am not probably updated.*

أ: وحايد وكعبه واللوطا وحبّه عظم. احنا نقولوا، «حبّه بـيض» ونقولوا،
«اللوطا.» مـثلاً downstairs, ا ... نقـولـوا، «التحت،» مـاش اللوط. الـوحـايـد
نقـولوا ... مـا نقـولوش الـوحـايـد [xxx]، «كـعبـه،» نقـولوا، «وحـده، زوج،
ثلاثه. les unités « مـا نقـولـوش، «الـكعبـه وكعبتين.» شـتـا الأّخـر ؟ et puis
ملـي جيت لهـنـانيـا ça fait عـشر سنـين ولاً مـانيش عـارف حداشن عـام even
الـdialecte هذاك شـويه تـغيّـر. كـاين شي كلمـات زادوا فـي الـdictionary
تـاع، تـاع هذاك الـdialecte، انـا I am not probably updated.

Vocabulary:

la région   *nfs*   the region

jaa جـا *v* to be located (as past tense or active participle); to come, come to, arrive at {*imperf:* iijii}

au sud d'Oran   to the south of Oran

même *adv* even

dialecte différent different dialect

wahraan وهـران *prop* Oran (city in western Algeria)

différent *adj* different

ʃii xaarjaaṭ, ʃii daaxlaat شـي خـارجـات، شـي داخـلات inside and out, all over (lit. some comings, some goings)

ʃtaa شـتـا *interrog* how; what, what is

ʃtaa hwa شـتـا هـو how are you (lit. what is it)

ʃtaa hwa laa شـتـا هـو لـها how are you (lit. what is it)

ʃḥaal شـحـال *interrog* how much, how many

ʃḥaal raahaa ssaaʕa شـحـال راهـا السـاعـه what time is it

alors *adv* so, then

Alger *prop* Algiers (capital of Algeria)

fraa فـرى *v* to finish, end s.t. {*imperf:* yəfrii}

donc *conj* then, so

un mélange *nms* a mixture

xalləṭ خلّـط *v* to mix, mix together {*imperf:* iixalləṭ}

301

spaanyooliyya سپانيوليه *nfs* Spanish (language)

et puis and then

mxalləṭ مـخلّط *adj* mixed, mixed together {*fs:* mxallṭa, *pl:* mxallṭiin}

mjalləṭ مـجلّط *adj* girded (with a sword) {*fs:* mjallṭa, *pl:* mjallṭiin}

mxalləṭ wə-mjalləṭ مـخلـط ومـجلُط all mixed up (lit. mixed and girded) {*fs:* mxallṭa wə-mjallṭa, *pl:* mxallṭiin wə-mjallṭiin}

très bien, même Alger very good, even Algiers

ceux qui font un effort those who make an effort

sinon conj otherwise

plutôt adv instead, rather

cent pour cent one hundred per cent

kaʕba كعبه *nfs* one (unit of counting)

lawṭaa لوطا *prep* downstairs; underneath

ʕḍam عضـم *nms* egg

təḥt تحـت *prep* downstairs; underneath

les unités nfp the units

et puis and then

ça fait that makes

ḥdaaʃən حداشـن *nms; form used in construct phrase* eleven

Notes:

1. The male speaker compares the Arabic spoken in his home city of Sidi Bel Abbès to that of Oran, saying /ḥanaa ʕadnaa *dialecte différent*, taaʕnaa, ʃwiyya ʕlaa taaʕ wahraan/ 'we have a different *dialect*, ours is, a bit from Oran's'. Sidi Bel Abbès is not far from Oran. There are, however, large differences between these citie in terms of history and geography. These differences play out in the kinds of language difference the speaker cites later in this selection. They occur even though the varieties of Arabic spoken in the two cities share a number of other features.

2. The statement /loo kaan nruuḥuu maa biinnaa w-biin *Alger* wəllaa biin a ... qṣanṭiina w-ʕannaaba, maa fraatʃ/ 'if we go ... from here to *Algiers* or to, ah ... Constantine and Annaba, it just doesn't stop' sums up language variation in Algeria. Conventional description divides the coastal region of Algeria into three linguistic sub-regions. One is dominated by Oran, another

by Algiers, and Constantine is the center of a third region.

3. The speaker ends his description of borrowed words in the Arabic of Sidi Bel Abbès with the statement /məʃ ʕaarəf tturk wəllaa. maaniiʃ ʕaarf mniin jaaybiinaa/ 'I don't know, the Turks or whatever. I don't know where we get it from'. His description is actually brief but accurate for Arabic as spoken in Sidi Bel Abbès and for SAA in general. Borrowings from French are common, as discussed previously (Note 1, Selection 5 and elsewhere). Spanish borrowings also occur, such as the North African Arabic /ṣəbbaaṭ/ '(pair of) shoes' (related to zapato 'shoe'). Borrowings from Turkish are most evident in the names of foods, such as /bəqlaawa/ 'baklava' (from baklava).

4. The statement /yəmmaa tə ... təsmaʕ l-waaḥəd mən ʕannaaba wəllaa mən suuq ahraas *plutôt*, maa təfhamluuʃ baalaak *cent pour cent*/ 'my mother ... hears a person from Annaba or, *rather*, from Souk Ahras, she won't understand him, you know, *one hundred per cent*' illustrates language variation in Algeria. From Sidi Bel Abbès to Annaba takes one from one end of Algeria to another. This may not look like much on a map. It is, however, approximately 1,000 km or 620 miles. This is roughly equal to the distance from New York to Charlotte, North Carolina or from Salt Lake City, Utah to Los Angeles.

We Have a Different Dialect

A: First of all, it is ... it is the ... the ... as they say, the location of, of our *region*, of the ... the city and of .... We are in the western part of Algeria, OK? Ah ... south of Oran, to *the south of Oran*. That means there is ... even we, we have, ah ... we *even* have a different *dialect*, ours is, a bit from Oran's.

B: Really.

A: A little bit different from Oran's. There are some words and some ... as they say, "inside and outside".

B: What are these words like?

A: It would make you dizzy. For example, they say ...

We say ʃtaa hwa? [what do you want?]. You understand?

They say, ʃtaa hwa laa [what do you want?]. OK?

We say, when we meet someone on the street or someplace, ʃhaal raahaa ssaaʕa? [what time is it?]. Us, we say, xayyii, ʃhaal raahaa ssaaʕa? [brother, what time is it?].

They say, ṣaahbii ʃhaal raahaa ssaaʕa? [buddy, what time is it?]

You understand? This is us and Oran, right?

B: Right.

A: So if we go ... from here to *Algiers* or to, ah ... Constantine and Annaba, it just doesn't stop.

B: [laugh].

A: You understand? So we have a *mixture* ... we mix in Arabic, we mix in maybe a little French sometimes, a little Spanish, *and then* there's what we inherited ... I don't know, from our ancestors, I don't know, the Turks or whatever. I don't know where we get it from.

B: [laugh].

A: [laugh]. We are ... mixed. [xxx] As they say, the situation is "all mixed up."

B: [laugh].

A: But ah ... We understand, we understand people from Oran, ah ... I mean, *very well*. Even *Algiers*, we also understand *quite well* [xxx] people who make an effort, *those who make an effort*. But *otherwise*, there are words we don't, don't understand. For example, my own mother, my mother ... hears a person from Annaba or, *rather*, from Souk Ahras, she won't understand him, you know, *one hundred per cent*. She'll say to you, "What is he saying?"

B: Really.

A: Yes, because there are ... what? As you say, whaayəd and lawṭa and we don't have those whaayəd or ...

B: What?

A: whaayəd and kaʕba, and lawṭa and ḥabba ʕḍamm. We say ḥabba bayḍ [egg], we say lawṭa [downstairs]. For example, downstairs, we say taḥt, not lawṭa. For whaayəd we say ... we don't say whaayəd. For kaʕba we say waaḥda, zuuj, θlaaθa [one, two, three]. *The units*. We don't say kaʕba and kaʕbateen. What else? And then, since I came here ten years ago or whatever, I don't know, 11 years, *even* the *dialect* has changed some. There are some words they've added to the ... to the *dictionary* of, of that *dialect*. *I am probably not updated.*

llahjaa taaʕnaa, taaʕ ʕənnaaba

This selection begins as a description of the Arabic of another urban center, Annaba. It soon shifts to the Arabic of Constantine. According to the male speaker, the Arabic of Constantine is even more distinctive than that of Annaba.

A: llahjaa taaʕnaa, taaʕ ʕənnaaba baayna.

B: ṣaḥḥ.

A: ʕannaa lhadra ... iiguuluulaa lbəldiyya, yahdur bə-lbəldiyya, yahdur fiihaa. hadrətnaa kiiʃ? kiimaa taaʕ əttwaansa, kiimaa taaʕ, taaʕ tuunəs.[1]

B: ttwaansa, eeh.

A: ah.

B: twəllii ... twaa ... ta ... təhdroo wə-tɣənneeyuu?[2]

A: nɣənneew. kiimaa ... *voilà*, kiimaa yəmmaa, yəmmaa. yəmma tguul, 'waah ʕliyya wə-ʕlaa ḥaalii,' ah?

B: kiifaaʃ ... waaʃ tquul?

A: 'waah ʕliyya wə-ʕlaa ḥaalii.'

B: ʕliyya ʕlaa ḥaalii.'

A: [laugh].

B: ah.

A: ah.

B: ṣaḥḥ.

A: hadrətnaa, hadrətnaa ḥluuwa.

B: eeh.

306

اللهجه تاعنا، تاع عنّابه

أ: اللهجه تاعنا، تاع عنّابه باينه.

ب: صحّ.

أ: عندنا الهدره ... يقولولها البلديّه، يهدر بالبلديّه، يهدر فيها. هدرتنا
كيف؟ كيما تاع التوانسه، كيما تاع، تاع تونس.[1]

ب: التّوانسه، ايه.

أ: اه.

ب: تولّي ... توا ... تـ .... تهدروا وتغنّيوا؟[2]

أ: نغنّيوا. كيما ... voilà، كيما يّما، يّما. يّما تقول «واه عليّ وعلى حالي.»

ب: كيفاش ... واش تقول؟

أ: «واه عليّ وعلى حالي.»

ب: «عليّ وعلى حالي.»

أ: [laugh].

ب: اه.

أ: اه.

ب: صحّ.

أ: هدرتنا، هدرتنا حلووه.

ب: ايه.

A: hadrətnaa, taaʕ ʕannaaba ḥluuwa.

B: ṣaḥḥ.

A: w-kiimaa ʃaabba, tʃaabəh ʃwiyya lə-qṣanṭiina. bə-ṣaḥḥ, ləqṣənṭiinii yahdər 'ttsaa-tsa'³ w-yahdər bə-ttsaa w-yahdər ...

B: bə-ttsaa-tsa, eeh [laugh].

A: fhəmtii?

B: taaʕ *la tchi tchi*.

A: ttsaa-tsa, *voilà*, 'zaarətsnaa lbaaraaka w-čuuzuu ʕandnaa.' ssaayaasa taaʕ lsaanhum ḥluuwa.

B: lsaan ḥluu, ṣaḥḥ.

أ: هدرتنا، تاع عنّابه، حلووه.

ب: صحّ.

أ: وكيما شابّه، تشابه شويّه لقسنطيمه. بصحّ، القسنطينيي يهدر بالتساتسه،³ ويهدر بالتسا، ويهدر ...

ب: بالتساتسه، ايه [laugh].

أ: فهمتي؟

ب: تاع *la tchi tchi.*

أ: التساتسه، *voilà*، «زارتسنا البـاراكه وجـوزوا عندنا.» السـياسـه تـاع لسانهم حلوه.

ب: لسان حلو، صحّ.

Vocabulary:

baayən بـاين *adj* distinct, evident {*fs:* baayna, *pl:* baayniin}

hadra هدره *nfs* speech, talk, conversation

bəldii بـلدي *adj* local, regional; traditional {*fs:* bəldiyya, *pl:* bəldiyyiin}

tuunsii تـونسي *adj* Tunisian {*fs:* tuunsiyya, *pl:* twaansa, *pl:* tuunsiyyiin}
voilà *presentative* there it is

waah واه *interj* oh dear, oh my (expression of dismay or unhappiness)

waah ʕliyya wə-ʕlaa ḥaalii واه عليّ وعلى حالي woe is me, oh dear

ḥluu حلو *adj* pleasant, nice; sweet {*fs:* ḥluuwa, *pl:* ḥəlwiin}
voilà *presentative* there it is
la tchi tchi *nfs* the rich, the bourgeoisie

zaarətsnaa lbaaraaka w-çuuzuu ʕandnaa زارتنا البـاراكه وجـوزوا عندنا we are blessed while you are visiting us (conventional formula of welcome)

saayaasa سـايـاسـه *nfs* skill, clever way of doing s.t.; policy; politics

Notes:

1. According to the male speaker, the Arabic of his home city Annaba is /kiimaa taaʕ əttwaansa, kiimaa taaʕ, taaʕ tuunəs/ 'like the Tunisians', in, in Tunisia'/. This is only natural. Language rarely follows political boundaries, and Annaba is nearer to Tunis than Algiers. This does mean that the speaker's Arabic is Tunisian. It shares features with Tunisian as it does with other varieties of Algerian Arabic.

2. The female speaker describes the Arabic spoken in Annaba as /təhdroo wə-tɣənneeyuu/ 'you talk and sing at the same time'. This is, of course, an exaggeration. Descriptions like this usually refer to differences in relative pitch, relative vowel length, intonation, and other features. Such differences do not usually affect comprehension. They do, however, play a role in the listener's attitude toward the speaker, since the listener may consider these differences charming or otherwise.

3. The male speaker calls the sound change of Constantinois Arabic /ttsaa-tsa/ 'the tsa-tsa'. The name indicates the pronunciation of /t/ as /ts/. Sound changes rarely occur in isolation, however. As the mimicked phrase /zaarətsnaa lbaaraaka w-čuuzuu ʕandnaa/ (we are blessed, since you are visiting us) demonstrates. The sound change called /ttsaa-tsa/ 'the tsa-tsa' in this case also entails the pronunciation of /j/ as /ǧ/ .

Our Dialect, in Annaba

A: Our dialect, in Annaba, it is distinctive.

B: Right.

A: We have a way of talking ... they call it "local talk". They speak local talk, he speaks it. Our way of talking is like the Tunisians', in, in Tunisia.

B: Tunisians, yes.

A: Right.

B: You end up ... you talk and sing at the same time?

A: We sing. It's like, there it is, it's like my mother, my mother. My mother says, waah Sliyya wə-Slaa haalii [woe, woe is me]. Right?

B: How ... what does she say?

A: waah Sliyya wə-Slaa haalii [woe, woe is me)]

B: Sliyya waa Slaa haalii, oh.

A: [laugh].

B: Right.

A: Right.

B: Yes.

A: Our way of talking, our way of talking is nice.

B: Yes.

A: Our way of talking, in Annaba, it's nice.

B: Right.

311

A: As beautiful as it is, it's a little like Constantine's. But a Constantinois speaks with the "tsa-tsa,". He speaks with "tsa". He speaks ....

B: With the "tsa-tsa," right [laugh].

A: You know?

B: Like the chi-chi.

A: The "tsa-,", *there it is.* [mimicking] zaarətsnaa lbaaraaka w-çuuzuu ʕandnaa [we are blessed, since you are visiting us]. Their way of talking is nice. They talk pretty.

B: A nice way of talking, right.

lḥayaat fə-lmaariikaan

This brief selection looks at women's lives in the US. It also provides an introduction to speech that contains larger amounts of French. This marks a shift from earlier selections, in which French usage consists of occasional words and short phrases.

a ... lḥayaat fə-lmaariikaan, a ... [clear throat] a ... lḥayaat ṣʕiiba fə-lmaariikaan, a .... *mais* bə-ṣṣaḥḥ *il y a un retour, il y a une certaine gratification, une certaine ... comment te dire, une admiration personnelle. C'est-à-dire que* bnii aadəm[1] *surtout* nnsaa, *je, je, je trouves surtout les femmes* iixədmuu fə-ddaar w-fə-zzənqa w-yəlthaaw[2] bə-ddraarii. *donc* a ... a ... lḥayaat taaḥḥum maaʃii kiimaa taaʕ zmaan llii lmraa kaant təqʕad fə-ddaar wə-rraajəl yəxdəm barra, ləmraa ʕandhaa ɣeer əddraarii wə-ddaar.[3] duuka ləmraa ʕandhaa *double* a ... *double travail.* ʕandhaa ddə ... təxdəm barra w-təxdəm fə-ddaar wə-trabbii ddraarii wə-tqarriihuum wə-ta ... *et caetera, et caetera. donc* ʕandhaa ... *il y a beaucoup de choses que la femme fait en ce moment* w-donc ddənyaa ṣʕiiba bəzzaaf. a ... *la femme* maa ʕandhaaʃ əlwəqt bəzzaaf l-nəfshaa.

الحيـاه فـي المـاريكـان

ا ... الحيـاه فـي المـاريكـان، ا... [clear throat] ا... ا ... الحيـاه صعيبـه فـي المـاريكـان، ا ...
il y a un retour, il y a une certaine gratification, une certaine ... بالصّحّ mais
surtout[1] بنـي ادم comment te dire, une admiration personnelle. C'est-à-dire
النّسـا، je, je, je trouve surtout les femmes, يخـدمـوا فـي الدّار وفـي الزّنقـه
ويلتـهاوا[2] بالدّراري. Donc ا ... ا ... الحيـاه تاعهم مـاشي كيمـا تاع زمـان اللّـي
المراه كـانت تقعـد فـي الدّار والرّاجل يخـدم ، المراه عندها غيـر الـدّراري
والدّار.[3] دوك المراه عندهـا double a ... double travail. عندهـا الـد ... تخـدم
بـرّت وتخـدم فـي الدّار وتربّي الـدّراري وتقـرّيـهم وتـ ... et caetera, et
il y a beaucoup de choses que la femme fait en ce عنـدهـا caetera. donc
moment ... donc و la femme ... ا.صعيبـه بـزّاف الدّنيـا مـا عندهـاش الـوقت
بـزّاف لنفسها.

Vocabulary:

je ... je ... je trouves surtout les femmes I ... I ... I find that women in
   particular

mais conj but, however

il y a un retour, il y a une certaine gratification, une certaine ...
   comment te dire, une admiration personnelle. *c'est à dire que*
   there is an exchange, there is a certain gratification, a certain ... a certain, how
   would I say it? a personal admiration. That is to say

il y a beaucoup de choses que la femme fait en ce moment there are a lot
   of things that a woman does these days

bnii aadəm بنـي ادم person, individual {*fs:* bnii aadma, *pl:* bnii aadmiin}

surtout *adv* especially

əlthaa b- بـ التهى *v* to be busy with; to care for {*imperf:* yəlthii, *imperf:* yəlthaa}

barra بَرّه *adv* outside; outdoors; overseas

double, euh ... double travail a double, ah ... double duty

qarraa قَرّا *v* to teach, educate {*imperf:* iiqarrii}

et caetera, et caetera. Donc and so on, and so on. So

donc conj then, so

la femme nfs the woman

Notes:

1. The form /bnii aadəm/ 'person, individual, lit. son of Adam' an unusual construction, a compound. SAA and certain other varieties of spoken Arabic treat this compound as a single unit. They mark gender and number the end of the form. The FS is, thus, /bnii aadma/ and the P is /bnii aadmiin/. In contrast, MSA treats this form as an idafa or construct phrase. It has the FS **bint** ʔaadam and the P **ʔabnaaʔ** aadam. In other words, MSA marks gender and number on the first noun of the construct, ibn.

2. The 3P imperfect verb /yəlthaaw/ 'they take care of' has the 3MS imperfect /yəlthaa/. Note, however, that forms of the verb /əlthaa/ with the imperfect final long vowel /aa/, as cited here, alternate with forms in which the imperfect final long vowel is /ii/. These have the 3MS /yəlthii/ and the 3P /yəlthiiw/. This variation in the imperfect final long vowel occurs only in Form VIII verbs, not in other verb forms. This may be because Form VIII is not especially productive in SAA.

3. The speaker describes women's lives in the old days as /ləmraa ʕandhaa yeer əddraarii wə-ddaar/ 'a woman has only the children and the home [to take care of]'. Her description is simpler than the reality. Child care, food preparation, and house cleaning are time-consuming at the best of times. In a pre-modern society, they are also hard physical work.

Women's Lives in America

Ah ... life in America, ah ... [clear throat] ah ... Life is hard in America, ah ... *But*, but there is a return, *there is a certain gratification, a certain ... how should I say it? a personal admiration. That is to say*, a person, *especially* women, *I, I, I find that women especially* work in the home and outside, and look after the children. *So*, ah ..., ah ... Their lives are not like in the past, when a woman stayed at home and the man worked outside the home, when a woman had only the children and the home [to take care of]. Now, a woman has *a double, ah ... double duty.* She has ... she works outside the home and works at home, she raises the children and educates them ... *and so on, and so on. So* she has ... *There are many things that a woman does these days* and *so* things are very difficult. Ah ... *A woman* does not have a lot of time for herself.

lɣurba ṣˁiiba

Another comparative selection, this one looks at life in the US and France for Algerians. The first female speaker notes the effects of racism and economic challenges.

A: lmaariikaan fiihaa waaḥəd … ḥaaja waaḥda taˁjəbnii fiihaa. lwaaḥəd ḥurr a … fii ləbbəstuu wəllaa fii haddərtuu[1] wəllaa fii … wə-yaˁnii yḥabb yəstaˁii … yətˁarrəf bə-nnaas, yətˁarrəf. maa yḥabbʃ, maa yḥabbʃ. wə-ḥnaa ka-jaazaaʔiiriyyiin, maa … yaˁnii maa yˁarfuuʃ mniin kii yʃuufuunaa haakdaa. ˁa-lwṣaa … lwṣaayəf ntaaˁnaa maa yˁarfuuʃ.[2] laa raanaa maariikaniyyiin, məʃii maariikaaniyyiin, *donc on est anonyme, voilà, c'est ça le trait principal.* llii maḥsuub a … iiḥəbb yədrəs w-yaˁnii maa fiiʃ maasaakiil[3] ilaa kaan a … kaan a … ləfluus mawjuudiin. wəllaa yəṭləb a … ilaa kaan *je ne sais pas, une bourse* wəllaa. ṣaˁb lwaaḥəd iikuun mə-lxaarəj, *mais* maḥsuub ilaa kaan ləfluus wə-kaan lʔiiraada lwaaḥəd ləmmaa yḥabb yədrus, yədrus, yənjaḥ. maa fiiʃ yaˁnii maʃaakiil taaˁ a … lmuuˁaalliim wəllaa lmədraasa wəlla. fiih qaawaaniin, kiimaa fii fraansaa wəlla, fə-fraansaa lmuuˁalliim yaˁnii ʃaxṣiyya a … staɣfər aḷḷaah yaa rabbii, kii llii huwwa *le Dieu ou quoi.*[4]

B: ṣaḥḥ.

A: hnaa maa kaaynʃ, ʃʃeex yaˁnii mən ənnaas, iijii yˁalləm, iiwaasii ʃəɣluu wə-xlaaṣ. *donc ça c'est un côté positif.* eeh, yaˁnii lwaaḥəd ilaa kaan ˁanduu haadəf, yaˁrəf lqaawaaniin w-yaˁrəf a … kiifaas[3] əssiira taaˁ əlʔaamriikaan, mumkən. yaˁnii fiih aamaal, ndunn ilaa kunt ruḥnaa, ruḥnaa l-fraansaa, kaant tkuun lḥaala aṣˁab.

B: bəzzaaf *le racisme* fii fraansaa.[5]

الغربه صعيبه

أ: الماريكان فيها واحد ... حاجه واحده تعجبني فيها. الواحد حرّ ا ... في
لبّسته ولاّ في هدّرته[1] ولاّ في ... ويعني يحبّ يستعيـ ... يتعرّف بالنّاس
يتعرّف. ما يحبّش، ما يحبّش. واحنا كجازائيريّين، ما ... يعني ما
يعرفوش منين كي يشوفونا هكدا. عالوصا ... الوصايف نتاعنا ما
يعرفوش.[2] لا رانا ماريكانيّين مشي ماريكانيّين، *donc on est anonyme,*
voilà, c'est ça le trait principal. اللّي محسوب ا ... يحبّ يدرس ويعني
ما فيش ماساكيل[3] الا كان ا ... كان ا ... الفلوس موجودين. ولاّ يطلب ا ...
الا كان *je ne sais pas, une bourse* ولاّ. صعب الواحد يكون مالخارج، *mais*
محسوب الا كان الفلوس وكان الايراده الواحد لمّا يحبّ يدرس يدرس،
ينجح. ما فيش يعني مشاكيل تاع ا ... الموعاليّم ولاّ المدراسه ولاّ. فيه
قاوانين، كيما في فرانسا ولاّ، ففرانسا الموعلّيم يعني شخصيّه ا ...
استغفر اللّه يا ربّي، كي اللّي هو *le Dieu ou quoi.*[4]

ب: صحّ.

أ: هنا ما كاينش، الشّيخ يعني من النّاس، ييجي يعلّم، يواسي شغله
وخلاص. *donc ça c'est un côté positif.* ايه، يعني الواحد الا كان عنده
هادف، يعرف القاوانين ويعرف ا ... كيفاس[3] السّيره تاع الآمريكان،
ممكن. يعني فيه آمال، نظنّ الا كنت رحنا، رحنا لفرانسا، كانت تكون
الحاله اصعب.

ب: بزّاف *le racisme* في فرانسا.[5]

319

A: *Oui, oui.*

B: [xxx]

A: lwaaḥəd kii yḥəbb yədrus wəllaa yḥəbb yə ... yəʃtaɣəl wəllaa, ṣʕiib ʕleeh ktiir ktiir. anaa nʃuuf llii mən ʕaaʔəltii fii fraansaa, maθalan nquul waaḥəd ṭəbiib, yəxdəm, haadaa wliid ʕammii. yəxdəm fii zuuj mustaʃfaat, məstaʃfaayaat? wə ... yə ... ʕanduu a ... yaʕnii *[les depenses] personnelles* taaʕuu. yəlḥaq, yaa rabbii, yəlḥaq. ʕanduu zuuj draarii bərk.

B: ʃuuf.

A: a ... yaʕnii lə ... maahuuʃ ʃaarii, mʔajjər bərk bass, bass.

B: *Il loue.*

A&B: [xxx].

A: *Tous les deux jours il dit, "Je vais acheter, je vais acheter." Mais* iissənnaa ḥattaa wlaaduu yəkkəbruu ʃwiyya. yaʕnii mumkən, haakdaak martuu yəmkən təqdər təxdəm. raahiyya qaaʕda fə-lbiit ʕlaa jaal ddraarii. wə-bə-ṣṣaḥḥ lɣurba ṣʕiiba.

أ: ‏*Oui, oui.*

ب: ‏[xxx].

أ: الواحد كي يحبّ يدرس ولاّ يحبّ يـ ... يشتغل ولاّ، صعيب عليه كتير
كتير. انا نشوف اللّي من عائلتي في فرانسا، مثلاً نقول واحد طبيب،
يخدم، هذا وليد عمّي. يخدم في زوج مستشفات، مستشفايات؟ يـ ... و
... عنده يعني ا ... *personnelles* [*les depenses*] تاعـه. يلحق، يا ربّي،
يلحق. عنده زوج دراري برك.

ب: شوف.

أ: أ ... يعني الـ ... ماهوش شاري، مأجّر برك بسّ، بسّ.

ب: ‏*Il loue.*

أ وب: ‏[xxx]

أ: ‏*Tous les deux jours il dit, "Je vais acheter, je vais acheter." Mais* يسنّى
حتّى ولاده يكبّروا شويّه. يعني ممكن، هكداك مرته يمكن تقدر تخدم.
راهي قاعده فالبيت فـالبيت على جال الدّراري. وبـالصّحّ الغربه صعيبه.

Vocabulary:

waṣf وصف *nms* description {*pl*: wṣaayəf}

donc on est anonyme, voilà, c'est ça le trait principal then a person can be anonymous, there it is, that's the principal feature

je ne sais pas, une bourse I don't know, a scholarship

muuʕaaliim موعاليم *nms* teacher {*pl*: muuʕaaliimiin}

staɣfər aḷḷaa استغفر الله I ask God's forgiveness (said when avoiding sin or the occasion of sin)

le Dieu ou quoi God or something

waasaa واسى *v* to do, to make {*imperf*: iiwaasii}

donc ça c'est un côté positif so that's a positive aspect

321

haadəf هـادف *nms* object, aim, goal {*pl:* hdaaf}

siira سـيـره *nfs* conduct, way of life {*pl:* siyar}

le racisme *nms* racism

oui, oui yes, yes

wliid ولـيـد *nms* child, son (diminutive of /wəld/) {*pl:* wliidaat}

wliid ʕamm ولـيـــد عـمّ cousin (father's brother's son) {*fs:* wliidət ʕamm, *pl:* wliidaat ʕamm}

[les depenses] personnelles personal [expenditures]

ʃaarii شـاري *nms* buyer, purchaser {*fs:* ʃaarya, *pl:* ʃaaryiin}

mʔajjar مـاجّر *adj* tenant, renter; landlord {*fs:* mʔajjra, *pl:* mʔajjriin}

il loue he rents

Tous les deux jours il dit, "Je vais acheter, je vais acheter." Mais
Every other day, he says, "I am going to buy, I am going to buy," But

biit بـيـت *nms* home, house; room {*pl:* byuut}

əssənnaa اسـنّـى [*also* əstənnaa] *v* to wait, wait for {*imperf:* iissənnaa}

Notes:

1. The forms /ləbbəstuu/ 'his clothing' and /haddərtuu/ 'his speech' in the phrase /fii ləbbəstuu wəllaa fii haddərtuu/ 'to dress as you like and to talk as you like, lit. in his dress and in his talk'. These forms derive from /ləbsa/ and /hədra/. The doubling of the consonant is due to the addition of a vowel-initial suffixed pronoun.

   The addition of a suffixed pronoun for some speakers results in minimal change, as in /ləbsətuu/ and /hədrətuu/. Minimal change, however, produces an unstressed short vowel /ə/ in the open syllable before the suffix. Other speakers of SAA avoid that unstressed short vowel. For some of these speakers, the combination of a form like /ləbsa/ or /hədra/ with a vowel-initial suffix produces forms like /ləbstuu/ and /hədrtuu/ that eliminate the short vowel. Other speakers use the forms heard here, with a doubled consonant before the short vowel.

   Note that similar variations occurs in SAA verbs. The first mention of these is Selection 6, note 7.

2. The main speaker explains her anonymity in the US by the fact that /lwṣaayəf ntaaʕnaa maa yʕarfuuʃ/ 'our features, they don't know them'. The comparison with France is implicit. There, persons of Algerian and North African origin are more numerous than in the US. The number of generalizations and even ethnic stereotypes supposed to describe them is, therefore, greater. American society, of course, stereotypes other ethnic groups.

3. The main speaker twice substitute /s/ for /ʃ/ in this selection. This occurs in /maasaakiil/ (for /maaʃaakiil/ 'problems') and again in /kiifaas/ (for /kiifaaʃ/ 'how'). The reason for this repeated substitution is not clear. Some sub-varieties of SAA regularly substitute /s/ for /ʃ/.

4. The main speaker describes a teacher in the French educational system with the phrase /kii llii huwwa *le Dieu ou quoi*/ 'as if he were God or something'. The exaggeration is obvious. At the same time, however, the French system differs from the American system. Instructors in that system are civil servants. They do not work with the same rules and constraints that govern instructors in the US. As a result, they may appear to have a lot of power.

5. The interviewer comments that /bəzzaaf *le racisme* fii fraansaa/ 'There is a lot of *racism* in France'. France is a multicultural society, but not very open toward cultural difference. Skin color, the basis of racism in the US, is less meaningful in France. Thus, mainstream French society requires that immigrants assimilate to French norms or at least demonstrate few differences in culture or religion.

Being a Foreigner Is Hard

A: America has one ... one thing I like here. You are free, ah ... to dress as you like or to talk as you like or to .... And, I mean, if you want ... to meet people, you can meet people. If you don't want to, you don't want to. As Algerians ... I mean, they don't know where we are from when they see us like this.... Our features, they don't know them. They don't see us as Americans or as non-American. *So a person is anonymous, that is the main thing.* A person who, I mean ... wants to study and, I mean, there are no problems if there is, ah ... there is, ah ... money is available. Or he asks for ah ... if there is. *I don't know,* a *scholarship* or whatever. It's hard to be from somewhere else, but, I mean, if the money and the will are there, a person who wants to study can study and be successful. There are no problem with, ah ... teachers or schools or whatever. There are laws. Like in France, or whatever. In France, the teacher is a person, ah ... God forgive me, o Lord, as if he were ... *God or something.*

B: Right.

A: They don't have that here. A teacher, I mean, is a regular person. He comes to teach, does his job, and that's it. *So this is the positive side.* Yes, I mean, if a person has a goal, he knows the rules, and knows how things are in the US, it's possible, I mean, there is hope. I think that if we had gone, we had gone to France, things would have been harder.

B: There is a lot of *racism* in France.

A: Yes.

B: [xxx].

A: A person who wants to study or wants to ... work, or whatever, it's really hard for him. I see members of my family in France. For example, let's say, a doctor, he has a job, this is my cousin. He works in two hospitals, hospitals? And ... I mean, *personal expenses*. Let him keep up, o Lord, let him keep up. And he has only two children.

B: Really.

A: Ah ... I mean. He's not a homeowner, just a renter, no more, that's all.

B: *He rents.*

A&B: [xxx].

A: *Every other day he says, "I'm going to buy, I'm going to buy."* But he's waiting for his kids to get a little older. I mean, it's possible, that way, it's possible for his wife to work. Now she's staying home because of the kids. Really, being a foreigner is hard.

ahl əttaṣawwəf

The male speaker in this selection touches on a range of religious and social practices that fall under the heading of Sufism. At one end of the spectrum, Sufi tariqas or orders provided religious, cultural, and political alternatives to the institutions of French colonialism through the 19th century. At the other end of the spectrum lie popular customs. These have survived,, even as the Sufi orders have become less influential and as institutional Islam frowns on certain popular customs.

A: haaðuuk ahl əttaṣawwəf haaðuuk.

B: ʃuuf.

A: haaðuuk llii ḥaafðuu ʕalaa, ʕalaa, ʕalaa ddiin taaʕnaa w-ḥaafðuu ʕa-lmuusiiqaa,[1] ḥaafðuu ʕa-lmaaluuf. lmaaluuf haaðaa lə ... lmuusiiqaa lʔandaluusiyya[2] taaʕnaa llii fii ddzaayər wəllaa fii tləmsaan wəllaa ʕannaa fii qṣanṭiina. ʃkuun ḥaafḍuu ʕa-lmaaluuf? lʕiisaawiyya wə-lḥanṣaaliyya,[3] fə-qṣanṭiina taaʕ əʃʃeex lḥanṣaalii. wə-lʕiisaawa? lʕiisaawa taaʕ əʃʃeex lhaadii mḥammad bən ʕiisaa llii kaan ... jaa mə-lmaɣrəb, skən fii məknaas ... faas, faas. mən ahl əttaṣawwəf, kaanuu yətəbbʕuuh. ahl əttaaṣawwəf, w-humma llii ḥaafðuu ʕlaa lə ... ʕlaa ddiin w-ʕlaa ttaaqaaliid jjaazaaʔiriyya w-ḥaafðuu ʕalaa, ʕa-lmuusiiqaa lʔandaluusiyya taaʕnaa kiimaa lmaaluuf wə-lmədḥ ddiinii wələ ... lḥawzii[4] llii ʕannaa [xxx]

B: ṣaḥḥ.

A: xaaṣṣatan lmədḥ, lmədḥ kiimaa taaʕ əlʔooliyaa[5] taaʕnaa. ʕannaa lʔooliyaa kiimaa siidii bən ʕabd ərraḥmaan w-siidii ərraaʃəd ... ah? w-siidii a ... wəʃ? ʕayn əssəkkuur w-ʕandək a ... fə-qṣanṭiina siidii bu ḥjaar,[6] haaðuuk ələ ... lʔoowliyaa ... w-fii ʕannaaba ʕannaa taanii ooliyaa taanii kiimaa raas əlḥamraa.[7]

B: sməʕt biihaa.

اهل التّصوّف

أ: هذوك اهل التّصوّف هذوك.

ب: شوف.

أ: هذوك اللّي حـــافظوا على، على، على الدّين تاعنا وحافظوا على الموسيقى،[1] حافظوا على المالوف. المالوف هذا الـ ... الموسيقى الاندلسيه[2] تاعنا اللّي في الدّزاير ولاّ في تلمسان ولاّ عندنا في قسنطينه. شكون حافظوا على الملوف؟ العيساويه والحنصاليّه،[3] في قسنطيه تاع الشّيخ الحنصالي. والعيساوه؟ العيساوه تاع الشّيخ الهادي محمّد بن عيسى اللّي كان ... جاء من المغرب، سكن في مكناس ... فاس، فاس، فاس. من اهل التّصوّف، كانوا يتبعوه. اهل التّصوّف، هم اللّي حافظوا على الـ ... على الدّين وعلى التّقاليد الجزائريّه وحافظوا على على الموسيقى الاندلسيه تاعنا كيما المالوف والمدح الدّيني والـ ... الحوزي[4] اللّي عندنا ..[xxx]

ب: صحّ.

أ: خاصةً المدح، المدح كيما تاع الاوليا[5] تاعنا. عندنا الاوليا كيما سيدي بن عبد الرّحمن وسيدي راشد ... اه؟ وسيدي ... ا ... واش؟ عين السّكور وعندك ا ... في قسنطينه سيدي بوحجر،[6] هذوك الـ ... الاوليا ... وفي عنّابه عندنا تاني اوليا كيما راس الحمرا.[7]

ب: سمعت بيها.

327

A: raas lḥamraa. kaanuu iijiiw lə ... taaʕ qṣanṭiina ydiiruu lʔaʕraabən təmmaa.

B: ʃuuf.

A: ah? əxt lfərgaanii zhuur.[8]

B: zhuur.

A: zhuur. kaanət kull ʕaam ddiir lʕarboon taaḥḥaa fii raas əlḥamraa.

B: ʃuuf.

A: kaanət ddiir lmaadda haaðiik. tʕarfii lmaadda?

B: *Non.*

A: ʃəftii kiifaaʃ? haadiik wəʃ iidiiruu ləkḥul, əl ... lkḥul, tʕarfii ləkḥul?

B: heeh, ləkḥul.

A: iidiiruuhaa fə-lmaa haaðiik w-iidiiruu lə ... fii ʕayn ... əʃʃwaafər, ʃɣul haaðaak lə ...

B: heeh.

A: w-iidiiruuh haak kbiir w-əlkull iidiiuruu ... yəmdḥuu, 'ḥayyaaw nzuuruu baabaanaa taaʕ ʕabd ərraḥmaan.'

B: heeh.

A: 'ḥayyuu yaa ziyyaar wiin ʃʃiix lladḥraʕ ḥnaa,' w-yətthawwluu.

B: ʃuuf.

A: kunnaa ḥnaa ṣɣaar nʃuufuuh.

B: eeh, eeh.

A: wə-ʕlaah nnaas yəthawwluu mənhaa?

B: ṣaḥḥ, ṣaḥḥ

328

أ: راس الحمرا. كانوا يجيوا الـ ... تاع قسنطينه يديروا العرابن تمّا.

ب: شوف.

أ: اه؟ اخت الفرقاني زهور.[8]

ب: زهور.

أ: زهور. كانت كل عام تدير العربون تاعها في راس الحمرا.

ب: شوف.

أ: كانت تدير المادّه هذيك. تعرفي المادّه؟

ب: Non.

أ: شفتي كيفاش؟ هذيك واش يديروا الكحل، الـ ... الكحل, تعرفي الكحل؟

ب: هيه، الكحل.

أ: يديروها في الما هذيك ويديروا الـ ... في عين ... الشّوافر شغل هذاك الـ ....

ب: هيه.

أ: ويديروه هاك كبير. والكلّ يديروا ... يمدحوا، «هيّوا نزوروا بابانا تاع عبد الرّحمن.»

ب: هيه.

أ: «هيّ يا زيّار وين شيخ الاضرع احنا.» ويتهوّلوا.

ب: شوف.

أ: كنّا احنا صغار نشوفوه.

ب: ايه، ايه.

أ: وعلاه النّاس يتهوّلوا منها؟

ب: صحّ، صحّ.

A: nnsaa yduuxuu w-yəbdaaw yə... lmuuṣaabaat[9] haaðuuk.

B: heeh.

A: tsəmʕii biihum ... lmuuṣaabaat yəbduu yʃuuɾuu ʕa-nnaas, yahdɾuu, yahdɾuu ʕa-lmustaqbəl, ʕa-*le futur* taaʕ ənnaas. kii ykuunu fə-l ... *in trance* kiimaa [noise] nguuluu *en anglais* ...

B: iih.

A: kii ykuunuu *in trance* yəbdaaw mən baʕd iiʃuufuu, kiifaaʃ ... *des images pour prédire le ... le futur.*

B: *Le futur.*

أ: النّاس يدوخوا ويبداوا يـ ... المصابات[9] هذوك.

ب: هيه.

أ: تسمعي بيهم ... المصابات يبدوا يشوروا على النّاس، يهدروا، يهدروا على المستقبل، عا *le futur* تاع النّاس. كي يكونوا في الـ... *in trance* كيما نقولوا *en anglais*.... [noise]

ب: ايه.

أ: كي يكونوا *in trance* يبداوا من بعد يشوفوا، كيفاش ... *des images pour prédire le le futur*.

ب: *Le futur*.

Vocabulary:

maadda مادّه *nfs madda* (kind of traditional eye makeup made from kohl)

taṣawwəf تصوّف *nms* Islamic mysticism, Sufism

maaluuf مـالوف *nms malouf* (kind of Arab-Andalusian music associated with Constantine and Algiers)

tləmsaan تلمسان *prop* Tlemcen (city in western Algeria)

ʕiisaawiyya عيساويه *prop* Isawiyya (Sufi brotherhood or order founded in the 16th century by Sheikh Muhammad Bin Isa)

ḥanṣaaliyya حنصاليه *prop* Hansaliyya (Sufi brotherhood or order with roots on the Moroccan-Algerian border)

ʃʃeex alhaadiii mḥammad bən ʕiisaa الشيخ الهادي محمّد بن عيسى *prop* Sheikh al-Hadi Muhammad Bin Isa (founder of the Isawiyya, the Sufi brotherhood named after him)

məknaas مكناس *prop* Meknes (city in central Morocco)

faas فاس *prop* Fes (city in central Morocco)

mədḥ مدح *nms* praise poetry

ḥawzii حوزي *nms haouzi* (kind of Arab-Andalusian music associated with Tlemcen)

siidii bən ʕabd ərraḥmaan سيدي بن عبد الرّحمن *prop* Sidi Bin Abd al-Rahman

331

(founder of a Sufi brotherhood or order)

ʕarbuun عـربون *nms* charitable donation (made in the name of a Muslim saint in the hope that the saint will grant a specific favor); pledge; earnest money; deposit, down payment {*pl:* ʕaraabən}

ʃfar شـفر *nms* eyelash {*pl:* ʃwaafər}

hayyaa هـيّى *interj* let's go, come on

zaar زار *v* to make a pilgrimage to the tomb of a Muslim saint; to visit (in general) {*imperf:* iizuur}

zaayər زايـر *nms* pilgrim (to place other than Mecca); visitor {*fs:* zaayra, *pl:* ziyyaar, *pl:* zaayriin}

ḍaarəʕ ضـارع *adj* humble, submissive {*fs:* ḍarʕaa, *pl:* ḍraʕ}

thawwəl تـهوّل [*also* thəwwəl] *v* to be alarmed, be frightened {*imperf:* yəthawwəl}

muuṣaab مـوصـاب *adj* touched, affected by God; possessed; afflicted, injured {*fs:* muuṣaab, *mpl:* muuṣaabiin, *fpl:* muuṣaabaat}

ʃaar شـار *v* to point at; to hint, infer {*imperf:* iiʃuur}

le futur *nms* the future

en anglais in English

des images pour prédire le ... le futur images to predict the ... the future

Notes:

1. As the male speaker states, the Sufi orders /ḥaafḏ̣uu ʕa-lmuusiiqaa/ 'preserved the music' of Algeria. In some Sufi orders, music is a key element of religious ritual. Traditional Algerian music and especially Andalusian music (see next note), thus, survived the colonial period.

2. Muslims and Jews who left Andalusia for North Africa at the end of the 15th century brought with them /əlmuusiiqaa laʔandaluusiyya/ 'Andalusian music'. This is a rich musical tradition that combined elements of Arabic and Islamic music with Christian and Jewish music. It is still heard in Algeria and the rest of North Africa in secular as well as religious contexts.

3. The male speaker names only two of the many Sufi orders, /lʕiisaawiyya wə-lḥansaaliyya/ 'the Isawiyya and the Hansaliyya'. The Isawiyya is the larger of the two. It has roots in Morocco, but spread from there through North Africa and into the Arab Middle East. The Hansaliyya is smaller. It,

too, originated in Morocco and had centers in Algeria and Tunisia.

4. Three types of traditional Andalusian music are named here. They are /lmaaluuf wə-lmədh ddiinii wələ ... lhawzii/ 'the malouf and the madh and the ... haouzi'. The term /maaluuf/ 'malouf' is a general term for secular and religious music of this type. Religious panegyric is /lmədh ddiinii/ ' madh'. It praises the glory of God, the qualities and deeds of the Prophet Muhammad, and those of other holy persons, the awliyaa. The form called /hawzii/ 'haouzi' is sung in the Arabic spoken in Tlemcen.

5. The term /ooliyaa/ (or /awliyaa/) 'awliyaa' (singular /waalii/) is often translated as 'saint'. These are usually persons who are remembered for their extraordinary piety or religious scholarship. Some awliya are known for the miracles they perform. The tomb of a waalii, often a small domed building, may become a center where people go to pray or to fulfill vows in hopes of a favor from the saint. These are popular practices, however, and are not sanctioned by contemporary institutional Islam.

6. The male speaker lists a number of awliyaa: /siidii bən ʕabd ərrahmaan w-siidii ərraaʃəd ... ah? w-siidii a ... wəʃ? ʕayn əssəkkuur. w-ʕandək a ... fə-qṣanṭiina siidii bu hjaar/ 'Sidi Bin Abd al-Rahman and Sidi Rashid, ah ... what? And Sidi ... and Ain al-Sekur. In Constantine there is Sidi Bou Hjar'. Some of these are well-known, while others have only local significance.

7. The saint known as /raas əlhamraa/ 'Ras al-Hamra' is also the namesake of the old Cap de Garde. It is a major landmark in Annaba , as it houses the lighthouse.

8. The identity of /əxt əlfərgaani zhuur/ 'El-Fergani's sister Zehour' is not clear from context. It seems like, however, that Zehour is the sister of al-Hadj Mohamed Tahar El-Fergani. His is a well-known performer of Algerian Andalusian music, especially that of the Constantine region.

9. The /muuṣaabaat/ are 'afflicted, touched by God' during the hadra, a religious ceremony that consists of prayers, litanies, and sometimes music. In other religious traditions, they might be called "touched by the spirit". Ecstatic religious experience is not uncommon, especially where religious ritual includes repetitive movement, chanting, or music. The effect on spectators, as the male speaker notes, may be frightening. The trance usually ends with the ritual itself.

333

Suffis

A: Those people, those are the Sufis.

B: Really.

A: Those are the one who preserved ... our religion and they preserved the music and they preserved the malouf. The malouf is ... our music from Andalusia in Algiers, in Tlemcen, or back home in Constantine. Who preserved the malouf? The Issawiyya and the Hansaliyya. In Constantine they followed the Hansali sheikh. And the Issawiyya? The Issawa follow Sheikh al-Hadi Muhammad Bin Issa who was ... he came from Morocco and lived in Meknes ... Fez, Fez. He was one of the Sufis, the Sufis followed him and they are the ones who preserved ... Islam and Algerian traditions. They preserved Andalusian music, like the malouf and the madh and the ... haouzi that we have [xxx].

B: Right.

A: Especially the madh, especially the madh of our awliyaa. We have awliyaa like Sidi Bin Abd al-Rahman and Sidi Rashid, ah ... what? And Sidi ... what? Ain al-Sekur and you have ... in Constantine there is Sidi Bou Hjar. Those are the ... the awliyaa ... In Annaba we also have other awliyaa like Ras al-Hamra.

B: I've heard of that.

A: Ras al-Hamra, people used to come ... to Constantine to fulfill their vows there.

B: Really.

A: What? Al-Fergani's sister, Zehour.

B: Zehour.

A: Zehour. Every year she used to fulfill her vow at Ras al-Hamra.

B: Really.

A: She used to put on that madda stuff. Do you know what madda is?

B: *No.*

A: Like this, see? This, what they do with kohl, ah ... kohl. Do you know what kohl is?

B: Yes, kohl.

A: They do it with water and they do ... the eye ... the edges of the eye, like that ...

B: Yes.

A: They do it like this, big. And everyone does ... they sing madh: "Let's make a pilgrimage to the shrine of our father Abd al-Rahman."

B: Yes.

A: "Let's go, pilgrims, to our sheikh, the sheikh of the humble ones, us." They get scared.

B: Yes.

A: We used to watch when we were little.

B: Yes, yes.

A: And why are people frightened by it?

B: Right, right.

A: Women get dizzy and the possessed women start up.

B: Yes.

A: You've heard about them ... The possessed women, they start pointing at people, they talk, they talk about the future, about people's *future*. When they are in the ... *in trance*, as we say *in English* ...

B: Yes.

A: When they are in trance, next they start seeing, how ... *images to predict the ... the future.*

B: *The future.*

maa ʕlaa baaliiʃ wəʃ raaḥ yəṣraa

The two male speakers in this selection describe the feelings of many young people in Algeria. Unemployment and underemployment, along with a severe housing crisis, have plagued the country. The official unemployment rate in 2003 had risen to 24%, hitting young people hardest.

A: a ... ljazaayər tsəmmaa maa, maa ʕandii ɣeer ... wəʃ nəḥkii mə-lməʕiiʃa?
puisque maa kaanʃ mʕiiʃa. raahii baayna, raahii baayna. məllii nnooḍuu wə-ḥnaa nruuḥuu nəqraaw, nxərjuu, nxəllṣuu lqraaya, nəbqaaw l-barra, maa ʕannaa waaluu. les moyens de distractions maa kaaynʃ, siwaa mə-lqraaya lə-ddaar, mə-ddaar lə-lqraaya. a ... même tsəmmaa lə ... lqraaya gaaʕdiin nəqraaw fiihaa zaayda haakðaak puisque l'avenir maa kaanʃ m-baʕd. a ... kaayən bəzzaaf llii a ... en chômage dərk, əlbaaṭaala, a ...même la chance taaʕ a ... txədmii bə-d-diplôme taaʕək¹ maa kaanʃ. lwaaḥəd yəqraa tsəmmaa huu maa ʕlaa baaluuʃ bə-lmustaqbəl taaʕuu wəllaa kaayən kaayən, wəllaa maa kaanʃ wəllaa.

B: ʃuuf.

A: eeh, ṭayyəb a ... tsəmmaa ʕandii ... ndiir riyaaḍa, nəlʕab a ... kurət yədd, nəlʕab kurət yədd ḍəmn əlfaariiq ... tsəmmaa a ... wjətt² l'équilibre taaʕii fii ... mmaalaa ... tsəmmaa fə-rriyaaḍa, wjətt l'équilibre maa biin ləqraaya wə-lmʕiiʃa hakkaak, tsəmmaa s-sport huwwa llii ʕaawənnii kuun maa jaaʃ kaayən s-sport, kuun lwaaḥəd hakkaak w-yəmruḍ wəllaa yəqləq wəllaa.

B: ṣaḥḥ.

A: eeh, rriyaaḍa hiyya llii ʕaawnətnii anaa, tsəmmaa biihaa ....

B: mziyya.

A: eeh, mziyya jaat fə-rriyaaḍa kaayna.

B: w-fayṣal, wəʃ iikuun lək?

338

ما على باليش واش راح يصرى

أ: ا ... الجزاير تسمّى ما، ما عندي غير ... واش نحكي ملمعيشه؟ *puisque* ما كانش معيشه. راهي باينه، راهي باينه. ملّي نّوضوا واحنا نروحوا نقراوا، نخرجوا، نخلّصوا القرايه، نبقاوا البرّه، ما عندنا والو. Les *moyens de distraction* ما كلنش، سوى مالقرايه للدّار، مالدّار للقرايه. ا ... *même* تسمّى الـ ... القرايه قاعدين نقراوا فيها زايده هكذاك *puisque* *l'avenir* ما كانش مبعد. ا ... كاين بزّاف اللّي ... *en chômage* درك، لبطاله ا ... *même la chance* ... تاع ا ... تخدمي بالـ*diplôme* تاعك[1] ما كانش. الواحد يقرا تسمّى هو ما على بالهش بالمستقبل تاعه، لا كاين كاين ولاّ ما كانش ولاّ.

ب: شوف.

أ: ايه، طيّب ا ... تسمّى عندي ... ندير رياضه، نلعب، ا ... كرة يدّ، نلعب كرة يدّ ضمن الفريق ... تسمّى ا ... وجدت*l'équilibre*[2] تاعي في ... امّالا تسمّى ... في الرّياضه. وجدت *l'équilibre* ما بين القرايه والمعيشه هكّاك، تسمّى الـ*sport* هو اللّي عاونّي. كون ما جاش كاين الـ*sport*، كون الواحد هكّاك ويمرض ولاّ يقلق ولاّ.

ب: صحّ.

أ: ايه، الرّياضه هيّ اللّي عاونتني انا، تسمّى بيها ....

ب: مزيّه.

أ: ايه، مزيّه جات في الرّياضه كاينه.

ب: وفيصل، واش يكون لك؟

339

A: wəld xaaltii fayṣal, wəld xaaltii. mən əṣṣɣər wə-ḥnaa maʕ baʕḍ.

B: eeh.

A: eeh, huwwa yəʕarrəf ruuḥuu dərk. ʕarrəf ruuḥək.

C: fayṣal, xallaṣt lʕaam llii faat, [xxx] *pendant* ʕaam.

B: leeh ḥabəst?

C: a ... dərnaa ʕaam w-naa *au chômage*, bii ... haaðii ʕlaa jaal a ... *erreur administratif* [sic], ʕaam wə-ḥnaa ḥaabsiin. yaʕnii lmʕiiʃa fə-ljazaayər, *c'est-à-dire on ne vit pas, on survit.* wiin maa kaaynʃ mʕiiʃa [xxx] lwaaḥəd *à l'aise*,[3] iiḥəss ruuḥuu *à l'aise* wəllaa ydiir wəʃ iiḥəbb wəllaa. *C'est-à-dire il se developpe comme qui ... comme il veut* wəllaa ḥaaja. a ... *à part que* raanii fə-s-*sport*, anaa *en même temps* mudarrəb w-laaʕəb fii qəsm awwal. a ... yaʕnii *à part* haaðii lə ... yaʕnii *l'occupation* taaʕii, taaʕ s-*sport* maa kaanʃ ḥaaja xraa. w-*bon*, lmʕiiʃa mʕiiʃa, maa ʕandəkʃ yaʕnii *l'embarras du choix* bəhaa tʕiiʃ kiimaa tḥəbb, raak *limité*, raak baayən zaʕmaa ʕandək s-*sport* taaʕək wəllaa qraaytək. *à part ça* maa ʕandəkʃ ḥaaja xraa wiin lwaaḥəd yəqdər iidiirhaa wəllaa yḥabb iiruuḥ plaaṣa xraa *où il se repose* wallaa [xxx] maa ydiir wəllaa. a ... *les moyens de distraction limités* bəzzaaf, a ... yaʕnii lwaaḥəd *n'est pas à l'aise chez soi.* haaðii hiyya.

B: xsaara.

A: tsəmmaa lwaaḥəd maa ʕanduuʃ *une raison, euh ... pour vivre* wəllaa.

C: *Il n'a pas des objectifs à long terme ... .*

A: *Objectifs* wəllaa ʕanduu haadəf hakkaa ... .

أ: ولد خالتي فيصل، ولد خالتي. من الصّغر واحنا مع بعض.

ب: ايه

أ: ايه، هو يعرّف روحه درك. عرّف روحك.

ت: فيصل، خلّصت عام اللّي فات [xxx] *pendant* عام.

ب: ليه حبست؟

ت: ا ا ... درنا عـام وانا *au chômage* بيـ ... هذي على جـال ا ...[sic] *erreur*
administratif، عام واحنا حابسين. يعني المعيشه في الجزاير، *c'est-à-dire*
on ne vit pas, on survit. وين ما كاينش معيشه [xxx] الواحد *à l'aise*،
C'est-à-dire il se ولاّ. يحـبّ وش يدير ولاّ *à l'aise*³ يحـسّ روحـه
comme il veut... developpe comme qui حاجه. ا ... *à part que* راني في
à part يعني ... ا اوّل. قسم في ولاعب مدرّب *en même temps*, انا sport الـ
هذي الـ .... يعني *l'occupation* تاعي، تاع الـ sport ما كانش حاجه اخرى.
و *bon*، المعيشه معيشه، ما عندكش يعني *l'embarras du choix* بها تعيش
كيما تحب، راك *limité*، راك باين زعما عندك الـ sport تاعك ولاّ قرايتك.
À part ça مـا عندكش حاجـه اخرى وين واحد يقدر يديرها ولاّ يحـبّ
les moyens ... ا. ولاّ ما يدير ولاّ [xxx] ولاّ *où il se repose* اخرى بلاصه يروح
de distraction limités بزّاف، ا ... يعني الواحد *n'est pas à l'aise chez soi*.
هذي هي.

ب: خساره.

أ: تسمّى الواحد ما عندهش *pour vivre... une raison euh* ولاّ.

ج: .... *il n'a pas des objectifs a long terme*.

أ: *objectifs* ولاّ عنده هدف هكّا ....

341

C: maa yǝqdǝrʃ, *voilà*. maa yǝqdǝrʃ iidiir haadǝf w-iisaṭṭruuh *parce que rien n'est sûr, c'est-à-dire*, ḥnaa fǝ-ljazaayǝr nxǝmmuu, *on vit le jour le jour*, yoom baʕd ... wraa yoom. maa nqǝdruuʃ ndiiruu *des projets* wǝllaa *des* ...ndiiruu a ... *projet*, kiifaah?[4]

A: mǝʃruuʕ.

C: mǝʃruuʕ zaʕmaa, a ... gaayǝl zaʕmaa *dans un an* wǝllaa *dans six mois* wǝllaa fii haakðaa ndiir ḥaaja. ḥaabb ndiir, nooṣǝlhaa, ndiirhaa. ʕala baaalii bǝllii maa ... *c'est pas sûr*, mǝnnaa l-ɣadwa maa ʕlaa baaliiʃ wǝʃ raaḥ yǝṣraa. *C'est-à-dire*, maa, maa ʕandǝkʃ ḥaaja *sûr, c'est pour ça que tu n'es pas à l'aise, tu n'est pas* ... maakʃ mhannii. *alors, c'est pour ça tu es toujours* mqallǝq a ... tǝ ... *on vit le jour le jour*, kiimaa jaat jaat. haaðii hiyya.

ج: ما يقدرش. *voilà*، ما يقدرش يدير هدف ويسطّره، *parce que rien n'est*

يوم بعد *on vit le jour le jour*، احنا في الجزاير نخمّوا، *sûr, c'est-à-dire*

... ا دنديروا ... ولاّ *des projets* نديروا *des* ... ما نقدروش. يوم ورا ...

projet، كيفه؟[4]

أ: مشروع.

ج: مشروع زعما، ا ... قايل زعما *dans un an* ولاّ *dans six mois* ولاّ في هاكذا

ندير حاجه. حابّ ندير، نوصلها، نديرها. على بالي بلّي ما ...*c'est pas*

sûr، منّا لغدوه ما على باليش واش راح يصرى *C'est-à-dire*. ما، ما

عندكش حاجه، *sûr, c'est pour ça que tu n'es pas à l'aise, tu n'est pas n'es*

... ا مقلّق *Alors. c'est pour ça tu es toujours* مهنّي، ما كش ... *pas à l'aise*

تـ ... *on vit le jour le jour*، كيما جات جات. هذي هيّ.

Vocabulary:

tsəmmaa تسمّى [*also* təmmaa; səmmaa; θəmmaa] *disc* I mean, that is to say
puisque *conj* since
qraaya قرايه *nfs* reading, studying; education
les moyens de distraction ways to relax
siwaa سوا *prep* other than; except
même *adv* even
zaayda زايده *nfs* extra, surplus
puisque l'avenir since the future
en chômage unemployed
même la chance even the chance
diplôme *nms* degree, university degree
kurət yadd كرة يدّ handball
l'équilibre *nms* balance
hakkaak هكّاك [*also* hakkaa; haak] *adv* thus, in that way
sport *nms* sport

kuun كون *part.* if

qləq قلق *v* to be uneasy, upset {*imperf:* yəqləq}

wəld xaala ولد خـالـه cousin (mother's sister's son) {*fs:* bənt xaala, *pl:* wlaad xaala}

xallaş خلّص *v* to finish, complete (s.t.); to pay, have paid {*imperf:* iixallaş}

au chômage unemployed

pendant prep during

erreur administratif administrative error

c'est à dire on ne vit pas, on survit that is, we don't live, we survive

à l'aise comfortable

c'est à dire il se developpe comme qui ... comme il veut that is, a person develops like someone who ... as he wants

à part que conj apart from

en même temps at the same time

à part prep separately, apart from

l'occupation nfs job

l'embarras du choix too much to choose from

limité adj limited

à part ça apart from that

où il se repose where he can rest

les moyens de distractions limités limited ways to relax

n'est pas à l'aise chez soi is not comfortable at home

une raison, euh ... pour vivre a reason, ah ... for living

il n'a pas des objectifs à long terme he has no longterm goals

objectifs nmp goals

voilà presentative there it is

saţţər سطّر *v* to trace out, outline (project, plan); to draw lines (on paper) {*imperf:* iisaţţər}

parce que rien n'est sûr, c'est à dire because nothing is certain, that is

on vit de jour le jour we live one day at a time

des projets projects

dans un an in a year

dans six mois in six months

c'est pas sûr it's not certain

yədwa غدوه *adv* tomorrow; the next day

c'est à dire that is, that is to say

sûr, c'est pour ça que tu n'es pas à l'aise certain, that's why you don't feel comfortable

maakʃ ماكش you (ms) are not

mhannii مهنّي *adj* calm, tranquil {*fs:* mhanniyya, *pl:* mhanniyyiin}

alors, c'est pour ça tu es toujours   so that's why you are always

mqalləq مقلّق *adj* upset, anxious {*fs:* mqallqa, *pl:* mqallqiin}

Notes:

1. The phrase /bə-d-*diplôme* taaʕək/ 'with your *degree*' illustrates the degree to which Arabic and French interact for some speakers of SAA. That is, the French word *diplôme* 'academic degree, diploma' has dropped directly into the Arabic phrase /bə-l ... taaʕək/ 'with your X'. Neither the Arabic nor the French portion of the phrase undergoes any change. Similar uses of French in verbs, rather than nouns, are seen in Selection 11, note 5, and Selection 28, note 6.

    Note that the amount and type of French used in speech varies according to the individual speaker of SAA. Not all speakers have the education or background to make extensive use of French. Some speakers who could use French make a conscious choice not to.

2. The form /wjett/ 'I found', with a final double /t/, derives from /wjedt/. The voiced stop /d/ of the verb stem /wjəd/ assimilates to the voiceless stop /t/ of the 1S perfect suffix. Assimilation of this kind, where the second of two consonants affects the first, is common in SAA. It tends to occur most often in high-frequency forms. See Selection 7, note 6, for the first description of it in this work.

3. The speaker changes reference here. He begins by talking about /waaħəd/ 'one, a person', with /[xxx] **lwaaħəd** *à l'aise*/ 'a person [xxx] *comfortable*'. He then shifts to address his listeners directly with the 2MS pronoun, in /maa ʕandəkʃ yaʕnii *l'embarras du choix*/ 'you don't have, I mean, *a lot of choice*'. Both usages are similar to English. That is, the speaker uses 3S and 2S pronouns to provide some distance from the topic, although he is speaking about himself. Note that speakers of SA and certain other varieties of Arabic may use /alwaaħid/ 'a person' to stand in for a variety of personal pronouns.

4. The speaker here asks for the Arabic equivalent of a French word, with the

question /*projet*, kiifaah?/ '*Project*, how do you say that?'. His question does not, of course, indicate that the speaker does not know SAA. Speakers who use more than one language commonly rely on one member of an equivalent pair, such as the pair *projet* - /məʃruuʕ/.

Between Today and Tomorrow, I Don't Know What Will Happen

A: Ah .... Algeria, that is, I don't, don't have anything but ... Should I talk about life there? *Since* there is no life. It's perfectly clear. From the time we get up, we go to school, we go out, we finish class and stay outdoors. We have nothing. There are no *ways to relax*, just from school to home, from home to school. Ah ... *even*, that is, the .... school, we just keep on studying more, like that, *since* there is no future later. Ah .... There are a lot of people who are ... *unemployed* now. Unemployment, ah .... There's not even a chance of ... your working with your *diploma*. A person goes to school, that is, he doesn't know about his future, whether there is one or not or what.

B: Really.

A: Yes, right, ah ... that is, I have ... I do *sports*. I play, ah ... handball. I play handball on the team ... that ... I found my *balance* in ...that is ... I mean, in sport, I found a balance between school and life like that. That is, *sports* are what helped me. If there were no *sports*, a person like that would get sick or upset or whatever.

B: Right.

A: Yes. *Sports* are what helped me to, that is, in them ....

B: A good thing.

A: Yes. It's a good thing there are *sports*.

B: And Faysal, what relation is he to you?

A: My cousin, Faysal is my cousin. We've been together since we were little.

B: Yes.

A: Yes, he will introduce himself now. Introduce yourself.

C: Faysal. I finished school last year, [xxx] for a year.

B: Why did you stop?

C: Ah ... We spent a year while I was *unemployed*, with... This was because of ... an *administrative error*. A year since we stopped. I mean, life in Algeria, *that is, we don't live, we survive.* Where there is no life a person [xxx] *comfortable*, he feels *comfortable* or does what he wants or whatever. *That is, he develops like someone who ... like he wants to*, or whatever. Ah ... *aside from* being in *sports*, a coach and a player at the same time, in the first division. Ah ... I mean, *besides* that ... I mean, *this work* of mine, in *sports*, there is nothing else. And, well, life is life, you don't have, I mean, *a lot of choice* to live the way you want. You are limited. You are, it's obvious. That is, you have your *sports* or your studies. *Aside from them* you've got nothing else, a place a person can do that, or he wants to go somewhere else *where he can relax*, or something [xxx] he can do or whatever. Ah ... *very limited ways to relax*, ah ... I mean, a person, *he can't be comfortable in his own home.* That's it.

B: What a shame.

A: That is, a person doesn't have *a reason ... to live* or anything.

C: *He has no long-term objectives....*

A: *Objectives* or he has a goal like that ... .

C: He can't, *there you are*, he can't set a goal and plan for it *because nothing is certain, that is.* In Algeria we think, *we live day by day*, day before, after day. We can't carry out *projects* or ... make, ah ... *Project*, how do you say that?

A: maʃruuʕ ['project'].

C: A project, that is, ah .... You say, that is *in a year* or *in six months* or whatever, something like that I will do something. I want to do it, I can reach it, I will do it. I know that it's not ... *it's not certain.* From today to tomorrow I don't know what will happen. *That is to say,* you haven't got, you haven't got anything sure. *That's why you're not comfortable.* You're not calm. So *that's why you're always* upset. Ah ... *a person lives day to day.* What happens, happens. That's all there is.

nta huwa lwahraanii, nta llii taʕrəf

*The final selection of this volume proposes a tour of Oran. The male speaker
uses a good deal of French. Where the French word or phrase is not a proper
name, it may be repeated in Arabic. This repetition is common where two
languages are used.*

A: fii wahraan nruuḥuu *le musée* taaʕ ... *le Musée d'Oran. le Musée* a ...
ʕand ... fiih ṣwaaləḥ bəzzaaf. a ... *c'est un très beau musée. w-à part le
Musée,* ʕannaa, ʕannaa *le Jardin Public. Le Jardin Public, il y a un petit
lac, il y a des canards.* kaayn lbraak beeḍ. ya ... b-ṣaḥḥ kaan ʕannaa
waaḥd əl ... *deux cents,* waaḥda lmiitiin braaka, klaaw[1] nnuṣṣ taaʕhum,
nnuṣṣhaa [laugh] klaawh.

B: [laugh].

A: maaʕleeʃ.

B: [laugh] yaa ... .

A: a ... w-kaayn, kaayn ʃʃwaada, ʃʃwaada ydaḥḥkuu. lə ... kaayn əz-*zoo,
zoo* ṣɣiir. *Le Jardin Public* mliiḥ, kaayn *le Jardin Public. A part le Jardin
Public* kaayən *le Stade, le Stade Municipal,* kaayn *le Stade du 19 juin*[2] *où
ils font tous les sports, football .... On peut aller faire un tour de ....* nḍərbuu
dawra l-ḥimrii.

B: wəʃ hiya ... ?

A: *Le quartier* ḥimrii, anaa zətt təmmak, nwurriilək wiin skənt, wiin, wiin
zətt.

B: aywa.

انت هو الوهراني، انت اللّي تعرف

أ: في وهران نروحوا تاع le Musée ... le Musée, le Musée d'Oran, عند ... عند
à part le musée, ... c'est un tres beau musée ... ا ، فيه صوالح بزّاف،
عندنا، عندنا le Jardin Public. le Jardin Public, il y a un petit lac, il y a des
canards. كاين البراك بيض، يا ... بصحّ كان عندنا واحد الـ deux cents,
واحده الميتين براكه، كلاوا¹ النّص تاعهم، نصّها كلاوه.

ب: [laugh].

أ: معليش.

ب: [laugh] يا ....

أ: ا ... وكاين، كاين الشّواده، الشّواده يضحّكوا. الـ ... كاين الـ zoo, zoo
صغيـــر. Le Jardin Public مليح، كاين A part le Jardin Public. le Jardin
Public كاين le Stade, le Stade Municipal, le Stade du 19 juin² où ils
font tous les sports, football ...On peut aller faire un tour de... نضربوا
دوره لحمري.

ب: واش هي ...؟

أ: حمري le quartier، انا زدت تمّاك، نوريّلك وين سكنت وين، وين زدت.

ب: ايوه.

A: aah ... ḥimrii w-kaayən *la Gare na* ... *Nationale. la Gare Nationale, c'est euh* ... *la structure* taaḥḥaa, a ... tguuliihaa jaaməʕ, ṭa ... mʃiitii lə ... *la gare* ... *la Gare Nationale?*

B: non.

A: *La gare* taaʕ ... *la gare d'Oran.* mniin twuṣlii gəddaam lbaab, tḥəsbii ʕliihaa jaaməʕ.[3] fiihaa *un minaret* w-kərʃəm beeḍ w-təlt qubbaahaat.[4]

B: ʃuuf.

A: mən baʕd, mən ... *de loin* tquulii bəllii jaaməʕ w-hiyya *une gare.*

B: iih.

A: tguuliilhaa jaaməʕ wa-ḷḷaah [laugh]. b-ṣaḥḥ mliiḥa *la gare.* w-nruuḥuu l-gəmbeeṭa. gəmbeeṭa, *c'est un beau quartier.* a ... w-jeey fəl ... *fə-nord* ... *nord-est d'Oran* w-*la vue* mən təmmaak ʃbaab, *très beau,* ʃabba, *la vue du port. le port* taaʕnaa mliiḥ. eeh, aʃḥaal -- ʕaarfa ʃḥaal? -- fiih wəllaa? ɣaaya kii lɣallaaya [laugh]. muur gəmbeeṭa ... yəmkən məm-baʕd gumbeeṭa nruuḥu lə ... ndərbuu dawra *le front de mer. Le front de mer* njəmmʕuu təmmaak barra, ndərbuu ... ʕannaa naḍra taaʕ *le port,* ndərbuulhaa *la crème. La crème* taaʕ wahraan wa-ʕannaa kriipuunii nguuluulaa.

B: heeh.

A: lkriipuunii taaʕnaa mṭarṭag. fiih waaḥd əl ... waaḥd əl ... *Le goût* taaʕ a... lliim. ntuumaa tguuluu lliim, lliimuun b-qaṣd əl ....

B: lqaarəṣ.

A: lqaarəṣ, ḥnaa nguuluu lliim.[5]

أ: ‫ا ... حمري وكاين ...‬ la Gare na ... Nationale. la Gare Nationale c'est euh

‫تاعها، ا ... تقويلها جامع، ط ... مشيتي الـ ...‬ la structure ‫... la ... la gare‬

Gare Nationale؟

ب: Non.

أ: La gare ‫تاع ...‬ la gare d'Oran. ‫منين توصلي قدّام الباب، تحسبي عليها‬ ‫جامع.[3] فيها‬ un minaret ‫وكرشم بيض وتلت قبّهات.[4]‬

ب: شوف.

أ: ‫من بعد، من ...‬ de loin، ‫تقولي بلّي جامع وهيّ‬ une gare.

ب: ايه.

أ: ‫تقوليلها جامع واللّه‬ [laugh] la Gare ‫. بصحّ مليحه ونروحوا لقمبيطه.‬ ‫القمبيطه،‬ c'est un beau quartier. ‫وجاي فلـ ... ا ... في‬ nord, nord-est ‫من تمّاك شباب,‬ très beau, ‫الشّابّة,‬ la vue ‫و‬ d'Oran la vue du port, le port، ‫تاعنا مليح. ايه، اشحال ــ عارفه اشحال؟ ــ فيه ولاّ؟غايه كي‬ ‫الغلاّيه‬[laugh] ‫. مور قمبيطه... يمكن ممبعد قمبيطه نروحوا الـ ...‬ ‫نضربوا دوره‬le front de mer. le front de mer ‫نجمّعوا تمّاك برّه، نضربوا‬ ‫... عندنا نظره تاع‬ le port ‫نضربوا‬ la crème. la crème ‫تاع وهران‬ ‫وعندنا الكريبوني نقولولها.‬

ب: هيه.

أ: ‫الكريبوني تاعنا مطرطق. فيه واحد الـ ... واحد الـ ...‬ le goût ‫تاع ا ...‬ ‫اللّيم. انتما تقولوا اللّيم، الليمون، بقصد الـ ....‬

ب: القارص.

أ: ‫القارص، احنا نقولوا اللّيم.[5]‬

B: [laugh].

A: ləkriipuunii mṭarṭag, mliiḥ. w-b-ṣaḥḥ yəḍurrnii lkriipuunii, yaʕṭii ... maa, maa ...

B: iih.

A: ləkriipuunii mliiḥ. *alors,* naakluu *un peu de* kriipuunii fə-*le front de mer.* mən baʕd, mən *le front de mer* nruuḥuu lə .... wiin, wiin nruuḥuu mən *le front de mer?* nruuḥuu lə ...

B: [laugh] nta huwa lwahraanii, nta llii taʕrəf.

A: ttaḥwiisa ɣaaya fii *le front de mer,* mliiḥ *le front de mer.* fiih, fii *le front de mer il y a plein de palmiers,* fiih *les palmiers* bəzzaaf, waaḥd ələ ... waaḥəd ... *la vue generale* taaʕ *le port* w-mən *le front de mer* tʃuufii lə ... *le mont* ... *la montagne* taaʕ siidii ʕabd əlqaadər l-foog w-*le Château* taaʕ *Santa Cruz* w-mʕaah *la Sainte Marie, c'est une très belle vue.*

B: ṣaḥḥ.

A: wa-ḷḷaah, *le front de mer* mliiḥ, mən *le front de mer* nruuḥuu *le jardin d'essai* .... *le jardin d'essai,* fiih a ... *les* ... *les murs,* ləḥyuuṭa məṣnuuʕiin, ṣənʕuuhum mə ... *les conquistadors, les Espagnols, durant l'invasion* taaʕ *les Espagnols.*[6] məm-baʕd nruuḥuu lə ... l-dərb əlhuud a... *l'habitation turque, pa ... le pacha, la mo ... la mosqué, euh ... bey, du bey, quelque chose comme ça. c'est très beau, on a...* ʕənnaa, ʕənnaa *des ... l'histoire formidable.*

ب: [laugh].

أ: الكريبوني مطرطق، مليح. وبصحّ يضرّني الكريبوني يعطي ... ما ...
ما ....

ب: ايه.

أ: الكريبوني مليح، *alors*. من ناكلوا *un peu de* كريبوني في *le front de*
mer. من بعد، من *le front de mer* نروحوا الـ ... وين، وين نروحوا من *le*
front de mer؟ نروحوا الـ ....

ب: [laugh] انت هو الوهراني، انت اللّي تعرف.

أ: التّحويسه غايه في *le front de mer*، مليح *le front de mer*. فيه, في *le front*
de mer il y a plein de palmiers فيه *les palmiers* بزّاف، واحد الـ ... واحد...
la vue générale تاع *le port* ومن *le front de mer* تشوفي الـ ... *le mont*
Santa Cruz تاع سيدى عبد القادر الفوق و *le château* تاع *la montagne*
ومعه *la Sainte Marie. c'est une très belle vue*.

ب: صحّ.

أ: واللّه، *le front de mer* مليح *le front de mer* من نروحوا *le* ... *le jardin*
jardin d'essai d'essai فيه ا ... *les murs* ... *les* ... الحيوطه مصنوعين ...
صنعوهم تاع *les conquistadors, les Espagnols. durant l'invasion* ... *les*
Espagnols.[6] من بعد نروحوا الـ ... لدرب الهود ا ... *l'habitation turque,* ...
pa ... le pacha, la mo ... la mosquée, euh ... bey, du bey quelque chose
des ... l'histoire عندنا، عندنا *comme ça. c'est très beau, on a* ...
formidable.

355

Vocabulary:

wahraanii وهراني *adj* Oranais (from Oran) {*fs:* wahraaniyya, *pl:* wahraaniyyiin}
le musée *nms* the museum

ṣaalḥa صالحه *nfs* good, material commodity {*pl:* ṣwaaləḥ}
le musée d'Oran. le musée the Oran Museum. The museum
c'est un très beau musée it's a very beautiful museum
à part le musée apart from the museum
le Jardin Public. Le Jardin Public, il y a un petit lac, il y a des canards.
    the Jardin Public. The Jardin Public, there is a small lake, there are ducks.

braak براك *nms; collective* ducks {*fs:* braaka, *pl:* braakaat}

byaḍ ابيض [*also* byaaḍ] *adj* white; fair-skinned {*fs:* beeḍaa, *pl:* biiḍ}
deux cents 200

ʃaadii شادي *nms* monkey {*pl:* ʃwaada, *pl:* ʃwaadii}
le zoo, zoo the zoo, a zoo
le Jardin Public the Jardin Public
le Jardin Public. A part le Jardin Public the Jardin Public. Aside from the
    Jardin Public
le stade, le Stade Municipal the Stadium, the Municipal Stadium
*le stade du 19 juin où ils font tous les sports, football .... on peut
    aller faire un tour de ....* the June 19 Stadium where they have all kinds of
    sports, football ... we can do a tour of ....

ḍrəb ضرب *v* to do, make; to hit, strike {*imperf:* yəḍrəb}

ḥimrii حمري *prop* Himri (neighborhood in Oran)
le quartier *nms* the neighborhood

zaad زاد *v; pre-verb* to be born; to do again (action of main verb); to continue to do
    (action of main verb) {*imperf:* iiziid}

wərraa ورّى *v* to show, demonstrate {*imperf:* iiwərrii}
la gare na ... nationale. la Gare Nationale, c'est euh ... la structure
    the Gare Nationale, the Gare Nationale, that's the ... structure
la gare ... la Gare Nationale the railway station ... the Gare Nationale
la gare *nfs* the railway station
la gare d'Oran the Gare d'Oran

ḥsəb ʕlaa حسب على *v* to believe (s.o. or s.t. to be) {*imperf:* yəḥsəb ʕlaa}
un minaret *nms* a minaret

356

kərʃəm كرشم *nms* window

qubba قبّ *nfs* dome {*imperf:* qubbaat}

de loin from afar

une gare *nfs* a railroad station

gumbeeţa گمبيطه *prop* Gambetta (neighborhood of Oran named for a 19th century French political figure)

c'est un beau quartier it is a nice neighborhood

nord ... nord-est d'Oran north ... north-west of Oran

la vue *nfs* the view

təmmaak تمّاك *adv* there, over there

ʃbaab شبـاب *adj* nice; pretty {*fs:* ʃaabba, *pl:* ʃaabbiin}

très beau very nice

la vue du port the view of the harbor

ɣaaya غايه *nfs* good, nice

ɣallaaya غلّايه *nfs* coffeepot (small with long handle) {*pl:* gallaayaat}

ɣaaya kə-lɣallaaya غايه كالغلايّه the best, the ultimate (lit. the greatest, like the coffeepot)

muur مور *prep* after; behind, in back of

le front de mer, le front de mer the seafront, the seafront

le port *nms* the harbor

la crème, la crème the ice cream, the ice cream

kriipuunii كريبوني *nms* créponnée (kind of lemon ice cream)

mţarţaq مـطرطـق *adj* great, wonderful; explosive

le goût *nms* the taste

liim ليـم *nms; collective* lemon (fruit) {*fs:* liima, *pl:* liimaat}

liimuun ليـمـون *nms; collective* lemon (fruit) {*fs:* liimuuna, *pl:* liimuunaat}

qaarəş قـارص *nms; collective* lemon (fruit) {*fs:* qaarşa, *pl:* qaarşaat}

alors so, then

un peu de a little bit of

le front de mer the seafront

taḥwiisa تحويسه *nfs* walk, stroll {*pl:* taḥwiisaat}

le front de mer il y a plein de palmiers the seafront there are plenty of palm trees

la vue générale the overall view

le port *nms* the harbor

le front de mer the seafront

le mont ... la montagne mount ... the mountain

siidii ʕabd əlqaadər سيـدي عبـد القـادر *prop* Sidi Abd El-Qadir (Algerian hero, namesake of mountain near Oran)

le château *nms* the Château

Santa Cruz *prop* Santa Cruz (Oran landmark named for Catholic patron saint of the city)

la Sainte Marie, c'est une très belle vue Sainte Marie, it's a very nice view

le front de mer the seafront

le jardin d'essai .... le jardin d'essai the jardin d'essai ... the jardin d'essai (experimental garden)

les ... les murs the ... the walls

les conquistadors, les Espagnols, durant les Espagnols the conquistadors, the Spanish, at the time of the Spanish

les Espagnols *nmp* the Spanish

dərb əlhuud درب الهـود *prop* the Derb (former Jewish quarter of Oran)

l'habitation turque, pa ... le pacha, la mo ... la mosqué, euh ... bey, du bey, quelque chose comme ça. c'est très beau, on a the Turkish residence ... the pasha ... the mosque ... the bey, of the bey, something like that. it's very pretty, we have

des ... l'histoire formidable. some ... a magnificant history.

Notes:

1. The form /klaaw/ 'they ate' derives from the verb /klaa/ 'to eat', with the imperfect /yaakəl/. That is, the perfect /klaa/ resembles a finally-weak verb. The imperfect /yaakəl/, however, resembles an initially-weak verb. One other verb of SAA, /xdaa/ - /yaaxəd/ 'to take' (also /xðaa/ - /yaaxəð/) has a similar perfect and imperfect.

2. The stadium known as *le Stade du 19 juin* 'the June 19 stadium" marks a turning point in Algerian history. On this date in 1965, Ahmed Ben Bella, the first president of Algeria, was overthrown in a coup led by Houari Boumediene. Boumediene went on to serve as president from 1967 to 1978.

3. Whether or not *la Gare d'Oran* looks like a mosque is a matter of opinion. The design of the building, however, incorporates the indigeneous and Islamic elements cited by the male speaker. This use of local tradition in non-local buildings is common in certain types of French colonial architecture

in North Africa.

4. The form /qubbaaḥaat/ 'domes', with /h/ preceding the feminine plural suffix /aat/, is a slip of the tongue. The singular /gubba/ 'dome' has several plural forms in SAA. The most commonly used of these are /qbəb/ and /qəbbaat/.

5. The two speakers produce three regional variants that mean 'lemon'. They are /liim/, /liimuun/, and /qaarəṣ/. Certain words and semantic fields appear to be more open to regional variation than others for reasons that are not clear. Citrus fruits are one of these fields in the spoken Arabic of North Africa.

6. The event the male speaker calls /l'invasion taaʕ les Espagnols/ occurred in 1509. The Spanish held the city until 1708 and again from 1732 to 1792.

You're the One From Oran, You're the One Who Knows

A: In Oran, we'll go the *Museum of... the Oran Museum, ... the Museum ...* It has ... there are a lot of things there, ah ... *It's a very beautiful museum.* And *besides the Museum*, we have, we have *the Jardin Public, the Jardin Public. There is a small lake. There are ducks.* There are white ducks .... Really, we used to have about ... *two hundred*, about two hundred ducks. They ate half of them, half of them [laugh], they ate them.

B: [laugh].

A: That's OK.

B: [laugh]

A: Ah .... And there are, there are monkeys. The monkeys are funny. The ... there is the *zoo*, a small *zoo. The Jardin Public* is nice. There is *the Jardin Public, besides the Jardin Public* there is *the Stadium, the Municipal Stadium.* There is *the June 19 Stadium where they have all kinds of sports, football ... we can do a tour of* ....We can do a tour of Himri.

B: That's that?

A: The Himri *neighborhood.* I was born there. I'll show where I lived, where, where I was born.

B: Yes.

A: Ah .... Himri and there is *the Gare ...Nationale. The Gare Nationale, it's ... the building* it's in, ... You'd say it is a mosque .... Have you been to ... *the railway station... the Gare National?*

B: No.

A: *The railway station* of … *the Gare National.* When you arrive at the door, you'd think it's a mosque. It has a *minaret* and white windows and three domes.

B: Really.

A: From a distance, from … *from a distance,* you'd say that it's a mosque but it's *a railroad station.*

B: Yes.

A: You'd say it's a mosque, by God [laugh]. Really, *the railroad station* is nice. And we will go to Gambetta. Gambetta, *it's a nice neighborhood.* Ah … and it's to the … to the *north … northeast of Oran.* And *the view* from there is beautiful, *very beautiful. The view of the port is* beautiful. Our *port* is nice. Yes. How much -- do you know "how much" -- there is or what? "Great like a kettle"[laugh]. After Gambetta, maybe after Gambetta we'll go to … we'll do a tour of the *seafront.* The *seafront,* we'll get together there outside, we'll do … We have the view of *the port.* We'll drop by for *ice cream,* Oranais *ice cream* and … We have *créponnée,* we call it.

B: Yes.

A: Our *créponné* is great. It has a … a *taste* of … ah … lemon. You call it <u>liim</u>, <u>liimuun</u>, that is …

B: <u>qaariṣ</u>.

A: <u>qaariṣ</u>. We say <u>liim</u>.

B: [laugh].

A: *Créponnée* is great. nice. But it hurts me. it gives … not … not ….

B: Yes.

A: *Créponnée* is good. So, we'll eat *a little bit of créponnée* on *the seafront*, afterwards, after *the seafront*, we'll go to .... Where, where will we go from the seafront? We'll go to ....

B: You're the one's who's Oranais, you're the one who knows.

A: A walk would be good on *the seafront*. *The seafront* is nice. There are, on *the seafront there are a lot of palm trees*, there are a lot of *palm trees*, some ... some .... *The overall view* of *the port*, and from *seafront* you can see *the Mount* ... *the Mountain* of Sidi Abd al-Qadir up there and *the Château of Santa Cruz* and nearby is *the Sainte Marie. It's a very beautiful view.*

B: True.

A: God, *the seafront is nice.* From the *seafront* we'll go to the *Jardin d'Essai*, the *Jardin d'Essai.* There are ... *walls*, walls made, they built them .... *The conquistadors, the Spanish,* during *the invasion of the Spanish.* Afterwards we'll go to ... to Darb al-Houd, ah .... *The Turkish residence ... the pasha ... the mosque ... the bey, of the bey, something like that. it's very pretty, we have* .... We have, we have, *it's very beautiful, we have ... a fantastic history.*

Glossary

Introduction

The glossaries for this work are divided into items from SAA and items from French. SAA entries appear in alphabetical order, rather than root order. SAA alphabetical order is based on the Arabic alphabet. Changes to the conventional ordering of the Arabic alphabet accommodate the sound system of SAA.

French lexical items appear in conventional alphabetical order. The French glossary is provided for those with little or no knowledge of French. For that reason, items in the form in which they are cited in the selection.

?	ء	ʃ	ش
aa	ا	ṣ	ص
a - ə	ا	ḍ	ض
ee	اي	ṭ	ط
oo	او	ọ̃ - ḍ	ظ
aw	او	ʕ	ع
u	ا	ɣ	غ
i	ا	f	ف
b	ب	v	ڤ
p	پ	q - g - k - ?	ق
t	ت	k	ك
θ - t	ث	l - ḷ	ل
j	ج	m	م
ḥ	ح	n	ن
x	خ	h	ه
d	د	uu	و
ð - d	ذ	w	و
r - ʁ	ر	ii	ي
z	ز	y	ي
s	س		

ʔ

ʔaaḍiifa قضيفه *nfs* velvet 26

ʔaal قال [*also* qaal; gaal] *v* to speak, talk {*imperf:* iiʔuul} 26

ʔafṭaan قفطان [*also* qafṭaan] *nms* caftan {*pl:* ʔafaaṭən} 26

ʔafṭaan ṣdər قفطان صدر [*also* qafṭaan ṣdər] caftan (worn as an underlayer) {*pl:* ʔafaaṭən ṣdər} 26

aa

aaxər اخر [*also* ooxər] *adj* other {*fs:* axraa, *pl:* axriin} 2

aañvastaa انڤاستى [*also* aanvastaa] *v* to invest in, put money into {*imperf:* yaañvastii} 21

lʔaandaaluus الاندالوس *prop* Andalusia (region of southern Spain) 2

aanvastaa انڤاستى [*also* aañvastaa] *v* to invest in, put money into {*imperf:* yaanvastii} 21

aanoñsaa انونصى *v* to announce, make public {*imperf:* yaanoñsii} 12

a ə i o

abb اب *nms* father {*pl:* abawaat} 18

ətʃraa تشرى *v* to be bought {*imperf:* yətʃraa} 15

ətṣraf اتصرف [*also* əṣṣref] *v* to be spent (of money) {*imperf:* yətṣraf} 7

iḥtiiyaaṭ احتياط *nms* reserve, supply {*pl:* iḥtiiyaaṭaat} 6

əxt اخت *nfs* sister {*fpl:* xwaataat} 15

arbaʕa اربعه [*also* rabʕa] *nfs* four, 4 6

arḍ ارض *nfs* land, plot of land, piece of real estate {*pl:* aaraaḍii} 6

asəm اسم *nms* name {*pl:* aasmaaʔ, *pl:* aasaamii, *pl:* smaawaat} 5

əssənnaa استّى [*also* əstənnaa] *v* to wait, wait for {*imperf:* iissənnaa} 33

iṣpaanii اصپانى *adj* Spanish, Spaniard {*fs:* iṣpaaniyya, *pl:* iṣpaan} 2

əṣṣref اصرّف [*also* ətṣraf] *v* to be spent (of money) {*imperf:* yəṣṣraf} 10

əksporṭaa اكسپرطى *v* to export {*imperf:* yəksporṭii} 21 ilaa الا *part.* if 19

əlthaa b- بـ التهى *v* to be busy with; to care for {*imperf:* yəlthii, *imperf:* yəlthaa} 32

aḷḷaa aʕlam الله اعلم God only knows (lit. God is the most knowing) (said of uncertain or undesirable outcome) 24

aḷḷaah yəhdii + **suffixed pronoun** الله يهدي God guide s.o. (i.e. to the right path, often said in criticism) 28

aḷḷah yəṣḍar الله يصضر [*also* aḷḷaah yəṣṭar] *v* may God protect 5

aḷḷah yəṣṭar الله يصطر [*also* aḷḷaah yəṣḍar] *v* may God protect 5

əllii اللي [*also* llii] *pro* who, what (definite relative pronoun) 1

immaalaa امّالا [*also* mmaalaa] *conj* so, therefore 6

anaa انا [*also* anaayaa] *pro* I (1S) 1

anaayaa انايا [*also* anaa] *pro* I (1S) 12

owwəl اول [*also* uwwəl; awwəl] *adj* first {*fs:* uulaa, *pl:* uuwliin} 2

ooxər اخر [*also* aaxər] *adj* other {*fs:* ooxraa, *pl:* ooxriin} 17

ookla اوكله *nfs* dish (speciality of the house or region {*pl:* ooklaat} 17

uwwəl اوّل [*also* awwəl; owwəl] *adj*

first {*fs:* uulaa, *pl:* uuwliin} 4

iiðaa اذا *conj* if; when, whenever 11

iiraanyoom ايرانيوم *nms* uranium 6

iiguullək يقولّك *disc* that is to say, I mean (lit. they tell you) 6

iimaam ايمام *nms* imam (Islamic prayer leader) {*pl:* ayma} 18

iinsaan اينسان [*also* insaan] *nms* person, human being {*pl:* naas} 9

iih ايه *interj* yes 7

eeh ايه [*also* iih] *interj* yes 8

b

baabaa بابا *nms* father {*pl:* baabaawaat} 8

baaraaka باراكه *nfs* divine blessing, divine grace 5

lbaarəḥ البارح *adv* yesterday; the previous evening 17

baaʃ باش [*also* bəʃ] *conj* for; so that, in order to 2

baaṭaaṭa باطاطه *nfs* potato 21

baaqii باقي *adj* rest, what stays, what remains; resting, staying, remaining 18

baalaak بالاك *adv* maybe, perhaps; about, approximately 15

baanaan بانان [*also* baanaanaa]

nms banana 5

baanaanaa بانانا [*also* baanaan]
nms banana 21

baayən باين *adj* distinct, evident
{*fs:* baayna, *pl:* baayniin} 31

bə-ddaat بالذات none other than, of
all people, of all things 14

bərbuuʃa بربوشه *nfs* couscous 17

barra برّه *adv* outside; outdoors;
overseas 32

barraad براد *nms* tea pot {*pl:*
braarəd} 23

bərk برك [*also* bark] *adv* only,
just 18

bərnuuṣ برنوص *nms* burnous (kind
of cape or hooded cloak) {*pl:*
braanəṣ} 15

bəzzaaf بزّاف *adv* a lot, very much 4

bəʃ باش [*also* baaʃ] *conj* for; so
that, in order to 7

bəʃʃaar ٰبشّار *prop* Béchar (city in
southern Algeria) 19

bə-ṣṣaḥḥ بالصّحّ [*also* b-ṣaḥḥ] *conj*
but (lit. with the truth) 5

baṭṭiix بطّيخ *nms* melon {*ms:*
baṭṭiixa, *pl:* baṭṭiixaat} 21

baʕdeen بعدين *adv* afterwards, then
12

bəkrii بكري *adv* earlier; in the old

days; at first 14, 17

bəldii بلدي *adj* local, regional;
traditional {*fs:* bəldiyya, *pl:*
bəldiyyiin} 31

bəllii بللي *conj.; after verbs of
speaking, thinking, etc.* that 11

bən fuulaan بن فولان so-and-so,
what's his name {*fs:* bənt fuulaan,
pl: bnuu fuulaan} 17

lbayyəɠ البيّض *prop* El Bayadh
(town in southwest Algeria) 25

beetoon بيتون *nms* concrete,
cement 5

b-ḥaal بحال *prep* like, as 19

b-ḥeet بحيث *conj* since, as, due to
the fact that 11

bdaa بدا *v* to start, begin {*imperf:*
yəbdaa} 7

braak براك *nms; collective* ducks {*fs:*
braaka, *pl:* braakaat} 36

b-ṣaḥḥ بصحّ *conj* but; actually (lit.
with truth) 1

byaa بغى *v* to want; to like, love
{*imperf:* yəbɣii} 25

blaa بلا *prep* without 18

blaad بلاد *nfs* country; region; city
{*pl:* bəldaan, *pl:* blaadaat} 6

bluuza بلوزه *nfs* blouse, woman's
shirt {*pl:* bluuyəz, *pl:* bluuzaat} 26

bnii aadəm ادم بني person, individual {*fs:* bnii aadma, *pl:* bnii aadmiin} 32

boomba بومبه *nfs* bomb {*pl:* boombaat} 13

buu بو *nms* father {*pl:* bwaat} 18

biit بيت *nms* home, house; room {*pl:* byuut} 33

biiskra بسكره *prop* Biskra (town in south central Algeria) 21

biin بين [*also* biinaat] *prep* among, between 6

biinaat بينات [*also* biin] *prep* among, between *with P noun or suffixed pronoun* 3

byaḍ ابيض *adj* fair-skinned; white {*fs:* beeḍaa, *pl:* biiḍ} 26

byaḍ ابيض [*also* byaaḍ] *adj* white; fair-skinned {*fs:* beeḍaa, *pl:* biiḍ} 36

p

pətrool پترول [*also* peetrool; piitrool] *nms* oil, petroleum 4

parlaamaan پرلامان *nms* parliament, legislature {*pl:* parlaamaanaat} 11

peetrool پترول [*also* pətrool; piitrool] *nms* oil, petroleum 4

plaastiikii پلاستيكي *adj* plastic, made from plastic {*fs:* plaastiikiyya, *pl:* plaastiikiyyiin} 21

plaaṣa پلاصه *nfs* place, location {*pl:* plaaṣaat, *pl:* plaayeṣ} 8

piitrool پيترول [*also* pətrool; peetrool] *nms* oil, petroleum 6

t

taabəlbaala تابلباله *prop* Tabelbala (town in west central Algeria) 25

taajriiba تاجيبه *nfs* experiment, trial {*pl:* taajaariib} 20

taaḥ- + suffixed pronoun with initial /h/ تاح [*also* taaʕ] *possessive adjective: invariable* of, belonging to 1

taaʕ تاع [*also* ntaaʕ] of, belonging to *possessive adjective: invariable* 1

taalət تالت *adj* third {*fs:* taalta} 23

taanii ثاني [*also* θaanii] *adj.; also adv* another; again {*fs:* taanya, *pl:* taanyiin} 12, 14

təbbaʕ تبّع *v* to follow, pursue; to imitate {*imperf:* iitəbbaʕ} 11

təḥt تحت *prep* downstairs; underneath 30

taḥwiisa تحويسه *nfs* walk, stroll {*pl:* taḥwiisaat} 36 taraab تراب *nms* earth, dust, dirt 6

təsʕiin تسعين *nms* ninety, 90 13

təsʕiinaat تسعينات *np* nineties 15

təsmiyya تسميه *nfs* name, naming practice {*pl:* təsmiyyaat} 17

taṣawwəf تصوّف *nms* Islamic mysticism, Sufism 34

taʕdaal تعدال *nms* straightening; pruning 21

təʕʕab تعبّ *v* to tire out, make tired, fatigue {*imperf:* iitəʕʕab} 16

təlgaaḥ تلقاح *nms* pollination 21

tamanraasət تمنراست *prop* Tamanrasset (city in southern Algeria) 22

təmmaa¹ تمّى [*also* tsəmmaa; səmmaa; θəmmaa] *disc* I mean, that is to say

təmmaa² تمّا [*also* θəmma; tsəmma; səmmaa] *adv* there, over there 20

təmmaak تمّاك *adv* there, over there 36

təngiiza تنقيزه *nfs* jump, leap {*pl:* təngiizaat} 25

tbaark aḷḷaah تبارك الله God bless s.o. (lit. God be blessed; said in admiration or irony, also against the evil eye) 25

tbəddəl تبدّل *v* to change (o.s. or one's clothing) {*imperf:* yətbəddəl} 26

tbərrək تبرّك *v* to be blessed, receive a blessing from {*imperf:* yətbərrək} 16

ttəkəl اتكل *v* to be eaten, be able to be eaten {*imperf:* yəttkəl} 17

tḥallaa تحلّى *v* to become sweet, make o.s. sweet {*imperf:* yətḥallaa} 17

txaaṭəb تخاطب *v* to become engaged (to be married to one another) {*imperf:* yətxaaṭəb} 15

txabbaa تخبّى *v* to hide, conceal oneself {*imperf:* yətxabbaa} 14

txədəm اتخدم *v* to be made, done, worked {*imperf:* yətxədəm} 15

txəlləṭ تخلّط *v* to be confused, mixed up; to be mixed, mingled {*imperf:* yətxəlləṭ} 12

traaḥ ʕlaa تراح *v* to slip away {*imperf:* yətraaḥ} 5

tsəmmaa¹ تسمّا [*also* təmma; θəmma; səmmaa] *adv* there, over there 19

tsəmmaa² تسمّى [*also* təmmaa; səmmaa; θəmmaa] *disc* I mean, that is to say 35

tʃiiʃa تشيشه [*also* dʒiiʃa] *nfs* dchica (kind of coarse-ground barley or wheat) 17

tʃiina تشينه‎ *nfs; collective* orange
(fruit) {*pl:* tʃiinaat} 6

tʕarrəḍ ʕlaa تعرّض على‎ *v* to attack,
assault {*imperf:* yətʕarrəḍ} 14

tlaata ثلاثه‎ [*also* θlaaθa; tlət;
θəlθ] *nfs* three, 3

tlaatiin ثلاثين‎ [*also* θlaaθiin] *nms*
thirty, 30

tlaaṭṭaaʃ تلاطّاش‎ [*also* tlaṭṭaaʃən]
nms thirteen 8

tlaaṭṭaaʃən تلاطّاشن‎ [*also* tlaṭṭaaʃ]
nms; form used in construct phrase
thirteen 8

tlət تلت‎ [*also* θəlθ; θlaaθa; tlaata]
nms three, 3 20

tləmsaan تلمسان‎ *prop* Tlemcen (city
in western Algeria) 34

tmar تمر‎ *nms; collective* dates (fruit)
{*fs:* təmra, *pl:* təmraat} 6

tməsxər تمسخر‎ *v* to trick, fool; to
laugh at, ridicule {*imperf:*
yətməsxər} 12

tmuuʃən t تموشنت‎ *prop* Temouchent
(variety of date); Temouchent (city in
western Algeria) 21

tnawwəḍ تنوّض‎ *v* to quarrel with one
another {*imperf:* yətnawwəḍ} 25

tneen اتنين‎ [*also* θneen] *nms* two,
2 17

thallaa fii تهلّى في‎ *v* to take care of,

care for {*imperf:* yəthallaa} 6

thəwwəl تهوّل‎ [*also* thawwəl] *v* to
be alarmed, frightened {*imperf:*
yəthəwwəl} 12

thawwəl تهوّل‎ [*also* thəwwəl] *v* to
be alarmed, frightened {*imperf:*
yəthawwəl} 34

twaḥḥaʃ توحّش‎ *v* to miss, long for
{*imperf:* yətwaḥḥaʃ} 29

turkii تركي‎ *adj* Turk, Turkish {*fs:*
turkiyya, *pl:* turk, *pl:* traak} 2

tuunsii تونسي‎ *adj* Tunisian {*fs:*
tuunsiyya, *pl:* twaansa, *pl:*
tuunsiyyiin} 31

tiiliifiizyoon تيليفيزيون‎ *nms*
television {*pl:* tiiliifiizyoonaat} 9

θ

θaar ثار‎ *nms* revenge, vengeance 25

θəlθ ثلث‎ [*also* tlət; θlaaθa; tlaata]
nms three, 3 17

θəmmaa¹ ثمّى‎ [*also* təmmaa;
səmmaa; tsəmmaa] *disc* I mean,
that is to say

θəmmaa² ثمّا‎ [*also* təmma; tsəmma;
səmmaa] *adv* there, over there 16

θlaaθa ثلاثه‎ [*also* tlaata; tlət;
θəlθ] *nfs* three, 3 15

θlaaθiin ثلاثين‎ [*also* tlaatiin] *nms*

thirty. 30 18

θneen اثنين [*also* tneen] *nms* two, 2 17

j

jaa جا *v* to come, come to, arrive at; to be located (past tense or active participle) {*imperf:* iijii} 1, 30

jaab جاب *v* to bring {*imperf:* iijiib} 2

jaaz جاز *v* to be permitted, allowed; to pass by, travel {*imperf:* iijuuz} 12

jaanuub جانوب *nms* south 19

jaahiliyya جاهليّه *prop* the Jahiliyya, pre-Islamic Arabia; ignorance, barbarism 22

jaay جاي *adj* coming, arriving {*fs:* jaaya, *pl:* jaayiin} 9

jəbhat lʔinqaaḍ جبهه الانقاض *prop* (Islamic) Salvation Front (*FIS, Front Islamique du Salut*) 13

jədd جدّ *nms* grandfather {*pl:* jduud, *pl:* jdaad} 25

jərf əttarba جرف التربه *prop* Djorf Torba (village near Béchar in western Algeria) 20

ljazaayər الجزاير [*also* ddzaayər] *prop* Algeria; Algiers *FS* 1

jəssəs جسّس *v* to spy, keep secret watch {*imperf:* iijəssəs} 10

jjəlfa الجلفه *prop* Djelfa (city and province in central Algeria) 29

jbəd جبد *v* to pull; to pull back {*imperf:* yəjbəd} 13

jbəd ruuḥ + suffixed pronoun جبد روح *v* to withdraw oneself {*imperf:* yəjbed ruuḥ-} 13

jbiin جبين *nms* forehead {*pl:* jbiinaat, *pl:* jbən} 26

jjaab اتجاب *v* to be brought {*imperf:* yəjjaab} 4

jraa جرى *v* to run {*imperf:* yəjrii} 9

joohar جوهر *nms* jewel, gem {*pl:* jwaahər} 26

juuz جوز [*also* zooj; zuuj; zawj] *nms* two, 2 17

jiiha جيهه *nfs* side; direction {*pl:* jiihaat, *pl:* jwaayəh} 6

ḥ

ḥaabəs حابس *adj* stopped, not moving {*fs:* ḥaabsa, *pl:* ḥaabsiin} 22

ḥaabb حابّ *adj.; also pre-verb* wanting, intending to; liking, loving {*fs:* ḥaabba, *pl:* ḥaabiin} 12

ḥaaja حاجه *nfs* thing, object {*pl:*
ḥaajaat, *pl:* ḥwaayəj} 8

ḥaaqiiqa حاقيقه *disc* actually, in
fact (lit. reality) 16

ḥaalaawiyyaat حالاويات *np* s.t.
sweet; candy; pastry 17

ḥaawaalii حاوالي *adv* about,
approximately 2

ḥabb حب *v.; also pre-verb* to want to;
to like, love {*imperf:* iiḥabb} 7

ḥabba حبّه *nfs* piece (of fruit); grain
(of wheat, etc.) {*pl:* ḥabbaat} 5

ḥattaa حتّى *adv* even 1

ḥattaa wə-loo حتّى ولو *conj* even if
11

ḥattaa w-maa حتّى وما *conj* even if
not 8

ḥariira حريره *nfs hariira* (kind of
North African soup) 19

ḥaddər حضّر *v* to make, cause to
appear, attend {*imperf:* iiḥaddər} 18

ḥagger حقّر *v* to despise, scorn. treat
with contempt {*imperf:* iiḥaggər}
11

ḥəlwa حلوى *nms* sweet pastry; candy
{*pl:* ḥəlwaat, *pl:* ḥaalaawiyyaat} 17

ḥanaa احنا [*also* ḥnaa; ḥnaayaa]
pro we, us (1P) 11

ḥanṣaaliyya حنصاليه *prop*
Hansaliyya (Sufi brotherhood or order

with roots on the Moroccan-Algerian
border) 34

ḥənnaa¹ حنّى *v* to apply henna
{*imperf:* iiḥənnii} 16

ḥənnaa² هنّا *nfs* grandmother {*pl:*
ḥənnaawaat} 17

ḥawzii حوزي *nms haouzi* (kind of
Arab-Andalusian music associated with
Tlemcen) 34

ḥbəs حبس *v* to make stop; to stop
o.s. {*imperf:* yəḥbəs} 29

ḥbiiba حبيبه *nfs* female friend;
female relative {*pl:* ḥbaabaat, *fpl:*
ḥbiibaat} 15

ḥdaa حدا *prep* next to

ḥdaaʃ حداس *nms* eleven

ḥdaaʃən حداشن *nms; form used in
construct phrase* eleven 30

ḥdaam حدام *prep* next to 23

ḥsəb حسب *v* to think, consider,
suppose {*imperf:* yəḥsəb} 7

ḥsəb ʕlaa حسب على *v* to believe
(s.o. or s.t. to be) {*imperf:* yəḥsəb
ʕlaa} 36

ḥeeṭ حيط *nms* wall {*pl:* ḥyuuṭ} 25

ḥḍar حضر *v* to attend, be present at
{*imperf:* yəḥḍar} 17

ḥkaa حكى *v* to say, tell {*imperf:*
yəḥkii} 8

ḥluu حلو *adj* sweet; pleasant, nice
{*fs:* ḥluuwa, *pl:* ḥəlwiin} 17

ḥmeeṣa حميصه *nfs* chickpeas
collective 9

ḥnaa احنا [*also* ḥnaayaa; ḥanaa]
pro we, us (1P) 5

ḥnaayaa حنايا [*also* ḥnaa; ḥanaa]
pro we (1P) 18

ḥwaayəj حوايج *np* clothes, clothing
14

ḥurma حرمه *nfs* woman; honor; what
is sacred or taboo {*pl:* ḥuuruumaat}
14

ḥuqd حقد *nms* hatred, malice 28

ḥuwwəs حوّس *v* to take a walk; to
make or take a tour {*imperf:*
iiḥuwwəs} 18

ḥuut حوت *nms; collective* fish {*fs:*
ḥuuta, *pl:* ḥuutaat} 5

ḥuulii حولي *nms* blanket, coverlet
{*pl:* ḥwaalii} 15

ḥimrii حمري *prop* Himri
(neighborhood in Oran) 36

ḥiiṭ حيط *nms* wall {*pl:* hyuuṭ} 5

X

xaarəj خارج *prep* overseas, outside
the country; outside 4

xaaṭ خاط [*also* xaatʃ; xaatʃii;
xaaṭər] *conj* because, due to the fact
that 15

xaaṭər خاطر [*also* xaatʃ; xaatʃii;
xaaṭ] *conj* because, due to the fact
that 23

xaatʃ خاطش [*also* xaaṭ; xaatʃii;
xaaṭər] *conj* because, due to the fact
that 8

xaaṭii + suff. pro خاطي it doesn't
concern s.o., leave s.t. alone
invariable 10

xaaldii (lxaaldii) الخالدي *prop*
Abdelkader El Khaldi (Algerian poet
whose lyrics continue to influence raï
music) 27

xəddaam خدّام *nms* worker,
employee {*fs:* xəddaama, *pl:*
xəddaamiin} 6

xəddəm خدّم *v* to employ, put to work
{*imperf:* iixəddəm} 20

xəddiimii خدّيمي *nms* small knife,
dagger (diminutive of /xudmii/) {*pl:*
xdaamaa} 25

xədma خدمه *nfs* work, job,
employment; task {*pl:* xədmaat} 7

xəṣṣ خصّ *v.; pre-verb* to be necessary
(for s.o. or s.t. to do action of the
main verb) {*imperf:* iixəṣṣ} 23

xaṭra خطره *nfs* time, moment {*pl:*

xaṭraat} 25

xalaaṣ خلاص *nms* pay, salary {*pl*} 7

xəllaa خلّى *v* to allow, let {*imperf*: iixellii} 11

xallaṣ خلّص *v* to pay, have paid; to finish. complete (s.t.) {*imperf*: iixallaṣ} 7, 35

xalləṭ خلّط *v* to mix, mix together {*imperf*: iixalləṭ} 30

xəmsiin خمسين *nms* fifty, 50 18

xamm fii- خمّ في *v* to think about, reflect on {*imperf*: iixamm fii-} 28

xdəm خدم *v* to weave; to do, make; to plant, cultivate, grow {*imperf*: yəxdəm} 15

xdəm خدم *v* to plant, cultivate, grow; to weave; to do, make {*imperf*: yəxdəm} 21

xdem خدم *v* to work; to do, make; to weave; to plant, cultivate, grow {*imperf*: yexdem} 6

xeer خير *nms* goodness, bounty 5

xfaafa خفافه *nfs* khfaf (kind of fried pastry) {*pl*: xfaaf} 9

xlaaṣ خلاص *interj* that's it; that's the way it is 2

xlaaṣ خلاص *v* to be ended, finished {*imperf*: yəxlaaṣ} 7

xmiira خميره *nfs* leavening; baker's

yeast 19

xooṣa خوصه *nfs* earrings, large earrings {*pl*: ?} 26

xudmii خدمي *nms* knife, dagger {*pl*: xdaamaa} 25

xuḍra خضره [*also* xuṭra] *nfs* vegetables *collective* 20

xuṭra خطره [*also* xuḍra] *nfs* vegetables *collective* {*pl*: xḍaarii} 5

xulṣa خلصه *nfs* salary {*pl*: xulṣaat} 23

xuu اخو *nms* brother {*pl*: xwaat, *pl*: xwaan} 18

xiima خيمه *nfs* tent {*pl*: xyəm} 22

d

d- د *part.* of, belonging to 15

daax داخ *v* to become dizzy; to feel ill {*imperf*: iiduux} 25

daaxəl داخل *adj* belonging to, part of; entering {*fs*: daaxla, *pl*: daaxliin} 13; *prep* within, inside 13

daar¹ دار *v* to do, commit; to make {*imperf*: iidiir} 6, 9

daar² دار *nfs* house {*pl*: dyaar} 8

daar b- دار بـ *v* to care for, tend {*imperf*: iiduur bi-} 25

daar ʕlaa دار على *v* to turn away from, turn one's back on {*imperf:* iiduur ʕlaa} 14

daaruuk داروك [*also* druuk] *adv* now 23

daaymən دايمـاً *adv* all the time, always 8

dəbbər دبّر *v* to conduct, direct, take care of {*imperf:* iidəbbər} 18

dəbbər raas- + suffixed pronoun دبّر راس to manage, work out; to do one's best {*imperf:* iidəbbər raas} 18

dərb əlhuud درب الهود *prop* Derb (former Jewish quarter of Oran) 36

dərrii[1] درّي *nms* child {*pl:* draarii} 7

dərrii[2] درّي *adj* atomic, nuclear {*fs:* dərriyya} 20

dərham درهـم *nms* derham (basic Algerian unit of currency) {*pl:* draaham} 7

daʕwaa دعوى *nfs* affair, matter, business {*pl:* dʕaawii} 8

dbəḥ ذبـح *v* to murder; to kill, slaughter {*imperf:* yədbəḥ} 13

ddaa ادّى *v* to take; to bring; to send {*imperf:* yəddii} 1

draaham دراهـم *np* money (from /dərham/ derham, Algerian unit of currency) 7

druuk دروك [*also* daaruuk] *adv* now 20

ddzaayər الدّزاير [*also* ljazaayər] *prop., FS*Algiers ; Algeria 1

ddzaayər lʕaaṣiima الدّزايـر العـاصيـمـه *prop* the capital Algiers 1

dzaayrii دزايري [*also* jazaayii] *adj* Algerian {*fs:* ddzaayriyya, *pl:* dzaayriyyiin} 2

dʃiiʃa تشيـشـه [*also* tʃiiʃa] *nfs* dchica (kind of coarse-ground barley or wheat) 19

dhaan دهـان *nms* butter; cooking oil, fat 22

doomaandaa دومـانـدى *v* to require; to ask for {*imperf:* iidoomandee} 21

durk درك [*also* duuk; duuka; durka] *adv* now 13

durka درك [*also* durk; duuk; duuka] *adv* now 29

duwaa دوا *nms* medication, medicine {*pl:* dwaayaat, *pl:* dwiyya, *pl:* dwaawii} 14

duuroo دورو *nms* douro (unit of currency equal to 5 centimres) {*pl:* dwaara} 9

duuk دوك [*also* durk; duuka; durka] *adv* now 11

duuka دوك [*also* durk; duuk;

375

durka] *adv* now 16

diimaa ديما *adv* always 7

diin دين *nms* religion (specifically Islam) {*pl:* dyaan, *pl:* dyaanaat} 16

dyaal ديال of; belonging to *possessive adjective; invariable* 7

ð

ðaak ذاك *pro* that (MS far demonstrative) {*fs:* ðiik, *pl:* ðuuk} 17

ððəkkar اذّكر *v* to remember, recall {*imperf:* yəððəkkar} 5

ðuuk ذوك *pro* that (P far demonstrative) {*ms:* ðaak, *fs:* ðiik}

ðiik ذيك *pro* that (FS far demonstrative) {*ms:* ðaak, *pl:* ðuuk}

r

raajəl راجل *nms* man, person {*pl:* rjaal} 11

raah راح *v* to go {*imperf:* iiruuh} 2

raas راس [*also* ʁaas] *nms* head {*pl:* ruus}

ʁaas راس [*also* raas] *nms* head {*pl:* ʁuus} 26

raas + suffixed pronoun راس self *invariable* 18

raa + suffixed pronoun را there is, there are *disc* 6

raay راي *nms* opinion {*pl:* ruyyaan} 13

raay راي *nms* raï (kind of Algerian popular music originating in Oran) 27

raayəh رايح *adj* going to, will; going, on one's way {*fs:* raayha, *pl:* raayhiin} 9

rabbamaa ربّما [*also* rubbamaa] *adv* maybe, perhaps 11

rabʕa اربعه [*also* arbaʕa] *nfs* four, 4

rəbʕiin ربعين *nms* forty, 40 18

rajjaʕ رجّع *v* to give, pay (money); to return, make return {*imperf:* iirajjaʕ} 7

rəkba ركبه *nfs* knee {*pl:* rkaayəb} 24

raməl رمل *nms* sand 22

rbaṭ ربط *v* to tie, tie up {*imperf:* yərbaṭ} 21

rdəm ردم *v* to bury, cover with (sand, debris, etc.); to fill up with earth (hole, etc.) {*imperf:* yərdəm} 24

rdiim رديم *nms* burial (in sand, debris, etc.) 24

rfiis رفيس *nms* rfiss (kind of savory pastry made with flat bread); rfiis (kind of sweet pastry) 17

roomaa رومـا *prop* Rome 1

roomaanii رومـانـي *adj* Roman {*fs:* roomaaniyya, *pl:* roomaan} 1

rubbamaa ربّمـا [*also* rabbamaa] *adv* maybe, perhaps 11

ruuḥ + suffixed pronoun روح self *invariable* 13

riiḥa ريحـه *nfs* smell, odor {*pl:* riiḥaat} 25

riiggaan رقّـان *prop* Reggane (city in south central Algeria) 20

riyyəḥ ريّح *v* to rest, relax; to be left to rest, left fallow {*imperf:* iiriyyiḥ} 9

riyyəḥ ريّح *v* to be left to rest, left fallow; to rest, relax {*imperf:* iiriyyiḥ} 21

z

zaad[1] زاد *v.; pre-verb* to do again (action of main verb); to continue to do (action of main verb) {*imperf:* iiziid} 23

zaad[2] زاد *v* to be born {*imperf:* iiziid} 36

zaar زار *v* to make a pilgrimage to the tomb of a Muslim saint; to visit {*imperf:* iizuur} 34

zaarətsnaa lbaaraaka w-çuuzuu

ʕandnaa زارتنـا البـاراكـه وجـوزوا عنـدنـا we are blessed, since you are visiting us (conventional formula of welcome) 31

zaahiya bəlʕaaruus زاهيـه بـالعـاروس *prop* Zahiyya Belarouse (Algerian television personality) 12

zaawra زاوره *nfs* bedcover, bedspread, blanket {*pl:* zaawraat, *pl:* zwaar} 15

zaawii زاوي *nms* descendant of the Prophet Muhammad {*pl:* zwii} 25

zaayər زاير *nms* pilgrim (to place other than Mecca); visitor {*fs:* zaayra, *pl:* ziyyaar, *pl:* zaayriin} 34

zaayda زايده *nfs* extra, surplus 35

zarbiya زربيـه *nfs* carpet, rug {*pl:* zraabii} 15

zaʕmaa زعمـا *disc* that is to say, I mean, that is to say; so, then; really 21

zənqa زنقـه *nfs* street, road; alley {*pl:* znəq} 10

zawj زوج [*also* zooj; zuuj; juuz] *nms* two 23

zruuf زروف *nms* zrouf (kind of jewelry worn on the head) {*pl:* zraarəf} 26

zzəwwəj تزوّج [*also* tzəwwəj] *v* to get married to s.o. {*imperf:*

yəzzəwwəj} 25

zmaan زمـان *adv* a long time ago; in the old days 1

zooj زوج [*also* zuuj; juuz; zawj] *nfs* two 7

zooj زوج *nms* husband, spouse {*pl:* zwaaj} 18

zurna زرنـه *nfs* zurna (kind of reed instrument) {*pl:* zurnaat} 16

zuuj زوج [*also* zooj; juuz; zawj] *nms* two 12

ziit ziituun زيت زيتون olive oil 24

S

saaʕa سـاعـه *nfs* hour {*pl:* swaayəʕ, *pl:* saaʕaat} 29

saawaa سـاوى *v* to form, put together, make up; to do, make {*imperf:* iisaawii} 27

saayaasa سـايـاسـه *nfs* skill, clever way of doing s.t.; policy; politics 31

səbb سـبّ *v* to insult, call s.o. a name {*imperf:* iisəbb} 23

saṭṭər سـطّر *v* to trace out, outline (project, plan); to draw lines (on paper) {*imperf:* iisaṭṭər} 35

saqsaa سـقسـى *v* to ask, inquire {*imperf:* iisaqsii} 29

səllək سلّك *v* to acquit, clear of an accusation {*imperf:* iisəllək} 25

səmʃ سـمـش [*also* ʃəms; ʃəmʃ] *nfs* sun 24

səmmaa[1] سـمّـى [*also* təmmaa; tsəmmaa; θəmmaa] *disc* I mean, that is to say

səmmaa[2] سـمّـا [*also* təmmaa; tsəmmaa; θəmmaa] *adv* there, over there 18

santitiizaar سـنتـتـيـزار *nms* synthesizer {*pl:* santitiizaaraat} 27

spaanyooliyya سـپـانيـوليـه *nfs* Spanish (language) 30

staɣfər aḷḷaa اسـتـغفـر الله I ask God's forgiveness (said when avoiding sin or the occasion of sin) 33

stəftaḥ اسـتـفتـح *v* to open (a ceremony); to start {*imperf:* yəstəftaḥ} 18

smaana سـمـانـه *nfs* week {*pl:* smaanaat} 8

sm- + suffixed pronoun + kiifaah اسـم ... كيـفاش what is s.o.'s name 24

sena سـنـه *nfs* year {*pl:* sniin} 6

suwwəl سـوّل *v* to ask, inquire {*imperf:* iisəwwəl} 23

suuliimaan lqaanuunii سـوليـمـان القـانـوني *prop* Suleiman the

Magnificent (lit. Suleiman the
Lawgiver; 16th century ruler of the
Ottoman Empire) 2

suuma سومه *nfs* price 4

siwaa سوا *prep* other than; except 35

siidii سيدي *nms* Mr. (title before
name of Muslim male saints);
respectful term of adddress 16

siidii ben ʕabd ərraḥmaan سيدي بن
عبد الرّحمن *prop* Sidi Bin Abd
al-Rahman (founder of a Sufi
brotherhood or order) 34

siidii ʕabd əlqaadər سيدي عبد
القادر *prop* Sidi Abd El-Qadir
(Algerian hero, namesake of mountain
near Oran) 36

siira سيره *nfs* conduct, way of life
{*pl:* siyar} 33

siimaan سيمان *nms* cement,
concrete 5

siineemaa سينيما *nfs* cinema,
movie theater {*pl:* siineemaat} 8

siyyaara سياره *nfs* car, automobile
{*pl:* siyyaaraat} 18

ʃ

ʃaabb xaald شابّ خالد *prop* Cheb
Khaled, Khaled (star of raï music) 27

ʃaadii شادي *nms* monkey {*pl:*
ʃwaada, *pl:* ʃwaadii} 36

ʃaar شار *v* to point at; to hint, infer
{*imperf:* iiʃuur} 34

ʃaarii شاري *nms* buyer, purchaser
{*fs:* ʃaarya, *pl:* ʃaaryiin} 33

ʃaaʃiya شاشيه *nfs* cap, skullcap
{*pl:* ʃaaʃiyaat} 26

ʃaaf شاف *v* to see, look at; to
consider, think {*imperf:* iiʃuuf} 2

ʃaamaal شامال *nms* north 20

ʃajara شجره *nfs* tree {*pl:* ʃjar} 6

ʃədd ʕlaa شدّ على [*also* ʃədd l-] *v*
to dress s.o., put on s.o.'s clothing or
headgear {*imperf:* iiʃədd ʕlaa} 26

ʃədd l- شدّ لـ [*also* ʃədd ʕlaa] *v* to
dress s.o., put on s.o.'s clothing or
headgear {*imperf:* iiʃədd l-} 26

ʃarrəb شرّب *v* to give s.o. to drink,
make s.o. drink {*imperf:* iiʃarrəb}
24

ʃəkwa شكوه *nfs* chekoua (kind of
bagpipe) {*pl:* ʃəkwaat} 16

ʃəms شمس [*also* səmʃ; ʃəmʃ] *nfs*
sun

ʃahriyya شهريه *nfs* salary {*pl:*
ʃahriyyaat} 6

ʃbaab شباب *adj* nice; pretty {*fs:*
ʃaabba, *pl:* ʃaabbiin} 36

ʃtaa¹ شتاة many, numerous;

dispersed, separate {*fs:* ʃtaat} 28

ʃtaa² شتا *interrog* how; what, what is 30

ʃtaa hwa شتا هو *how* are you (lit. what is it) 30

ʃtaa hwa laa شتا هو لها *how* are you (lit. what is it) 30

ʃḥaal شحال *interrog* how much, how many 30

ʃḥaal raahaa ssaaʕa شحال راها الساعه *what* time is it 30

ʃeex شيخ *nms* religious scholar or leader; chief, headman; holy man; title of respect {*pl:* ʃyuux, *pl:* ʃyaax} 18

ʃeex alhaadiii mḥammad bən ʕiisaa (əsseex) شيخ الهادي محمّد بن عيسى *prop* Sheikh al-Hadi Muhammad Bin Isa (founder of the Isawiyya, the Sufi brotherhood named after him) 34

ʃraa شرى *v* to buy, purchase {*imperf:* yəʃrii} 9

ʃriif شريف *nms* descendant of the Prophet Muhammad; noble {*pl:* ʃərfaa} 25

ʃṭəḥ شطح *v* to dance {*imperf:* yəʃṭəḥ} 16

ʃɣul شغل *prep* like, as, in the form of; a kind of, type of 6

ʃfaa شفى *v* to remember, recall

{*imperf:* yəʃfaa} 5

ʃfar شفر *nms* eyelash {*pl:* ʃwaafər} 34

ʃkuun شكون *interrog* who 10

ʃkuun llii شكون اللي *conj* anyone who, someone who; who is it that *conj* 10

ʃhaar شهار *nms* month {*pl:* ʃhuur, *pl:* ʃhur, *pl:* ʃhahraat} 10

ʃwiyya شويّه *nms* a little (of anything); a short time 9

ʃuuf شوف *interj* really, my goodness 15

ʃii شي *nms* matter, situation; thing, object {*pl:* aʃyaa} 2

ʃiibaanii شيباني *nms* elderly man {*pl:* ʃiibaaniyyiin, *pl:* ʃyaab, *pl:* ʃwaabiin} 25

ʃiix شيخ [*also* ʃeex] *nms* religious scholar or leader; chief, headman; holy man; title of respect {*pl:* ʃyuux, *pl:* ʃyaax} 18

ʃii xaarjaaṭ, ʃii daaxlaat شي خارجات، شي داخلات inside and out, all over (lit. some comings, some goings) 30

ṣ

ṣaab صاب *v* to find, discover
{*imperf:* iiṣiib} 4

ṣaaḥəb صاحب *nns* follower,
adherent; entrusted with; friend {*pl:*
ṣḥaab} 14

ṣaaḥba صاحبه *nfs* female friend
{*fpl:* ṣḥaabaat, *fpl:* ṣaaḥbaat} 15

ṣaalḥa صالحه *nfs* good, material
commodity {*pl:* ṣwaaləḥ} 36

ṣəbb صبّ *v* to fall (rain) {*imperf:*
iiṣəbb} 21

ṣadaqa صدقه *nfs* charity, alms 25

ṣəddər¹ صدّر *v* to export {*imperf:*
iiṣəddər} 6

ṣəddər² صدّر *v* to seat in the place of
honor, place up front {*imperf:*
iiṣəddər} 26

ṣbəḥ صبح *v* to become {*imperf:*
yəṣbəḥ} 14

ṣbuḥ صبح *nns* morning; dawn {*pl:*
ṣubḥaat} 9

ṣpaanyoolii صپانيولي *adj* Spanish,
Spaniard {*fs:* ṣpaanyooliyya, *pl:*
ṣpaanyool} 2

ṣraa صرى *v* to happen, occur
{*imperf:* yəṣraa} 14

ṣḍar صضر [*also* ṣṭar] *v* to protect
(of the deity); to cover, conceal
{*imperf:* yəṣḍar} 5

ṣṭar صطر [*also* ṣḍar] *v* to protect
(of the deity); to cover, conceal
{*imperf:* yəṣṭar} 5

ṣʕiib صعيب *adj* hard, difficult {*fs:*
ṣʕiiba, *pl:* ṣʕaab} 4

ṣmaʁ اصمر [*also* ṣmar] *adj*
dark-skinned, dark *FS* {*fpl:* ṣamʁaa,
pl: ṣamaʁ} 26

ṣmar اصمر [*also* ṣmaʁ] *adj*
dark-skinned, dark *FS* {*fs:* ṣamraa, *pl:*
ṣamar} 26

ḍ

ḍaarəʕ ضارع *adj* humble, submissive
{*fs:* ḍarʕaa, *pl:* ḍraʕ} 34

ḍənn ظنّ [*also* ðənn] *v* to think,
consider, deem {*imperf:* iiḍənn} 11

ḍrəb ضرب *v* to do, make; to hit,
strike {*imperf:* yəḍrəb} 36

ḍlam ضلم *v* to oppress {*imperf:*
yəḍlam} 14

ṭ

ṭaab طاب *v* to boil, be on the boil; to
cook, to be cooking; to ripen, be ripe

Glossary (IPA)

{*imperf:* iiṭiib} 23

ṭaaḥ طاح *v* to fall, drop {*imperf:* iiṭiiḥ} 4

ṭaaləb طالب *nms* person with Islamic religious education, religious scholar {*pl:* ṭəlba} 18

ṭaaləʕ طالع *adj* coming, arriving {*fs:* ṭaalʕa, *pl:* ṭaalʕiin} 7

ṭəbəl طبل *nms* drum {*pl:* ṭbuul} 16

ṭarz طرز *nms* style, design {*pl:* ṭruuz} 26

ṭərgii طرقي *adj* Tuareg (nomadic, Berber-speaking peoples of the southern Sahara) {*pl:* ṭərgiyya, *pl:* ṭwaarəg} 22

ṭəlləʕ طلّع *v* to promote, elevate {*imperf:* iiṭəlləʕ} 21

ṭʕaam طعام *nms* couscous (cooked and ready to eat); food 17

ṭfəl طفل [*also* child] *nms* {*fs:* ṭəfla, *pl:* ṭfaal} 15

ṭləʕ طلع *v* to rise, go up, ascend {*imperf:* yəṭləʕ} 14

ṭmaʕ fii طمع في *v* to desire, covet aspire to {*imperf:* yəṭmaʕ fii} 25

ṭnaaʃ طناش [*also* ṭnaaʃən] *nms* twelve 8

ṭnaaʃən طناشن [*also* ṭnaaʃ] *nms;* *form used in construct phrase* twelve 8

ṭowwəl طوّل *v* to take, require a long time {*imperf:* iiṭowwəl} 15

ṭoolga طولقه *prop* Tolga (town in southeastern Algeria) 21

ṭoomaaṭiiʃ طوماطيش *nms* tomatoes *collective* {*fs:* ṭoomaaṭiiʃa, *pl:* ṭoomaaṭiiʃaat} 21

ṭiqniyya طقنيه [*also* təqniyya] *nfs* technique {*pl:* ṭiqniyyaat} 8

ṭiyyəb طيّب [*also* ṭayyəb] *v* to cook, prepare (food) {*imperf:* iiṭiyyəb} 9

ð̣

ð̣add ضدّ *prep* against 14

ð̣ayyəf ضيّف *v* to host, treat as a guest {*imperf:* iið̣ayyəf} 22

ð̣ð̣ərr اظّر *v* to be forced to, compelled to {*imperf:* yəð̣ð̣ərr} 28

ð̣iif ضيف *nms* guest {*pl:* ð̣yaaf, *pl:* ð̣yuuf} 23

ʕ

ʕa عل [*also* ʕlaa; ʕal] *prep* at, about (of time); incumbent on, necessary; on, at; concerning 7

ʕaʔiiʔ عقيق [*also* ʕaqiiq] *nms* beading, beads 26

382

ʕaaʔiila عائيله [also ʕaayla; ʕaayiila] nfs family {pl: ʕaaʔiilaat} 10

ʕaajuuz عاجوز nfs mother of the bridegroom; old woman {pl: ʕjaayəz} 15

ʕaad عاد adv just now, only now 16

ʕaaʃiyya عشيّه nfs late afternoon, early evening {pl: ʕaaʃiyyaat} 9

ʕaaṣər عاصر nms afternoon prayer (Islamic); afternoon {pl: ʕaṣaarii} 18

ʕaamaar + suffixed pronoun + maa عامار ما never (lit. in s.o.'s life) 14

ʕaawəd عاود v.; pre-verb to re-do, replace; to do again (action of following imperfect verb); to begin, start (to do the action of the following imperfect verb) {imperf: iiʕaawəd} 7, 8, 27

ʕaawəd taanii عاود تاني also, too, as well 19

ʕaayeʃ عايش adj living, residing {fs: ʕaayʃa, pl: ʕaayʃiin} 8

ʕaayla عايله [also ʕaaʔiila; ʕaayiila] nfs family {pl: ʕaaylaat} 10

ʕaayiila عائيله [also ʕaayla; ʕaaʔiila] nfs family {pl: ʕaayiilaat} 7

ʕaddəl عدل v to straighten, make s.t. straight; to prune {imperf: iiʕaddəl} 21

ʕad + suffixed pronoun عند [also ʕand; ʕan] prep to have 15

ʕarbuun عربون nms charitable donation (made in the name of a Muslim saint in the hope that the saint will grant a specific favor; pledge); earnest money; deposit, down payment {pl: ʕaraabən} 34

ʕarjoon عرجون nms date palm branch with date cluster {pl: ʕaaraajən} 21

ʕars عرس nms wedding party, wedding fesitivities {pl: aʕraas} 15

ʕarʃ عرش [also ʕaarʃ] nms tribe; throne {pl: ʕraaʃ} 16

ʕarḍa عرضه nfs invitation {pl: ʕarḍaat} 18

ʕaʃra عشره nfs ten 9

ʕal عل [also ʕlaa; ʕa] prep at, about (of time); incumbent on, necessary; on, at; concerning 9

ʕam-baal- + suffixed pronoun عم بال [also ʕlaa baal] in s.o.'s opinion, s.o. thinks 4

ʕand + suffixed pronoun عند [also ʕad; ʕan] prep to have 1

ʕan + suffixed pronoun عند [also

ʕad; ʕand] *prep* to have 17

ʕannaaba عنّابه *prop* Annaba (city in eastern Algeria) 1

ʕayyəṭ عيّط *v* to call (by the name of); to call out, shout {*imperf*: iiʕayyəṭ} 5

ʕrəḍ عرض *v* to invite {*imperf*: yaʕraḍ} 15

ʕraq عرق *v* to sweat, perspire {*imperf*: yaʕraq} 24

ʕḍam عضم *nms* egg 30

ʕṭaa fii اعطى في *v* to give s.o. victory over (of the deity) {*imperf*: yaʕṭii fii} 25

ʕqal اعقل *v* to recall, remember {*imperf*: yəʕqal} 28

ʕlaa على [*also* ʕal; ʕa] *prep* incumbent on, necessary; on, on top of; at, about, around (of time) 9

ʕlaa baal على بال aware of, alerted to 17

ʕlaa jaal على جال *conj* because of, due to *conj* 10

ʕlaa ḥsaab على حساب according to 15

ʕlaa xaaṭər على خاطر [*also* laa xaaṭər: laa xaaṭʃii; laa xaaṭs] *conj* because, due to the fact that *conj* 18

ʕlaaʃ علاش *interrog* why, for for reason

ʕlaah علاه *interrog* why, for what reason

ʕutmaanii عتماني [*also* ʕuθmaanii] *adj* Ottoman Turkish {*fs*: ʕutmaaniyya, *pl*: ʕutmaan} 2

ʕuula عوله *nfs* provisions, supplies 23

lʕiiraaq العراق *prop* Iraq 21

ʕiisaawiyya عيساويه *prop* Isawiyya (Sufi brotherhood or order founded in the 16th century by Sheikh Muhammad Bin Isa) 34

ʕyaa عيى *v* to be, become tired, ill {*imperf*: yaʕyaa} 25

ɣ

ɣaadii غادي *part.* will (expresses future) *pre-verb; invariable* 25

ɣaaz غاز *nms* gas, gasoline; gas, gaseous element {*pl*: ɣaazaat} 6

ɣaaʃii غاشي *nms* people, group of people, crowd 17

ɣaanii غاني *adj* rich, wealthy {*fs*: ɣaaniyya, *pl*: aɣniyaa} 6

ɣaaya غايه *nfs* good. nice *invariable* 36

ɣaaya k-əlɣallaaya غايه كالغلايه the best. the ultimate (lit. the greatest, like the coffeepot) 36 ɣaayṭa غـايـطـه *nfs* ghayta (kind of reed instrument) {*pl:* ɣwaayəṭ} 16

ɣədwa ه غدو *adv* tomorrow; the next day 35

ɣars غرس *prop* ghars (variety of date) 21

ɣarnaaṭa غرنـاطـه *prop* Granada (city in Andalusia in Spain) 2

ɣaṭṭaa غطّـى *v* to cover, conceal {*imperf:* iiɣaṭṭii} 24

ɣallaaya غلّـيـه *nfs* coffeepot (small with long handle) {*pl:* gallaayaat} 36

ɣeer غـيـر *prep* only, just 5

ɣras غرس *v* to plant, sow {*imperf:* yəɣras} 21

ɣmar غمـر *v* to cover, bury; to flood, inundate {*imperf:* yəɣmar} 20

ɣnaa غنـى *v* to be or become rich {*imperf:* yəɣnii} 14

f

faat فـات *v* to pass, elapse (of events, time) {*imperf:* iifuut} 15

faatḥa فـاتحـه *prop* the Fatiha (first sura of the Qur'an, recited on formal occasions) 18

faariina فـارينـه *nfs* flour 9

faas فـاس *prop* Fes (city in central Morocco) 34

faakiya فـاكيـه *nfs* fruit {*pl:* fwaakiih} 5

fəttət فتّـت *v* to break into small pieces, crumble {*imperf:* iifəttət} 22

farkət فـركـت *v* to search (violently or roughly) {*imperf:* iifarkət} 29

fəʃtii فشتـي *nms* lie, untruth; untrue, lying 12

faṣəl فصـل *nms* term, semester; section, part {*pl:* fṣuul} 9

fə-lʔaaxər فـالاخـر [*also* fə-llaxxər] at the end, in the end 2

fə-lɣaaləb فـالغـالب in general, mostly 15

fəlfəl فـلفـل *nms* pepper (spice and vegetable) *collective* {*fs:* fəlfla, *pl:* fəlflaat} 21

fə-llaxxər فـالاّخّـر [*also* fə-lʔaaxər] in the end, finally 12

ftəḥ فتـح *v* to start, begin; to open {*imperf:* yəftəḥ} 18

ftəl فتـل *v* to roll (into beads of couscous); to spin (into thread) {*imperf:* yəftəl} 17

fraa فـرى *v* to finish, end s.t. {*imperf:* yəfrii} 30

friik فـريـك *nms* frik (kind of coarse-ground wheat or barley) 17

fwaad فواد *nms* internal organs, entrails, guts {*pl:* fwaadaat} 25

fumm فمّ *nms* mouth {*pl:* fwaam} 25

fii ʕood في عود *conj* instead of, rather than *conj* 7

fiilaaḥa فيلاحه *nfs* agriculture, farming 20

fiilm فيلم *nms* movie, film {*pl:* aflaam} 8

fiiniiqii فينيقي *adj* Phoenician {*fs:* fiiniiqiyya, *pl:* fiiniiqiyiin} 1

v

varsaa ڤرسى *v* to put; to pour {*imperf:* iivarsii} 20

vwaayaajaa ڤواياجى *v* to travel {*imperf:* iivwaayaajii} 29

vooṭaa ڤوطى [*also* vuuṭaa] *v* to vote {*imperf:* iivooṭii} 13

vuuṭaa ڤوطى [*also* vooṭaa] *v* to vote {*imperf:* iivuuṭii} 11

g, q

gaadər قادر *adj* strong, powerful; able {*fs:* gaadra, *pl:* gaadriin} 25

qaaduus قادوس *nms* pipe, drainpipe {*pl:* quwaades} 7

qaarəṣ قارص *nms* lemon (fruit) collective {*fs:* qaarṣa, *pl:* qaarṣaat} 36

gaazooz قازوز *nms* carbonated soft drink 18

gaaʕ قاع *adv* all; every, each; not at all, never (with negative constructions) 6, 9

gaaʕət قاعت *adv* all; every, each; not at all, never (with negative constructions) 21

gaaʕətiik قاعتيك [*also* gaaʕiitiik] *adj* all; every, each; not at all, never (with negative) 9

qaaʕəd قاعد *adj* staying, remaining {*fs:* qaaʕda, *pl:* qaaʕdiin} 8

gaaʕiitiik قاعيتيك [*also* gaaʕətiik] *adv* not at all, never (with negative); all; every, each 21

qaafiila قافيله *nfs* caravan {*pl:* qwaafəl, *pl:* qfuul} 18

gaal قال [*also* qaal; ʔaal] *v* to speak, talk {*imperf:* iiguul} 5

qaam قام *v.; also pre-verb* to begin (to do s.t.); to get, stand up; to revolt, rebel {*imperf:* iiquum} 3

qəddaaʃ قدّاش *interrog* how much, how many

qəddaam قدّام *prep* in front of 5

garanṭeeṭa گرنطيطه *nfs garantita,*

carantita (kind of pastry made from chickpea flour) 9

qarraa قرّا *v* to teach, educate {*imperf:* iiqarrii} 32

gəṣba قصبه *nfs gesba* (kind of reed flute) {*pl:* gəṣbaat} 27

gaṣṣər قصّر *v* to talk, chat; to pass, spend the evening {*imperf:* iigaṣṣər} 22

gəṭṭaaʕ قطّاع *nms* cutter, person who cuts {*fs:* gəṭṭaaʕa, *pl:* gəṭṭaaʕiin} 21

qafṭaan قفطان [*also* ʔafṭaan] *nms* caftan ({*pl:* qfaaṭən} 26

gəlluuz قلّوز *nms guellouz* (kind of drum) 27

gaməḥ قمح *nms* wheat 21

qbaaylii قبايلي *adj* Kabyle, of or from Kabylia (region of west central Algeria) {*fs:* qbaayliyya, *pl:* qbaayliyyiin} 3

qdər قدر *v* to be able to {*imperf:* yəqdər} 8

qraa قرا *v* to study, get an education; to read {*imperf:* yəqraa} 8, 14

qraaya قرايه *nfs* reading, studying; education 35

qriib قريب *nms* close relative {*pl:* qraab} 18

griib قريب *adv* nearly,

approximately 29

qṣəd قصد *v* to mean, intend {*imperf:* yəqṣəd} 1

qṣamṭiina قسنطينه [*also* qṣanṭiina] *prop* Constantine (city in eastern Algeria) 1

qṣamṭiinii قصمطيني *adj* Constantinois (from Constantine, city in eastern Algeria) {*fs:* qṣamṭiiniyya, *pl:* qṣamṭiiniyyiin} 3

qḍaa قضى *v* to shop; to buy, get {*imperf:* yəqḍii} 5

qʕad قعد *v.; also* pre-verb to remain; to sit; to continue (to do s.t.) {*imperf:* yəqʕad} 1

gləb قلب *v* to reverse, turn upside down {*imperf:* yəgləb} 23

qləq قلق *v* to be uneasy, upset {*imperf:* yəqləq} 35

qubba قبّه *nfs* dome {*imperf:* qubbaat} 36

gumbeeṭa گمبيطه *prop* Gambetta (neighborhood of Oran named for a 19th century French political figure) 36

qunṭaar قنطار *nms* hundredweight (traditional measure of approximately 100 pounds) {*pl:* qnaaṭiir} 17

quunbuula قونبوله *nfs* bomb, explosive device {*pl:* qaanaabəl}

20

qiiṭaaʕ قيطاع *nms* segment, section
{*pl:* qiiṭaaʕaat} 15

k

kaaθaafa كاثافه *nfs* capacity;
thickness, density 17

kaar كار *nms* bus {*pl:* kiiraan} 18

kaaskrooṭ كاسكروط *nms* sandwich,
snack {*pl:* kaaskrooṭaat} 9

kaaʃ كاش [*also* kəʃ] *part.* some,
any 7

kaaməl كامل *adj* all, entire
invariable {*fs:* kaamla, *pl:* kaamliin}
18

kaamyaa كاميا [*also* kaamyuu]
nms truck {*pl:* kaamyuwaat} 18

kaamyuu كاميو [*also* kaamyaa]
nms truck {*pl:* kaamyuwaat} 18

kaayən كاين *adj.; existential; also
invariable* there is, there are {*fs:*
kaayna, *pl:* kaayniin} 5

kərʃəm كرشم *nms* window 36

kəsra كسره *nfs* flat bread {*pl:*
kəsraat, *pl:* ksuur} 17

kəʃ كاش [*also* kaaʃ] *part.* some,
any 12

kaʕba كعبه *nfs* one (unit of counting)
30

kəmm كمّ *nms* sleeve {*pl:* kmaam}
26

kbiir كبير *nms* adult, grownup; large
{*fs:* kbiira, *pl:* kuubaar} 18

ktəl قتل *v* to kill, murder {*imperf:*
yuktəl} 25

kdəb ʕlaa كذب على *v* to lie, speak
untruthfully to s.o. {*imperf:* yəkdəb}
8

kriipuunii كريبوني *nms créponnée*
(kind of lemon ice cream) 36

klaa كلى *v* to eat {*imperf:* yaakəl} 9

klaaṭaa كلاطى *v* to explode, blow up
{*imperf:* yəklaaṭii} 28

knaadsa كنادسه *prop* Kanadsa (city
near Béchar in western Algeria) 20

lkuθra) الكثره *nfs* mostly (lit. the
majority) 15

kurət yadd كرة يدّ handball 35

kurruusa كرّوسه *nfs* car; horse-drawn
cart {*pl:* kraars} 18

kusksii كسكسي *nms* couscous 19

kulləʃ كلّش *nms* all, everything 4

kuun كون *part.* if 35

kii كي *conj* when, whenever; like, as
5

kii كي *conj* like, as; when, whenever
16

kiifaaʃ كيفاش [*also* kiifaah]

interrog how; how much (also exclamatory) *conjunction* 2

kiifaah كيفاه [*also* kiifaaʃ] *interrog* how; how much (interrogative or exclamatory) 12

kiif kiif كيف كيف just alike, the same 15

kii ... kii كي ... كي *conj* the same for ... as for ... 16

kii llii كي اللي *conj* as if, like 6

kiimaa كيما *prep* like, as *conj* 5

1

laa baas لا باس *interj* fine, all right (general response to "how is s.o. or s.t.?"); rich, well-off *invariable* 20

laa baas bii + noun or suffixed pronoun لا باس s.o. or s.t. is fine, all right (general response to "how is s.o. or s.t.?"); rich, well-off 20

laataay لاتاي *nms* tea 22

laa xaaṭər لا خاطر [*also* ʕlaa xaaṭər; laa xaaṭʃ; laa xaaṭʃii] *conj* because, due to the fact that 18

laa xaaṭʃ لا خاطش [*also* laa xaaṭər; ʕlaa xaaṭər; laa xaaṭʃii] *conj* because, due to the fact that 7

laa xaaṭʃii لا خاطشي [*also* laa xaaṭər; ʕlaa xaaṭər; laa xaaṭʃ] *conj*

because, due to the fact that

laazəm 1 + suffixed pronoun لازم لـ *pre-verb; invariable* it is necessary for (s.o. to do action of main verb) 24

laazem لازم *adj.; also invariable preverb* it is necessary that 7

laazma لازمه *nfs* necessary thing, requisite {*pl:* lwaazəm} 15

ləbsa لبسه *nfs* piece of clothing; costume {*pl:* ləbsaat} 26

ləṣṣəq لصّق *v* to stick on, attach to, glue on to {*imperf:* iiləṣṣəq} 14

ləmmaa لّما *conj* when 1

lawṭaa لوطا *prep* downstairs; underneath 30

lḥag لحق *v* to catch up with, overtake; to reach, arrive at {*imperf:* yəlḥag} 24

lḥaq لحق *v* to reach, arrive at; to catch up with, overtake {*imperf:* yəlḥaq} 9

lḥaq ʕlaa لحق على *v* to keep up with, be on top of {*imperf:* yəlḥaq ʕlaa} 3

lḥamdu ḷḷaah الحمد لله thank God, thanks be to God (indicates or responds to fortunate event) 8

lgaa لقى *v* to find, encounter {*imperf:* yəlgaa} 21

lgaḥ لقح *v* to pollinate {*imperf:*

yəlgəh} 21

ḷḷaah iixallii- يخلّي الله thank you (lit. may God keep s.o.) 15

ḷḷaah yarḥam + suffixed pronoun يرحم الله God rest s.o.'s soul, (lit, may God have mercy on s.o.; said after mention of deceased's name) 25

llii اللي [also əllii] *pro* who, what (definite relative pronoun) 7

loo لو *part.* if 11

liʔannuu لانه *conj.; invariable* because 10

liim ليم *nms; collective* lemon (fruit) {*fs:* liima, *pl:* liimaat} 36

liimuun ليمون *nms; collective* lemon (fruit) {*fs:* liimuuna, *pl:* liimuunaat} 36

liyanna لين [also liʔanna] *conj* because 10

m

mʔajjar ماجّر *adj* tenant, renter; landlord {*fs:* mʔajjra, *pl:* mʔajjriin} 33

mə- م [also mən; məm-] *prep* from, of 4

maa ما *nms* water {*pl:* myaa} 7

maaḥabba ماحبّه *nfs* affection, love 23

maa daam مادام *v.; invariable, also conjugated, also takes suffixed pronoun as long as* 18

maadda مادّه *nfs* madda (kind of traditional eye makeup made from kohl) 34

maarʃii مارشي *nms* market (large or European-style marketplace) {*pl:* maarʃiyyaat} 4

maariikaan (lmaariikaan) الماريكان *prop* America *FS* 9

maa zaal ما زال *v.;invariable, conjugated, or with pronoun suffix* still; not yet 13

maa + suff. pro + ʃ ما – ش [*also* muu + suff. pro + ʃ] s.o., s.t. is not 6

maa : ما – ش ʃ not 1

maaʃii ماشي *part.; negates nominal structures* not 12

maaʃiina ماشينه *nfs* machine, engine, machinery {*pl:* maaʃiinaat} 4

maaʕliiʃ ما عليش [*also* maʕliiʃ] it's nothing, don't worry, it's OK 17

maa kaaʃ ما كانش [*also* maa kaaʃ] there was not, there were not; s/he is not, it is not 9

maa kaaʃ ما كاش [*also* maa kaanʃ] he is not, she is not, it is not; there was not, there were not 15

maakʃ ماكش you (ms) are not 35

maakla ماكله *nfs* food, nourishment {*pl:* maaklaat, *pl:* mwaakəl} 17

maaluuf مالوف *nms malouf* (kind of Arab-Andalusian music associate d with Constantine and Algiers) 34

maanaaʃ ماناش we are not 22

maanuuʃ مانوش [*also* maahuuʃ] he is not; it (ms) is not 1

maaniiʃ مانيش I am not 6

məjbuud مجبود *nms* gold thread; thread 26

maḥsuub محسوب *disc* that is to say, I mean (lit. considered to be) 18

məxduum مخدوم *adj* woven: made. done {*fs:* məxduuma, *pl:* məxduumiin} 15, 26

mədḥ مدح *nms* praise poetry 34

mədd مدّ *v* to give {*imperf:* iimədd} 21

məddarrəg مدرّق *adj* having hidden, concealed o.s. {*fs:* məddərrga, *pl:* məddərrgiin} 29

mərqa مرقه *nfs* stew (any dish that has a sauce or gravy); sauce, gravy {*pl:* mərgaat} 19

məzraʕ مزرع *nms* planted field; farm {*pl:* maazaariiʕ} 14

məzwəd مزود *nms mezoued* (kind of bagpipe) {*pl:* mzaawəd} 16

məʃ ماش [*also* maaʃ] *part.* not 7

məʃii ماشي [*also* maaʃii] *part.* not 13

məṣṣ مصّ *v* to absorb, suck up {*imperf:* iiməṣṣ} 24

maṣṭfaa bəm- braahiim مصطفى بن براهيم *prop* Mustafa Ben Brahim (19th century Algerian poet whose work is considered an early source of raï music) 27

məṣɣar مصغر *nms* young person; bull calf {*pl:* mṣaaɣar} 16

mədṭarr مضطرّ *adj* forced to. compelled to {*fs:* mədṭarra, *pl:* mədṭarriin} 10

maṭraḥ مطرح *nms* mattress {*pl:* mṭaaraḥ} 15

maʕa baʕḍ + plural suffixed pronoun مع بعض ... بعض + baʕḍ with one other, together 28

maʕruuḍ معروض *adj* invited {*fs:* maʕruuḍa, *pl:* maʕruuḍiin} 18

maʕʃər معشر *nms* kinfolk; group; community {*pl:* mʕaaʃər} 18

maɣrəbii مغربي *adj* Moroccan {*fs:* maɣrəbiyya, *pl:* mɣaarba} 19

maqruuṭ مقروط *nms maqrout* (kind of confection made with dates, also pastry filled with this confection) 21

məkruus مكروس *nms* young adolescent, young teenager {*pl:* mkaars} 18

makla ماكلة *nfs* food, edible item; meal {*pl:* maklaat, *pl:* mwaakəl} 9

məknaas مكناس *prop* Meknes (city in central Morocco) 34

məllii مللي *conj* when, at the time that; since. from the time that 5, 12

məm مم [*also* mən; mə] *prep* from, of 14

məm-baʕd ممبعد [*also* mən baʕd; m-baʕda; m-baʕd] after *conj* 1

mən taḥt l-taḥt من تحت لتحت secretly, furtively, (lit. from underneath to underneath) 25

mənjəm منجم *nms* mine, pit, source of minerals {*pl:* maanaajəm} 20

mən jiiha من جيهه on the one hand; as for, as to (lit. from one direction) 6, 15

mən jiiha xraa من جيهه اخرى on the other hand (lit. from another side) 6

mənsuuj منسوج *adj* woven (fabric) {*fs:* mənsuuja, *pl:* mənsuujiin} 26

mən ṭaraf من طرف on the side of, on the part of 14

mən mefruuḍ من مفروض it is

supposed, it is assumed 11

mənnaa هنّا *adv* beginning now, from now; from here; over here 8, 16

mənhee منهي *adv* there, over there 16

mən hnaa l-hnaayaa من هنا لهنايا from here to there 25

m-baʕd مبعد [*also* məm-baʕd; mən baʕd; m-baʕda] after *conj* 9

m-baʕda مبعد [*also* məm-baʕd; m-baʕd; mən baʕd] after *conj* 9

mbliisii مبليسي *adj* hurt, wounded {*fs:* mbliisiyya, *pl:* mbliisiyyiin} 25

mjalləṭ مجلّط *adj* girded (with a sword) {*fs:* mjallṭa, *pl:* mjallṭiin} 30

mxalləṭ مخلّط *adj* mixed. mixed together {*fs:* mxallṭa, *pl:* mxallṭiin} 30

mxalləṭ wə-mjalləṭ مخلّط ومجلّط all mixed up (lit. mixed and girded) {*fs:* mxallṭa wə-mjallṭa, *pl:* mxallṭiin wə-mjallṭiin} 30

mraa مراه *nfs* woman {*fpl:* nsaawiin, *fpl:* nsaa} 16

mrabbii مربّي *nms* breeder, raiser (of livestock) {*pl:* mrabbiyyiin} 19

mrassəm مرسّم *adj* composed; appointed {*fs:* mrassma, *pl:* mrassmiin} 27

mziyya مزيّه *adj* merit, superiority;

thankfully, fortunately 25

msaḥ مسح *v* to wipe, wipe off
{*imperf:* yəmsaḥ} 24

msiid مسيد *nms* mosque {*pl:*
msaayəd} 9

mʃaa مشى *v* to go; to go away, leave
{*imperf:* yəmʃii} 13

mṭarṭaq مطرطق *adj* great,
wonderful; explosive 36

mʕa مع *prep* at, about, around (of
time); with 9

mʕaz معز *nms* goat {*pl:* mʕiiz} 22

mʕa llaxxər مع الآخر finally, in the
end 14

mʕammar معمّر *adj* full, filled up
{*fs:* mʕammra, *pl:* mʕammriin} 29

mefruuḍ مفروض *nms* supposed,
assumed; it is supposed, it is assumed
also pre-verb 11

mqalləq مقلّق *adj* upset, anxious {*fs:*
mqallqa, *pl:* mqallqiin} 35

mliiḥ مليح *adj* good, nice {*fs:*
mliiḥa, *pl:* mlaaḥ} 4

mnəssəj منسّج *adj* woven 15

men jiiha من جيهة on the one hand
(lit. from a side) 6

mniin منين *interrog* when; from
where, whence 25

mhannii مهنّي *adj* calm, tranquil {*fs:*

mhanniyya, *pl:* mhanniyyiin} 35

mwaa موا *nfs* mother {*pl:* maawaat}
26

mwaaləf mʕa موالف مع used to,
accustomed to {*fs:* mwaalfa mʕa, *pl:*
mwaalfiin mʕa} 4

mooʃ مهوش [*also* muuʃ] *part.* not
negates non-verbal structures 17

muur مور *prep* after; behind, in back
of 36

muu + suff. pro + ʃ مو – ش [*also*
maa + suff. pro + ʃ] s.o., s.t. is not
8

muuʃ مهوش *part.* not *negates
non-verbal structures* 9

muuʃkila موشكله [*also* muuʃkiila]
nfs difficulty, problem {*pl:*
maaʃaakəl} 8

muuʃkiil موشكيل *nms* {*pl:*
muuʃkiilaat, *pl:* mʃaakəl}

muuʃkiila موشكيله [*also* muuʃkila]
nfs problem, difficulty {*pl:* mʃaakəl}
7

muuṣaab موصاب *adj* touched,
affected by God; possessed; afflicted,
injured {*fs:* muuṣaab, *mpl:*
muuṣaabiin, *fpl:* muuṣaabaat} 34

muuʕaaliim موعاليم *nms* teacher
{*pl:* muuʕaaliimiin} 33

muukkəl ʕlaa موكّل على

representative of, for {fs: muukkla ʕlaa, pl: muukkliin ʕlaa} 18

muuhəmm (lmuuhəmm) المهمّ disc the point is, the essential thing is (resumptive) 5

muuhuuʃ موهوش [also maahuuʃ] he is not; it (ms) is not 8

miiziiriya ميزيريه nfs destitution, extreme poverty; misery, despair 4

mya ميه nfs hundred {pl: miyaat} 21

n

naaḍ ناض v to get up, be up; to jump {imperf: iinuuḍ} 9

naaga ناقه nfs female camel {pl: nyaag, pl: nuug} 22

naayeb نايب nms deputy, representative {pl: nuwwaab} 11

nəḥḥaa نحّى v to take away, remove {imperf: iinəḥḥii} 6

naḥḥaa نحّى v to eliminate, remove (i.e., from a post) {imperf: iinaḥḥii} 13

naʕma نعمه nfs grain, cereal (especially couscous); prosperity 17

nəggəz نقّز v to hop, leap {imperf: iinəggəz} 25

nta انت pro you (2MS) 14

ntaaḥ- + suffixed pronoun with initial /h/ نتاح [also ntaaʕ] of, belonging to *possessive adjective; invariable* 15

ntaaʕ نتاع [also taaʕ] of, belonging to *possessive adjective; invariable* 15

ntahək انتهك v to infringe, violate {imperf: yəntahək} 14

ntuumaa انتوما pro you (2P) 29

ntii انت you (2FS)

njəm نجم v to be able to *also pre-verb* {imperf: yənjəm} 28

nḥaa انحى v to attack, assail {imperf: yenḥii} 11

nxəṭab انخطب v to get engaged (to be married) {pl: yənxaṭab} 15

nxal نخل nms palm trees *collective* {fs: nəxla, pl: nəxlaat} 21

ndaar اندار v to be made, done, prepared {imperf: yəndaar} 17

nsəj نسج v to weave {imperf: yənsəj} 26

nʃaa ḷḷaah ان شاء الله God willing, if God wills (of hoped-for event) 8

nʃəf نشف v to dry up, become dry {imperf: yənʃəf} 24

nʕaṭaa انعطى v to be given {imperf: yənʕaṭaa} 12

nqaal انقال v to be said; to be able to

be said, be sayable {*imperf:* yənqaal}
12

nqəʃ نقش *v* to hoe; to chisel, engrave
{*imperf:* yənqəʃ} 25

nqəṣṣ انقصّ *v* to be cut, cut short
{*imperf:* yənqəṣṣ} 17

nhaar نهار *nms* day {*pl:* nhaaraat}
9

nowwəð̣ نوّض *v* to awaken, wake o.s.
up {*imperf:* iinowwəð̣} 9

h

haad هاد [*also* haað] *pro* this
(invariable near demonstrative) 1

haadaa هدا [*also* haad; haað;
haaðaa] *pro* this (MS near
demonstrative) {*fs:* haadii, *pl:*
haaduu} 2

haadaak هداك [*also* haadaaka;
haaðaak; haaðaaka] *pro* that (MS
far demonstrative) {*fs:* haadiik, *pl:*
haaduuk} 11

haadaaka هداك [*also* haadaak;
haaðaaka; haaðaak] *pro* that (MS
far demonstrative) {*fs:* haadiika, *pl:*
haaduuka}

haadaay هداي [*also* haaðaaya;
haadaa; haaðaa] *pro* this (MS near
demonstrative) {*fs:* haadiyya}

haadəf هادف *nms* object, aim, goal
{*pl:* hdaaf} 33

haadum هدم [*also* haaduu; haaðuu;
haaðum] *pro* these (P near
demonstrative)

haaduu هدو [*also* haaduu; haaðuu;
haaðum] *pro* these (P near
demonstrative) {*ms:* haadaa, *fs:*
haadii}

haaduuk هدوك [*also* haaduuka;
haaðuuk] *pro* that (P far
demonstrative) {*ms:* haadaak, *fs:*
haadiik} 14

haaduuka هذو [*also* haaðuu;
haadum; haaðum] *pro* these (P far
demonstrative) {*ms:* haadaa, *fs:*
haadii}

haadii هدي [*also* haaðii;
haadiyyaa; haaðiyyaa] *pro* this
(FS near demonstrative) {*ms:* haadaa,
pl: haaduu} 4

haadiik هديك [*also* haadiika;
haaðiik; haaðiika] *pro* that (FS far
demonstrative) {*fs:* haadaak, *pl:*
haaduuk} 1

haadiika هديك [*also* haadiik;
haaðiik; haaðiika] *pro* that (FS far
demonstrative) {*fs:* haadaaka, *pl:*
haaduuka}

haadiyaa هديا [*also* haadii; haaðii]
pro this (FS near demonstrative) {*ms:*

haadaay, *pl:* haaduu} 7

haað هَاذ [*also* haað] *pro* this (invariable near demonstrative) 13

haaðaa هَذا [*also* haadaa; haaðaayaa; haadaay] *pro* this (MS near demonstrative) {*fs:* haaðii, *pl:* haaðuu} 2

haaðaak هَذاك [*also* haadaaka; haadaak; haaðaaka] *pro* that (MS far demonstrative) {*fs:* haaðiik, *pl:* haaðuuk} 5

haaðaaka هَذاك [*also* haadaaka; haadaak; haaðaak] *pro* that (MS far demonstrative) {*fs:* haaðiika, *mpl:* haaðuuka}

haaðaay هَذاي [*also* haadaa; haadaayaa; haaðaa] *pro* this (MS near demonstrative) {*fs:* haadiyyaa} 18

haaðum هَذم [*also* haaduu; haaðuu; haadum] *pro* these (P near demonstrative) 29

haaðuu هَذو [*also* haadum; haaduu; haadum] *pro* this (P near demonstrative) {*ms:* haaðaa, *fs:* haaðii} 13

haaðuuk هَذوك [*also* haaduuka; haaduuk; haaðuuka] *pro* that (P far demonstrative) {*ms:* haaðaak, *fs:* haaðiik} 6

haaðuuka هَذوك [*also* haaduuka;

haaduuka; haaðuuk] *pro* that (P far demonstrative) {*ms:* haaðaaka, *fs:* haaðiika}

haaðii هَذي [*also* haadii; haaðiyyaa; haadiyyaa] *pro* this (FS near demonstrative) {*ms:* haaðaa, *pl:* haaðuu} 6

haaðiik هَذيك [*also* haadiika; haadiik; haaðiika] *pro* that (FS far demonstrative) {*ms:* haaðaak, *pl:* haaðuuk} 4

haaðiika هَذيك [*also* haadiika; haadiik; haaðiik] *pro* that (FS far demonstrative) {*fs:* haaðiika, *pl:* haaðuuka} 5

haaðiyaa هَذيا [*also* haadii; haadiyyaa; haaðii] *pro* this (FS near demonstrative) {*ms:* haaðaaya, *pl:* haaðuu} 12

haa + suffixed pronoun هَا look here; here is, here are 8

haak هَاك [*also* hakkaa; hakkaak] *pro* thus, in this way 25

haakdaa هكدا [*also* haakðaa] *adv* thus, in this way 29

haakdaak هكداك [*also* haakðaak] *adv* thus, in that way

haakdaak هكداك *adv* like that, in that way 2

haakðaa هكذا [*also* haakdaa] *pro* thus, in this way 29

haakðaak هكذاك [*also* haakdaak]
pro thus, in that way

haanaa هانا here I am 8

hadra هدره *nfs* speech, talk,
conversation 31

hakkaa هگّا [*also* hakkaak; haak]
adv thus, in this way 12

hakkaak هگّاك [*also* hakkaa; haak]
adv thus, in that way 35

hal اهل *nms* family, relatives,
relations {*pl:* aahaalii} 17

ham هم [*also* huuma; humm(a);
hum] *pro* they (3P) 21

hayyaa هيّى *interj* let's go, come on
34

hdər هدر *v* to speak, talk {*imperf:*
yəhdər} 28

hrab هرب *v* to run away; to escape
{*imperf:* yəhrab} 25

hnaayaa هنايا [*also* hnaa] *adv*
here 16

heeh هيه *adv* there, over there 19

hum هم [*also* huum(a); ham; humm]
pro they (3P) 13

humm هِمّ [*also* huum; ham; huuma]
pro they (3P) 7

huwa هو [*also* huu; huwwa] *pro* he
(3MS)

huwwa هوّ [*also* huu; huwa] *pro* he

(3MS) 3

huu هو [*also* huwwa; huwa] *pro* he
(3MS)

huum هوم [*also* humm(a); ham;
huuma] *pro* they (3P) 1

huuma هوم [*also* humm(a); ham;
huum] *pro* they (3P) 2

hii هي [*also* hiyya; hiya] *pro* she
(3FS)

hiya هي [*also* hiyya; hii] *pro* she
(3FS)

hiyya هيّ [*also* hii; hiya] *pro* she
(3FS) 4

w

wo-ʔillaa والّا [*also* wəllaa] *part.* or
something like that, or whatever (at
end of sequence) 15

waajəd واجد *adj* ready, available,
prepared {*fs:* waajda, *pl:* waajdiin}
13

waaḥəd واحد *nms* someone, a certain
person; oneself 12

waaḥəd + **plural noun** واحد some,
approximately, about; a, an (indefinite
article) 1

waaḥd aaxər واحد اخر other;
another *pro., adj* {*fs:* waaḥd ooxraa,
pl: waaḥd ooxriin} 13

397

waaḥd w-səbʕiin واحد وسبعين 71
(kind of tea) 23

waasaa واسى *v* to do, to make
{*imperf:* iiwaasii} 33

waaʃ واش [*also* wəʃ] *interrog* what
15

waaqiil واقيـل [*also* waaqiilaatən]
disc maybe, perhaps; apparently 21

waaqiilaatən واقيـلاة [*also* waaqiil]
disc maybe, perhaps; apparently 15

waaləd والد *nms* parent, father {*fs:*
waalda, *pl:* waaldiin} 9

waaləf mʕa والف مـع *v* to be or
become used to, accustomed to
{*imperf:* iiwaaləf mʕa} 5

waaləm والـم *v* to be flattering,
suitable {*imperf:* iiwaaləm} 26

waaluu والو *part.* nothing, not a
thing 6

waalii والي *nms* holy person; saint
(in Islamic context) {*pl:* wulyaa} 16

waah واه *interj* oh dear, oh my
(expression of dismay or unhappiness)
31

waah ʕliyya wə-ʕlaa ḥaalii واه علي
وعلى حالي woe is me, oh dear 31

wəjjəd وجّد *v* to prepare, make
preparation {*imperf:* iiwəjjəd} 9

wəddər ودّر *v* to lose, misplace
{*imperf:* iiwəddər} 28

wərraa ورّى *v* to show, demonstrate
{*imperf:* iiwərrii} 36

wəzən وزن *nms* influence; weight,
poundage 13

wəʃ واش [*also* waaʃ] *interrog* what
8

wəʃnuu واشـنـه [*also* waaʃnuu]
interrog what 17

waṣf وصف *nms* description {*pl:*
wṣaayəf} 33

wədʕiyya وضعيـه *nfs* situation,
position {*pl:* wədʕiyyaat} 7

wə-laa ولا there has to be 7

wəld xaala ولد خالـه cousin
(mother's sister's son) {*fs:* bənt
xaala, *pl:* wlaad xaala} 35

wəllaa ولا *conj* or 3

wəllaa ولّى [*also* wullaa] *v* to end
up; to become; to return; to start (as
pre-verb) {*imperf:* iiwəllii} 5

wəllaa ولّى [*also* wullaa] *v* to
become; to end up; to return; to start
(as pre-verb) {*imperf:* iiwəllii} 6

wəllaa ولّى [*also* wullaa] *v* to start
(as pre-verb); to end up; to become; to
return {*imperf:* iiwəllii} 8

wəllaa ولا [*also* wə-ʔillaa] *part.* or
something like that, or whatever (at
end of sequence) 8

wəllaa ولّى [*also* wullaa] *v* to

return; to start (as pre-verb); to end up;
to become {*imperf:* iiwəllii} 9

wahraan وهران *prop* Oran (city in
western Algeria) 30

wahraanii وهراني *adj* Oranais (from
Oran) {*fs:* wahraaniyya, *pl:*
wahraaniyyiin} 36

wjaah وجاه *nms* region {*pl:* ?} 25

wjəd وجد *v* to find, come across
{*imperf:* yuujəd} 13

wdən ودن *nfs* ear {*pl:* wədniin} 26

wraa ورا *prep* behind, in back of 11

wsiila وسيله *nfs* means, way {*pl:*
wsaayəl} 18

wṣəl وصل *v* to reach, arrive at
{*imperf:* yuuṣəl} 26

w-kiifaaʃ mənnaa وكيفاش منّا and
so on (lit. and how from here) 21

wliid وليد *nms* child, son (diminutive
of /wəld/) {*pl:* wliidaat} 33

wliid ʕamm وليد عمّ cousin (father's
brother's son) {*fs:* wliidət ʕamm, *pl:*
wliidaat ʕamm} 33

wuddii ودّي *nms* my friend, pal, buddy
(ms) 25

wullaa ولّى [*also* wəllaa] *v* to
become; to end up; to return; to start
(as pre-verb) {*imperf:* iiwullii} 2

wullaa ولّى [*also* wəllaa] *v* to

return; to start (as pre-verb); to end up;
to become {*imperf:* iiwullii} 8

wiin وين *interrog* where, the place
that *conjunction* 5

u

uusaada وساده [*also* wsaada] *nfs*
pillow {*pl:* uusaayəd} 15

uuliid وليد [*also* wliid] *nms* child
{*pl:* uuliidaat} 15

i

iiðaa اذا *conj* if; when, whenever 11

iiraanyoom ايرانيوم *nms* uranium 6

iiguullək يقولّك *disc* that is to say, I
mean (lit. they tell you) 6

iimaam ايمام *nms* imam (Islamic
prayer leader) {*pl:* ayma} 18

iinsaan اينسان [*also* insaan] *nms*
person, human being {*pl:* naas} 9

iih ايه *interj* yes 7

y

yaa wuddii يا ودّي o my friend (term
of address) 7

yaʕnii يعني *disc* I mean; that is to

say (lit. it (ms) means) 1

yəmmaa يمّا *nfs* mother; s.o.'s mother (reference clear from context) {*pl:* yəmmaat} 5

yoom يوم *nms* day {*pl:* yyaam} 8

yuunaan (lyuunaan) اليونان *prop* Greece 1

l'affection   affection 23

Alger   *prop* Algiers (capital of Algeria) 30

alors   *adv* so, then 19, 20, 25, 30, 36

des animés   cartoons 9

les animés   *nmp* cartoons 9

août   *nms* August 24

barrage   *nms* dam 20

les barrages   *nmp* the roadblocks 29

barrages   *nmp* roadblocks 29

bon   *interj* then; all right 25, 27

budget   *nms* budget 20

le budget   *nms* the budget 23

les camions   *nmp* the trucks 29

Canada   *prop* Canada 21

carrément   *adv* straight out 25

des casse-croûtes   snacks 9

c'est   it is 19

c'est   they are, lit. it is 25

charbon   *nms* coal 20

le château   *nms* the Château 36

cinquante   50 24

Clauzel   *prop* Clauzel, Bertrand (1772 - 1842; governor-general of Algeria from 1835 - 36) 5

d'abord   *adv* first, at first, first of all 23

les dattes   *nfp* dates 21

déjà   *adv* already 28

des   of the (indefinite article) 6

deux cents   200 36

devoirs   *nmp* homework 9

différent   *adj* different 30

diplôme   *nms* degree, university degree 35

donc   *conj* then, so 20, 30, 32

ensemble   *adv* together 28

les environs   *nmp* the surrounding area 20

les Espagnols   *nmp* the Spanish 36

Europe   *prop* Europe 6

expert   *nms* expert 27

extraordinaire   *adj* extraordinary 25

la femme   *nfs* the woman 32

film   *nms* movie 8

les films   *nmp* the movies 8

le FIS   *prop* FIS (*Front Islamique du Salut, Islamic Salvation Front*) 13

le futur   *nms* the future 34

la gare   *nfs* the railway station 36

une gare   *nfs* a railroad station 36

gâteau   *nms* cake 18

les gâteaux   *nmp* cakes 21

gaz *nms* gas, natural gas 7

général *nms* general 5

le goût *nms* the taste 36

le gouvernement *nms* the government 28

la graisse *nfs* fat 19

les groupes *nmp* the groups 28

guerre *nfs* war 28

juste *adv* right, just 25

l'équilibre *nms* balance 35

l'espace *nms* space 21

l'exportation *nfs* the export 21

l'histoire *nfs* the story 25

limité *adj* limited 35

mafia *nfs* mafia 14

mais *conj* but, however 7, 12, 13, 20, 21, 32

marché *nms* market 5

Marseille *prop* Marseille (city in southern France) 21

des médecins some doctors 24

un mélange *nms* a mixture 30

même *adv* even 20, 21, 24, 29, 30, 35

un minaret *nms* a minaret 36

le mouvement *nms* the movement 21

le musée *nms* the museum 36

normal *adj* normal 7

le nylon *nms* nylon (as in cording); plastic bag 21

des nylons nylons; plastic bags 21

objectifs *nmp* goals 35

les palmiers *nmp* the palm trees 21

pardon *nms* excuse me 25

parfois *adv* sometimes 28, 29

pendant *prep* during 35

la période *nfs* the time 21, 24

peut-être *adv* maybe 24

la plage *nfs* the beach 24

les plages *nfp* the beaches 29

plutôt *adv* instead, rather 27, 30

les poclains *nmp* the bulldozers (Fr. brand name) 21

le point *nms* the point 28

le port *nms* the harbor 36

la production *nfs* the production 21

des projets projects 35

protocole *nms* formalities 23

publicité *nfs* commercial, advertisement 21

la publicité *nfs* commercial, advertising 21

puisque *conj* since 35

la **quantité**   *nfs* the quantity 21

le **quartier**   *nms* the neighborhood 36

quatrième   *adj* fourth 23

le **quatrième**   *adj* the fourth 23

le **racisme**   *nms* racism 33

la **récolte**   *nfs* the harvest 21

la **région**   *nfs* the region 30

le **remède**   *nms* the remedy 24

un **reportage**   *nms* a news report 21

le **rhumatisme**   *nms* rheumatism 24

la **sauce**   *nfs* the sauce 22

sec   *adj* alone, with nothing else 24

sinon   *conj* otherwise 30

soit   *conj* either 17

sport   *nms* sport 35

surtout   *adv* especially 20, 32

synthétiseur   *nms* synthesizer 27

la **taguela**   *nfs* *taguela* (kind of bread cooked in hot ash) 22

la **tchi tchi**   *nfs* the rich, the bourgeoisie 31

la **télévision**   *nfs* television 12

télévision   *nfs* television 29

tellement   *adv* so much 21, 24

la **température**   *nfs* the temperature 24

le **temps**   *nms* time 22

TF1   *prop* TF1 (French television channel) 21

les **traditions**   *nfp* the traditions 22

le **traitement**   *nms* the treatment 24

les **transports**   *nmp* transportation 20

les **uniformes**   *nmp* the uniforms 29

les **unités**   *nfp* the units 30

les **Vandales**   *nmp* the Vandals 1

les **villes**   *nfp* the cities 29

voilà   *presentative* there it is 31, 35

le **voyage**   *nms* the trip 29

la **vue**   *nfs* the view 36

zéro   *nms* zero 6